RECREATION And LEISURE:
Issues In An Era Of Change
Revised Edition

RECREATION and LEISURE:

Issues In An Era of Change
Revised Edition

edited by

Thomas L. Goodale

and

Peter A. Witt

VENTURE PUBLISHING
State College, Pennsylvania

Design by Marilyn Shobaken

Design Assistance by Sandra Sikorski

Proofreader Susan Lewis

Production Assistance by Bonnie Godbey

Library of Congress Catalogue Card Number 85-50103

ISBN 0-910251-10-X

Distributed outside North America
by E. & F. N. Spon. Ltd.
11 New Fetter Lane
London, England EC4P 4EE

OTHER BOOKS FROM VENTURE PUBLISHING

To Leisure: An Introduction by John Neulinger

Recreation Planning and Management edited by Stanley R. Lieber and Daniel R. Fesenmaier

Playing, Living, Learning — A Worldwide Perspective on Children's Opportunity to Play by Cor Westland and Jane Knight

Values and Leisure and Trends in Leisure Services by the Academy of Leisure Sciences

Marketing Parks and Recreation by the National Park Service

Vandalism Control Management for Parks and Recreation Areas by Monty L. Christiansen

Winning Support for Parks and Recreation by the National Park Service

Leisure in Your Life: An Exploration, Revised Edition by Geoffrey Godbey

Leadership and Administration of Outdoor Pursuits by Phyllis Ford and James Blanchard

Private and Commercial Recreation edited by Arlin Epperson and Frank Guadagnolo

CONTENTS

ISBN 0 419 13800 5

Distributed outside North America
by E. & F.N. Spon Ltd
11 New Fetter Lane
London, England EC4P 4EE

PREFACE

The litany of issues which confront and confound as the 21st century approaches can begin at any point and proceed in any sequence. The problems are complex and interwoven. Together they suggest that a variety of difficult tasks may be at hand; together they spur us to think about needed changes and about transformations as dramatic as at any time in our history. Because of its presumed centrality to peoples' lives, the park and recreation movement cannot escape this kind of scrutiny, reflection, and questioning. Indeed, the park and recreation movement must undergo such scrutiny to help deal with some of its basic dilemmas, contradictions, and incongruities.

Too little is said about current philosophic and directional difficulties which face the movement. In cataloguing our current status, too little attention has been paid to the essential issues of raison d'etre and the impact of burgeoning social issues and ills on current and future practices. Too little is said about the basic forces that are shaping society and generating questions about the park and recreation purpose. There are exceptions, of course. Still, most of the questioning is about issues like proliferation of programs and services, clarification of mandates, sources of financial support and the like. Many reviews of the park and recreation movement have concentrated on cataloguing numbers, current legislation or the size, location, and responsibilities of park and recreation services and education curricula.

Although allusions are often made to basic issues facing the profession and the movement (for these are different), more energy seems to be given to extolling the virtues of legislative victories and programmatic successes. Professionalism, registration/certification, accreditation and professional preparation receive more attention than more fundamental issues. Emphasis remains on how more than what, and what more than why. The search for stability via institutionalization draws attention away from currents of flux and change, shades of dissatisfaction and misgivings, and the forces within our political, social, and economic systems which can hinder or help us be what we purport to be. A few examples are briefly sketched below.

Gradually but unstintingly, our modes of living and thinking must change. Especially at the individual level, there is already much change in evidence. But, inevitably, change is more difficult and consequently slower for our agencies and institutions. From this pattern, as from others, emerges a sense of lag, and for many, a diminution in congruity. We are, in the main, certain that the agencies which we serve and which serve us must change markedly. But we are much less certain of what those changes should be. Still, we would like to respond of our own volition since we know unabated problems only make matters worse up to the time alternatives are shrunk and change forced upon us. Too, there is no virtue in doing the right or required thing under duress.

There is much current interest in community development, local autonomy and control, returning resources and responsibility to neighborhoods and local associations in the recreation field. There is also heightened interest in volunteers serving the field in various capacities. But how do we weigh the antecedents of this rebirth of interest? Surely some weight must be given to economic restraints. Perhaps some of this interest is only recognition of a growing spirit of independence among the people, or at least a growing disenchantment with organizational and institutional provisions of service. Surely there is some basis for the renewed interest in the philosophy of individual workers and agencies in the recreation field; perhaps there is a growing feeling of uncertainty, inadequacy, and humility in the face of so much to do. Still, that is received with equanimity since there are still so many so dedicated to building the recreation profession; the church, if you will, but not the creed. Such issues as these point to serious and difficult questions which the movement and profession must ultimately address. For example:

A. — There is a growing concern in many areas of human services over the proliferation of service providers, the overlapping of service provision efforts, and the scope and breadth of service involvements in the everyday lives of individuals. Coordination, integration, systems planning and other methods have been mentioned as potential means for controlling, limiting, and making service efforts more efficient. Where, then, do recreation and leisure services fit in the overall scheme of human services and human welfare?

B. — Basic to the above is the question of who are or should be the prime recipients of leisure services: the poor, the middle class, urban dwellers, institutional residents? If leisure services increasingly come under the ruberic of enabling services, should efforts be directed toward those who are the least fortunate? Who is to be enabled — and enabled to do what?

C. — What are the expected outcomes of leisure experiences? How do these relate to concern for the quality of human life? Can we mandate what people should do according to some notion of social utility, personal well-being, wholesome involvement, human experience? Can we trust that people know what they want or do they need to be told (led or directed or counseled)?

D. — How can the powerful establishments which shape our values (the advertising establishment, the welfare establishment, the corporate establishment) be made to understand the vital nature of recreation, creative involvement and all forms of endeavors promoting spiritual, emotional and social development? Can the more traditional sources of values such as the family, church and community be revitalized? Does the recreation movement have a stake in all this? Does it matter whose values prevail? What are our values and how committed are we to realizing them?

E. — Do recreation services create a self-perpetuating need for continued service provision? To what extent are recreation services used as instruments of social control? To what extent do recreation organizers create or manipulate needs? To what extent should they? And on whose behalf?

F. — Should recreation agencies devote the bulk of their energies to stimulating and supporting those recreational opportunities which are least demanding of elaborate and specialized facilities and which are least consumptive of durable and nondurable goods? Perhaps we have become so enchanted with things that we have lost sight of the fact that the greatest recreational resource we have is ourselves and our families and friends, and there is little else that we need. Are we culpable for that?

G. — Have we abandoned ourselves as resources in favor of resources provided by public and private agencies, thus willfully becoming dependent on those only too happy to foster dependency as it contributes to the agency's growth and longevity? Exclusive of those whose roles change due to political and economic forces, are there park and recreation agencies consciously striving to reduce their size but not necessarily their significance?

H. — Should the recreation and park agency become the community's outstanding example of harmoniously living in and parsimoniously sharing our finite resources? A commitment to that course would affect nearly every service and every operation of the agency. It may even mean a shift in emphasis from parks to the whole environment. Whatever became of the environmental movement?

I. — With the environmental as well as monetary cost of energy, especially fossil fuels, how much longer should we build and maintain artificial ice rinks, heated swimming pools, and other facilities and operations which make heavy energy demands? Even assuming the financial means to continue such practices, do they not foreclose options for those who follow? Further, does this tacitly endorse the right of the wealthy, whether individuals, communities, or nations, to consume resources critical to the well being of all.

J. — Given the current economic situation and projections of it well into the future, what responses are required of the recreation field? Increased reliance on revenue generated by fees and charges may further imbalance services in favor of those with the ability to pay. Increased reliance on high salaried, full-time staff along with increased professionalization and unionization of what was previously volunteer, part-time, and seasonal work may deprive many of involvement which could add meaning to their lives. It may also deprive many of needed, however limited, income. It most certainly drives up the cost of service. Whatever the case, clearly the economics of the steady state or the conserver society will require major changes in the park and recreation field.

K. — What is the balance of benefits to the public, as opposed to an individual "professional," from accreditation, registration, and certification? Whose interests does a profession serve? What are the advantages of professional versus volunteer leadership? Are there personality and socialization factors that selectively bias the perception and attitudes of recreation professionals?

Questions about the recreation and park field, then, come pouring out. The essence of them all is the search for ways to respond to the many problems which confront us all and ways to provide leadership in ameliorating these problems and establishing new modes of living and thinking. How do we turn problems into opportunities and capitalize on them for the common good?

In some ways it is easy to agree with Gray and Grebin when they state that: ". . . our contribution (as a movement) has been somewhat minimal in terms of providing leadership for the main current of social progress in America and somewhat marginal to where the action is."[1] It is also easy to agree when they express their view of the plight of creative leaders in the movement who "describe their sense of isolation because they dare to be innovative and because they defy the party line."[2] Although these observations are relatively recent, the problems raised are long standing. They remain unresolved still.

It is no wonder, then, that "value crises" has become such a fashionable, if not always fully fathomed, topic. It is no wonder, then, that our age is characterized as one of uncertainty and anxiety. A spate of books are addressed to the end, decline, demise, twilight, challenge, crisis, and failure of one (damn) thing after another. And all of that literature reveals a deep concern for human well-being *in the long run*. Are we a people whose short-sightedness or lack of will leads inevitably to the precipice?

We are fortunate to have such concerns as they are reserved only for those who can afford them. Our affluence, our conveniences, our transportation and communication ability, our high levels of education, our ability to produce beyond our ability to consume; these are prerequisites to our anxiety. These attainments have always been viewed as ends, and in the main we have attained them, however poorly their benefits may be distributed. Now we regard them as means to an end. And the question before us is, "to what end?" That has been the main item on our agenda for at least the last quarter century. Answers, typically, refer to freedom, releasing human potential and creativity, and the like.

How much agreement there is on such answers is a mystery, given the mega-structures and mountainous proprietary interests contingent upon the absence of freedom and the atrophy of human potential and creativity. And we must look further to determine what it is we have the freedom, potential and creativity to do. That leisure and recreation are important to attaining desired ends, whatever those ends might be, is widely recognized, or, perhaps more precisely, is widely assumed. We need clarification and agreement about those ends, then ways of determining our contribution toward meeting them.

So whether we speak of the economy, energy, or consumption; population, or urbanization; growth or stasis; the rights of the collective or those of the individual; the virtues of work or of leisure; the search for escape or for identity, meaning, and involvement; we are speaking of the right things. No doubt we will continue speaking of these things for some long time. Meanwhile, some outlines for leadership and action are before us, ill-focused though they may yet be. It is time to begin addressing the important issues and responding to them, particularly among those engaged in parks, recreation, and leisure services who have joined hands in holding out the promise of a new, and somehow better order for us all.

THUS THIS BOOK

Some eight years ago, in the midst of a discussion about the literature in the recreation field, we uncovered a mutual and long-held interest in trying to put together a book about issues facing the field. In recent years we have witnessed the publication of some very good books on recreation and leisure — and some very bad ones. However good or bad one judges some or all of the literature in the field to be, still there remained a gap in that too seldom are issues raised or argued forcefully enough that they cannot be readily dismissed. We believe the task of presenting issues an important one, whatever the subject or applied field.

Venture Publishing Incorporated encouraged our venture into issues facing the field, thus making it their own. Together, the editors and publishers believed the book would help fill a void in the literature of the recreation and leisure field. Most books in the field are introductions, regardless of titles or prefatory claims. The periodical literature, with few and recent exceptions, has been oriented toward practical program and administration matters or toward data-based, quantitative research. Again, one's opinion of the literature is not our concern; rather it is the absence of issues and arguments on matters that do concern us.

The textbook approach may be ill-suited to a time in which the consensus on nearly every subject, including leisure and leisure services, is shrinking. Most extant views and underlying assumptions are being challenged by professionals, students, and an increasingly aware citizenry. A renewed humanistic spirit seems to be both cause and effect of the questioning attitude, along with the sobering effect of environmental degradation, energy consumption, urban congestion, slowed economic growth, and related phenomena. There is still some "living in the past," or in a present shored up by optimism and perhaps naivete.

The first edition of our compilation of issues appeared in 1980. The belief in the importance of presenting issues was shared widely enough to venture forth with this revised edition. The first edition was picked up in quite diverse quarters and used in a variety of ways. That is understandable since its focus is not a particular subject but rather an exploration of issues facing those involved in the park, recreation and leisure service domain, expansive a domain as it is. One of the results of the first edition was to strengthen our conviction about the importance of addressing issues. Particularly in education settings, issues draw us away from techniques and tools and toward discussion, reflection, argumentation and debate. Issues underscore the importance of education rather than training and help develop the ability which marks the educated person; the ability to think and reason, to sift, to weigh, and to judge. For judge we must, and *then* we must act. There are no greater responsibilities than those, and they must be done in that order. "Look," as the saying goes, "before you leap."

Another result of the first edition has been a substantial revision. Ten chapters from the first edition do not appear here, not for want of merit but for want of time to make substantial revisions or for want of the editors' abilities to weave a coherent fabric through them all. Four chapters have been substantially revised. Ten new chapters have been added. Among them are several chapters by authors whose contributions we solicited for the first edition but whose commitments precluded it. Finally, materials in this edition are organized in three sections rather than four.

Each of the chapters is perceptive and timely, and is based on wide-ranging study and experience of an objectively viewed North American scene. Each is forward looking as well as a reflection on our present and past experiences. Much of the material also has a timeless quality as some of the issues and concerns are related to, if not in fact derivatives of, such enduring themes as Mill's liberty, Rousseau's social contract, Marx's class struggle, Veblen's leisure class, Durkheim's anomie, Riesman's lonely crowd, Jacob's cities, Ward's habitat, Weber's protestant ethic, Ellul's technological society, and much more.

The book is unique in another way. Each chapter is a mini-treatise. In that sense, it is analytical but not methodological; empirical, but not laden with data on a cross-section of the population at a given time. In each piece, the reasoning for the view taken is developed in order to generate thought, reflection, and even argument. No one (including ourselves) will agree with all of the positions or arguments here. Indeed, there are clear disagreements among the authors represented. That is as it should be.

The chapters raise and explore all of the issues outlined above. The contributions are the out-growth of each author's concerns and convictions and could easily stand alone as separate, important contributions to the overall literature in our field. Together they form a composite that should contribute significantly to understanding and working through the vital and important issues that face our field in an era of change.

This is neither a "how to" book nor a mere compendium of current thinking or practice. Neither diatribe nor mainstream, it is an exploration of concerns, issues, assumptions, values, and perceptions which underlie our efforts to serve. There are no answers; there are no easy answers anyway. But there are many suggestions, and much to think about.

Over eight years ago, when we began inquiring about the interests of potential contributors, we distributed a few pages of text describing our rationale for the book and the style and tone we hoped to develop. In the main, we suggested that with the rapid pace of our lives and rapid change of our society and culture, time must be found to step back, pause, and reflect. Our analogy is that of finding an eddy; a respite from the rapid current of the mainstream.

When one finds one's self in an eddy aside from the mainstream, one generally feels alone. Any who feel that way can rest assured that there is much company. In fact the eddy may be crowded; it may even be the new mainstream. If so, perhaps it will run slower and deeper. If in it there is some groping for principles and purposes around which to order congruent personal and professional lives, then fine. It may result in less drifting with the current, or thrashing about.

TLG
PAW

REFERENCES

1. Gray, David S. and Greben, Seymour. "Future Perspectives." *Parks and Recreation*, 1974 (July). p. 31.
2. *Ibid.*, p. 32.

SECTION ONE

Clarifying Concepts:
The Ongoing Struggle
For Understanding

INTRODUCTION

Most books on almost any subject begin by defining the basic terms to be utilized and making distinctions between key concepts that need to be introduced. Books on recreation and leisure follow this general pattern. Unfortunately, after reading most definitions of terms like *play*, *recreation* or *leisure*, the reader is often left with the vague sense that though much has been said, little has been communicated, and definitional and conceptual understanding continues to be elusive.

No doubt the haze surrounding the terms and concepts essential to understanding the field of recreation and leisure allows us the latitude to continue in our individually chosen paths, however divergent those paths may be. But if the field of recreation and leisure is to advance and mature, we must continue the struggle for clarity. Seeking clarity is a process that ultimately forms the basis for practice and evaluation of whether services or systems have met stated goals and objectives.

One of the purposes, then, of this opening section is to focus attention on some of the basic concepts that are used in our field. For example: Arnold (1) delves into the background and interrelationship of recreation, leisure and play; Farina (2) examines time and free time; Bregha (3) and Goodale (4) analyze obligation and freedom; Smith (5) looks at pleasure; and Bishop and Jeanrenaud (7) and Michaelis (6) assess play and creativity. Witt and Ellis (8) summarize attempts to operationalize the concept of leisure. Mannell (9), in the chapter concluding this section, wonders about the desirability of the social and psychological engineering applications which may result from our quest.

The combined efforts of the above authors add considerable support to material contained in later sections of the book which notes the crippling consequences of failing to come to grips with defining our terms or clarifying our concepts. Thus, the wrestling with meaning sets the stage and tone for efforts in the other sections of the book to describe needed services and professional practices.

1

Several other themes emerge through the articles in this section. One of these is the necessity to balance objective and subjective conceptualizations and evidence for our key concepts and terms. Farina (2), for example, points out the extraordinary complexity of the concept of time. In a society such as ours — technologic, interrelated, and interdependent — time as a quantity is inescapable. As a commodity measurable with uncommon precision, we know the mechanistic, objective side of time well. Godbey's (17) discussion of "time deepening" or Sessoms' (16) delineation of life span, life cycle concepts are examples of further efforts to understand time and the patterns of time usage that occur over a person's life.

On the other hand there is the subjective, aesthetic and experiential side to time. While more difficult to grasp it may be far more important because the "problem of leisure" is perhaps not so much a problem of quantity of time but of quality. This is clear, as Farina (2) points out, in the two most common qualifiers attached to the word time, as in "free" time and "leisure" time. Beyond any objective meaning these adjectives are laden with qualitative, evaluative and emotive content. Ultimately, Farina suggests that leisure is probably better understood in relation to freedom rather than time.

Freedom thus becomes another dominant theme of this section. Bregha (3) raises the issue of whether we are dealing with freedom *from,* i.e. freedom from work and other obligations, or freedom *to,* i.e. freedom to choose what to do. Bregha ultimately asks: How much freedom do we really have? What are the conditions of freedom? What are the internal as well as external barriers to choosing freely?

The fragile nature of freedom *to* becomes a dominant issue for several other authors in this section as well. For example, Michaelis (6) describes the conditions that can destroy playfulness as one moves through childhood and into adulthood, while Bishop and Jeanrenaud (7) discuss the many potential roadblocks to creativity and the difficulty in its preservation. Witt and Ellis (8) discuss the centrality of perceived freedom in attempts to measure whether an individual is experiencing leisure. In Section Three, Reynolds (23) points to the social control potential of our service system as a significant negative influence on the freedom *to,* while Lord, Hutchison and Van Derbeck (22) chastise professionalism per se for presenting significant restraints on leisure and the ability to choose.

The goal of leisure is another dominant theme. Bregha (3) notes that goal-less leisure is a contradiction and that time uses are not equal in quality, morality or social relevance. Smith (5) makes a

leisure ⟶ happiness
means   end

similar observation in stating that not all intellectual pleasure (thinking) is good because the product of it may be twisted or destructive. This is also noted by Goodale (4) in his discussion of the strong link in Aristotle's philosophy between leisure, ethics and the exercise of virtue. Thus, we are once again involved in the age-old task of distinguishing means from ends. To Aristotle, happiness was the end and leisure in the sense of freedom *to* was an essential means. But Aristotle clearly separated leisure from amusement and recreative pastime.

In the words of poet Alexander Pope: "Amusement is the happiness of those who cannot think." That is one way to summarize Aristotle's philosophy on that subject. It is also an appropriate summary of Smith's (5) analysis of the "Biological Basis of Pleasure" and its implications. Smith raises several issues related to the goal of leisure and its end, pleasure, by discussing the neurophysiologic evidence which points to human beings as distinguishable from other animals by their ability to derive pleasure from thought. He describes the fact that too many of us involve ourselves in sensate, hedonistic and even narcissistic pleasures, increasingly ignoring the potential of deriving pleasure through thought. These pursuits he sees as sub-human and not in the best interests of human development and purpose. Whether this is only a value judgement or has basis in declining culture and fulfillment is a matter of opinion. Those who seek sensory pleasures, which probably includes us all to greater or lesser degrees, could reply to the effect that we are, after all (or merely) human. But then there are those who have suggested that in light of the many problems and challenges confronting man, being only (or merely) human may not be enough.

Smith's discussion of the biological basis of pleasure also points to the potential for recent research into brain functioning to supply important new information about the purpose and value of play and leisure. Michaelis (6) also sees the potential descriptive value of this emerging information, noting the primacy of the right brain and of the affective, non-rational model of thinking to play and creativity. The ultimate need to integrate right and left, cognitive and affective, and rational and non-rational elements also brings us back to the objective-subjective distinction regarding leisure.

As a fitting conclusion to the section, Mannell (9) raises questions concerning the emergence of "experience" as the focus and objective of recreation and leisure services. Psychic rather than material gratification has increasingly become the motivation of what advertisers tell us is the "now" generation and social critics tell us is the "me" generation. Mannell thus warns us against the

3

"Psychologization of Leisure Services" where "experience engineers" manipulate "psychic loadings" and the like. How far is it from here to the "feelies" and "solidarity services" of Huxley's Brave New World?

In total, the time has come to think seriously about what and how we think, about what we mean, what we intend, what we do and what happens as a result. Leisure, recreation and play can and often do mean and imply different things; means and ends of service delivery need to be distinguished; and the disparity between objective and subjective experience resolved.

T.L.G.
P.A.W.

Chapter One

The Dilemma of Meaning

Serena Arnold

Almost everyone believes that he or she has an adequate understanding of the words leisure, recreation and play. Even though we may have carefully and logically thought through their meanings, we can find ourselves unable to interpret what others may be implying by their usage. Many persons will have ready definitions and argue that leisure is time off the job, time free from requirements of life and time in which they may choose to do what they like. Recreation will be reported as closely allied with sports and games, and if you ask for an identification of recreations, more often than not you will be provided with the names of diversions perceived as means for escape from routine. It will be asserted that play is an activity of children, the opposite of work or the antithesis of attention to duty. Some have suggested that play is the work of children. We frequently hear that Americans work hard at their play and their work is their recreation. At the same time, some persons will assert that they have no time for leisure.

If the reader feels comfortable with our more common definitions of leisure, recreation, play, and also the word work, and believes that he or she can precisely understand what the authors of chapters within this book have meant in their usage, there is no reason to pursue further the following material. If, on the other hand, there are inconsistencies in meanings, a simple exercise of categorization of what each writer tends to be implying by use of these terms will illustrate clearly a need for greater precision in definition.

The purpose of this article, therefore, is to search for clarity, in our understanding of the words leisure, recreation and play, as well as work. If those words are ambiguous and we are unsure of our symbols, it will follow that our thinking will be illogical and our intent confusing. Particularly is this true when we attempt to carry out research pertaining to leisure, recreation or play. If we are to communicate with any degree of scientific intent, we must come to grips with semantic representations. For there is ample evidence that we use words when we think. Imagine if you will, how much confusion could be engendered if a chemist left us to surmise what he meant when he said, "You will be using $C_3H_3 (NO_2)_2$ in this experiment?"

Our ability to communicate through symbols is a definite attribute that separates human beings from other creatures. Words are symbols, just as the number two is a symbol. If we fail to understand the meaning of the symbols we use, there is little hope for an orderly comprehension of conceptual realities or actions. In other words, it is essential that we think through what we mean when we speak or write about leisure, recreation and play, just as you would need to know that our chemist was speaking of nitro glycerine. While the consequences might be different, the needs are similar.

To assert that recreation is re-creation, leisure is free time and play a non-productive activity, and all three have their opposites in work, is to compound errors made in the 18th and 19th centuries in which these terms were used in relation to industrialized production. Knowledge of how words have developed into present day terminology will come from tracing their historical significances and symbolic usages. It clarifies where we are and what needs to be done to properly understand what is being said or written. The science of semantics provides us the tools.

Only recently have there been serious attempts to analyze the discrete meanings of leisure, recreation and play. For the most part, these terms have been used with emotive intent rather than by reason of their symbolic content — that is, the signs they contain (significance). Many of us have not been aware that there is a difference between what is loosely meant by a term and its symbolic meaning or significance. The two approaches are often confused, just as the definition of a word is often confused with a description of what it represents. Some persons find it difficult to accept the fact that a standard dictionary does not contain definitions, but rather synonyms.

Culminating from centuries of usage and changing moral codes and mores, the terms we are discussing have undergone a variety of adaptations resulting in a mixture of imprecision. To bring concrete thinking out of generalizations and to separate meanings present a formidable task. While the English language is considered to be rich and expressive from a literary view, ambiguous terms with imprecise connotations are precarious for scientific applications. So much of what has been written concerning leisure, recreation and play fits better into journalistic convenience than into a scientific mode that provides us explanations. For these reasons, attempts have been made to coin new terms or find a single representative term, but none has gained wide acceptance. For a time, I advocated coining the term Ludinetics for academic study of recreation; the logic being that the Latin *ludus,* for play and *etics,* the study of, made operational sense. However, I soon reasoned that with such esoterics, I could not avoid confronting the hackneyed terms I wished to clarify; therefore, the dilemma was merely exacerbated.

The field of recreation is not alone with semantic difficulties. Traditional disciplines are still fraught with agonies of definition. In medicine, for example, the term sick has no precise meaning, nor have the terms illness, handicapped or health. Recently, 25 physicians were interviewed and asked to define sick. The resulting conclusion was that the term meant "something was not working." For the medical profession, the word had meaning only to the extent that it was broken down into referents and these referents isolated and made definitive through laboratory investigation. Viability and respectability of any field is not found in its designation *per se,* but rather by the specificity of its concepts and concreteness of its research. It is by such contributions to knowledge that more preciseness and better research is developed. Testing, substantiated by competent observers, is a continuing process in every viable field.

One of the immense challenges for recreation professionals is to understand the field so well that they are capable of delimiting terms into elements that are applicable to research methods. One law of research is that when a problem is stated as a generalization, the resulting conclusion can only be a greater generalization. The umbrella under which we presently reside as a profession is far too expansive for concrete research purposes. As long as recreation is anything done for pleasure within free time, as long as leisure is wedded to time, and as long as play is activities of fun and games, there are no boundaries. We may find solace in designing facilities and developing and managing parks and playgrounds, but how do we evaluate them in terms of purpose? What specifically, were our aims, objectives or goals?

It seems to me that all facets of the field of recreation, leisure and play are infested by our looseness of meaning in the terms presently being applied. As the title of this publication suggests, we are in an era of change and if we fail to update our concepts of what we mean by recreation, leisure and play, there are reasons to believe that our efforts to become a mature profession will become less effective rather than more. We have been saying this for years, but the difficulties we face are much older and more far-reaching. It means setting aside traditions within our profession, becoming radical, perhaps, in changing our ways of thinking and daring to challenge the *status quo.* As I travel about the country, I cannot avoid contemplating how it happens that our concepts of children's playgrounds show very few differences from those established in 17th century Boston. Resisting change is a human foible and fear its strongest ally.

The intent of this article, therefore, is a limited investigation into the history of the terms we habitually apply to our field and a search for the sources from which they have emanated. Such a review may seem dull and academic, for there are many who shy away from semantics, believing that expediency is a more practical and rewarding enterprise. In passing, however, the very connotation of freedom with which we have traditionally interpreted leisure and recreation may well have a bearing on the maddening increase in misuse of park and recreation amenities. At one time, historically speaking, leisure was license; campus, playground; ludicrous an aspect of play; games the fetes of gladiators within Roman colosseums. Residuals from the past in respect to language are especially slow to disappear.

Academic study of recreation, leisure and play is little more than a few decades old. During this time research consisted predominantly of descriptive studies depicting the status quo. Considerable emphasis was placed on leadership, administration and management practices, but these studies were predicated on the premise that recreation was understood through spiritual and moral values or a contributing factor to self-improvement or prevention of social ills.

Of late, there is greater frequency of studies directed toward basic research. Hopefully, we have passed the stage where we carried out surveys in which we asked a constituency, "What does recreation (or leisure or play) mean to you?" Within such quests, we learned that our constituency knew no more than we about definitions. Again, through a process of maturing, we went on many searches to discover what persons did for their recreations, and furthermore, what constituted their leisure pursuits. We did discover one essential fact from these efforts, however, and that was that our population reported activities as broad as life itself. I well remember a nation-wide study to discover the most popular recreation of the American people. The finding showed that swimming headed the list. When I investigated further, it was revealed that the study was conducted during July and August. On the other hand, I also found that the researcher failed to instruct his population as to the meaning of recreation. Again, an erroneous premise that everyone knows its meaning.

Another example of lack of interpretation may be found in the statement "leisure is one of our leading industries." An exciting statement, is it not, but if analyzed, one must ask the question, is leisure a commodity to be bought and sold in the marketplace? Is leisure a thing, and if so what are its referents? Inasmuch as the fast food industry is included in the research that reported on the economic value of leisure, one could well ask the question, does eating out mean an increase or decrease in the amount of leisure one has? Clearly, it depends upon the definition given to leisure. If we consider leisure as the opposite of employment for financial gain, then leisure must be exchanged for the time taken to earn enough money to pay for eating out. This dichotomy would not occur if we ceased using time as a measure for leisure or as a thing to be calculated as a leisure referent.

There are numerous examples of failing to clarify meaning. A recent review of 123 studies of play revealed that only 19 authors attempted to define the term within their methodology. To say that we expect everyone to know what is meant by play, is to avoid the issue. Additionally, to state that play-recreation-leisure is simply an attitude, a way of life, or a state of mind, is to provide richness through poetics, but little in substance. A fair and unbiased illustration is to review all of the so-called theories of play and compare the differences.

Our dilemma, therefore, lies in subjectivity without definition. We have been unable to name recreation, play or leisure as a thing that can be counted or measured. In an effort to quantify recreation experiences, I was a participant in an effort to experiment with use of sphygmomanometers to measure changes in blood pressure during periods of play activity, but conclusions were invalid due to contaminating influences by members of the research team. Apparently, play, according to our definition, could not be superimposed by persons outside and apart from the players themselves and neither could there be interference with the progress of play. All participants expressed the loss of freedom and an absence of a "spirit of play," hence the technique was abandoned.

There is instructive value in recognizing our limitations in terms of being able to gain accurate information on human behavior under controlled conditions. Objectivity is illusive at best, and if we do not recognize subjectivity for its tell-tale signs, we will go blithely on our way believing that defining terms is an inconsequential exercise. We must know, however, that we are not alone with our problems of definition and meaning. Ogden and Richards stated the problem concisely when they wrote:

"... the approach to meaning, far more than the approach to such problems as those of physics, requires a thorough-going investigation of language. Every advance in physics has been at the expense of some generally accepted piece of meta-physical explanation which had enshrined itself in a convenient, universally practiced symbolic shorthand. But the confusion and obstruction due to such shorthand expressions and to the naive theories they protect and keep alive is greater in psychology, and especially in the theory of knowledge, than elsewhere; because no problem is so infected with so-called metaphysical difficulties — due here, as always, to an approach to a question through symbols without initial investigation of their function."[1]

The authors could have written equally well for recreation. Only in the last few years are we becoming aware of our own symbolic shorthand. In a field as subjective as recreation, evolving as it did through a type of missionary zeal and moralistic appeal by enthusiastic supporters, generalizations were acceptable. To sever our ties with emotionally laden nomenclature requires awareness of words and their meanings. By this I do not mean to debase emotionality in any sense of the word; I only plead for knowing the difference between an emotionally laden term and an objective one and their different uses. Linguistic modes are powerfully contageous and there needs to be a few iconoclasts who question and resist the prevailing influence. To listen as well as to read words with acute awareness of their referents and symbols is similar to the mathematician who responds to equations and understands their symbols as meaningful or not. Let us begin now by exploring the meanings of our terms as they originated.

RECREATION AS AN ABSTRACTION

The term recreation is an abstract symbol and thus resists modeling into a series of sub-referents without resorting to further abstractions. In this sense, it could be argued that recreation has no meaning in reality because it does not represent a description of a thing or object. It eludes measurement or quantification. Furthermore, its boundaries are unlimited in terms of the number of referents that could be brought to mind. The word could be said to be a conditional symbol of varying magnitude, as on a continuum. It raises problems not unlike those associated with beauty or pleasure, it becomes a plaything of the mind.

If we assert that recreation represents revitalization of the individual because he has participated in certain activities, we place upon the symbol a qualitative measure, a degree of worth or value — hence a morality. The assumption implies that creativity is good and non-creativity is bad, at least it suggests that non-creativity is not recreative. The question arises, how did recreation become associated with good or bad?

As an English word, it arose from Middle English of the 14th century and was adopted from Old French. Remembering our history, this was a period of moral upheaval that gave rise to the Reformation. Originally, however, the term recreation stemmed from Latin, *recreatio*. From the history of the English language, we find that literary words stemming from French and incorporated into English were expressions of the upper class. Thus recreation had use, not to peasants and laborers, but to those who enjoyed the privileges of higher social position. If there were a word in the idiom of commoners that connoted recreation in the sense of refreshment, revitalization, or entertainment, it has eluded me. All of these words, including amusement, were of French-Latin extraction. On the other hand, the Germanic "rest" is likely from Germanic *"rast"* which referred to ceasing work or the absence of motion — to be at ease.

In Latin, *recreatio* carried a connotation of restoration or recovery from something. Its root is in the word *re-creo* (to create again) to refresh, invigorate, or revive. Further references include such inferences as to amuse oneself after obligation: *laxandi levandique animi gratia,* having to do with pleasant respite. Without neuroscientific evidence, the word with which we are dealing has a metaphysical content. If we are to accept the various synonyms given, we would need to substantiate activity as a means for attaining relaxation or rest. The assumption would produce a dichotomy: rest from activity or a cessation of movement on the one hand and diverting activity on the other.

In the study of word meanings, and accepting the canon that thought is dependent upon symbols, we should try to find a word to mean the opposite of recreation. If we selected the referent, revitalization or refreshment, the antonyms fatigue and exhaustion would come to mind. If, however, we accept the Latin root *creare,* the antonym would be to exterminate or annihilate. Further, the Latin word *creo* has the meaning of bringing forth and quite clearly symbolizes work (fabricate). With the root word for recreation relating to work, it would require considerable imagination to establish re-creation as the antithesis of work. Furthermore, in usage, the word create was associated with the Divine Creator and re-create with being re-born of the spirit, of being made anew or cleansed of sin. In this sense, the word recreation was ontological rather than a name for some activity as such. In essence, then, it was a word associated with the nature of being, or reality.

During the 16th and 17th centuries, recreation began to be used to represent activities that provided both spiritual and physical refreshment for industrial workers after hours of debilitating toil. It was during the industrial revolution when the word became a referent for both a state of being and activities of a diversionary nature which were espoused by advocates as essential to maintaining health of workers confined in factories for the majority of their waking hours. In Germany, and to a lesser degree in England, physical exercise was promoted and took root among groups outside of factory workers, *per se*. The saying, "healthy body, healthy mind" became an acceptable precept. In England, field sports were widespread means for diversionary activity and were for a time discouraged or prohibited by entrepreneurs because workers would leave their machines to participate in group contests. In 19th century United States, social problems attributed to child labor and tenement living led to the advent of the "play movement" which was to prosper and include more than sports and more than activities only for children. By this advent, however, recreation did not lose its moral connotation, but rather the notion of recreation being a curative process for unfavorable conditions was strengthened. With secular support, recreation became popularized on the basis of being a preventive and as such was useful to satisfy the emotive needs of entrepreneurs, the moralistic interests of reformers, and the philosophic proclivities of intellectuals. From these early stages, Patrick proposed the "recreation or relaxation theory of play" and recreation as opposed to work became an ingrained notion in this country.[2] While I find no support for such liberties with word meanings and no precedents set in our language stemming from other languages, particularly from Latin or Greek, we seem to persist in choosing work as the antonym for recreation as well as for leisure or play. If we were to continue to depend on the general population for assistance in defining recreation, we would have paid little attention to those who have insisted that their work was their recreation.

LEISURE IDEALS

Turning to Greece and particularly the writings of Aristotle for discourses on leisure and its ideal, we find that leisure was a basis for culture. Historically and profoundly, leisure was a way of personal growth and social attainment of the "good life," particularly in Athens during the 5th century B.C. This was the period often referred to as the "Golden Age" or the "Age of Pericles," the time during which the Parthenon was constructed and various intellectual and aesthetic advances were made. The importance of Greek culture to any study of Western civilization and Occidental thought cannot be minimized. Our system of reasoning is of Greek origin, to say nothing of political influences on our own form of government or on arts and sciences. Approximately 10 percent of the English language is Greek, including much of our nomanclature associated with leisure. The Greek term *schole* (leisure) has since evolved into words such as school, scholar, scholastic, and a host of terms we use in daily conversation. Curiously, however, we possess no counterpart to the Greek *ascholia* (un-leisure) which of course was the antonym for leisure and necessary to the Greeks to insure clarity.

Athenian society was centered around leisure, or in our terms, centered in freedom from labors associated with everyday maintenance necessities. At this point, we must keep in mind that during this period of Greek history, there was no industrial manufacturing as such. The social system was supported by a slave population which was rationalized as essential to citizen freedom to reach a state of *arete* (the nearest English translation being virtue). *Arete* represented "excellence in all things" and, in the Homeric period, symbolized the ideal for which all citizens must strive; attainment of the highest good of which humans were capable. Leisure, therefore, was "opportunity" for realization of that ideal. The complexity of meaning of the term *schole* was in the wholeness of its concept, in its life-giving inferences and universality. More recently, Jaegar, in his scholarly work, explored these concepts fully, relating them to the central meaning of the term culture.[3] Pieper also asserted that leisure was the basis of culture and implied that the term recreation as commonly used in our society had been erroneously attached to leisure due to the fact that it reflected certain states of prescribed activity.[4] DeGrazia also supported the same contention.[5]

In classical Greece, leisure was not time available to be employed, nor was it a means to an end outside and apart from itself. It would have been incomprehensible to Aristotle for a person to state, "Now I have leisure for some activity." Neither was work considered the opposite of leisure, for the word work was *erg,* the root meaning for output of energy, in other words, a system of measuring expenditure of energy. A state of toil, (our term for labor) can be found in the Greek counterpart: slave. Thus we draw from early Greek culture our emotive referents associated with distaste for work and labor, representing something somewhat less than the good life and in itself demeaning to the human spirit.

Although we cling with passion to the idea of freedom, we also center our lives around work, and in our attempts to integrate the two — freedom and work/labor, we have created a dichotomy of semantic complexity which contributes to misunderstandings and inconsistencies. The framers of our Constitution, many of whom were scholars of Greek, held that the pursuit of happiness was the American ideal, but did not anticipate that Americans would become slaves to technology rather than technology replacing the slavery of Athens. We have great difficulty conceiving of a highly advanced civilization where labor was not the center of life. In this sense we have adopted Greek terms, but turned full circle from their meanings.

Finding referents by which to clarify the Greek meaning for leisure requires study of the first chapter of Aristotle's *Metaphysics*.[6] There is evidence that the important referent for *schole* is found in the word contemplation. This term does not, however, symbolize inactivity by posturing oneself as the Thinker, but rather it meant to observe, view, behold. Contemplation has a close association, etymologically, with Greek *theoria* from whence we draw our word theory. *Theoria* referred to being a spectator at festivals and it is interesting that during the Periclean period, poor people were given money or "passes" by government to attend the theater. The *theorikos* were those who traveled to see men and things and reflect upon them as one would speculate or postulate an explantion for a phenomenon. In our modern sense, it would apply if we attended the World Series baseball games to reflect on the scene in order to gain insights into the character of American culture.

Contemplation meant more than merely reflecting on phenomena and perceiving man's place in the scheme of things; it carried the connotation of participation-reflection. Attendance at a festival such as the Olympian Festival was a highly religious experience and a culmination of all that was Greek. The *theorikos* were persons of action, and through their beholding of phenomena, innovations within the culture arose. Thus, philosophy was an action oriented process which to the Greeks was fundamental to knowledge. To dissuade ourselves of the notion that contemplation did not result in action and that leisure was inaction, we need only to turn to archaeological discoveries that clearly reveal the Greeks' contribution to technology. Brumbaugh published an impressive account of machines, gadgets and a variety of inventions that were precursors of our clocks as well as mechanical toys.[7] Leisure, then, fits well into the Greek scheme of aesthetics as experiential integration of thought and action. An idea alone was insignificant without action.

In Latin derivations of leisure we find that important diversions occurred which affected our current concepts of leisure. The dominance of Rome over Greece was military and economic rather than intellectual. Greek philosophers and teachers perpetuated their system of education and left lasting marks on Roman literature, religion and language. While the Greeks were profoundly aesthetic and idealists for the most part, the Romans, above all else, were pragmatic — or as we say, practical. Therefore, any infusion of ideals held in regard to leisure by the Greeks was selectively accepted in terms of how these ideals could become subservient to practicality and applicable to a pragmatic philosophy. As was said by a Roman general, "Greeks die in bed, while Romans die on the battlefield."

Leisure, in the modern sense, came from Latin *licere* and by way of French *leisir,* Middle English *licere,* to its present spelling. The root word, *licere,* meaning to be permitted, evolved into the word license. Leisure literally meant "permission" as applied to "opportunity" afforded that was free from a legal occupation. Roman intellectuals such as Cicero and Ovid, however, invoked *otium* as signifying the idea of leisure. *Otium* was associated with contemplation and opportunity for freedom from time as well as freedom from occupation. As we have the word "leisurely" to describe a manner, there was the Latin *otiose.* There was also the word *vaco* which symbolized emptiness, to be free from, and as Cicero used the word, to have occasion for something, or to have leisure. Our word vacation comes from the same root. The English phrase, "free living" could be represented by *licentia* which for Ovid implied dissoluteness or licentiousness.

The counterpart for Greek *schole* was the Latin *schola* and, according to classical references, *ludus literarum* and *ludus discendi,* literally mean to be free of books. Later, *schola* was to become associated with a sect of scholars or disciples, and thus the word discipline referred to activities at *schola.* In this sense, learning and scholarship were representative of leisure as well as the absence of a legal occupation. Much later, *schola* came to indicate a place where learned lectures and discussions took place and hence disciplines as studies.

For some time after Greece was conquered by Rome, young Roman patricians were sent to Athens for schooling and *ludus* (play) became a referent for schooling and learning. From this emerged our word campus as the center of learning — playground. It is highly instructive to us in the field of recreation that both leisure and play in the Greek and Roman sense were linked closely to education or learning. Contemplation or reflection would take place only when a condition of leisure was experienced. Leisure could not be forced, it could not occur under servitude, it was non-material and therefore a non-business-like condition. It was opportunity for knowledge and culturation. *Artes liberales* has the meaning of leisure in its finest sense.

We must remember that Roman writers such as Ovid, Seneca, Virgil and Cicero were profoundly affected by Greek culture, and therefore reflected a selective point of view. Their philosophies do not necessarily reflect the thinking of either the populace or the ruling classes. It was after disintegration of the Roman Empire that *otium* was considered circumspect in terms of Christian moral codes. Christian adherents who wrote had witnessed license within leisure as it had been practiced, and condemned festivals and spectacles during the waning years of Roman civilization. On the other hand, *otium* was to fuse with the contemplative life within monasteries and continued to have an association with learning and discipline. Leisure was strictly controlled within monastic life and the doctrine of work was to become a means for purification of the spirit. The word work took on attributes of being a preventive as well as a cure for transgressions in both individuals and social groups.

Centuries later, the economist Veblen attached to leisure the notion of free time and created the term "leisure class."[8] From his treatise by the same name and through the respect given to his theories by sociologists, Veblen left his mark on American thinking in regard to leisure. At this time, and henceforward, leisure became synonymous with free time, unproductiveness and absence from the necessity to work; in fact as unwillingness to work, or laziness. Many became disdainful of the wealthy who had freedom from toil, while others envied their comfortable position in society. This was a popularized ideality not unlike that held by Puritans of New England. It may have been, as Hall suggested, that opposition to pursuits of the wealthy was not so much that the pursuits themselves were evil, but that envy resulted in recriminative acts against the group that had opportunity to pursue interests that the less advantaged would have liked to pursue.[9]

On the other hand, Veblen's influence on writers in the field of recreation and leisure brought about the common definition of leisure still being published in Fairchild's *Dictionary of Sociology* in which it is defined as time remaining after the necessities of life are attended to,[10] hence the notion that leisure as time is quantitatively determined. Any semantic faithfulness to its roots and origin has been abrogated. Without removing leisure from time as a referent, without discontinuing to use the phrases, "leisure time," "free time," "using leisure" and a host of other phrases propositional to quantities of time, leisure will continue to be considered a commodity to be used, bought or sold. In this sense, time becomes the central issue and not leisure. From a point of language, time and leisure are anomalies, just as "good leisure" or "bad leisure" are anachronisms for those of us who prefer to maintain that leisure is an experience. It becomes our problem, if we believe this, to sort out referents that hold true to the classical notion of *arete*.

PLAY AS A SYMBOL

There is no single idea to be expressed by the word play, any more than for the words discussed previously, but the concept of play is far more universal than either leisure or recreation. While the other two terms applied only to humans, play extends to include animals. It is therefore instructive to keep in mind the juncture with the gamboling and frolicking of animals as well as humankind.

The English word play etymologically came from Anglo-Saxon *plega* and *plegan,* literally symbolizing play and to play. The word came from those commoners of Britian and not from the litany of aristocracy, therefore it has no equivalent in French, Latin or Greek word roots. While I know of no author who has undertaken an analysis of recreation and leisure to any exhaustive degree, Huizinga has provided us with a classic treatise on play.[11] I often lament that among the readers of his work, by far the greater number are outside the field of leisure and recreation. My own research tends to support Huizinga's contention that the word, stemming from German idioms and fusing with English, provides us with many more referents than simply to move swiftly, frolic, or play a game for amusement. Etymologically, the word encompasses the whole spectrum of ways of playing, modes of playing and conditions of playing. Bringing together referents from a variety of languages, the case may be established that play has a focal meaning of a harmonious mix of sheer fantasy and powerful realism. A review of some 52 referents supports this contention.

There appears to be a generic term for play that represents all play and all forms of play. The basic Greek word was *paidia* (play), which referred to the play of children, with its roots in child *(pia)*. In literary usage, however, *paidia* had an extended meaning to represent the belief that one must be as a child to play. This influence is illustrated by Plato when he wrote, ". . . man is God's plaything, and that is the best part of him." He noted that life must be lived as play, playing certain games, making sacrifices, singing and dancing, then man will be able to propitiate the gods . . ." In this discourse, Plato was referring to a much higher order of play than mere "child's play."

We find the same extended usage for play in association with education and culture, for we find the same root in *paideia*. There is no doubt that the Greeks considered education as a life-long concern integrated into community and *arete*. According to some authorities, the word *paideia* literally meant culture.[12] It is apparent from Plato's writings that learning and play were inseparably bound together, that the former was a natural outgrowth of a play motive in life, and that play extended from the child's level to the highest realms of aesthetic and religious experience. Symbols referring to play were for the most part derivations of *paidia*. Suffixes were to indicate playing, playful, plaything, attendance at school, rearing of children, teaching and instruction, as well as to take part in festivals (which included athletics and drama-poetry along with music and dance). The Greeks attached no morality to play and there was no antonym to connote "unplay." Curiously, they had no linguistic equivalent to our word game or sport. For the Greeks, there was only the Olympian Festival and no such expression "Olympic Games." While they may have not understood play any better than we, they recognized it in all aspects of life and nurtured it.

Not unlike classical Greek, but even more inclusive, we find that in Latin there was one universal word to express the whole realm of play, that being *ludus*. The word stem comes from *ludere,* of which *ludus* is a referent. Play was not drawn from the root for child, but rather from a breadth of concepts and at all ages and all levels of society. *Ludus* covered aspects of drama, gambling, games, festivals, athletics, school and learning, satire and comedy, as well as activities associated with parades and public celebrations for amusement. Other derivations cover the realm of unreality or conditions illusionary or fanciful. Cicero used the word *ludimagister* or schoolmaster, hence a direct link with education as was the case with leisure and the Greek derivations.

The word *alea* represented a game of dice and later was to become a referent for chance or hazard. To play, *ludo,* indicated that one could play in a variety of ways, including dice, for purposes of amusement, to banter in conversation, or deceive or delude another with tricks. In classical Latin, there was no word for game in the literal sense, only *ludus*. Game is of English origin as is the term sport. Although we loosely term festival and circuses of Roman times as "public games" they are literally known as *ludus* (play).

Curiously, we find only faint tracings of the original, classical Latin *ludus* in the Romance languages. Our words ludicrous, ludibrious and other derivations carry overtones of play, but in a limited sense. Interestingly, we have a game called *Ludo,* which is related to parcheesi and carries the notion of play. Backgammon is often given as the source for game, or originally, *gammon,* but this may only be claimed due to the sound-alike effect.

It seems that in our search for meaning of recreation, leisure and play, we find a central theme among all characteristics indicated in the historical tracings of those languages most nearly associated with our own. This theme converges in play, the phenomenon most interesting and intriguing to me. It would appear, then, that play is the experience attributed to recreation and sought through leisure. By systematized observation and autobiographic investigations, we are able to distinguish play from among other behaviors, be it animal or humankind. When you and I play, we are conscious of the experience and are not self-deceiving. By focusing on play to understand concepts generally associated with leisure and recreation, there is no linguistic violence committed against the other terms. The major handicap that I have found is in derisive connotations of an emotive nature among those who fail to understand the universality and significance of play. I am convinced that these handicaps will pass if we become more committed to a research approach.

Of the three terms, play is the most immediately recognized as action oriented. It is the most universal among all cultures, for all languages have a symbol for play, both written and spoken, and no society in the history of written language has ignored play. In a literal sense, we can accept the common phrase, "Americans work hard at their play," as being linguistically correct — we put a great many ergs into it. If, on the other hand, such play is more of a fetish, then there may be a different assessment made. The fact that the word play comes to us through the language of "common folk" and subjugated peoples, helps explain emotive responses to it by intellectuals and upper classes in England and thence America. It might be said that in more recent times, only the disenfranchised person played (including children and animals) while the more advantaged recreated and had leisure.

CONCLUSIONS

This has been a very cursory treatment of the evolution of terms in the field of recreation, but nevertheless, it should provide evidence that we are truly faced with a dilemma as to the meanings of the words central to any discussion of recreation, leisure or play. My theme has been a plea for semantic understanding to clarify intended uses of these terms, especially as we attempt to carry out, through research, assessments of what the field is contributing to society. It has been my contention that we unknowingly add to misunderstanding by failing to clarify our definitions, both among ourselves and with the public. We are often like the person, who, when asked what he meant by a certain statement has responded by saying, "You know what I mean" or "I know what I mean, I just can't explain it." If we fail to know the meaning of words necessary to explain a point, then we can presume that the person's thinking is fuzzy. Fuzzy thinking generally produces fuzzy notions, for when we think we use symbols (words).

It is not surprising that we resist being asked to explain what we mean. Not only are we verbally bombarded with words through television and radio, but we are also surrounded by the printed word for most of our waking hours.

To listen carefully and analyze what we hear may soon become a lost art, and then when someone errs and says, "There has been a breakdown in communication," it will be a fact and not just an excuse for failure. Sometimes when we ask for clarification we become more confused and then simply shut down our ears in defense. As an illustration of defending oneself from onslaughts of words which have no meaning for us, a lady clerk in a large office where there were a number of other workers, was asked, "How can you concentrate on what you are doing when there is so much conversation going on around you?" Her answer was, "I don't hear them. I turn it off."

How many of us truly listen and analyze what a politician is saying during campaigns? How many analyze the words he uses? Rather, too many persons take in superficial impressions of how he looks at people, his dress, and how convincingly he delivers his words. Long ago, despots learned the art of orating without using words that had clear-cut and precise meanings and were able to evade or shelter the facts. For example, for a time Americans were not at war in Vietnam, we were maintaining a police action and many less discerning persons believed it.

Too often the journalistic mood of the writer arises and colorful words are sprinkled across the pages. They read so well, it is hoped that no one will question their accuracy. How delightful it sounds when we sell recreation and leisure as a vehicle for contentment and happiness. Who can be against happiness, against joyful living, against satisfaction with oneself? The gritty part comes when someone asks us to explain what we mean. It has often been said that the person who asks another for clarity is the worst sort of bore, if not simply rude. Only a few of us have lost enough timidity to insist.

As children we learned our language first by imitation and we often misled our parents by using words that they should have realized we did not understand. We also learned to use words in a correct sense without knowing their meanings, to say nothing of skipping the hard ones in our school texts. It is well understood that language is highly contagious, and we must guard against adopting jargon and nonsense statements without examination.

Influences have been many and varied as to reasons for our dilemma in meaning. Not the least of them stems from emotionally laden explanations of the importance of recreation, leisure and play by the early founders of the recreation movement. During the beginning stages of any social movement, stimulating emotional responses among people is far more productive in drawing attention and adherents than any intellectual approach could possibly be. Today, however, recreation has gained acceptance as an institution in America and it is now time for dispassionate analysis. Changes in methods of communication are coming so rapidly that we will be forced to play catch-up to be understood. If we believe, as our early leaders did, that recreation, leisure and play contributed to fulfillment of living, then we need to ask "how" and "why." This can happen only by developing new theories and testing them through research. In light of present individual and social needs, we must not only recognize the holes in other's symbolic reasoning, but also in our own.

REFERENCES

1. Ogden, C. K. and Richards, P.A., *The Meaning of Meanings, A Study of the Significance of Language Upon Thought and the Science of Symbolism,* New York, Harcourt Brace, 1923 p. 12.
2. Patrick. George T.W., *The Psychology of Relaxation,* Boston, Houghton Mifflin, 1916. p. 15.
3. Jaeger, Werner, *Paideia: The Ideals of Greek Culture* (Gilbert Highet trans.), New York, Oxford University Press, 1939.
4. Pieper, Josef, *Leisure: The Basis of Culture,* New York, The New American Library, 1963.
5. deGrazia, Sebastian, *Of Time, Work and Leisure,* New York, The Twentieth Century Fund, 1962, p. 264.
6. Aristotle, *Metaphysics,* Chapter 1.
7. Brumbaugh, Robert S. *Ancient Greek Gadgets and Machines,* New York, Thomas Cromwell Co., 1966, pp. ix-x.
8. Veblen, Thorstein, *The Theory of the Leisure Class,* New York, The Macmillan Co., 1899.
9. Hall, Thomas Cuming, *The Religious Background of American Culture* Boston, Houghton Miffin, 1930, Chapter 1.
10. Fairchild, Henry Pratt (Ed.), *Dictionary of Sociology,* New York, Philosophical Library, 1944, p. 175.
11. Huizinga, Johan, *Homo Ludens: A Study of the Play Element in Culture,* Boston, Beacon Press, 1955, Chapter II.
12. Jaeger, Werner, *Op.Cit.*

Chapter Two
Perceptions of Time

John Farina

Time, as a concept, has caused insomnia to philosophers, artists, and social and physical scientists from the beginnings of recorded thought. Yet for the ordinary man the concept itself presents no problem. He knows what time it is — he received a watch for Christmas. He knows when he starts and quits work — he punches in. He knows when the buses, trains and aircraft come and go. He has a fair sense of what sixty miles per hour means both objectively and subjectively. The calendar gives him some idea where he is on the continuum of history. On occasion he has too much time and, perhaps more frequently, he has not enough time.

It seems, however, that the most illuminating observations on time have been recorded not by common men but by uncommon men, not by scientists, social or physical, but by artists and philosophers.

Lao-Tse the Chinese mystic simply noted that, "Time is a state of the mind." Omar Kayam indicated the finality of the progress of time in his beautiful verse:

The Moving finger writes, and having writ,
Moves on; nor all your piety nor wit,
Shall lure it back to cancel half a line,
Nor all your tears wash out a word of it.

In a related vein Henry Dobson answers a rhetorical question regarding time. "Time goes you say? Oh no! Alas, time stays, *we* go."

Omar Ibn Al Halif notes that regardless of whether we go or time goes, time does not come back:

"Four things come not back:
The spoken word
The sped arrow;
Time past;
The neglected opportunity."

Einstein speaking of visiting friends lingering (this is the artistic Einstein) states; "They remind me of time — always going but never gone."

The pace of time is beautifully contrasted by Shakespeare and Oscar Wilde speaking of its slowness and Herrick and Tennyson speaking of its inexorable speed.

Macbeth laments:

"Tomorrow and tomorrow and tomorrow,
  Creeps in this petty pace from day to day,
  to the last syllable of recorded time:"

And Oscar Wilde's sad, sad lines from the "Ballad of Reading Gaol":

"All that we know who lie in gaol,
  Is that the walls are strong;
  And every day is like a year,
  A year whose days are long."

Contrast this tragic slowness of time with the light hearted challenge of the swiftness of time as presented by Herrick in his cavalier sonnet:

"Gather ye rosebuds while ye may,
  Old Time is still a-flying,
  And this same flower that smiles today,
  Tomorrow will be dying."

Tennyson's *Ulysses*, referring to the swift passage of time, bemoans the brevity of opportunity that the limits of just one life time impose:

"Life piled on life were all too little;
  And of one for me — little remains,
  And vile it were for some three suns,
  To store and board myself."

Marcel Proust lucidly explicates the relativity of time:

"The time which we have at our disposal every day is elastic;
  the passions that we feel expand it, those that we inspire
  contract it; and habit fills up what remains."

In this day of such concepts as space-time, time-motion and the theory of relativity, the most appealing literary reference to time comes from Lewis Carrol. In *Alice in Wonderland*, that rich source of creative thought, the Mad Hatter speaks with Alice:

"If you knew Time as well as I do you wouldn't talk about wasting it. It's him."

"I don't know what you mean," said Alice.

"Of course you don't" the Hatter said, tossing his head contemptuously, "I dare say you never spoke to Time."

"Perhaps not," Alice cautiously replied; "but I know I have to beat time when I learn music."

"Ah! That accounts for it," said the Hatter. "He won't stand beating. Now if you only kept on good terms with him, he'd do almost anything you liked with the clock. For instance, suppose it were nine o'clock in the morning, just time to begin lessons; you'd only have to whisper a hint to Time and round goes the clock in a twinkling! Half-past one, time for dinner!"[1]

What, then, is this slippery concept time which has been so diversely described? A half facetious (and therefore more than half wise) definition states that: "Time is the diminution of the future by the accumulation of the past."[2]

Historically, man has in fact judged time by periods or intervals. The earliest such intervals were marked by natural events such as night and day; Spring, Summer, Winter; full moon, new moon; planting and harvest; etc. It is somewhat ironical that just as man achieved precision and accuracy in the measurement of intervals by the development of chronometers and by observations of the solar system, the concept of the relativity of time (subjectively recognized by artists throughout history) was proposed by physical scientists. It is therefore necessary to attempt to relate the views of the philosopher-artists on the one hand and the physicists on the other hand before we can present a comprehensive social concept of time.

While physicists have long used time as a basis for measuring motion — miles per hour for speed of motion or feet per second as a measure of acceleration — they now view time as a concept without which motion and change cannot exist. Time by definition now represents, rather than simply measures, change or motion. Two or more differing and non-simultaneous images are required in the perception of motion; non-simultaneous means time. For the physicist, time is inextricably bound to change and motion. For the social scientist, this change and motion is also seen in terms of the activity of people, of process, of social change and interchange, and of the interaction of people.

Yet the social concept of time seems inextricably bound to our value system. Thus George Woodcock, writing on the tyranny of the clock, suggests that the clock was the most important instrument of the Industrial Revolution.[3] George Soule, suggests that "The American Attitude" includes enslavement by and reverence to the clock. This he relates directly to economic attitudes characteristic of the Protestant Ethic.[4] Thus we spend, waste, exchange, buy, hoard, sell, forget, save, use, kill, structure, beat, and pass time. Time itself; marches, flies, plods, creeps, passes by, and escapes. All these terms relate directly to action and process. While to the economist and worker time is money to be saved, spent or wasted just as material goods, time is also a dimension of activity, change, or process. In turn, time has several dimensions, including duration, intensity, extensity, quantity and quality.

DIMENSIONS OF TIME

Duration

This attribute of time may be viewed as a continuum extending from the infinite past to the infinite future. The present is an infinitesimal moving interval proceeding at a regular and unfailing pace from the past to the future. Time as the accumulation of the past by the diminution of the future fits this notion beautifully. Thus duration is measurable in terms of the regular passage of the present along the continuum of duration. Indeed this measurement has been so operationally accurate and economically useful that it has been literally reified in terms of an interval scale — the clock. This approach to time synchronizes smoothly with the notion of money, also an interval scale, to represent materially the value of man's time. Thus a man might say, "My time is worth $10.00 an hour."

There is, however, a subjective aspect of duration. The psychologists point out that time which is occupied with much pleasant activity tends to seem shorter than time which is devoid of meaningful activity. For example: one hour of playing baseball seems shorter than one hour of waiting for a bus. In retrospect, however, the reverse is true. The time which was occupied seems longer on recall than does that time which was relatively unoccupied.

Intensity

Since time is inextricably bound up with action, the subjective experience of any given action over a period will vary in intensity. What we must recognize is that regardless of the precise indices of time we use, we are in fact dealing with perceptions and feelings. De Grazia notes:

"Thus by using a strictly quantitative assembly-line conception time — time as a moving-belt of equal units — one ignores the significance of much activity. A moment of awe in religion, or ecstasy in love, or orgasm in intercourse, a decisive blow to an enemy, relief in a sneeze, or death in a fall is treated as equal to a moment of riding on a bus or shovelling coal or eating beans."[5]

We can note the same intensity differential almost daily — bases full, two out, last of the ninth inning, the home team 2 runs behind, the count on the batter 3 and 2 — is a significantly more intense moment than a ninth inning with 2 out nobody on and the home team leading 10-0. The subjectivity is clear in this illustration for in addition to the different intensity potential which is inherent in the setting and structure of the activity there is a distinguishable subjective intensity difference for the pitcher and outfielder, for the team managers and the umpires, for the players and the spectators, and among the spectators depending upon their emotional commitment to either team or the amount of their bet on the outcome of the game.

Extensity and Quantity
Under this heading consideration is given to the extent to which identifiable blocks of time are available. For example that block of time called a life time has doubled in western civilization during the past 1,000 years. This greater life expectation is increasing in extensity, i.e. it is becoming available to more people in more areas of the world.

Again — in western civilization — that block of time we identify as "work-time" is becoming more brief and this shortening of work time as a quantity of time is becoming more extensive. The obvious corollary is that non-work time increased in direct proportion to the decrease in work time. Again, speaking in terms of extensity, if we view non-work time as being mostly leisure time (as some do) we can state that, in Western Civilization at least, this is the age of mass leisure. No longer, as in Veblen's day, is leisure so restricted in extensity or so limited in quantity that we can speak of the leisure class. There is no longer a class identified by the fact that it alone has quantities of leisure.

Thus when we speak of time in terms of extensity, we are referring to the extent of the distribution of identifiable blocks of time. When we speak of time as quantity, we are speaking of the variations in measurement of particular blocks of time. Thus the 35 hour work week refers to the quantitative aspect of work time. The availability of the thirty hour work week to a given number of office workers refers to the extensity of this particular block of time.

Quality

The quality of time refers to those conditions that make it possible to classify a period as: work, leisure, free time, idleness, etc. To a great extent the quality of time is culturally determined and inextricably dependent upon values. Most societies tend to dichotomize time and the tendency of western civilization is to do so in terms of work and non-work. To a large extent this particular dichotomy dates from the Industrial Revolution and is a reflection of the Protestant Ethic.

Other societies employ different dichotomies: e.g.

African Bushmen — Women's activities and Men's activities.
Plains Indians — Peace and War.
Baluchi of Pakistan — Obligatory and time of free will. Here the emphasis and status is on the latter.
In one respect the Baluchi point of view is easier for us to understand than is the view of the Plains Indians for, like us, they distinguish between an area of sober, mundane, practical activity and an area of play or free will.[6]

Work and Obligated Time

Work time in our society is that time required for maintenance or for material improvement of self and dependents. It is literally time spent in return for money or its equivalent. It is time *spent* to fulfill the obligation of monetary reward. One man spends his money for another man's time while reciprocally the other man spends his time for another man's money.

Obligated time may be divided into two types, although these are not always mutually exclusive:

1. Sleep and personal maintenance time. This would include time involved in personal toilet and for eating. Non-essential eating time can, however, on occasion be viewed as free time, leisure or recreation.
2. Non-work obligatory time. This involves time committed to one's primary role expectations outside the sphere of gainful employment. It is adequately illustrated by such characteristic suburban activities as upping and downing storm windows and screens, mowing the lawn, driving junior to his music lesson, the trip to the shopping centre and sundry obligatory "voluntary" activities. These may or may not be satisfying modes of

behavior. No judgment is being passed on the value of these activities. For some they may challenge the mentality or spirit or simply be pleasant in themselves; for others they may be dull and "plonking."[7]

IDLENESS, RECREATION, FREE TIME, LEISURE

Idleness

In general use, idleness is a term of eprobrium although it can be an alternate for recreation, free time and leisure. It found wide currency following the Protestant Reformation when it was generally used in reference to non-workers. As recreation came to be viewed as a contributor to greater productivity, the term idleness was reserved for those non-workers who were not refreshing or recreating themselves for more efficient work. Today the term has lost currency outside puritan oriented religious groups.

All four of the terms listed above represent the non-work side of our time dichotomy. We must recognize, however, that leisure is not the antonym for work but rather is the positive counterpart. The opposite of work is unemployment.

Recreation

This term in our society has been implicitly identified with the work category of time although it is popularly believed to represent the non-work category of time. Professional recreation workers identify recreation as activity indulged in voluntarily for the satisfaction derived from the activity itself and leading to revitalization, or recreation, of mind, body or spirit. In fact this is a limiting definition in terms of pre-determination as it is only by the result (revitalization) that recreation can be identified.

Nonetheless, our society assumes that certain types of activity are potentially recreative; music, sports, drama, cinema, social events, etc. Public, private and commercial organizations providing opportunities for these types of activities have proliferated in recent years. The question raised by the definition of recreation is: recreation or revitalization for what? Recreation promoted by business and industrial concerns, recreation as a medical prescription, and recreation as an adjunct to our educational system all emphasize the potential of such activities for revitalizing the individual so he can work more efficiently.

Will the role of leisure in relation to work undergo a basic change? Up to now our leisure as well as most other activities of our life has been work-oriented. Leisure is often thought of in terms of "recreation" — i.e., activities to be engaged in during non-work hours which will refresh or "recreate" the individual so that he may be a more effective worker upon his return to his job. Otherwise, it is regarded as idleness. With increasing leisure, will new types of pursuits emerge — goal-directed, useful, long-term, satifying in nature — around which man may also focus his energies and ambitions? Will work once again in human history become a means to other ends — as visualized in Thomas More's *Utopia* — rather than an end in itself?[8]

Free Time

In general usage free time is considered as residual time after we take account of work-time, sleep-time and time for personal care. More precisely, free time may be considered as that time during which one is relatively free of primary role expectations. This approach ties the concept of free time into the theoretical framework of role theory. It derives from the notion that free time is time which is not restricted by occupational and family duties and obligations. Other obligations and duties then are considered secondary to an individual's family and occupational roles. Indeed occupational role may be considered as subsidiary to family role or as a specific aspect of that central role. Free time, then, is time during which one is relatively free of economic, social, or physical restriction or compulsion.

As with duration, free time and obligatory time can be conceived as the extremes of a continuum. Thus we may view time as relatively free or relatively obligatory. In terms of this conceptualization, absolutely free time is an ideal and probably unattainable.

Free time allows for relatively preferential behavior while obligatory time involves the expectation of a particular kind of behavior. During obligatory time an individual acts with reference to the norms and primary expectations of his occupational and family roles. While role expectation is not absent in free time there is not the same intensity of obligation to assume specific role behavior. If obligations to assume specific roles or to meet specific role expectations are present then the time during which such a role is performed is less free than when such obligations do not exist. During free time there is a greater opportunity for a person to select from a wide range of choices of behavior as he or she may pursue goals not necessarily related to economic or family expectations. It must be recognized that the individual is seldom, if ever, free of structural expectations. During free time he comes under the pressure of different norms which might be quite as restrictive as those operating during obligatory time.

Free time then presents the opportunity to exercise preferential behavior. The range and quality of choice may vary considerably in terms of the quantity and quality of time available. There is a difference in the quality of behavioral opportunity after ten hours of strenuous work and after eight hours of refreshing sleep. Also there is a great difference in the range of choice offered during a 15 minute free period at a factory ten miles from home and a free afternoon at a summer resort.

Leisure

Leisure, as opposed to recreation, does not describe activities and as opposed to free time is not time. The term "leisure time" as differing from "leisure" describes a particular type of time. On this basis *leisure* should perhaps be more logically compared with *freedom*, i.e. the two modifiers in the terms "free time" and "leisure time" warrant comparison.

Leisure has become a recent concern of the modern social science scholar whereas previously it was primarily the domain of the philosopher. We are not, however, dealing with a new concept but rather with a reconceptualization of a construct which has been a subject of philosophic discussion since the Golden Age of Greece. Most discussions of leisure take Aristotle's ideas as the point of departure.

Aristotle viewed leisure as, "a condition or state, the state of being free from the necessity to labor."[9] On occasion he used the term in such a manner as to suggest that it involved a time element, that is, the time during which one was in the particular condition or state referred to as leisure. The essential terms in this definition are "freedom" and "necessity." We must not be misled into believing that labor, in the sense of strenuous physical activity, is excluded from Aristotle's notion of leisure. What is excluded is the *necessity* or obligation to labor.

It must be noted, however, that freedom from the opportunity to labor does not constitute leisure if the necessity to labor is present. Thus the unemployed do not necessarily have leisure.

Pieper, commenting on Aristotle's view noted: "The provision of an external opportunity to leisure is not enough; it can only be fruitful if man himself is capable of leisure and can as we say occupy his leisure."[10] This suggests a value placed on the manner in which leisure is occupied: i.e. "fruitfully." Leisure thus has a positive connotation. If a man is free from the necessity to labor

31

and does not employ himself "fruitfully" he is more likely referred to as idle than as at leisure.

A definition of leisure devoid of value is that offered by the *Oxford English Dictionary*: "The state of having time at one's disposal; time which one can spend as one pleases; free or unoccupied time."[11] This definition includes the notion of leisure as a state and of its freedom. It adds, however, the non-judgmental element of choice of use of time without specifying that the choice must be "fruitful" in order to qualify as leisure.

Thus we find a consensus that leisure is characterized by freedom, a sense of freedom that is in the mind of man as differing from environmental or socially determined freedom. This freedom can be considered an opportunity to act as one pleases with the limits imposed by environment and social context. The idea that the action must be "fruitful" appears too judgmental and value oriented to be an essential aspect of the concept. In given circumstances, if we leave the judgment of leisure to criteria external to the concept, then we may speak of fruitful or non-fruitful leisure according to context.

When we divest the view of Aristotle and its restatement by Pieper of the value element, there remains the clear implication that activity is an aspect of leisure. The time during which one is in the state of leisure must be "occupied."

This occupation of time may include overt activity and also such "leisurely" pursuits as counting clouds on a sunny afternoon, or quiet meditation, or contemplation. Indeed Pieper considers the notion of non-activity an essential of leisure.

"Leisure is a form of silence, of that silence which is the prerequisite of the apprehension of reality: only the silent hear and those who do not remain silent do not hear. Silence, as it is used in this context, does not mean 'dumbness' or 'noiselessness;' it means more nearly that the soul's power to 'answer' to the reality of the world is left undisturbed. For leisure is a receptive attitude of mind, a contemplative attitude, and it is not only the occasion but also the capacity for steeping oneself in the whole of creation."[12]

Pieper adds that this ideal state of leisure contributes to happiness. The element of freedom as a precondition to leisure is explicated by Kaplan[14] in terms of social role obligations. He suggests that during leisure a man can choose to assume obligations "voluntarily, and with pleasanter expectations than, for example, going to work on January 2 to which he is formally committed for a long period of time."[13] Our conceptualization of free time borrows the notion of freedom from social role obligation. We are, however, impressed with de Grazia's concern regarding the loss of free time by increasing family role expectations.[14] Our notion of leisure, however, goes further. Leisure is that time when one is free from the necessity of fulfilling primary role expectations. This means time not restricted by the demands of occupational and family duties and obligations. Clearly this concept does not limit leisure to free time.

It is possible to achieve leisure within the context of primary role obligation if the need or demand to act in a particular manner is not present. Thus a professional man may choose an activity while performing his professional role which is not necessary or demanded of him at that time. A worker on an assembly line lacks this choice. Similarly, a father may feel obliged to play ball with his son, which we would consider non-leisure, or he may choose to join his wife on the patio for a gin and tonic which would be leisure. The differentiating factors are the element of necessity and the element of freedom of choice.

Man is faced with an ever increasing block of time which is potentially free. Whether he keeps it free and is able to free himself to enjoy leisure is the challenge of our age. Meeting this challenge will not be facilitated by simplistic and often contradictory notions of time, of leisure, and of freedom. Conceptual clarity is essential in the use of designations. Games, play, idleness, contemplation, leisure, recreation, sports and cultural activities are clearly related terms. Yet just as clearly they are not synonymous or interchangeable when we want words to work with the precise denotations that are essential to knowledge building.

A more hopeful factor that might contribute to meeting the challenge is how man chooses to occupy his ever increasing potential inherent in free time. In a society of increasing unemployment, rapid replacement of workers by automation, earlier retirement, later entry to the work force, innumerable make-work jobs, and increasing income maintenance programs, it seems ridiculous to be concerned with full employment. Rather, maximum non-employment might be a more reasonable goal for a post industrial society. Certainly, this would satisfy an essential precondition to a leisure society and free man's potential to occupy his time constructively and productively in terms of the quality of life. Towards this end, *time* is of the essence.

REFERENCES

1. Carroll, Lewis. *Alice's Adventures in Wonderland.* New York: The Modern Library, 1920. p. 94.
2. Author unknown.
3. Cited in: Kaplan, Max. *Leisure in America: A Social Inquiry.* New York: John Wiley and Sons, 1960. p. 265.
4. Soule, George. "The Economics of Leisure." *The Annals of the American Academy of Political and Social Science,* (September, 1957). pp. 16-24.
5. de Grazia, Sebastian. "How People Spend Their Time." In: Kleemeier, Robert W. (Ed.). *Aging and Leisure.* New York: Oxford University Press, 1960. p. 142-43.
6. Donahue, Wilma, et. al. (Eds.) *Free Time.* Ann Arbor, Michigan: University of Michigan Press, 1958. p. 10-11.
7. A favorite Stephen Potter word meaning just what it sounds like.
8. Donahue, *Op. Cit.* p. 130.
9. de Grazia, Sebastian. *Of Time, Work, and Leisure.* New York: The Twentieth Century Fund, 1960. p. 11.
10. Pieper, Joseph. *Leisure: The Basis of Culture.* New York: Pantheon Books, 1952. p. 71.
11. *Oxford English Dictionary.* Toronto: Leland Publishing Company, 1957.
12. Pieper, *Op. Cit.* p. 52.
13. Kaplan. *Op. Cit.* p. 23.
14. de Grazia. *Op. Cit. Chapter III.*

Chapter Three
Leisure and Freedom Re-examined

Francis J. Bregha

In reviewing some current definitions of leisure, one finds that many link leisure with freedom, even if only in the form of "free time." Two examples will suffice. De Gazia describes leisure as "the state of being free from the necessity to labor."[1] Neulinger affirms: "Leisure has one and only one essential criterion, and that is the condition of perceived freedom."[2]

Whether freedom is analyzed as an actual state of being or as a perception by an individual or a group, as suggested by Neulinger, it is evident that for many conceptual thinkers in our field, there is a profound and intimate relationship between leisure and freedom. How free do we need to be to enjoy leisure? Is professional intervention in leisure services enhanced or limited by the ethos of freedom? Does freedom, in fact, mean the ability of doing what one wants to do when one wants to? And if so, is leisure one of several possible outcomes of such an ability? Where do such questions lead us?

At this point, a word of caution: The purpose of this chapter is to raise questions more than to suggest answers. It is quite true that this old philosophical method of inquiry is rather unfashionable in our technological age in which answers have market value whereas questions tend to irritate. Moreover, we live at a time in which most believe that there must be an answer to everything, the growing evidence to the contrary notwithstanding. Therefore, this text should be read as an invitation to stop, to think, even to look into our own spiritual mirror and to reflect on the questions and answers that we find there.

It is a generally accepted belief that, as children, we first discover freedom, its delights and dangers, in playing. As formal education gradually replaces play, we all experience constraints, some of us rebelling, some adapting. Our freedom, as grasped and developed in childhood, is beginning a long process of adjustment that will last our entire life. But it is particularly in the world of modern work that the freedom of most of us will be subjected to its most severe restrictions. Whether because of standardization and uniformization of both products and production or whether because of the complex hierarchies of our bureaucracies, we can seldom, if ever, do what we would like. There is little place for a free, creative act, except perhaps one that brings in a new routine. Opportunity to do that is reserved for only a few. Hence, some people are actually unlearning the little freedom that may have survived their preparation for the working place. Freedom, like anything that is not exercised, atrophies. In Max Weber's words, "one does not work to live, one lives to work."[3] Marx spoke of alienation and Pieper brilliantly exposed the modern situation in *Leisure: The Basis of Culture*.[4] Finally, in old age many of us fall victim to institutional confinement, poverty or unkindly restrictive expectations of the younger generation. By that time, freedom may not have survived, even in memory or dreams.

If leisure and freedom are as closely related as current descriptions suggest, how can leisure survive whenever freedom is progressively curtailed, shrinking from birth to death? There is no freedom and therefore no leisure for those subjected to a routine, be it at work or elsewhere. Nor is there leisure for a prisoner, whether of conventions, social pressures or exhausted imagination. There is no leisure for anyone who has not maintained his freedom. Would, therefore, the maintenance of freedom throughout our lifetime not be the first and most important precondition of leisure; a sine qua non for its successful practice? Similarly, does such reasoning not suggest that, to be a professional in leisure services, means, among other things, the urgent need for helping people to rediscover their freedom, to define and maintain it? Surely a noble task, yet also one that is bound to lead to confusion if performed by those who are not free themselves.

ABILITY TO EXPERIENCE LEISURE

Going back to our initial question, whether leisure be the outcome of an ability to do what one wants to in a specific situation, one discerns the pivotal importance of the term "ability." It means several things: firstly, the possession of those qualities that enter into being able to do what one wants, essentially knowledge to compare options and then physical and spiritual capability to act on them; secondly, it suggests the availability of means required by such an option; thirdly, it connotes power and strength necessary for acting at all and living with the outcome of our own actions.

Let us look more closely at all three. Firstly, the possession of qualities that enter into being able to choose what one wants to do includes more than information on what is available or permissible. Something deeper is required: the knowledge of oneself as well as of one's milieu; the knowledge of what is good and what is wrong;

the knowledge of various possibilities and of their consequences. Indeed, were such knowledge absent, then every choice would of necessity be a blind one, contradicting the very ability that is required. Thus leisure is linked to knowledge and to wisdom, both of which form part of the ability to choose with intelligence and responsibility. Furthermore, this analysis suggests the need of education for leisure. Throughout history we have increasingly accepted education for work: in fact, the working force in our century is vastly better prepared, more educated for work than ever before. Can humanity be left to its own devices in regard to leisure if we wish to occupy our leisure with intelligence and responsibility?

Secondly, there is the question of means. Throughout history, wealth was perceived as leading to leisure. The poor classes were excluded. Property and leisure went hand in hand, as noted in the expression "the leisure class." Leaving aside, then, the necessity for providing means to everyone who aspires to leisure, still a considerable undertaking even in our prosperous society, there remains the problem of our ability to use available means effectively and responsibly. The presence of means, however, is not sufficient. On top of it, man must have mastery over the means that his concept of leisure demands. Hence leisure cannot exist without training, apprenticeship, or whatever form of preparation the mastery over means may call for. Nor can it exist without a socially conscious management of means, especially for their conservation.

Thirdly, the ability to do what one wants is related to power and strength to act. Since few forms of leisure, except contemplation, can be practiced without at least passive consent of our neighbors or civic authorities, the ability we are seeking here addresses itself to the need for power arrangements that permit the seeker to proceed without fear or punishment. The incapacity to enjoy leisure may in many instances be due to the constant pressures exercised by modern states and their authoritarian institutional structures upon individuals, especially if those states are totalitarian or collectivist in character. Therefore, beyond knowledge, both practical and ethical, beyond accessibility to means and mastery over them, the ability that gives birth to leisure must also be based upon our secure power and strength to enjoy leisure in peace.

Assuming for a moment that such an ability can be developed and maintained through our lives, a phenomenon of extreme rarity in all history, what are the critical points at which our present world threatens to separate leisure from its roots in individual freedom? This is the most difficult part of our analysis as it forces us to reach beyond symbols with which we are increasingly bombarded in our communications-mad society, and to pierce through the thousand and one mirrors used by politicians, salesmen and propagandists of all hues to disorient us.

MANIPULATION AND LEISURE

The most obvious threat to leisure comes from manipulation of any kind, the problem being simply that few people know how much they are being manipulated. Many people do not know what they want. Quite practically, they want what they know — or what someone else shows or tells them. Although education may be presented sometime as an attempt to "draw out" the best that there is in us, in its actual form of schooling, training, or apprenticeship it clearly implies the transmitting of knowledge and skills from the outside to a more or less willing and ready learner.

Our economy may be painted in the bucolic colors of a free market in which free agents freely compete for the best supply-demand interaction — yet a moment of observation shows the ruthless manipulation of everyone by everyone else, the weakest, i.e. the poor, the unemployed, the consumers, holding the short end of the stick while the strongest, i.e. vertically integrated monopolies, are getting richer. One does not need to study Galbraith; personal experience is sufficient to show that, in our economy, there is little place for leisure rooted in freedom. In fact, all known economic systems use blatant manipulation to achieve their ends.

In politics, of course, manipulation parades as propaganda, lobbying, pressure groups and, in extreme cases, as brainwashing or psychiatric treatment. At a more subtle level, none of us is exempt from some degree of political manipulation since we all deal in power relationships in our daily lives. There is no reason to think that leisure services are less receptive to bribery by politicians than other services, or that leisure professionals would confuse persons and principles or policy and expediency less frequently than anyone else. The freedom to act politically in Canada and the United States often reduces itself to biased reacting, to voting against rather than for something, to fighting first for self-interest and only second for common good. In short, manipulation in politics is easy because we offer it great opportunity and expect, even perversely enjoy, being manipulated by our leaders.

Manipulation, besides going unrecognized fully by many, presents the further threat of succeeding so well in some instances that the Orwellian 1984 is suddenly perceived as enduring social reality. "War is Peace," "Freedom is Slavery," and the brain-washed public is no longer able to discern even the sharpest value opposites. Manipulation, of course, thrives on gullibility and aims at the total elimination of all freedom, hence of all leisure, however cleverly labeled in the new doublespeak. The emergence of religious and ideological cults of exotic nature, effectively enslaving their adherents in a web of preposterous and sometimes dangerous beliefs; the amazing scope of phony commercial and financial operations; the readiness to accept as true the most clearly distorted news stories — an acquired taste to which a whole new industry is catering — are only a few current examples of the extreme situations created by successful manipulation in our midst.

We can now perceive the importance of what used to be called "inner strength," "independent judgement," even "character" before our times produced more ambiguous terms. These qualities constitute our defense against manipulation. Hence the ability to be independent, self-sufficient in judgement and its expression, is a fundamental condition of both freedom and leisure.

Beyond the massive manipulation by major forces to which we are subjected as learners of life, as consumers and as citizens, a variety of threats can make enjoyment of leisure problematic or impossible. A host of them reside actually in our very minds: feelings of guilt, especially when not working at something useful; fears reflecting religious or moral norms that appear contradicting what we wish to do; even the prosaic lack of imagination that instead of leisure in freedom generates idleness in boredom. These obstacles are as difficult to overcome as the more visible ones, created by explicit manipulation. Yet, no one is free who fears freedom; no one can be at leisure who feels guilty before an offered opportunity. The Greek advice of knowing oneself first of all remains valid today since the true independence needed for satisfying pursuit of leisure can never be achieved unless we get rid of what distorts us from within. Thus leisure frequently has to take the form of liberation, starting inside oneself.

Finally, environmental factors have to be considered. In a city where there are insecurity, noise, pollution of all sorts and hectic activity in all public places, leisure will be difficult, if not impossible, as no one can be at one with oneself in such conditions. Nor will a sensitive human being be able to enjoy leisure wherever nature is destroyed, exploited and beauty denied by functional utilitarism. This describes so many of our modern surroundings that one can well raise the question: What chance for leisure here? There may be freedom though that freedom may only mean freedom to adapt or undertake the titanic task of environmental change. There may be "leisure activities" and "leisure facilities" — and yet little leisure can ever be experienced there. It is so because true leisure, like true freedom, can exist only in peace; in peace with oneself but also with one's surrounding.

LEISURE: AN IMPOSSIBLE GOAL?

The picture of leisure that is emerging from this discussion shows how difficult, fragile, almost impossible leisure is for modern man. Much less free than superficially believed, much more manipulated than publicly admitted, much less educated than generally thought, modern man appears to be lacking precisely those components of leisure that make it such an exacting state of being; self-knowledge and inner peace. Yet, were these two qualities added to those that we have identified as the basis of freedom, leisure would still not automatically follow. Boredom could still be with us, because leisure, to express freedom, requires choice; choice, in turn, requires awareness of preferences, hence a sense of direction, ultimately a goal. In other terms, leisure is as much freedom to something as it is freedom from something. Goalless leisure, then, is a contradiction which illustrates, even in our times, the difference between leisure and idleness.

These goals, of course, can be many. It is precisely the essence of leisure that they be almost without number since they define what is most personal, most unique in every one of us. At the same time, one suspects that these unique goals are not equal — in quality, morality or social relevance. Nor are they defined out of a vacuum. Besides individual predispositions, they reflect cultural influences and values constantly being absorbed and transformed. Leisure goals thus illustrate a state of a society, probably better than any other single indicator. Obversely, the state of a society is perhaps the greatest determining factor in shaping the leisure goals of its members. Using other terms: how well freedom fares in a given society will be the first measure of leisure opportunities in it.

One indirect result is that this diversity of leisure goals makes leisure as a social phenomenon so hard to grasp, to analyze and to classify. The study of commonalities leads to the development of theories — the study of unique particularities tends to resist scientific approach. Therefore, those social sciences that deal with leisure should not be astonished when their attempts at predicting or controlling, valid as these goals may be in regard to other phenomena, produce quite problematic results.

Much more important, though, is the inability of modern man to conceive worthwhile goals for himself. And yet, without a goal, he is condemned to an unleisurely life. As abhorrent as such a sentence might be to him, he falls victim to the all pervasive sickness of our times: the confusion of means and ends.

He starts with viewing education as a means to obtaining a job, then sees a job as means to securing a livelihood, considers work as means to getting rich, uses money as means to buy what he deems necessary or what would give him status and, finally, even that hardly acquired status becomes means to differentiating himself, a means to establishing his identity. Such a man lives in the world of means. There are no ends in his life that he does not use as means to still other ends and so, in growing confusion, his life results in what a poet once quite rightly described as "one damn thing after another."

Leisure, like freedom, is an end in itself. If perceived as means, it should be called recreation — a worthwhile but quite utilitarian concept. We do not occupy our leisure in order to become healthier or more productive. Leisure allows us to be free, to be what we want to be. Hence the importance of examining our own thoughts, desires and hopes and reflecting whether our lifestyle translates them or not into a coherent, meaningful life: an enterprise in which leisure counseling and education for leisure ought to play a role. The invitation to look into a spiritual mirror, issued at the beginning of this essay, is in fact a daily challenge. The questions that we shall find there, may not be answered immediately or by our effort alone. We need others as others need us. Beyond individual answers, we require societal ones and the understanding of their meaning. In this perspective, leisure professionals are both interpreters and builders of their communities.

It is for this reason that Aristotle's remark in his *Politics* remains so pertinent: "That is the principal point: with what kind of activity is man to occupy his leisure."[5] He, over 2,000 years ago, as well as Pieper more recently, saw that activity related to divine worship. Leisure was part of celebrating God, exactly as Psalm LXV, II has it: "Have leisure and know that I am God."

This view is no longer shared by most contemporary analysts of leisure. Leisure's link to religion has been gradually weakened as religious festivities, rites and feasts occupy less and less of a place in our lives. Instead, modern technology has multiplied the means available for the pursuit of secular leisure while saying very little about their value or moral direction. It should be clear that we are possibly the first generation that faces a peculiar problem in regard to our leisure. As long as leisure found its origin in God and its expression in partaking in worship, its morality was beyond reproach. Now that a divorce has taken place and leisure is linked to freedom rather than to God, a vast question mark as to its ultimate purpose is before us. Who is to guide us through the maze of good and evil now that God is absent and freedom is perceived in many ways? This brings us back to the dichotomy of freedom *from* and freedom *to*. Historically, we have found it easier to define and to fight for freedom *from*. Although this process is far from finished in most of the world, in Canada and the United States the emphasis is slowly shifting towards the consideration of freedom *to*. Since the 1960's, significant sections of our population, particularly women, youth and some minority groups have raised new questions that can be answered only in terms of freedom *to* — hence the considerable increase in conflicts over values. And also, therefore, such an explosion of new, morally untested leisure pursuits.

Is one type of leisure activity as good as any other? Are we to assume that, since leisure is the highest expression of our freedom and freedom, in turn, thrives best in our leisure time, there is not — there cannot be — an ethical conflict? Are leisure and freedom so good per se, in their essence, that neither can give birth to evil, under any circumstances? These questions flow naturally from linking leisure with freedom and necessarily lead into an examination of the moral dimensions of leisure. To say that modern leisure derives its meaning from personal self-fulfillment reached in various ways during free time is clearly no longer sufficient. All of us who in the past have been tempted into perceiving the ultimate goal of leisure in the Maslowian concept of self-actualization surely realize by now that such self-actualization cannot take place in a moral vacuum. The ethics of leisure, including the reconciliation of individual and collective goals within a coherent value system, thus form part and parcel of every serious inquiry into the nature of our freedom.

To sum up: leisure undoubtedly is the most precious and also most fragile expression of our freedom. Freedom remains leisure's pre-condition, its rewards being that freedom can flower best in pursuits that are leisurely. Whereas the maintenance of freedom becomes, then, our constant task and the defining of freedom *to* our greatest challenge, leisure itself still depends as much on the knowledge and wisdom entering into our options, on our ability to choose goals that will bring us happiness, on our inner strength and independence that affirm our unique character, and finally on an environment that is conducive to leisure because it offers peace, per chance beauty and quiet enjoyment.

REFERENCES

1. DeGrazia, Sebastian. *Of Time, Work and Leisure.* New York: The Twentieth Century Fund, 1962. pp. 13-14.
2. Neulinger, John. *The Psychology of Leisure.* Springfield, Illinois: Charles C. Thomas, 1974. p. 15.
3. Cited in Joseph Pieper. *Leisure: The Basis of Culture.* (Tr. by Alexander Dru). New York: Pantheon Books, Inc., 1952. p. 20.
4. *Ibid.*
5. Cited in *Ibid.*, p. 55.

Chapter Four
If Leisure is to Matter
Thomas L. Goodale

Judging from the number of new periodicals with "leisure" in the title, or the pervasive use of the term in the literature and in conversation, or the jargon of leisure studies, leisure education, leisure research, leisure counseling, leisure services, etc., we are moving into the age of leisure at last. Unfortunately, that would be a hasty judgement because leisure is more common in our literature than in our lives and because the term leisure is usually used as little more than a substitute for words we have grown tired of.

Frequently, leisure is used where recreation would serve better; as in the phrase leisure services. Often leisure means no more than free time; as in the phrase leisure time. In addition, the term has been resurrected from antiquity to refer to a state or condition; that is, where one is at. When one is at leisure one is in a relaxed, contemplative condition. If we convey no more than one of these meanings when we say leisure, then we burden ourselves with being concerned about what is, per se, not very important. If this is all we mean, then leisure doesn't matter — not yet.

MISAPPROPRIATING ARISTOTLE'S THOUGHT

There is deeper meaning which does not come to the surface in most talk and writing about leisure. To find it requires a more careful examination of Aristotle's thought, and the thoughts of those like Pieper[1] and de Grazia[2] who have tried to guide us to and through Aristotle's philosophy. With few exceptions, our encounters with Aristotle's thought, as interpreted by many of those writing about leisure, are not very satisfying. Leisure seems simple, impossible, and unrelated to our lives. There is too little congruence between what we read and hear of it and what we experience everyday.

Seldom do we reflect on the complexity and subtlety of philosophical thought. Understanding Aristotle's writings is at best difficult. His style, as his subject, does not readily yield understanding. Too, there are few among us who read him in the original. Rather, what we read are translations, of which there are many, and notes and interpretations, also in great number. Indeed,

Aristotle spawned an industry, as the shelves of any respectable library attest. Obviously, there are differences in the translations, notes, and interpretations. As a simple example, depending on the translation, Aristotle wrote either "one swallow makes not a summer" or "one swallow makes not a spring." The message, if not the season, is of great importance to us as is noted later. Surely, "leisure" is a much more complex notion than spring or summer. In fact, one of the better known translators, Benjamin Jowett, notes that Aristotle's "leisure" is "one of the most difficult notions to translate into English words and modes of thought."[3]

Aristotle was a product of a milieu so foreign to ours as to seriously tax our ability to comprehend. Consequently, it seems folly to wrench small bits of his writings from their context, transport them over twenty-three centuries, and set them down in an inhospitable place. This is especially hazardous as it is frequently noted that in Aristotle's thought, the existing order — that is what was — was an essential element in his thinking about what ought to be. The result is that there is much in Aristotle's writing that, quite simply, doesn't fit our time at all, some notions about women, friendship and love, slavery and citizenship, for example. He argues that friendship is a relationship between men exclusively, since it requires awareness and return of mutual affection. In relations between unequals, such as rulers and subjects or men and women, "the more useful of the two should receive more love than *he* gives."[4] And he writes, "Domestic authority is the best model for aristocracy, for the authority of the husband is founded on the superiority of his abilities and virtues."[5] One of Aristotle's contemporaries, a man named Aleman, in wishing to compliment some girls, could find no other way to refer to them except as "female boyfriends."[6] In Aristotle's Greece, women were simply not men's equals.

But all men were not equal either. Clearly leisure was not possible for all; or even many. As is widely known, Aristotle's concept of leisure, indeed many argue Greek civilization itself, was built on the backs of slaves. In most Greek cities of the time, slaves plus a few thousand non-voting metics and freemen, out-numbered citizens by ratios varying between 4:1 and 20:1.

In the context of the times, that posed no ethical dilemma. Citizens, in order to have time for government, war, literature, and philosophy, must have someone attend to their material concerns. To have leisure, one must be free from economic tasks. It is not necessary to be wealthy, but one must have means. Aristotle, if anything, was a preacher of moderation. To him slaves were animate tools, and he foresaw the machine age in recognizing inanimate slaves. He was, by all accounts, good to his slaves and to his women. But leisure was not for them; it was only for citizens. "Because mechanics and laborers cannot practice virtue while leading the life of mechanics and laborers they will not be included in the category of citizens."[7] Further, while slaves could enjoy "inferior pleasures . . . who will ascribe the happiness of a man to him who, by his character or condition, is disqualified from manly pursuits?"[8]

THE IMPORTANCE OF WORKING WELL

In the literature about recreation and leisure, one brief passage from Aristotle's voluminous writings is frequently cited. It is from *Politics, Book VII.*

> Nature herself . . . requires that we should be able not only to work well, but to use leisure well; for as I must repeat once again, the first principle of all action is leisure. Both are required but leisure is better than occupation and is its end.[9]

Translators differ. Elsewhere one finds:

> Nature requires not only that we should be properly employed, but that we should be able to enjoy our leisure in an honorable way.[10]

There is agreement, however, that being able to work well, or to be properly employed is so evident as to be a foregone conclusion. Although that part of the passage is often neglected in the recreation and leisure literature, we are reminded of it in so many other ways.

It is said, for example, that Aristotle died of a stomach ailment aggravated by overwork.[11] Pieper, in referring to Aristotle's maxim, "we are unleisurely in order to have leisure," writes that the maxim is more weighty because Aristotle was, ". . . a cool-headed workaday realist."[12] Further, there is no mistaking the closing verses of Genesis, Chapter I and the opening verses of Chapter II. On the sixth day God reviewed his work and saw that it was good; on the seventh day, he rested from his work. Too, it seems clear that Jesus was proud of the fact that he could make a table because he was a carpenter.[13]

In *Politics, Book X*, Aristotle notes the role of rest and recreation. They are good, but not the highest good.

Happiness then, cannot consist in mere recreative pastime; for it is absurd to think that all our serious exertions and strenuous labors should terminate in so frivolous an end. We do not labor that we may be idle, but, as Anarchis justly said, we are idle that we may labor with more effect; . . . The weakness of human nature requires frequent remissions of energy; but these rests and pauses are only the better to prepare us for enjoying the pleasures of activity. The amusements of life, therefore, are but preludes to its business, the place of which they cannot possibly supply; and its happiness, because its business, consisting of the exercise of those virtuous energies which constitute the worth and dignity of our nature.[14]

Rest and amusement are preludes to, and cannot replace business or happiness, the latter flowing from the former if by business we understand the exercise of virtuous energies.

VIRTUE, ETHICS AND LEISURE

Matters of virtue are found throughout Aristotle's *Politics*. This is so because Aristotle wrote *Politics* in conjunction with *Ethics*. He considered them part of one work. It is in *Ethics* that he identifies happiness as the highest good, it being an end in itself. And the wellspring of happiness is virtue. Happiness doesn't come cheap; one has to be virtuous. That is the often repeated message of *Nicomachean Ethics*; happiness derives from a lifetime of virtue.

The proper good of man consists then in virtuous energies, that is in the exercise of virtue continued through life; for one swallow makes not a summer; neither does one day, or a short time constitute happiness . . . The multitude, indeed, pursue different pleasures, because they do not rightly apprehend in what true pleasure consists. But pleasure, strictly so called, is the delight of a virtuous man whose life needs not an appendage of false joys, containing the perennial spring of true pleasure in itself . . . In the estimation of a wise man, virtue is pleasant because it is honorable and good; his happiness is one regular whole; not broken and disjointed.[15]

Of course, Aristotle did note that leisure was better than work, or at least better than work done by non-citizens, and he clearly linked leisure with the contemplative life but, again, in far more complex ways than we generally understand, because contemplation was inextricably bound to the divine in man; to the somehow transcendent soul. Difficult a time as scholars have had with the notion of leisure, it is as nothing compared to this. For Aristotle's notion of contemplation was linked to his notion of God and God's own sense of pleasure. To illustrate:

> Contemplation . . . is possible only by virtue of the divine element in man. We ought then not confine our thoughts to the ephemeral, but so far as possible we ought to seek immortality.[16]

> The life of good conduct — of morally good action — is the best human life, the completest expression of human nature . . . But there is in man an element which is either itself divine or the most godlike of elements in man: *vous*, or whatever that should be called whose nature it is to rule us and to take thought of things noble and divine. And in the activity of this element — in contemplation — man experiences the completest felicity.[17]

Work, leisure, contemplation and happiness are not the simple matters, at least in Aristotle's argument, that we sometimes make them out to be. In most contemporary discussions or writings about leisure, little is said about virtue and less about the divine. The omissions destroy the meaning.

We Without Means
Leisure in the Aristotelian sense is troublesome enough for us on the most secular of grounds; i.e. having means. If to be at leisure one must have means, then what are we to do? Those without means, which is nearly all of us, are simply going to have to work. If, as de Grazia suggests, work and leisure live in two different worlds and free time lives in the world of work,[18] then what are we to do? We live in a world of work and we have no reason to think we should not. We are workers and have no reason to think we should not be, not because Calvin walks in the land but because the world's work (dare we say God's work?) remains to be done. Quite evidently, then, work will require us to exercise our virtuous energies moreso than in the past.

If as Pieper writes, "Leisure . . . (is) utterly contrary to the ideal of 'worker' in each of its three aspects . . . . as activity, as toil, as a social function,"[19] then what are we to do? We have no recourse but to reject Pieper's characterization of the "worker."

> The 'worker' it has been seen in our brief analysis of that significant figure, is characterized by three significant traits: an extreme tension of the powers of action, a readiness to suffer in vacuo unrelated to anything, and complete absorption in the social organism, itself rationally planned to utilitarian ends.[20]

The description is not without merit, historically at least, including the recent past. It seems ill-fitted to the present and in any case there is no reason to cling to the characterization. Where it still fits perhaps it should not. Perhaps one of our major tasks is to assure that it does not. As long as we must work we must rid ourselves of hostility toward it. If leisure is to be a possibility for us, then it must infuse our work. Much more is involved here than the concepts of fusion or extension between work and non-work activities and roles. Our work should be what we choose to do; what we and others consider important. It should so absorb us, as W. H. Auden suggested, that in doing it we are, in essence, praying.[21] Would that Gibran's phrase, "Work is love made visible," was applicable. For if it is not, there seems little hope for leisure.

THE DIVIDING OF TIME . . .

A world of work such as ours suggests, a priori, that the most we can attain is free-time. So leisure as free-time becomes the focus. But free-time is not a goal; per se it is not important and it cannot shoulder the burden too readily placed upon it. What is usually meant by free-time is time free from work and other obligations. But even if by leisure we mean nothing more then free-time, ours is still not an age of leisure and there seems little prospect of it. "One widely current illusion about the future needs to be dispelled. This is the illusion of great affluence and leisure . . . . obtained via projections of increased productivity."[22] Productivity gains have not matched expectations for the past several years. Unemployment in mature economies has been increasing. The inanimate tools that Aristotle anticipated have not set us free; they have set us to work as servo-mechanisms. Sometimes they have set us aside. People now become redundant, a presumably sophisticated but actually grotesque way of saying unemployed. Economic and material growth was to have solved the problems of the unemployed and the poor. It has not, and it cannot, even if growth were to continue as in previous decades, and that seems most unlikely.

Free-time unavoidably carries with it a connotation of subservient worth and value. That is a handicap and a burden. It is undermined by its own definition; it is unobligated time and it is free from work. But who is ever free from work and other obligations? Because one has some discretion about how his or her time may be used does not make it unobligated. In fact, the reverse is true. It is only when we have the opportunity to choose that our obligations become fully apparent. That, as noted later, is consistent with

Aristotle's thought. Surely there is no end to the worthwhile work that must be done. Besides, do not each of us always have obligations to ourselves and to the cosmos and to most everything in between? Further, and particularly disconcerting about the notion of free-time, is that it perpetuates the dichotomy between work and leisure as free-time. The dichotomy deals leisure a heavy blow; probably a fatal blow. Jacques Ellul notes it well, among literally scores of other commentators.

> To assert that the individual expresses his personality and cultivates himself in the course of his leisure is to accept the suppression of half the human personality. History compels the judgement that it is in work that human beings develop and affirm their personality . . . When the human being is no longer responsible for his work and no longer figures in it, he feels spiritually outraged . . . The annihilation of work and its compensation with leisure resolves the conflicts by referring them to a subhuman plane . . . To gamble that leisure will enable man to live is to sanction the dissociation I have been describing and to cut him off completely from part of life.[23]

The work leisure dichotomy does violence to our nature in so many ways, ". . . for one swallow makes not a summer; neither does one day, or a short time constitute happiness . . ." Evenings, week-ends and holidays, however lengthened, are insufficient. A recent study in England revealed that a disproportionate number of suicides were committed on Sunday. Psychologists suggested that perhaps some of the victims of their own hand were not capable of facing another week of work.

AND OF LIVES

Much of the difficulty we face has been attributed to the factory system and the dehumanization of work, but people in comfortable highrise office towers show signs of a similar malaise. The factory system is, however, partly responsible for "the leisure problem" and for creating the work-leisure dichotomy, because it forced a separation; where one lived and where one worked became quite distinct, making the division of time a simple matter. Since then, the separation has been carried much further. Now we believe that working and living should be separate. One appeal of the suburbs, for many at least, is that they are not close to work. The space, and the time needed to traverse it, provides insulation between home and work, leisure and work, living and working. We are not supposed to take our work home; what goes on at the plant or office is supposed to be left at the plant or office. We can and do work at home, but that is a different matter. It is more imperative that one does not take home to work in the sense that one's activities and affairs outside are not to influence work at the plant or office. So half our lives, for a period of 40 years or more, is supposed to be unrelated to the other half. It is errant nonsense of course. It is probably impossible as well. And to be constantly suppressing half of one's life inevitably carries a heavy psychological cost.

This is not just a matter of playing different roles. Even if it were, why must we be constantly playing roles? The main difficulty is that the roles have become not simply unrelated but worse, incompatible. Ruben Nelson makes the case powerfully, illustrating it with the story of a space engineer caught up in a project requiring long hours of hard work. On returning home, he was always surprised to find that his wife seemed just as tired as he was. He didn't think she had much to do but she claimed she had more to do than she had time for. So he arranged to take a day off and spend it with his wife — not on a dinner or family picnic, however. He did a time and motion study of her day. He determined conclusively that his wife's complaints of being overworked were unjustified, and henceforth paid no attention whatever to her complaints.[24]

PERSONS OR OBJECTS

Surely we all recognize how inappropriate was his response. But we also recognize that his response was not inappropriate to the world of work. So we have come to see ourselves and others in two lights — as persons in our private lives, and as things or objects in our public or working lives. We have come to live by two sets of rules — those for the role of worker, functionary, agent, official or whatever role we play in our public lives, and those for the role of parent, friend, spouse, lover or whatever roles make up our private lives. But the roles are incompatible. We cannot reconcile them.[25]

Publicly, as objects, we seek to maximize our profits, importance and status; in part by externalizing our costs and wastes. "Let the buyer beware." Don't require the vendor to be forthright. That is why we are advised not to do business with friends or relatives; the roles are incompatible. Privately, as persons, we share our profits and strengths, and internalize our burdens and those of others — that is what friendship is about. To Aristotle, the first characteristic of friendship was, "the promotion of another's good for his own sake."[25] Publicly, we are unrestrained except by law and regulation: sometimes not even that restrains us. For surely billions of dollars are spent each year to change, avoid or circumvent the law, always to the spender's advantage. Sometimes we are merely rule obeyers ("I'm only doing my job. Don't blame me, I don't set policy.") which is "an organized form of non-responsible behavior."[27] Publicly, as objects, we know only institutional restraint and avoid even that when we can. Privately, as persons, we restrain ourselves; we recognize and exercise personal responsibility. A place where personal responsibility no longer exists would be a good working definition of hell.

MEANING AND MATTERING

The notion of free time diverts our attention from problems which free time cannot resolve. The dichotomy of work and leisure as free-time, the abandonment of people to incompatibly split lives, and the subsidiary value of free time is destructive as it recognizes — even emphasizes — selves as public "things" rather than private "persons." This creates not only confusion but also cynicism because we know that much of our work has lost its meaning; much of what we do does not seem to matter and so with our lives. That applies as often to those engaged in providing human services as it does to those providing goods or services for profit. Galper,[28] for example, notes that social workers are aware that many social services are of little benefit to people, thus they experience a sense of the limited value of their work. While individuals often feel the urgency and crisis, their institution often does not. As persons, they often feel that whatever they do will make little difference and they become dissatisfied with their own inadequate performance. Still, as things, they receive recognition and promotion in the system, perhaps for having resigned themselves to making the best of a situation which may be impossible. They learn not only that much of what they do may not matter, the institution conveys to them that it doesn't matter that it doesn't matter. Is it any wonder then that fatalism is on the rise, with not only more bingo and gambling in the usual sense but also with astrology and Tarot cards, religious and other cults (some of which have remarkably nasty streaks) and in privately and, increasingly, publicly sponsored lotteries, nearly all of which have been vastly more productive than their sponsors ever dreamed? There are even state organized lotteries for getting children into decent schools and those with too limited income into decent housing. What an incredible perversion. The losers are expected to blame their desperate situation on luck rather than on the failure of systems and institutions. As Cohen notes:

In the context of competitive culture the idea of luck may serve as a convenient stabilizer, convenient, that is, to the 'lucky ones' at the same time stultifying initiative and independent thinking. Daily emasculation of the reflective processes of millions, whose horoscopes are cast in the daily press, produces a potentially pliable mentality that sees the futility of social intervention if everything is ordained in the stars.[29]

Perhaps Cohen has cause and effect in reverse order, but it does seem that fatalism and a sense of futility go together.

Finally, the dichotomization of work and free-time, the subservience and the abandonment suggested in the notion of free-time; the fractioning of whole persons and whole lives as though no more than whole numbers, exacerbates what is generally regarded as the period of crisis in which we now find ourselves. Walter Lippmann addressed the issue directly, as noted in the editor's preface to his *A Preface to Morals*.

Thus, Lippmann indicates, business, the family and the other preoccupations of men's daily lives are, in effect, religion's "lost provinces." This loss has inevitably made life seem less meaningful to many men. For with each province now autonomous, each having its own standards and its own modes of thought, there is no longer any strong central theme in men's lives; nothing seems to be organically related to anything else, and so nothing seems to be terribly important.[30]

Tillich, in *The Courage To Be*, comes to the same conclusion. He notes that the anxiety characteristic of our era is that of emptiness and meaninglessness, placing us " . . . under the threat of spiritual non-being."[31]

So the final problem with the notion of leisure as time free from work and other obligations is that it does not matter. It is without value or meaning. If we have a leisure problem it is not because we have too much free time, or too little work. What we have is too little meaning in our free time and in our work; in sum, in our lives.

In only one sense is free-time a useful notion: the sense of discretion about its use. The opportunity and ability to choose is important. There is no other road to virtue because, to cite Aristotle once more, when he summarizes his argument about the relation between virtue and voluntary and involuntary acts: "The habit of moral virtue implies the deliberate preference of one kind of conduct to another; and deliberate preference implies freedom of choice."[32]

IF LEISURE IS TO MATTER

Leisure is a useless notion if by it we mean merely free time or some contemplative state. Still, the Aristotelian view may inform and encourage us if we keep his context. The context is virtue. The world of action is an essential corollary. If happiness is the highest good and the product of contemplation, so it is also the result of action; the exercise of virtuous energies. Well being and well doing are parts of a whole; complementary and synergistic. That, not surprisingly, is more compatible with our experiences than merely contemplating, even though such experiences may be pitifully infrequent. For who has not felt the peace and joy of having done something truly worthwhile, having done it well, and knowing it?

Aristotle concerned himself with whole men leading whole lives. He saw clearly that happiness was unattainable otherwise. Only if we perceive our lives, including our work, congruently, can we come to grips with Aristotle or with an endless collection of scholarly thought since his time.

What those in the recreation or leisure service fields should do about all this is not entirely clear. It is characteristic of our time, perhaps because we are only beginning to understand the crises before us, to have some ideas about what needs to be done without yet knowing what to do. The recapture of selves as persons rather than things; the exercise of virtue through a lifetime; the reintegration of all aspects of life into a varied but congruent whole; the recovery of meaning; these are the tasks before us all.

If leisure is to matter, these tasks must be addressed more directly, and probably more radically, than in the past. Until then, the judgement that leisure has arrived is not only premature but also misleading, with consequences which can only be dire.

REFERENCES

1. Pieper, Joseph. *Leisure: The Basis of Culture*. (Alexander Dru, trans.) New York: Pantheon Books, 1952.
2. de Grazia, Sebastian. *Of Time, Work and Leisure*. New York: The Twentieth Century Fund. 1960.
3. Steward, J. A. *Notes on the Nicomachean Ethics*. New York: Arno Press, 1973. p. 446.
4. Kierman, Thomas P. (Ed.) *Aristotle Dictionary*. New York: Philosophical Library, 1962. p. 137-138.
5. Gillies, John. *Aristotle's Ethics*. (John Gillies trans.) London: Routledge, 1886. p. 138.
6. Durant, Will. *The Life of Greece*. (The Story of Civilization: Part II), New York: Simon and Schuster, 1939. p. 301.

7. Kierman, *Op. Cit.*, p. 149-150.
8. Gillies, *Op. Cit.*, p. 361.
9. Kaplan, Justin (Ed.). *The Pocket Aristotle*. (W. E. Ross trans.) New York: Pocket Books, 1958. p. 336.
10. Durant, *Op. Cit.*, p. 533.
11. Kierman, *Op. Cit.*, p. xii.
12. Pieper, *Op. Cit.*, p. 21.
13. Nash, J. B. *Philosophy of Recreation and Leisure,* Dubuque, Iowa: Wm. C. Brown Co., 1973. p. 222.
14. Gillies, *Op. Cit.*, p. 360.
15. *Ibid.* p. 169-170.
16. Ferguson, John. *Aristotle*. New York: Twayne Publishers, 1972. p. 138.
17. Rees, D. A. (Ed.). *Aristotle: The Nicomachean Ethics,* (A Commentary by the late H. H. Joachim) Oxford: Oxford University Press, 1951. p. 287.
18. de Grazia, *Op. Cit.*, p. 7-8.
19. Pieper, *Op. Cit.*, p. 40.
20. *Ibid.*, p. 39.
21. Auden, W. H. "Culture and Leisure." *Ekstics*, (144, Feb., 1966). p. 418-420.
22. Boulding, Kenneth. "The Future of Personal Responsibility." *American Behavioral Scientist,* (15:3, Jan./Feb. 1972). p. 352.
23. Ellul, Jacques. *The Technological Society*. (John Wilkinson, trans.) New York: Random House, 1964. p. 339-400.
24. Nelson, Ruben F. W. *The Illusion of Urban Man*, Ottawa: Information Canada, 1976. p. 34.
25. *Ibid.*
26. Ferguson, *Op. Cit.*, p. 137.
27. Nelson, *Op. Cit.,* p. 56.
28. Galper, Jeffrey H. *The Politics of Social Services*. Englewood Cliffs, New Jersey: Prentice-Hall, 1975. p. 58.
29. Cohen, John. *Chance, Skill, and Luck: The Psychology of Guessing and Gambling*. Baltimore: Penguin Books, 1960. p. 66.
30. Lippmann, Walter. *A Preface to Morals*. New York: Time Inc., 1964. p. xiii.
31. Tillich, Paul. *The Courage to Be*. London: Nisbet and Comp., Fontana Library, 1952. p. 57.
32. Gillies, *Op. Cit.*, p. 194.

Chapter Five

On the Biological Basis of Pleasure: Some Implications for Leisure Policy

Stephen L. J. Smith

More often than not current speculations about the nature and value of leisure are either variations on a theme by Aristotle or a quantitative simulation of Veblen's observations of society. Many of our ideas about leisure are still strongly rooted in a school of thought 2300 years old or in the much more recent and mechanistic view that leisure is the leavings of time. We find ourselves in this condition because, it seems, we have forgotten a fundamental aspect of leisure: pleasure. Examine any recent article on any aspect of leisure and you will likely find a discussion of human rights, human dignity, social improvement, environmental quality, political action, holism, humanism or any of a shoal of other currently popular phrases and ideas. But you will find few, if any, references to pleasure. To ignore pleasure is a serious flaw. Pleasure is not trivial. It is absolutely essential to leisure, recreation and play, and we know very little about it. It is the answer to "why people play"; it is the reason for leisure and recreation. In this sense, "pleasure" has a much broader connotation than it does in Freud's concept of "pleasure principle" or in Aristotle's distinction between "pleasure" and "joy." Pleasure is used here to include happiness, joy, fun, sensuality, amusement, mirth and tranquility. These diverse emotions share one common quality — they make a person "feel good"; that is, they give pleasure.

Too often we try to better understand *why* humans play and recreate by ignoring pleasure and instead concentrate on the social structures that merely *shape* play, recreation and leisure. Much that has been learned by social scientists is useful for solving certain problems, but their work is neither fundamental nor universal. The subject which seems to offer more for the etiology of recreation, and thus pleasure, is neurophysiology.

Neurophysiology, the study of the nervous system, treats physical processes which are independent of the temporarily prevailing economy, political system or social mores. These external forces will result in different stimuli being perceived by the nervous system and in different material being learned, but the neurological processes of a person in the United States are the same as those of a person in the People's Republic of China. There is a common denominator in recreation which makes historical and cross-cultural studies academically meaningful and intriguing. That common denominator is pleasure — and pleasure is a neurophysiological phenomenon.

SOME BACKGROUND ON THE STUDY OF LEISURE

A major step forward in the objective study of pleasure was made in 1954 as the result of an experimental error. James Olds,[4] a psychologist, was working on the mechanisms involved in the alerting response, the changes in an animal when it goes from a drowsy state to an alert state. Olds already knew that the process was due to some sort of electrical activity in a portion of the brain called the reticular activating system. He was working with a group of rats in which electrodes had been implanted in the reticular system to study in detail certain aspects of their alerting responses. The stimulation was not a particularly pleasant experience — with one apparent exception. One rat, when its electrodes were activated, showed no signs of alerting. It did exhibit a peculiar form of behavior, however, that caught Olds' attention. When removed from the corner of the cage where the electrodes were activated, the rat would try to return to that corner. Olds began to close the switch that excited the electrodes whenever the rat was in the corner and observed that the rat never wandered very far away. It stayed in the corner — apparently waiting for the next charge to its brain.

Examination of the rat by a curious Olds and his research team revealed that the electrodes had been incorrectly positioned. Instead of exciting the reticular activating system, they were stimulating an adjacent area called the limbic system. Very little was then known about the limbic system; some researchers, though, suspected that this primitive part of the brain was involved in several forms of behavior. This bit of serendipity implicated the limbic system as the biological basis of pleasure. In fact, a portion of the limbic system is now called the pleasure area of the brain. The process of pleasure-seeking the rat exhibited is called intra-cranial self-stimulation.

This form of direct pleasure stimulation of the limbic system quickly became an exciting new field for experimenters. For example, Olds devised an experiment to test the relative strength of the pleasure drive in rats. He gave the test animals one hour a day to obtain intra-cranial stimulation of the pleasure area or to eat. They consistently chose self-stimulation. The drive was so strong that the test animals completely forewent food. One animal starved to death; the researchers discontinued their experiments when other animals lost up to a third of their body weight.

The limbic system, with little change in structure and virtually no change in function, also exists in the human brain. So, as one would expect, work on other species eventually led to studies on human beings. Some notable experiments were with mental patients of Robert Heath at the Tulane School of Medicine. Heath provided his patients with a set of implanted electrodes and a button. He noted that the patients used the buttons frequently. According to them, it felt good and made them feel happy. The improvement in their moods ranged from general pleasure, through intense excitement, to a profound euphoria that lasted anywhere from a few hours to several days. The variation depended on the strength and duration of the charge and the portion of the limbic system being activated.

Years of work and experimentation on these pleasure areas have determined that the pleasure drive is one of the strongest drives in animals (at least for vertebrates). Direct limbic stimulation offers the most powerful drive seen in animals, in the sense that "with the electrodes squarely in a pleasure area and a lever to activate them, the animal wishes to do nothing but press the lever and has no desire to engage in any other behavior whatever."[5] Direct stimulation of the pleasure areas is such a powerful drive that it overwhelms the desire for water, food, mating or protection of the young. What is being observed is "not merely pleasure in any parochial sense but what is clearly the ultimate pleasure, the font of all behavior."[6]

Intra-cranial self-stimulation clearly represents a totally new type of behavior although the idea of seeking pleasure is well-known in psychology and philosophy. However, no one could seriously suggest this kind of stimulation is "normal" behavior. Yet the pleasure areas of the brain, whether that of rat or man, are normally stimulated through our senses and internal nerve receptors in our daily round of activities. Indeed, the idea of seeking pleasure is a well-known idea of psychology and philosophy.[7]

SENSORY PLEASURE STIMULATION

Common experience tells us that not all sensory stimuli are pleasurable. Many mild stimuli and very sharp, intense stimuli are unpleasant; even painful. These forces activate another part of the limbic system which registers pain, but since we are dealing with recreation, and thus pleasant feelings, our focus is on the pleasure area. It was a similar interest in voluntary behavior (motivated by pleasure) which led Campbell, who had been studying intra-cranial stimulation (along with many other experimenters), to consider peripheral or sensory stimulation of the limbic system.

This new line of work did not rely on wires and electrodes or the conventional rewards of food, water or sex for a deprived animal but on mere sensory stimulation of a healthy animal in a homeostatic environment. Campbell hoped to prove experimentally that animals would voluntarily engage in some behavior which would yield no reward other than the pleasure of doing that particular act. In humans we can call this play, leisure or recreation. Campbell's experiments included successful sensory stimulation (using a small external electrical "tickle") of fish, newts, terrapins and a crocodile. The most significant successes, however, were with squirrel monkeys. His animals were kept in a light environment with food, water, room to play and mate, noise and human activity. Campbell provided his monkeys with a 500 watt lamp that would light whenever the monkeys touched a capacitance rod. The advantages of the rod included the fact that it had no moving parts to wear out, but most importantly, it made no noise and, in general, was a rather dull plaything. During the initial test sessions when the lamp was not attached to the rod the monkeys touched the rod about 30 times in 15 minutes. As Campbell describes their behavior, "unless it (any new object) proves edible or can be made love to, the new object is soon tired of and ignored."[8] After the lamp was attached, the monkeys required several sessons to learn how to "operate" the switch and the lamp. Once this education was accomplished they began touching the rod at the rate of 300 to 500 times in a 15 minute test.

The lamp used provided pure white light, which is not a stimulus readily analogous to the monkeys' usual range of experiences. There is no reference or symbolism to meat or mate or to free existence in the wild. All that was operating was a meaningless flash of white light directly into the eyes. Unlike intra-cranial stimulation which so absorbs an animal that it never stops voluntarily, peripheral or sensory stimulation will eventually become boring. When a white light was made available continuously the monkeys stopped flashing it within two hours. The same tapering-off or boredom was observed with any color light of equal brightness. However, when the color of light was changed every 15 minutes the monkeys kept flashing the light for over four hours. Such behavior is not unknown in humans. Manufacturers in recreation and other fields understand the value in bringing out the same old product in a new container or new form. Boredom haunts all forms of recreation from television to sex.

Psychologists, too, have discussed motivation based on intrinsic factors and pleasure seeking. White's conceptualization is one of the most insightful, although not physiologically based.[9] White notes that conceptualization of intrinsic motivation is needed to account for both actual behavior and the improvements in behavior animals and humans learn as they cope with their environment. The new conceptualization White suggests is "competence" — the ability of an animal to effectively cope with its environment. Learning, exploring, playing and thinking are among the activities that increase competence. White described these competence-increasing activities as "motivated in their own right;" that is, there is no motivation for them other than the feeling of satisfaction derived from their performance. White is heading straight for the recognition that pleasure is basic, that it is an element that cannot be simplified or explained by a still simpler concept. However, he stops short and calls the satisfaction of activity not pleasure or fun, but a "feeling of efficacy." This phrase obscures the fundamental reality of fun and the fundamental importance of pleasure. White does acknowledge however that efficacy shows itself most clearly in the fun of play.

The point to be drawn from these ideas is that animals do engage in behavior solely for the pleasure derived. In fact, most activities in which an animal engages in the natural world, eating, copulating, or exploring, are done for pleasurable stimulation only. Fortunately, some of these activities keep the animal alive. The pleasure derived from eating concomitantly provides nourishment. But, and it is a critical distinction, an animal does not eat to get nourishment; it eats to get pleasure. If an animal's mouth is "numbed" so that there is no taste or feel of food sensed during the eating, an animal may starve to death. Research by Ziegler[10] indicates that over-eating may be due to a malfunctioning of the trigeminal nerve which registers oral tactile sensations such as kissing, smoking and eating. In his experiments the destruction of the trigeminal nerve not only stopped the sending of the pleasurable feelings of eating, but also stopped any interest in eating. The strength of the drive for pleasure through other forms of behavior, especially exploration, has been experimentally documented as early as the 1940s and 1950s by researchers such as Whiting and Mourer,[11] Montgomery and Markman,[12] and Berlyne.[13]

When a healthy animal reaches satiation (stops receiving pleasure) from eating or any other activity, such as looking at a flashing light, it does not stop behaving; it seeks out something new. If it did not constantly seek new stimuli that lead to pleasure it would die. For however pleasurable or beneficial any single act may be, it will not maintain homeostatis for the animal over any length of time (i.e., keep it alive). This is the fatal characteristic of intracranial self-stimulation: animals will push a lever until they drop. This also suggests, physiologically, the fundamental reason for most (perhaps even all) animal behavior — it is an unending search for renewed pleasure. Survival is not the motivation for the actions of an individual animal; the motivation is the seeking of pleasure.

The biological basis of pleasurable feeling (sensory and proprioceptive stimulation of the limbic system) is the same for all vertebrates and this necessarily includes man. Whatever one's feelings about an immaterial part of humans, a spirit, soul or whatever, man in his body and its processes is an animal. We feel pleasure in the same way that animals do.

THE HUMAN DIFFERENCE

There is one difference, however, in the ways that humans can attain pleasure. This is a way of seeking pleasure which makes some of us most of the time, and all of us part of the time, different from animals. We can obtain pleasure from thought, from the use of the tertiary portion of the human cortex — that part associated with creative thought and symbolic reasoning. Animals do not because they cannot. This includes the dolphins and whales whose large cortices are the subject of much popular speculation. There is no evidence that the crustaceans use their large convoluted cerebrums for pleasure; they are too busy using their brain for the pursuit of the simpler pleasures of food, breathing and the companionship of their own kind.

The potential of conscious thought to control the older parts of the brain is a common experience. Almost all of us have experienced psychogenic insomnia — those nights when excited or angry thoughts have overwhelmed the call for sleep. This same barrage of electrical activity can be directed into the pleasure areas.

This organization and function of the brain provides the only unqualified, non-solipsistic and non-mystical difference between man and animal. The unique characteristic of Homo sapiens is that members have the potential for achieving pleasure from thought. To the degree that someone actualizes this potential and seeks pleasure from mental activity, he is acting human. To the degree he seeks sensory pleasure he is acting subhuman. These are unpleasant words, but we must face the truth, even if unpleasant, if we are to progress as human beings. The truth is: members of Homo sapiens often engage in decidedly sub-human acts.

With this simple distinction we can now perceive a pattern in recreation activities which is more basic than existing classification schemes such as the familiar indoor/outdoor dichotomy. Recreation activities, or anything else an individual does for fun or pleasure, can be placed on a continuum from purely sensory to purely intellectual and thus on a spectrum of sub-human to human activity.

This difference is not, in the first place, a philosophical one but an objective one (although there are many philosophical implications). In a rather over-simplified way the difference between acting human and acting sub-human is how you seek pleasure: stimulation by the cortex (human) versus stimulation by the peripheral receptors (sub-human).

While pleasure-seeking runs the gamut from sensual to intellectual, it can be approximated by three separate types of behavior. These three ways of pursuing pleasure have rather indistinct boundaries, but still provide a useful scheme for identifying different forms of pleasure-seeking behavior which is independent of prevailing social and political conditions. The three types of pleasure-seeking can be given the labels of (1) sensory, (2) expressive-cortical and (3) intellectual cortical. The basis for differentiation is the relative importance of the cortex in generating the feelings of pleasure.

SENSORY RECREATION

Sensory activities include many popular and traditional activities: eating, some forms of children's play, much music (especially such primitive forms as rock), vandalism, hunting, sports, snowmobiling, flirting and rape. These apparently unrelated activities are grouped together because a person finding pleasure in any of them does so because the activity stimulates the peripheral receptors. Physical play, sports, hunting and snowmobiling involve the pleasurable use of muscles which is sensed by the proprioceptors (nerves sensing muscular movement).

Eating, drinking, loud rhythmic music and similar activities provide direct stimulation of the senses and, with allowances for variations in personal tastes, provide pleasure for all people. Other activities are enjoyable because of the visceral or autonomic pleasure they provide. David Klein, a professor at Michigan State and a commentator for National Public Radio in the United States, has suggested the great popularity of snowmobiling in states like Michigan is due to the feeling of danger and personal confrontation with power it provides. These visceral pleasures (such as the tightening of the stomach) offset the blandness and tedium of jobs such as those on Michigan's automobile assembly lines. Klein suggested that snowmobiling could be greatly reduced (if this were deemed socially or environmentally desirable) by making snowmobiles safe, slow and quiet. Similarly, Campbell observed that the pleasure of mountain climbing comes primarily from the danger involved. Although the use of muscles, eyes, ears and nose must also provide pleasure it is the difficulty and challenge which draws climbers to their sport; thus "despite its apparent masculinity it reduces to the fairground mentality."[14]

Much so-called sexual pleasure also stems from the "fairground mentality." Caressing, kissing and intercourse provide many pleasurable stimuli, but not all apparently sexual activity is truly sexual. The first adolescent contacts between boys and girls generate great feelings of excitement and pleasure, but these are largely autonomic, arising from the pleasurable sensations in changes in the heart rate, respiration rate and movement of the stomach and intestines. Because these early pleasures (which also typically accompany any new contact between adults which has sexual overtones) are primarily autonomic, they inevitably decline as the two people become more familiar with each other. The mystery and intrigue is gone; sex becomes routine; the flame has gone out of their romance. Some change is necessary to rekindle the feelings: having sex in more exotic or naughty ways, in semi-public places or with new partners. Truly sexual feelings intensify with familiarity as the couple begins to draw together emotionally and become more skilled in their caresses. In brief, much so-called sexual attraction is basically pleasurable fear — like a roller coaster ride. In fact, a roller coaster is a not-unknown analogy in describing many love affairs.

EXPRESSIVE-CORTICAL RECREATION

The next group of recreation activities, expressive-cortical, are based on a mingling of man's sensory and intellectual characteristics. The expressive-cortical activities are those which use creative thought to produce something which also gives sensual pleasure (e.g., classical music) or which adds a major intellectual dimension to a sensory experience (e.g. winetasting). The arts and crafts: painting, sculpture, composing music, film-making, calligraphy and all the rest; sex based on emotional closeness; and certain occupations such as medicine and engineering provide this type of pleasure. Physical artifacts are used to give expression to an activity which is predominantly intellectual.

This category has especially confused borders. A composer of a piece of classical music will probably be closer to enjoying an intellectual-cortical pleasure than a sensual pleasure although his music can give sensual pleasure. The performer of that piece and the audience will tend to be successively more drawn to the sensual character of the music. However, some mathematicians, for example, who have a taste for classical music have occasionally described perceiving profound mathematical structures in a musical movement. On the other hand, Einstein described some of his early ideas about relativity as mental dance images. His intellectual reveries took on, in his mind, sensual qualities. Beethoven, near the end of a lifetime composing powerful, sensual music, completed several works while deaf. His pleasure in the Ninth Symphony could hardly be called sensual since he lacked the sense to appreciate it. Similarly Adolf Gottlieb, a 20th century abstract expressionist, produced some of his best pieces after he became blind.

Some types of children's play are expressive-cortical. Any parent who has watched children play has seen them first enjoy physical activity with a plaything and then grow bored as they exhaust the initial possibilities for pleasure. Children will then attempt to renew the fun of the activity or plaything by increasing its complexity, by changing the rules of play, by using the toy for fantasy or, if all else fails, by taking the toy apart to see how it works. The phenomenon is one where a child can easily obtain pleasure from sensory stimulation, and when he grows bored, will seek new pleasure by changing the form of play. The change that overcomes boredom is the change that allows the child to use his intelligence and creativity. These observations are probably the objective origins of the play theories of Berlyn,[15] Maddi,[16] and Ellis.[17]

INTELLECTUAL-CORTICAL RECREATION

Intellectual-cortical, the final category of pleasurable behaviors, seems to belong to the realm of the thinkers. Actually, everyone obtains some pleasure from intellectual activities — those activities which provide pleasure without the use of sensory stimulation. Only a few people, however, derive most of their pleasure from such sources. They form an elite in any society which is regularly singled out for admiration or, as often happens, suspicion and ridicule. These are the philosophers, theologians, linguists, mathematicians, logicians, certain historians, theoretical physicists, mystics, and, at times, politicians. Any motor behavior associated with their seeking pleasure is only ancillary. Some physical action is necessary to obtain information, education or the resources to keep alive; their pleasure comes from their minds and not their actions.

The development and nurturing of a human mind capable of human pleasures is one of the greatest responsibilities a society faces. It would be a mistake, though, to believe that all intellectual pleasures are necessarily lofty and virtuous. There are a great many bad philosophers and theologians. Many intellectuals are as silly as non-intellectuals. The vast potential of the creative intellect can also be turned to fantasizing and daydreaming, which are surrogates for sensory pleasure. Still, other humans develop elaborate, twisted political philosophies which give intellectual pleasure but all too often find ultimate expression in sub-human, destructive terrorism and war. Fascism and the twisted science developed under Hitler are probably the major examples from this century.

Not all intellectual pleasure is constructive, creative, enduring and socially desirable. Only intellectual activities, however, have the potential for becoming so. Sensory pleasure virtually never does. Apparent exceptions are individuals such as the Wright brothers who experienced an exquisite aesthetic reaction as well as physical thrill in their early experiments with flight. But even in such cases the work is preceded by long periods of intellectual study and analysis which either gave or promised future pleasure and contributed the requisite scientific basis for a lasting contribution.

A FEW IMPLICATIONS

The identification and classification of phenomena is basic to any discipline, profession or body of practitioners. Researchers and academics are still searching for a paradigm which will help guide work and provoke questions for future study of recreation, leisure and play. Such a paradigm may be built out of the common denominator of these phenomena or pleasures. This chapter has described in brief terms some of the physiological importance of pleasure and in doing so pointed out an important dichotomy in the search for pleasure, vis., an objective difference between human and sub-human pleasures. This difference is based on the origins of the stimuli received by the limbic system.

If a society holds the philosophy that the state not only exists to them as human as they can be, to emphasize and nurture good and enduring human values, then those social institutions that provide leisure services should take a careful look at their programs. Public recreation agencies, park departments, athletic leagues, youth groups, churches and schools (including universities) have the responsibility to evaluate their offerings in terms of their location on the sub-human to human spectrum. Few people would seriously suggest that we should not worry about preserving open-space natural beauty; nor would they suggest that we can completely ignore physical health. The issue is one of relative emphasis, of budgets and of program resources. A flat statement that all recreation and park agencies are emphasizing the subhuman in us by virtue of their sensory-oriented programming is unwarranted. But we do have the responsibility to take a critical look at programs and honestly evaluate just what part of our human/animal personality we are developing and whether this is the appropriate role of a public or educational agency. Surely, the magnitude of sports programs in most schools deserves special attention. A comparison of the institutional support for intercollegiate and intramural sports with cultural recreation at the same institutions should be made and interpreted in light of the concepts argued in this paper. Societies and governments which provide so much support and place so much attention on events such as the Olympic games are highlighting and promoting sub-human behavior. Considering the recent events of terror, retribution, resource boycotts and other global acts of sensory pleasure-seeking (in the name of whatever ideology), the emphasis given the Olympics and world-champion prize fights is disturbing, to say the least.

The same pattern can be found at local levels. Recreation is often claimed to be a deterrent to juvenile delinquency. The causes of delinquency, as with most social problems, are diverse and diffuse. But it seems almost paradoxical to think that a recreation program which emphasizes some forms of sub-human behavior is going to have broad success in eliminating other forms of sub-human behavior. Fights and riots which too often accompany sporting events and rock festivals are evidence that sensory recreation may not be such a cure-all for socially undesirable forms of sensory recreation. On the other hand, rare indeed are plays, classical music concerts, lectures or other intellectual events which are followed by violent forms of sensory-oriented behavior.

All this is but one aspect of the new approach to recreation. There are many others, some philosophical, some scientific. A biological approach to recreation will place many familiar phenomena in new contexts and will challenge quite a few of our old comfortable beliefs about sports, athletics, arts, the humanities and science. It suggests that there is indeed something special and unique about being human — and that many people (perhaps most) do not act "humanly" for much of their lives. We have much, much more to learn about pleasure, the manifold ways people pursue it and the implications for fields of inquiry from management to evolution to theology. Through it all, the image of man as constantly striving to be happy, and being most human when he is pursuing "human" pleasures is an optimistic and hopeful image of humanity.

REFERENCES

1. A few of the many different approaches can be read in the works of the following authors: Veblen, Thorstein. *The Theory of the Leisure Class*. New York: The American Library, 1953; de Grazia, Sebastian. *Of Time, Work and Leisure*. Garden City, New Jersey: Doubleday and Company, 1964; Pieper, Joseph. *Leisure: The Basis of Culture*. New York: Pantheon Books, 1952; Linder, Steffan. *The Harried Leisure Class*. New York: Columbia University Press, 1970; Brightbill, Charles. *The Challenge of Leisure*. Englewood Cliffs, NJ: Prentice-Hall, 1960; Dumazedier, Joffre. *Toward a Society of Leisure*. New York: The Free Press, 1967; Martin, Alexander Reid. "Leisure and Our Inner Resources." *Parks and Recreation*. March, 1975, pp. ia-ff.
2. Kuhn, Thomas. *The Structure of Scientific Revolutions*. Chicago: University of Chicago Press, 1970.
3. A recent example is the debate over the acceptability of hang-gliding in the National Parks. Questions on appropriateness were raised in a *New York Times* editorial by Ronald Taylor, November 11th, 1975, "National Park Policy."
4. Olds, James and Milner, Peter. "Positive Reinforcement Produced by Electrical Stimulation of Septal Area and Other Regions of Rat Brain." *Journal of Comparative Physiology and Psychology,* 47, 1954, p. 419. See also Olds, James. "Differentiation of Reward Systems in the Brain by Self-Stimulation Techniques." In *Electrical Studies on the Unanesthetized Brain*. New York: Hoeber-Harper, 1960. pp. 17-49.
5. Campbell, Herbert. *The Pleasure Areas*. New York: Delacorte Press, 1973. p. 25.
6. *Ibid.,* p. 24.
7. Among these would be Freud, Sigmund. *Beyond the Pleasure Principle*. James Strachey (Translator). New York: Liveright, 1961; Szasz, Thomas. *Pain and Pleasure*. New York: Basic Books, 1975; Heath, Robert (Ed.). *The Role of Pleasure in Behavior*. New York: Hoeber-Harper, 1964.
8. Campbell, *Op. Cit.,* p. 49.
9. White, P.W. "Motivation Reconsidered: The Concept of Competence." *Psychological Review*, 66, 1957, pp. 297-333.
10. Ziegler, H.P. "The Sensual Feel of Food." *Psychology Today,* August, 1975, pp. 62-67.

11. Whiting, J.W.M. and Mourer, O.H. "Habit Progression and Regression — A Laboratory Study of Some Factors Relevant to Human Socialization." *Journal of Comparative Psychology*, 36, 1945, pp. 229-253.

12. Montgomery, D.C. and Markman, J.A. "The Relationship Between Fear and Exploratory Behavior." *Journal of Comparative Physiology and Psychology*, 48, 1955, pp. 254-260.

13. Berlyne, D.E. "Novelty and Curiosity as Determinants of Exploratory Behavior." *British Journal of Psychology,* 41, 1950, pp. 68-80.

14. Brown, Evelyn. "An Ethological Theory of Play." *Journal of AAHPER,* September, 1968.

15. Berlyne, D.E. *Conflict, Arousal and Curiosity.* New York: McGraw-Hill, 1960.

16. Maddi, S.R. "Exploratory Behavior and Variation-seeking in Man." In *Functions of Varied Experience.* Edited by D.W. Fiske and S.R. Maddi. Homewood, Illinois: Dorsey Press, 1961.

17. Ellis, M.J. *Why People Play.* Englewood Cliffs: Prentice-Hall, 1973.

Chapter Six
Fantasy, Play, Creativity and Mental Health

Bill Michaelis

"... with my anti-experimental bias I don't save myself from trouble, but it does have a lot of sideways opening effects."
Gregory Bateson[1]

One of the ten rights of children as declared by the United Nations is the "right to full opportunity for play and recreation." The right to play should be also fully extended to adults. To discover what this means, it is important to reexamine the nature of play and to ask if our services are in line with our professional and theoretical knowledge. Our job as play professionals is not just to provide activities, teach skills, or fill people's time. It is also to educate them for leisure. Everything that we do, from the environments that we create for people to the type of leadership that we provide, should have this focus. The objective of leisure education is for people to have an understanding and actualization of the play experience in their lives. But what is play?

There are strong threads of interconnection between play and several other important concepts, notably fantasy, creativity, mental health and the "flow" phenomenon. Each of these has its own intracacies and muddled complexity. Each has relevance for human happiness. This chapter will explore those connections and suggest specific implications for the leisure services field.

PLAY AND MENTAL HEALTH: THE PRIMACY OF RIGHT BRAIN PROCESSES

A widely accepted definition of leisure is that it is primarily an existential state, a way of looking at the world. Gunter describes it this way: Leisure is "... a subjective state of the individual in his involvement with certain kinds of time, activity or lifestyle. This position is best known through the works of DeGrazia but it also permeates the work of other well known writers."[2]

DeGrazia himself would say that leisure has nothing to do with time or activity.[3] Play might also be viewed primarily as a 'mindset' (or a heartset). Some of its most significant components are fantasy, imagination and openendedness.[4] But there is more.

There has been much recent research on left and right brain functions. Psychologists tell us that we have primarily two modes of thinking. They are: (a) our right brain *primary* processes — our non-rational, dreamlike, emotional symbolizing modes; this is the powerful stuff of our tears, laughter, anger, hopes, fears, loves, loneliness and, yes, our play. And (b) our left brain *secondary* processes — our cognitive, reality-based, rational modes; this is our organizing, planning self.

Although play certainly contains aspects of rational planning, its magic and power lies in its attention to right brain, primary process elements. Eli Bower noted, ". . . that, for play and life in general, it is the primary process mode that is generally the more powerful, pervasive and satisfying of human symbolizing experiences, although secondary processes do serve an important organizing and planning function in our lives."[5] Bower also notes that a *balance* of both primary and secondary modes is necessary for mental health.

Erik Erickson confirms that play serves a very important mental health function. He reports that in a 30-year follow-up of people who had been studied as children, those subjects who felt they had had the most interesting and fulfilling lives were the ones who had managed to keep a sense of playfulness at the center of things.[6] Unfortunately our educational and leisure oriented institutions give too little attention to play and the right brain functions. Most people are taught to put away the "child" as they are subtly socialized into mass society.

PLAY AND CREATIVITY

Arieti describes the creative act in similar terms. He, too, uses the dualism of primary and secondary processes, but he postulates a third mode which he calls the *tertiary* process. He states that the task of this process is to fuse the irrational with the rational processes and thus produce an integrative balance and the magic synthesis of creativity. Both Bower and Arieti advocate that greater attention be paid to primary process development, the stuff that is the magic and power of play. Arieti states it this way: ". . . A society that urges the young to 'stop daydreaming and pay attention,' to 'stop playing and get to work,' is not one that encourages magic at all."[7]

Further evidence linking the right brain elements of play to creativity comes from the identification of blocks to creative lifestyles. Psychologists identify some of the main blocks to creativity as 1) the reluctance to play, 2) sensory dullness, 3) an impoverished fantasy life; 4) the reluctance to "let go", and 5) an impoverished emotional life.[8]

Corrine Hutt, in a series of longitudinal studies of 3-7 year olds, has shown that the opportunity for inventive and exploratory play affects a child's later creativity and social interaction. Feitelson and Ross also found that creativity is encouraged by the development of imaginativeness in play.[9] Bower summarizes our task when he states that ". . . a society concerned with producing a fair amount of creative and imaginative adults must protect the play modalities of childhood."[10]

PLAY, DREAMS AND FANTASY

Dreams and Daydreams as Play
Internalized fantasy or dreaming as a form of "play" has long been supported as valid by many play theorists. Sutton-Smith speaks of adult daydreaming as playing around in the head.

> "Play seems to parallel dreams in that it contains at least two types of processing: on the one hand the quite mundane assimilation of daily events and on the other the fairly elaborate and vivid construction of imaginary companions and the like."[11]

As children, most of us lived in a "never-never land" where we externally acted out our fantasies. It may have been the backyard, the imaginative worlds of dolls or cars, the forts built on bunk beds, the pickup games where the rules constantly changed, or the abandoned lot down the street. In many ways the whole world was accessible and limited only by imagination. We were not locked into a narrow conceptualization of everyday objects. A table would be a fort or, turned upside down, a ship or a motorcycle. But as we grew, powerful social forces buoyed by peer and adult pressure told us (overtly or covertly) to put aside that childlike freshness and creativity. Expressions of external fantasy were generally no longer legitimized or encouraged: play became more structured and reality became secondary process oriented. Bower suggests that much of the pain in growing up is the pull between the childlike fantasy and feelings of primary process and the demands of rational secondary process realities. It is clear, however, that as children grow to adulthood more of their fantasy and primary process activity is relegated to dreams and daydreams or internalized play. But these are still play and they do serve an important subconscious and conscious right brain function. But what if they are blocked?

Blocked Dreams (Internal Play) Lead to Dysfunctional Behavior
Recent dream research indicates that smooth functioning in the "awake, rational reality state" is influenced by the integrative primary process function that is performed while we sleep. During sleep there are times when we wiggle our eyes and possibly dream a little. This wiggling has been called by sleep researchers rapid eye movement (REM). We know that if we consistently wake people up during REM, they will become irritable, dysfunctional, disoriented and even hostile in their waking state. Dreams seem to serve an important left and right brain integrative and sorting out process.[12]

This process that night dreams accomplish occurs in a subconscious state. But isn't the daydreaming that Sutton-Smith describes as one form of adult play also accomplishing this "sorting out" (bridging) process in a more conscious awake state? And isn't the spontaneous make-believe fantasy play that children externally act out also accomplishing this?

The Importance of Daydreams, Fantasy and Make Believe Play
Jerome Singer states that the nurturing of fantasy in our lives is vital for mental health.

"Fantasies and daydreams, far from being irrelevant and insubstantial, may be the foundation of serenity and purpose in our lives . . .

. . . those who have trouble using fantasy to enrich their experience or as a substitute for aggression run the risk of serious trouble at each stage of their lives . . . A well developed fantasy life seems to be partly responsible for independence, tranquility and realism."[13]

But the encouragement of fantasy still frightens a lot of people. Sutton-Smith, however, suggests strong linkages between fantasy and the development of creativity.

"Teachers, even of middle-class background, still ask me whether a child with high levels of fantasy is not in danger of a nervous breakdown. The answer is no; in most cases, he is only in danger of becoming an outstanding scientist, writer, scholar, or perhaps even an international chess player."[14]

But what if people have difficulty with daydreaming, fantasy and make believe play?

Blocked Fantasy and Make Believe Play Leads to Dysfunctional Behavior

Singer details studies with aggressive delinquents, drug abusers, and overweight people, among others, that seem to indicate a close relationship between their "problems" and their lack of elaborated fantasies. He suggests that the aggressive group may never have had the early contacts with adults that allowed them to try out in play and fantasy the complex and relatively self-controlled behavior of adults. The drug (including alcohol) abusers more than nonusers were found to be:

> ". . . subject to boredom and mind wanderings and their fantasies, though frequent, tend to be fleeting and undeveloped. They are not as interested in inner consciousness as in blotting things out or developing external sensations. Marijuana users were found to be the exception to this research and were generally found to be interested in expanding both their internal and external awareness."[15]

Singer also reports studies of school-age children and adults which indicate relationships between healthy fantasy development and behavior.

The development of imaginative play, which allows the exercise of right brain functions, becomes increasingly important in light of the often reported negative effects of heavy television viewing on children. Dr. Lawrence Friedman points out that regular television viewing has rendered children passive, thus denying them normal outlets for their fantasy and aggression. "All television, except in small doses, feeds children ready-made fantasy, at a time when *fantasy making* is crucial for their development . . ."[16]

It has been suggested that the power and magic of play lies in its attention to primary process right brain functions, and the balanced integration of these functions is necessary for health and creativity. Further evidence for this position comes from the phenomenological investigations of the psychologist Mihaly Csikszentmihalyi into "flow" experiences. Simply put, "flow" is enjoyment, and although enjoyment is made up of both rational (left brain) and non-rational (right brain) elements, it is argued that "flow" is also mostly influenced by the primary process, right brain mode. A look at the reported experiences and identified qualities of the phenomena suggests why.

TOWARD HIGHER CONSCIOUSNESS —
THE FLOW EXPERIENCE

Csikszentmihalyi was interested in the feelings that emerged from activities found to be rewarding in and of themselves. He studied people in a variety of work-play settings — surgery, different sports, rock-climbing and artistic pursuits — and discovered that as individuals became totally immersed in a sport or creative act, they lost a sense of time and the external world and they experienced an ecstatic "flowing" feeling. His investigations indicated that this feeling approximated an "altered state of being" for those subjects.[17]

> "In this state the person loses a self-conscious sense of himself and of time. He gains a heightened awareness of his physical involvement with the activity. The person in flow finds, among other things, his concentration vastly increased and his feedback from the activity enormously enhanced."[18]

Certain elements always emerged from the different descriptions. One of them was a merging of self with the environment or action with awareness.

> "One of the rock climbers put it this way: 'You are so involved in what you are doing you aren't thinking of yourself as separate from the immediate activity' . . . ."[19]

Another element was the dreamlike sense of time.

> "In flow there is a sense of being lost in the action . . . . 'Time passes a hundred times faster. In this sense it resembles the dream state,' said a chess player. Sometimes the centering of attention produces a spatial alteration akin to the changed sense of time."[20]

In addition to a loss of self and time consciousness, a merging of action and awareness and a centering of attention on a relatively isolated and limited stimulus field, three other core qualities emerged. In the flow state, the subjects felt under control of self and environment, their activity was self-chosen and intrinsically motivated, and they received immediate and unambiguous feedback regarding their actions.

In addition to the peak arousal experiences of flow, there is also *micro flow* which is a small scale example of the same phenomena. Dr. Csikszentmihalyi's studies identify six areas of microflow in descending order of reported frequency: a) social involvement (i.e., browsing, talking, etc.); b) kinesthetic (running, touching, moving, etc.) c) imagining type behavior; d) attending behavior (i.e., TV, radio, reading); e) oral pleasures, and f) creative work (i.e., writing, sewing, playing music, etc.)[21]

Play and Flow: Differences and Relationships

What is the relevance of the flow phenomena? In one sense, it appears to be closely related to the existential attitude by which play and leisure were defined earlier.

Although the two concepts are closely aligned, there are some differences. Sutton-Smith states that "... flow is a state of integration with reality, play is not."[22] Dr. Csikszentmihalyi clarifies this distinction and the relationship between the two concepts, especially emphasizing the *quality of playfulness* vs. trying to identify any one activity as *play:*

> "Flow describes a *process* of involvement in a given reality while playfulness refers to one's attitude towards the reality in which one is involved. One can experience flow in a routine activity whose goals and rules are consistent with the paramount reality; in such a case there would be flow without playfulness. Or one could shift one's perspective on what goals and rules applied in a situation, without experiencing the intense involvement that characterizes flow. But, by and large, the two processes tend to evoke each other. The intensity of flow brings into question the value of everyday reality, while playfulness usually provides the kind of opportunities for action that make flow possible."[23]

It is clear that flow is one of the higher forms of pleasure, and it can occur in a wide variety of work/play activities that are not limited to any set time frame. Comprehending this holistic aspect of flow quite naturally leads to a greater understanding of the weakness of the traditional work-play dichotomy, and the application of the flow experience principles has tremendous potential for both personal pleasure/play and professional practice. We can learn how to increase flow in our own lives and in the lives of the people with whom we work and serve.

APPLICATIONS

Csikszentmihalyi, the trio of Ellis, Witt and Aguilar, and this author, have all suggested ways of applying what we know about flow.[24] The flow studies suggest that in addition to changing environments (i.e., home, job, associates), there are several principles that will increase the potential for flow, pleasure and playfulness:

1. An activity ought to have a broad enough range of complexity and challenge so that one can fine-tune the balance between the perceived difficulty of the task and one's skill level (or the skill level of one's client). If the challenge is too difficult, it will cause anxiety. If it's too easy, the result will be boredom. If the challenge is fine-tuned, flow can occur. Among other things, this implies leadership and rule flexibility, and multi-skill level options for all ages in leisure service programs. For example, this was certainly one of the advantages and playful attractions of the New Games Movement.

2. Attention needs to be focused, the stimulus field narrowed, and one's awareness merged with the activity in order to facilitate flow. Have you ever been totally absorbed in the concentration of the moment in a good ping pong rally, a musical piece, or a video game? When working with participants, one must first attract their attention. Ellis, et al, point out that being keenly aware of a client's preferences and using degrees of novelty and dissonance are extremely useful in gaining attention.[25,26] As this author pointed out in an article on game change and leadership, once attention is gained, limiting distractions along with fine-tuning the complexity of the task, provides greater access to flow, and very often playfulness.[27]

3. There is a need to focus on the process of being and doing the activity in the *present*. This implies minimizing: a) time consciousness; b) focusing on outcomes; and c) the promise of future extrinsic rewards. It also implies the elimination of a destructive anxiety-provoking competitive/comparative atmosphere. There is greater potential for flow, play and leisure when one is in the moment and neither racing nor chasing.[28,29]

4. There is a need to relax more and to become more aware of one's body and senses. The ability to achieve flow is enhanced by a relaxed body, an alert mind, and general sensory awareness. Stress gets in the way. Dr. Jim Polidora, a professor at the University of California-Davis Medical School and a holistic play practitioner, uses guided imagery, dance therapy, the eastern martial arts, massage, yoga, and many

other techniques to help people reduce stress and actualize the play experience in their lives.[30] These methods have tremendous implications for the leisure service profession, but are still under-utilized.

5. Finally, for all of the above, there is a need for *immediate* and ongoing, positively reinforcing feedback about our relaxing and focusing on the process, and information or modifications that help us fine-tune and be in the moment.[31]

Looked at from another angle, the steps just presented could be described as key elements of leisure education. By incorporating these steps into their lives, people can maximize the play state — the higher consciousness of flow. The ultimate result of understanding "the fun in fun" may be an increase in healthier, happier people and a redefinition of the work ethic.

BLOCKED FLOW

The flow experience is a form of higher consciousness accessible to all people. At least part of its power comes from its relationship to the right brain, primary process mode of symbolizing. The chess player, described earlier, referred to the time alteration experience in flow as a dream-like state. If dreams and daydreams are forms of internal play that serve an important, integrative mental health function in human beings, then it may be logical to assume that make believe play and flow serve some of the same functions in a more activity oriented conscious state.

Further suggestive evidence for the connection of flow to such primary process activities as dreams, daydreams and make believe play comes from looking at what happens to people when their flow is blocked. Csikszentmihalyi discovered that when the people he studied attempted to inhibit their preferred forms of flow, for example daydreaming, talking, gaming, or watching, or when they were blocked in some other ways, they became very irritable, and experienced a wide range of mental health difficulties.[32] This mental health dysfunction is consistent with research cited earlier on blocked primary process (right brain) activities such as dreaming, fantasy and make believe play.

INTERRELATIONSHIPS

It has been suggested that the power and magic of play lies in its attention to the primary process mode of symbolizing, and that the active functioning of this mode, as evidenced in such things as dreams, daydreams, fantasy, make believe play and flow, is crucial for mental health. Also, the playful exercise of this mode is a key element in creativity. Mental health, then, might be more broadly defined as the actualization of a creative lifestyle — a lifestyle that is open to growth, sensitivity, and the universal quest for love and human happiness. Each of the concepts of fantasy, play, creativity, and mental health is complex, but they are indeed interrelated. It should be clear that one common denominator for creative lifestyles is play.

The understanding of the nature of play has important implications for enriching our lives and improving practices in the leisure services field. The job of all professionals in the field, as noted earlier, is to be leisure educators. If leisure service professionals are to help in the facilitation of creative lifestyles and human happiness, the environments and programs that they provide and the tools and leadership techniques that they use must be consistent with the theoretic understanding of play.

IMPLICATIONS: BRIDGING THE GAP BETWEEN THEORY AND PRACTICE

It is clear that more people today are engaging in more activities that have play and leisure potential.[33] Our complex, rapidly changing world makes the job of educating people about play that much more important. Too often the values of play that are professed by the leisure profession are not reflected in services. It is important for professionals to understand their clients' needs and to help meet them. But for leisure educators, there is a greater task: to provide not only for *what is* but also models for *what can be*. All programs, in reality, should be geared to educating people about healthy play values.

Leadership is increasingly important because it is clear that the people who take part in leisure service activities are also constantly being influenced by strong social forces that often confuse or distort healthy play values. For example, in an increasingly rapid-paced, depersonalized, technological, consumer oriented society such as ours, forces such as conspicuous consumption, escapism and self-destruction through media, drugs, and obligatory mass leisure, all have an influence on play values. Urbanism, the highly structured product orientation of capitalism, sexism, cultural stereotypes of such groups as the disabled, and early parental mixed messages such as withholding play as punishment or using it as a reward, also confuse the conceptions and values of play for many people.[34] And although it is changing, the work ethic is still alive and well. Leisure education cannot be viewed in a vacuum, and all of the above factors, as well as many others, make the job of value leadership that much more important. A more careful look at children's play and socialization further illustrates this point.

Play and Socialization
Recall that Bower suggested that a society concerned with producing a fair amount of imaginative adults must protect the play modalities of childhood. As children we had tremendous potential creativity within us and exercised it because in a very existential way we knew what play was all about. We had adventures, challenged ourselves, played made-up games with made-up rules, explored new areas of the world in our heads and through participating in activities. We knew what play was about because it included such elements as flexibility, change and spontaneity. Fantasies were allowed and feelings were exercised. Play had a healthy air of unreality about it; often loose and open-ended. Play was not without its "serious" moments, difficulties or hurt feelings, but things were worked out because we wanted to keep playing. For the most part we provided support for each other's play.[35] If lucky, we might have had support for playfulness from some significant adults in our lives. But something happened, to many of us, at least.

As we grew older, powerful social forces began to influence playtime and thus our conceptions of both play and the world. The message was to grow up and put aside that child self.[36] The abuses of two forces in particular have a very strong influence on children. The first is the existence of very structured, highly competitive, adult dominated youth sports leagues that emphasize a win-at-all-cost ethic. And the second is the power of the plug-in drug, television. Both of these forces, youth sports and television, can be playful, positive educational tools, but there is increasing evidence of their abuse. This abuse has had a strong influence on children's abilities to conceptualize and operationalize play alternatives.

More and more evidence continues to accumulate about the negative effects of heavy T.V. viewing on such things as creativity, the development of reading skills, the communicative emotional climate of the home, self-image, and healthy nutritional habits.

Studies have also suggested links between heavy viewing and increased fears, violence and reality distortion.[37] And this is to say nothing of the exponential proliferation of media in general during the 1980's in the form of VCR's, video games, cable TV, etc. The effects of this proliferation on the development of healthy play patterns are not yet known, but the yellow caution flag is up.

The abuses of youth sports are also well documented. The "pro model" of big money, rigid structure and narrow definition of winning that includes only those with the highest score has filtered down to youth, with a strong push from the media. Although there are many well-meaning, caring adults in youth sports, there are also those whose expectations of children are too high; they crush individuality and promote conformity by attempting to create little five and six year old warriors. They lose sight of the playful developmental process that is the true power of youth sports, and often their 'products' are increased violence, cheating, concern with bigger trophies and an increasing number of young athletic dropouts. Those who most need the positive reinforcement of healthy activity are often the first cut or spend most of their careers on the bench. Too often this aspect of childhood play has become over-institutionalized and "adultocentric."[38]

Most professionals would state that they would like to have a hand in facilitating more creative, independent individuals. However, too many leaders and programs foster dependence on structure and experts and create a group think mentality. All people have the potential for creative, playful independence, but they are subtly socialized out of the magic, creativity, flexibility and individuality that is play. Children often buy into the media, abusive youth sports and other influencing social forces because they perceive very few alternatives. After all, adults *are* modeling their options. So children begin to perceive play as a narrow set of behaviors. Self-developed fantasy and pick-up games are things to be put aside. Play is to be structured to provide instant gratification or is something to pay for. Although there are many positive exceptions, leisure services still mainly reflect the confusing social forces influencing leisure rather than contributing to building a healthier future.

AND A CHILD SHALL LEAD

The main job of the leisure service profession is values leadership and that must include the nurturing of the positive child self and right brain elements for old and young alike. Education, for example, for all its innovations, is still mostly cognitive and career oriented, and based on faith and fear; drill and grill. Yet, the development of the affective primary process mode is crucial for creativity and mental health. And the operationalization of this leadership challenge and its programmatic manifestations will take many forms.

There is much to be done. In the broad sense, the profession must refocus its attention on play as seen from the child's perspective. Traditional offerings, even of the most competitive type, still have an important place in the scheme of things. But the abuses must be eliminated and the value focus must once again be on the *process* of enjoying, on the playfulness that is central to our profession. Or, as Ellis et. al., would say, we must see facilitating flow as an important and legitimate goal of our services.[39] Leaders must ask what's best for the development of mental health, human happiness and creativity. What messages are we giving people? Rather than running the serious risk of having "free" time dominated by left brain secondary processes and the stresses and anxieties that may accompany them, people need to be reminded not to take play too seriously. The non-rational 'unreality' of it is important. The magical right brain elements are the factors that free us from the boxes that we are in.

Meeting this challenge will require leadership; leadership that does not just provide what people have been taught to want, but expands into the areas where there is presently very little being done. There is still, for example, a paucity of cultural arts offerings in most public programs. It is clear that the full range of arts provide the much needed exercise of the right brain elements. They need as much (if not more) attention as sports programs currently command. Related activities such as intramural-type programs, movement education, theater, imagination and fantasy games, and the acclimatization movement in outdoor education all have potential to put people in touch with themselves and with the total environment. Important leisure education messages come from all of these activities. That is: "It's okay to touch, to move, to feel, to dream, to giggle, to play, and to create adventure in one's daily life."

THE FUTURE: THE CREATION OF DIVERSE MODELS

People need options. It is interesting to note that some of the most innovative models for the encouragement of healthy play values come from outside the mainstream of the leisure services profession. These alternatives not only provide some future direction for the parks and recreation movement, but also help to remind those in leadership positions of the nature and importance of play. Not only are these programs important as models in and of themselves, they also contain many elements from which leisure service professionals can learn. One does not necessarily have to always run, for example, a "New Games" program, but New Games leadership principles have broad based leisure education applications in schools, community centers, industry and many other areas of the public and private sector. What follows are a few short examples of alternatives. Additional information is available from the organizations themselves.

Adventure Playgrounds

What Adventure Playgrounds do is provide the space, materials and caring supervision for children to *create* and *own* their play experiences. In another article, this author has written extensively on the many growth and development values of Adventure Playgrounds.[40] The Adventure Playgrounds movement has been alive and well in Europe for over forty years, but has grown very slowly in the U.S. for a number of reasons, not the least of which is the power of the playground equipment industry in leisure service professional circles. However, with a little imagination the developmental, design, and child-centered leadership principles of Adventure Playgrounds can be applied in a variety of settings.

Project Adventure
Urban Outdoor Adventure Center

This rapidly growing movement has been described as both a "fun form of anxiety" and "adventure for big folks."[41,42] However, people of *all* ages and abilities have been playing Adventure Games, taking part in ropes courses, and sharing initiative activities for some time now. Using activities that involve cooperation, initiative, challenge, risk and fantasy, the ultimate goal of the Adventure movement is to put people in touch with their physical selves, their abilities, and their feelings, as well as to connect with the people around them. There is probably no better short term way of getting in touch with the concept of 'flow' than through adventure activities. The U.O.A.C. has been particularly innovative in its use of adventure as a juvenile diversion tool and for team building in industry.

New Games

New Games continues.[43] The New Games Foundation has trained over 30,000 people in the last ten years in a style of play and leadership that encourages participation, community, and creativity. The Foundation offers a variety of services and has published *More New Games*[44] which details its philosophical underpinnings and the leadership techniques which have led to its success. And a key to that success has been that New Games and New Games leadership provide ready access to flow and playfulness.[45]

Cooperative Games
Playfair
Project PLAE

The Cooperative Games Movement pioneered by Terry Orlick, focuses on the *process* of enjoyable challenges.[46,47] In recent books, he shares a wide variety of resources, including international games, self-refereed intramural programs, cooperative games for all ages, and academic learning experiences. The focus is on playing and winning *together* to build positive self-concepts. One of the special features of Orlick's books is a section that details ways to modify traditional sports to rekindle a play and process focus. This is especially useful, given our sport-oriented culture, as an entree to games flexibility when working with community groups.

The Playfair group has been very successful in bringing cooperative play to college orientations throughout the U.S.[48] In the area of integrative arts, two recent works by Bob Gregson provide scores of nurturing creative arts ideas.[49] Gregson was one of the founders of 'Sidewalk' in Hartford, Connecticut, and has been very active in the children's museum movement.

Project PLAE (Play and Learning in Adaptive Environments) is an extremely creative community based program that is successfully using the interrelated arts and flexible environments as mainstreaming vehicles.[50]

The Family That Plays Together . . .

A recently formed San Francisco based creative play, community development and leisure education organization, *The Family That Plays Together,* has as its chief purpose the fostering of healthy family play as one part of a community-wide family support network.[51] Using a synthesis of the best of the above movements and fifteen years of finely tuned facilitation skills, T.F.T.P.T. . . . has a variety of vehicles to accomplish its objectives. These include The Family Funforall, Family Fun Festivals, family leisure education workshops for professionals and lay people, presentations and consulting. In both direct service and training, there is a strong emphasis on empowerment and intergenerational play.

CONCLUSIONS

The above are just a sampling of the many innovative play/leisure education models that exist. Yet, there is always room for more flowers to bloom. In fact, it might be suggested that an international computerized clearinghouse be established to connect the organizations and to provide information about them to interested parties. Until that time, leisure service professionals are fortunate to have a recently developed compendium of almost one hundred of the world's most progressive children's play programs. *Playing, Living, Learning: A Worldwide Perspective on Children's Opportunities to Play,* by Westland and Knight[52] contains a summary of the major issues related to children's play, as well as descriptions of healthy play programs related to nature, games, adventure, the arts, toys, culture, education, the family, mobile opportunities, and playstreets.

People need a variety of play options, and the gap between theory and practice needs to be bridged if the profession is serious about helping people actualize the play experience, and ultimately achieve greater "flow" in their lives. The challenge for the profession will be to create flow inducing environments. Initially, people may want just "more of the same" but once they appreciate the excitement, fun, and energy of these options, they will demand more. And leisure services will be transformed into a more viable vehicle for human happiness.

Csikszentmihalyi tells us that the evolutionary significance of play is not that it maintains an already existing reality, but that it provides alternatives to it. How, in fact, do we free ourselves in general for a more playful view of the world — to know that the rules are freely chosen and can be changed?[53] Sutton-Smith reminds us of the power of play.

When different groups celebrate together, when parents and children play together, they bring to their lives the kinds of vividness which we have earlier called play or flow. These have in them the seeds of a life which is more interesting and more connected in an age when many of the older forms of connections no longer seem so available or so meaningful.[54]

Teacher, let me swim in a puddle,
Let me race a cloud in the sky,
Let me build a house without walls

But, most of all . . .
Let me laugh at
Nothing things.[57]

REFERENCES

1. Bateson, G. "Both sides of the necessary paradox: Meditations on George Bateson and the death of the bread and the butterfly." *Harpers*, 1973.
2. Gunter, B.G. "Properties of the Leisure Experience" in: Ibrahim, H. and Crandall, R. *Leisure: A Psychological Approach*. Los Alamitos, California. Hwong Publishing Co. 1979. pp. 3-43.
3. deGrazia, S. *Of Time, Work and Leisure*. New York: Anchor-Doubleday, 1962.
4. Beryne, D.E. "Laughter, Humor and Play." In: Lindzey, G. and Aronson, E. (Eds.). *Handbook of Social Psychology*. Reading, Massachusetts: Addison Wesley, 1968.
5. Bower, E. "Plays the Thing." In: Bower, E. *Games in Education and Development*. Springfield: Charles C. Thomas, 1974, pp. 10-11.
6. Bruner, J. "Play is Serious Business." *Psychology Today*. 8, (January), 1974, pp. 81-83.
7. May, C. "Study of Creativity and Sense of Magic." Review of: Arieti, S. *Creativity: The Magic Synthesis*. In: *Sunday Los Angeles Times Book Review Section,* January, 1977.
8. Kaufman, L. "Blocks to Creativity." Handout in E. Bower's Class, University of California, Berkeley School of Education, 1970.
9. In: Sutton-Smith, B. "The Useless Made Useful: Play as Variability Training." *School Review*. 83, (February), 1975. pp. 197-214.
10. Bower, *Op. Cit.,* p. 11.
11. Sutton-Smith, *Op. Cit.*
12. Bower, E. et. al. *Learning to Play/Playing to Learn*. Berkeley, California: University of California, Berkeley Creative Arts Printing, 1974. pp. 8-21.
    sity of California, Berkeley Creative Arts Printing, 1974. pp. 8-21.
13. Singer, J. "Fantasy, the Foundation of Serenity." *Psychology Today*. 10, (July) 1976. p. 32.
14. Sutton-Smith, *Op. Cit.,* pp. 197-214.
15. Singer, *Op. Cit.*
16. Caplan, F. and Caplan, T. "Creativity Through Play." *The Power of Play*. Garden City: Anchor Press, 1973, pp. 149-179.
17. Csikszentmihalyi, M. *Flow: Studies of Enjoyment*. Public Health Service Report: University of Chicago, 1974.
18. Furlong, W. "The Flow Experience: The Fun in Fun." *Psychology Today*. 1976 (June). pp. 36.
19. *Ibid*. p. 37.
20. *Ibid*. p. 37.
21. Csikszentmihalyi, M. *Beyond Boredom and Anxiety*. San Francisco: Jossey-Bass, 1976. See Also Csikszentmihalyi, *Op. Cit.,* 1973 and Furlong, *Op. Cit.,* 1976.
22. Sutton-Smith, B. "Play as Flow and Innovation: The New Meanings." Address at Press Conference, Frankfurt, Germany, March 12, 1979 (excerpted from *T.A.A.S.P. Newsletter,* 1979/80 p. 12.
23. Csikszentmihalyi, M. "Some paradoxes in the definition of play" in . . . Cheska, A. *Play as Context*. West Point, N.Y. Leisure Press, 1981. pp. 24-25 (Proceedings of the 5th. annual meeting of T.A.A.S.P.).
24. Csikszentmihalyi, *Op. Cit.*
25. Ellis, G., Witt, P. and Aguilar, T. "Facilitating Flow Through Therapeutic Recreation Services." *Therapeutic Recreation Journal*. Second Quarter, 1983. pp. 6-15.

26. Michaelis, B. "Flow/New Games." *New Games Foundation Newsletter*. San Francisco, California. Summer, 1977.
27. ----"It Power! — A Game Detergent." *New Games Foundation Newsletter*. San Francisco, California. Winter, 1978.
28. Ellis, et. al. *Op. Cit.*
29. deGrazia, S. *Op. Cit.*
30. Polidora, J. *Course Syllabus and Reading Guide for Behavioral Biology 451.* University of California, Davis Medical School, 1977.
31. Ellis, et. al. *Op. Cit.*
32. Csikszentmihalyi, M. *Op. Cit.,* 1974 and Furlong, *Op. Cit.,* 1976.
33. Glasser, W. "Needed for America: The Kind of Recreation that Frees the Mind." *U.S. News and World Report.* (May 23) 1977. pp. 74-76.
34. Gunn, S. "Blocks to Play." National Recreation and Parks Association Congress, Las Vegas, Nevada. October, 1977.)
35. Cf: Hawes, B. "Law and Order on the Playground." In: Bower, E. *Games in Education and Development.* Springfield, Charles C. Thomas, 1974. pp. 12-22.
36. Montague, A. "Don't Be Adultish." *Psychology Today.* 11 (August) 1977. p. 46.
37. Comstock, G. *Television and Human Behavior: The Key Studies.* The Rand Corporation, 1975.
38. Orlick, T. *Winning Through Cooperation.* Washington, D.C.: Acroplis Book Co., 1978.
39. Ellis, et. al. *Op. Cit.*
40. Michaelis, B. "Adventure Playgrounds: A Healthy Affirmation of the Rights of the Child" *Leisure Today. J.O.P.E.R.* October, 1979. pp. 55-58.
41. *Cowstails and Cobras.* c/o Project Adventure, P. O. Box 157, Hamilton, Massachusetts 01936.
42. Urban Outdoor Adventure Center, 198 Seal Rock Drive, San Francisco, CA 94121.
43. Cf: Fluegelmar, A. *The New Games Book,* Garden City, New York. Dolphin-Doubleday, 1976.
44. Fluegelman, A., Ed. *More New Games.* New York: Doubleday, 1981.
45. Sutton-Smith, B., "Play as Flow . . ." *Op. Cit.*
46. Orlick, T. *The Cooperative Sports and Games Book I & II.* Westmaster: Pantheon, 1979, 1982.
47. Michaelis, B. and Michaelis, D. *Learning Through Non-competitive Activities and Play.* Belmont, Cal.: Pittman Learning. 1977.
48. Weinstein, M. *Playfair.* Impact Publishers. P. O. Box 1094. San Luis Obispo, CA 93406. 1980.
49. Project PLAE. 1824 A Fourth Street, Berkeley, CA 94710.
50. Gregson, B. *The Incredible Indoor Games Book* and *The Outrageous Outdoor Games Book.* Belmont, Cal.: Pittman Learning. 1982.
51. Michaelis, B. "The Family That Plays Together: Programming, Marketing and Delivering Family Play Ideas." *California Parks and Recreation.* Winter, 1984. pp. 38-42 (For further information about T.F.T.P.T., write: Michaelis, 338 Reichling Avenue, Pacifica, CA. 94044).
52. Westland, C. and Knight, J. *Playing, Living, Learning: A Worldwide Perspective on Children's Opportunities To Play.* State College, Pa.: Venture Publishing, 1982.
53. Csikszentmihalyi, M. "Some Paradoxes . . ." *Op. Cit.*
54. Sutton-Smith, B. "Play and Flow . . ." *Op. Cit.*
55. Cullum, A. *The Geranium on the Window Sill Just Died, But Teacher Went Right On.* Holland: Harlin Quest, 1971.

Chapter Seven

Creative Growth Through Play and its Implications for Recreation Practice

Doyle Bishop and Claudine Jeanrenaud

A cherished belief among many play specialists is that play enhances the development of creativity.[1] The fact is, the paths to play have many dead ends, detours, and debris that discourage instead of enhance the development of creativity. These bad road conditions are numerous and often not easily visible until it is too late. The traffic engineers, road crews, and patrolmen who manage the journey through play (i.e. parents, teachers, recreation leaders, therapists, and others) must work hard to remove these roadblocks. If they do not, play experiences will almost certainly help to make non-creative children and later adults.

We propose to demonstrate these roadblocks with a general model of the stages, or choicepoints, involved in play. This model is the authors' integration of diverse ideas about play as well as some that, up to now, have not been closely linked to play. The model is the result of the authors' many discussions between themselves and with students. The detailed ideas included in the model are not novel; we have borrowed heavily from previous research and theory. What is original is the particular ways in which we have tried to integrate the ideas to provide one view of play and its link to creativity.

It seems to us that our emphasis, in the model, on the importance of exploratory behavior and its balance against too much or too little directiveness and structure, as a path to creative growth, provides a focal point for examining some possible limitations of current recreation practice. In the last part of the chapter we explore those limits. But first it is important to look at the path to creative growth and the ways in which it can be blocked.

The main ideas from previous work that we have relied on are those of Hutt[2] and Linford and Jeanrenaud,[3] who laid the groundwork for viewing play as a series of critical stages; reinforcement theorists such as Hull[4] and Skinner[5], whose principles of learning help to show how movement through the stages of play can be enhanced or retarded; arousal theorists, particularly Berlyne,[6] and Fiske and Maddi,[7] whose ideas about concepts like novelty, complexity, curiosity, and exploration help to define the distinctive crossroads on the path through play; personality and development theorists like Piaget,[8] Harvey, Hunt and Schroder,[9] and Eysenck,[10] whose ideas illustrate how different combinations of persons and environments, for both players and managers, can produce different outcomes at the different stages of play; and some investigations of play and creativity such as those by Torrance,[11] Lieberman,[12] Sutton-Smith,[13] and Bishop and Chace,[14] which have demonstrated that play is a powerful medium for inhibiting or enhancing creative potential. These authors and works are mentioned here so that the rest of the paper can proceed without continual reference to previous literature.

Refer to the diagram in Figure 1. For our purposes, a journey through play begins at:

THE ATTENTION STAGE

There is a story about an old farmer who used to periodically whack his mule on the snout with a stick of firewood. When asked why he did this, the farmer replied, "I can't l'arn him nuthin if'n I don't first git his attention!" Now, we do not recommend the whack-between-the-eyes method to get a kid started at play. But the farmer's wisdom, verified repeatedly by psychological research, is sound in principle: In order to begin learning anything, the person must first pay attention to some object or situation. No attention, no learning. No learning, no creativity.

NOVELTY

Novelty, or the extent to which an object differs, relatively or absolutely, from what has occured before, helps to gain one's attention. So does the *intensity* of the object or situation — how much it stands out from the rest of its environment. Things that are familiar or plain will not grab our attention very often or for very long. How many of you have noticed the light bulb in your ceiling lately? If you have, our guess is that it had stopped producing light. When was the last time you marvelled at a gray cement wall that you passed?

Those with an economic motive, like toy manufacturers, understand very well the old farmer's wisdom. Have you ever seen a child in a department store, grasping towards a brightly-colored toy and throwing a temper tantrum, because his mother is trying to pull him away? If so, you have witnessed first hand the significance of the attention stage of play.

Figure 1

Model of the Behavioral Stages and Blocks to Creativity Through Play

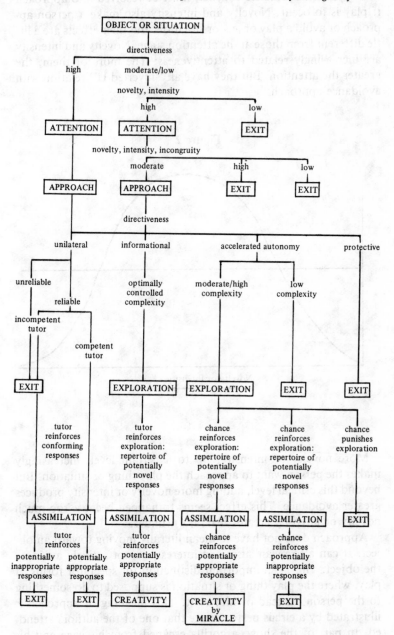

CURIOSITY

The *approach-avoidance conflict,* must be resolved into approach if play is to occur. Novelty and intensity also make a person approach or avoid a play object or situation. But their effects are a little different from those at the attention stage. Novelty and intensity are increasingly related to attentiveness: The more of them, the greater the attention. But they have an "inverted U" relation with avoidance-approach.

Figure 2

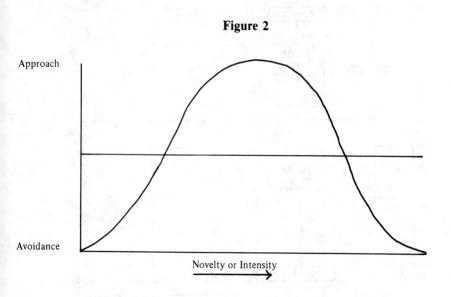

More novelty or intensity, up to a certain level, increasingly makes the person want to approach the play thing or situation. But beyond this critical level, adding more novelty or intensity produces greater avoidance. This effect seems to happen because too much novelty or intensity creates fear, not wonder.

Approach does not have to mean literally moving toward an object. It can also mean sustained interest, or not actively avoiding the object. This is an important distinction for spectator forms of play, where the play thing or situation is supposed to do something to the person, instead of him to it. This meaning of approach is illustrated by a circus performance that one of the authors attended. In part of the show, a gorilla escaped from his cage and his trainer to create havoc and fear among the other circus performers in the arena. This display riveted the interest of the children in the audience, who seemed delighted by these antics, until the gorilla leaped over the arena wall into the spectator section! The younger children, terrified, then began crying, clinging, and in some cases running for the exit. Soon the "gorilla" took off his hooded mask to reveal a man in a gorilla costume. The children immediately composed themselves and either returned to their seats or went over to the man-gorilla to get a closer look. Clearly, the children's approach tendency was close to or at the peak of the "inverted U," before the "gorilla" jumped out of the arena. The, novelty and intensity were just too high and avoidance reactions followed. Finally, the object was transformed to one that was relatively familiar but still somewhat novel — enough to produce literal approach and even touching.

This example demonstrates that approach (or avoidance) can be psychological as well as physical. The example also shows that distance between player and object and the presence of barriers between them can affect the amount of approach or avoidance.

In summary, if you present a child with optimum amounts of novelty, intensity, distance, and barriers in a play situation, he will be inclined toward curiosity; he will resolve the approach-avoidance conflict in favor of approach.

EXPLORATORY PLAY

Exploration is the manipulation of the new object or situation in order to discover its properties. Berlyne distinguishes between two kinds of exploration: a) specific exploration, aimed at finding a single answer to a problem or challenge and b) diversive exploration, aimed at finding in the environment elements that can produce excitement or distraction. Exploration is the means (not necessarily conscious or deliberate) by which the individual acquires a wide range of information; it adds to the person's repertoire of possible ideas and responses. The availability of this repertoire at a later time makes it possible for the person to produce many ideas or actions in a given situation; this potential is a necessary, though not sufficient, condition for creativity to occur.

The *complexity* of the play thing or situation determines how much the person will explore it. A complex thing has many different parts and/or unusual arrangements or combinations of parts; so certain kinds of novelty affect exploration too. An object or situation that has many things to see, hear, touch, smell, taste, and manipulate, especially in unusual ways, is more complex than one with fewer of these features and is more likely to encourage exploration.

Imagine a cuckoo clock with a dial that permits choosing the cycle in minutes with which the cuckoo sounds. Now add complexity by providing three doors and three "cuckoos" — a bird, a lion, and an old car — with an unpredictable pattern of which one will come out of which door. Add more by allowing the three cuckoos to do different things when activated — the lion can croak like a frog or toot like a car's horn, the bird can roar like a lion or moo like a cow, and the car can bark as well as squirt water from a radiator leak. As more and more features like these are added and the child has some way of influencing, though not precisely determining, their occurence, the frequency and duration of exploratory play should increase.

These rules about complexity and exploration hold, of course, only if the parts of the object did not produce so much intensity or novelty that an avoidance reaction occured. Given that approach takes place, then complexity should be increasingly related to exploration.

ASSIMILATION

Assimilation or consolidation play is the repetition of behaviors or situations, which, during the exploratory stage, appeared challenging or were reinforced; such repetition permits the child to assimilate or master the behavior or situation. As a rule, unless other people impose the constraints that we discuss later, the child's assimilation play does *not* involve 100% repetition. Complete repetition of behavior, all the time, would seem to discourage the development of creative abilities. The natural tendency of the child, according to Freud and Piaget, would be to make subtle transformations in his play or the situation. These transformations are the child's attempts to bring the object or situation within his range of comprehension or ability. These attempts are not diversive exploration but are forms of specific exploration that result in *mastery*; this word, although a good one to describe the outcome, does not necessarily mean that the child is diligently striving to master some specific skill, like a high school student strives to memorize the parts of the body for an anatomy course. Mastery or comprehension tend to follow (if not interfered with) not necessarily by the child's design or intent but often simply as a result of practice.

Assimilation play, along with formal training, helps the individual acquire proficiency in various responses; this proficiency is the other necessary condition for creativity.

CREATIVITY

Creativity is the production of *novel* responses that have an *appropriate* impact in a given context. If several truckloads of creativity were dumped in your front yard, this definition probably would not help you to identify it. But the definition does neatly summarize, if somewhat cryptically, the essence of extensive research and writing about creativity. Most people would probably agree that redundancy of ideas or products is not creative, but neither is novelty for novelty's sake; if the idea or product does not resolve some problem or affect established beliefs or practices, it is regarded as *not appropriate* and thus not creative, *for the given context,* although it might be appropriate in another place or time.

Our concern is to outline the general conditions that are likely to enhance or, more often, inhibit the person's ability to make novel *and* appropriate responses. According to the definition, if either of these abilities fails to develop, the person will be incapable of creative performance.

The first condition for creativity, the ability to make novel responses, comes primarily from the *exploratory play* experiences of the person; the attention and approach experiences are critical as well, but mainly because exploratory play cannot occur without them. In exploratory play the child learns the many different things that the environment can "do" and the many things that he can do to it. Over time, in many exploratory play situations, he accumulates a repertoire of potential responses that he can call upon, if and when he needs to. The more responses he accumulates, the greater the probability that at least one of them will be novel in some context, sometime. Also, the more there are the greater the possibility of combining several to yield a novel pattern of behavior, even though one response would not be novel in the given context. In short, exploratory play, by providing many potential responses, helps make the person *potentially creative,* in that he is able to emit those responses in some future context.

Exploratory play probably also increases the person's *motivation* to make novel responses, or at least reduces his fear of making them. Studies of humans and other animals suggest that fear of novelty is an acquired drive and that it is greatest in animals whose early environmental experiences are impoverished. We believe it was Piaget who said, "the more a child has seen and heard, the more he wants to see and hear." And we would add that this probably applies to the stimuli produced by the child's own responses.

The second condition for creativity, the ability to make appropriate or useful responses, comes primarily from the *assimilation-play* experiences of the person. It is during assimilation play that the person develops, through repetition and transformation, specific, known skills. He is not trying to find out all the things that the environment can do or that he can do to it, as in exploration; he is perfecting, within the limits of his existing abilities, his understanding of or skill at some particular situation or task. He is figuring out how to hammer a nail, throw a football, ride a bike, or why mother insists that he eat with a fork, not his hands, why he goes to the dentist, or later how a barometer, carburetor, or electric motor works.

In short, there is a kind of learning, distinct from exploration, that results in the acquisition of particular performance skills that are, or are intended to be, thorough and permanent. The more thorough and permanent the skills developed in a given domain of performance, the more likely it is that the person can make *appropriate* responses, and thus is *potentially creative,* in that domain. And the more frequently specific-skill learning is concentrated in one domain, the less potential creativity the person has in other domains: It is not likely that a professional novelist will help to invent a new breed of computers, and we would not expect an electronics engineer to win the Nobel prize for literature.

To briefly summarize, these are the major stages. By successfully progressing through these stages repeatedly, on many encounters with the environment during development, the person would become creative. Progression can be blocked, however, by environmental, social, and personality factors; the more often this happens, the less creativity will develop. We have seen how the degree of novelty, intensity, incongruity, and complexity affect these stages. Now we will look at some other factors that can block the development of creative ability.

BLOCKING PROGRESS TOWARD CREATIVITY

Control can be exercised by parents, older friends or relatives, teachers, etc. For lack of a better word on which most people can agree, they will be referred to as tutors. Tutors, then, can exercise control either directly on the child by means of directives and/or reinforcements (rewards and punishments), or indirectly through manipulation of the child's play environment, including its degree of novelty, complexity, intensity and incongruity.

Control can be exercised with over-directiveness, underdirectiveness or moderate directiveness. Over-directiveness can take several forms. The tutor can draw the child's attention against his will, and show him how to handle an object or situation *before* the child has had time to be curious about it or to explore it. For instance, the tutor may say this to the child: "Here, come with me, I want to show you something: see this plane? I want you to play with it, and I'll show you how to hold it. . .." This condition is called unilateral since all the information passes from the tutor to the child, and none from the child to the tutor. If the plane flies and does not crash, the condition is considered as reliable.

Under this form of over-directiveness, reinforcement is contingent upon conformance to directions. So punishment might sound like this: "How many times must I tell you not to hold your ball with your left hand?" Because both curiosity and exploration were circumvented, the behaviors displayed during assimilation play are limited to the motions dictated by the tutor. Consequently, the child becomes fearful, dependent upon his tutor's instructions, initiative, conforming and non-creative.

If the tutor's directives are unreliable, i.e. produce undesirable outcomes or contradict previous directions, the child faces a multiple conflict: following directions does not necessarily lead to desirable outcomes; not following them certainly leads to punishment. Besides having missed exploration, the child has no alternative solutions to the tutor's instructions. Consequently, he reacts with distrust and anger towards the tutor, and might try to oppose him. Often, therefore, behaviors opposed to directions and that escaped punishment are perceived as rewarded, even though they may be regarded as inappropriate by his society. So, the child might become rigidly anti-authoritarian and non-conforming — but not creative.

The tutor can also provide unnecessary assistance. For example, he might say this: "Here, this is too hard for you, I'll do it!" Under these *protective interpersonal* conditions, the tutor is over-responsive to the child's wants. While the tutor might interfere at any stage of the child's experience he tends to do so mostly when the child meets his first obstacle during exploratory play, thus preventing assimilation play. Therefore, while the development of novel responses might not have been affected as severely as under unilateral conditions, acquisition of proficient responses, whether appropriate or not, will have been inhibited.

One response, however, will have been fully explored and assimilated: manipulation of the tutor in order to elicit his assistance. The child might, therefore, become an expert at social manipulation, but without confidence in his own ability to achieve anything. So, he remains dependent on others to be creative in his place.

Under-directiveness occurs when the tutor exercises no control over the child. This is considered to be the *accelerated autonomy* condition. Spontaneous attention, curiosity, exploratory and assimilation play all occur, but in the absence of any guidance by the tutor. Reinforcement is dispensed by the environment. Behavior is rewarded whenever environmental consequences are pleasant, and punished whenever environmental consequences are adverse.

For instance, a child's attention has been caught by a toy which is lying on a table. He decides to explore the toy. Because he is too small to reach it, he grasps the table cloth and pulls on it until the toy falls on the floor. If the toy breaks, the child's behavior has been punished. If not, the child's behavior has been rewarded and table cloth pulling might become one of his favorite play activities.

As this example illustrates, the absence of adult guidance makes it difficult for the child to learn about his society's sense of appropriateness. So while he might have developed a wide repertoire of novel responses, few of them will be appropriate, thus limiting his creativity.

Moderate directiveness, as in the *interpersonal informational* condition, is most likely to lead to creativity. The tutor manipulates the environment so as to provide the child with an environment structured in such a way that the child will almost always proceed through a progression of experiences.[15] Although the child's approach and exploration are experienced as spontaneous, they actually follow a predetermined path leading to the discovery of appropriate responses.

For instance, if the tutor decides that the child will learn about cooperation, he sets up a game where success depends directly on the degree of cooperation between the players. He does not tell the child what to do. The child's desire to succeed motivates him to test alternative approaches, including the cooperative one. The consequences of the various approaches are compared. This information is stored and thus becomes available for combination with previously stored information, so that conceptual links can be drawn. In other words, the seeking of alternate solutions has been elicited, and concept formation made possible.

To that, the tutor may add social reinforcement by congratulating profusely the child for cooperating or initiating exploration. So, the behaviors likely to be learned during assimilation play are those rewarded during exploration as well as exploration itself. The child thus develops a wide range of appropriate and novel responses, the two necessary skills for creativity.

Table 1

Illustration of the Skills Developed under Each
Control Condition, and the Resulting Creativity

Control Conditions	Creative Skills		Resulting Creativity
	Novelty	Appropriateness	
Unilateral			
reliable	−	+*	−*
unreliable	−	−	−
Protective	+	−	−
Accelerated			
Autonomy	+	−	−
Informational	+	+	+

*Note: + means existing skill; − means absent skill.

In summary (see Table 1), of the control conditions discussed above, only the last one offers the opportunity to develop both novel and appropriate responses. The unilateral condition, by bypassing exploratory play and emphasizing assimilation play, encourages the development of appropriate responses (at least when the tutor is competent), but discourages the development of novel responses. The protective condition allows some exploration, but no assimilation. Therefore, while some novel responses might develop, neither appropriate nor inappropriate learning occurs. Finally, in the accelerated autonomy condition, exploration and assimilation both take place, but the absence of guidance results in the learning of many inappropriate responses.

PERSONALITY OF PLAYER AND TUTOR

The environmental effects and tutoring practices that we have outlined are probably determined, in part, by the personality characteristics of both learner and tutor; some effects of personality are undoubtedly independent of what is actually present in the environment or what the tutor intends *at any given time*. On the other hand, the stages that we have discussed obviously help to shape the personalities of people in some ways. So movement through the stages and the participants' personalities are in a dynamic relationship; they influence one another. This dynamic interplay continues throughout development, which, though concentrated in one's early years, probably is a lifelong process.

The player or learner will be motivated or able to notice, approach, or explore things depending, in part, on his past experience in doing so. Some kids will approach and explore things that other kids will not even notice or will be frightened by. Piaget's phrase, "the more he will want to see and hear," is highly relevant to this point; so is the added notion: the more he will *be able* to see and hear. Fiske and Maddi's idea of high- and low-activation people (seekers or avoiders of stimulation) could be an example of a pertinent personality characteristic, which presumably develops out of experience.

Eysenck's introverted and extraverted types, which he believes are largely inherited, are other examples. The introvert has a nervous system characterized by high levels of cortical arousal and low levels of reactive inhibition (mental fatigue or boredom); the extravert is just the reverse. These differences suggest that introverts should be less impulsive, more conscious of details, more persistent at various tasks, and more capable of long-term memory than extraverts; these hypotheses have been supported by a variety of studies. Extraverts, because of their high boredom potential, presumably would attend to and approach novel stimuli more than introverts but would engage in less detailed exploration and less consolidation play. This reasoning would conclude that, given the same developmental circumstances, introverts have a better chance of becoming creative than extraverts.

Now consider the personality of the tutor. Even with the best of intentions for the outcome of his tutoring, what he can actually *do* will be partly dictated by his own personality. In fact, his intentions — what he thinks should be done — will be somewhat preconditioned by his personality. This, to us, is a vital point for the management of play experiences: A tutor, say a recreation leader, cannot simply decide to manage play for the betterment of the player and expect to do so entirely on the strength of his own motivation and game skills. His personality might be such that he cannot recognize or manage the delicate balance between exploratory and consolidatory play. If his aim is the enhancement of creativity, he will almost certainly fail (unless someone else plugs the holes that he leaves).

A highly extraverted tutor, for example, if Eysenck's meaning of extraversion is correct, would probably emphasize a great variety of novel but, for learning purposes, superficial experiences in play. This approach, if prolonged or used often enough, seems likely to produce a jack-of-all-trades-but-master-of-none kind of player. Such persons, though often interesting, are hardly models of creative production.

Because tutors were once players and learners, their personalities have been shaped by the developmental experiences that we have described. The methods of control used by tutors, outlined previously, were derived largely from the childhood training conditions described by Harvey, Hunt and Schroder.[16] Those authors claim that the different training conditions produce distinctive adult personalities, ranging from the highly concrete, authoritarian, rigid person to the highly abstract, open-minded, adaptive one. What this means, in our terms, is that tutors who were frequently exposed to directive, unilateral methods of control in their development are likely to become concretistic, authoritarian personalities who, as tutors, will employ directive, unilateral methods of control.

SUMMARY

We have not tried to give a precise and exhaustive rendering of relevant personality characteristics. We have merely attempted to point out the importance of personality, for both player and tutor, and to suggest a few directions for further thought and research. The reader might have concluded by now that in order to promote creativity in others a tutor must be creative himself. We do not disagree with that conclusion. Unfortunately, telling would-be tutors to ''be creative'' is about as helpful as telling an alcoholic that he really ought to stop drinking. Clearly, it is easier said than done.

We have presented a model of stages of play, which is really a view of developmental experience adapted to play, in order to reveal various roadblocks to creativity. Figure 1 summarizes this model. We have not often referred to Figure 1 throughout our discussion. We hope that the figure, bolstered by the text, adequately summarizes our major points: a) the critical stages of play or, more generally, development, b) the dynamics between these stages and personality development, and c) the many roadblocks to creativity as well as the nature of the singular path that is likely to lead to it.

Recreation rhetoric sometimes extols the joys and wonders of play and its role in creative development. And researchers, including ourselves, have often looked to play as one source of creative behavior. We do not wish to squelch pretty thoughts or discourage positively-oriented research. But perhaps an alternative view should be heard and researched: If our model is somewhere along the right lines, the greater miracle is that anybody at all ever becomes creative.

IMPLICATIONS

This chapter has referred to childhood learning and experiences and their effects on later creativity. But "later" actually never comes. Recent research findings are beginning to re-emphasize what many individuals have always known but some of our institutions forgot: the need for creative development continues throughout the life cycle right up until death and, so far as we know, perhaps beyond it. Thus, fundamental ideas about the paths to creativity are relevant to adult behavior and development. And the recreation professionals who develop recreation institutions, programs, and the training of other recreation professionals are heavily implicated in that process, whether they want to be or not. Sometimes it seems that they do not want to be.

Recreation personnel are supposed to be "people-oriented." In their personal lives they most clearly are. Both casual observation and psychological test data show that recreation personnel are about as extraverted as you are likely to find. But in their professional lives — what they do on the job, what they write books about, and what they try to teach others to do — many seem to show greater concern with things like organizational charts; staff assignments; budget preparation, defense, and allocation; facility or resourse design and maintenance; and the rules and regulations that shall govern people's recreation behavior. These activities smack of a love for *things* and their orderly arrangements rather than a genuine concern for people as such. It is fair to ask whether anyone, recreation professional or otherwise, can really be genuinely concerned with *people*. Perhaps most of us are only capable of being genuinely concerned with a person or two. As is often suggested, if you discover that your true friends can be counted on one hand, do not be dismayed — feel fortunate.

Nevertheless, one must wonder what this heavy emphasis on things and abstract process is doing to recreation's potential for fostering creative growth in child and adult participants. In the terminology of the model presented above, the recreation field sometimes seems like the unilateral, reliable (?), competent (?) tutor who reinforces conforming responses and expects participants to assimilate the response alternatives proffered. The sterility of many recreation programs and places and the apparent lack of concern for exploration (by professionals or by the public they serve) is notable. Perhaps most or all recreation professionals occasionally allow, consciously or unconsciously, exploratory behavior to appear. But, often, these instances seem too infrequent and too superficial.

Some counter arguments to this characterization of the recreation field need to be acknowledged. First, organizational charts, budgets, rules, etc. are necessary and serve valuable functions. It is hopelessly idealistic to imagine that parks, playgrounds, recreation centers, and some resources can manage themselves. We might be surprised, however, at the positive outcomes that would follow a loosening of the reins in some instances. Total loosening, or a *laissez-faire* philosophy, in addition to being disastrous in some ways, will not promote creative growth in participants, as we tried to show by the accelerated-autonomy form of directiveness. Partial loosening of the tight structure of planning and programming might, of course, lead to *less well-managed* outcomes. But as our model also shows, well-managed tasks constitute only a necessary, not a sufficient condition for creative development of players.

Second, there is the claim, related to that of poorly managed outcomes, that people will "muck things up" (the environment, facilities, other participants' recreation) if recreational experiences are de-controlled. This rationalization for emphasizing institutionalized processes in recreation reminds us of the one used by some hunters to justify the killing of other animals for "sport." The hunted animals, it is claimed, are deficient in natural predators or sustenance, so if men do not kill them, they will die anyway from overpopulation or competition for scarce resources. Some of these benevolent-minded sportsmen do not appear to question how their prey came to be in this unnatural predicament in the first place. Perhaps because of the actions of previous "benevolent-minded" men? To what extent does the perceived need to regulate recreation experiences stem from some consequences of having regulated them in the past? Is it possible that some "mucking up" behaviors are exploratory forms of protest against institutionalized processes that were conceived in order to prevent people from "mucking things up?" There is evidence that this is exactly what happens in some types of regulated work situations, such as assembly lines. It is ironic that the recreation profession promotes itself as the opposite of such situations, as the guardian of people's leisure — the freedom from constraints and from the necessity to be occupied. Exploratory behavior is an important quality of leisure, and, if our model is correct, is essential to one of the outcomes of leisure —

creative growth. Yet, such behavior is often blocked by the very people who claim to be leisure specialists.

The irony of the discrepancy between recreation's words and deeds can be seen another way. It can be fairly said that recreation is not alone among the service professions in its bureaucratized ways. Medicine treats patients' diseases pretty well but often makes the recipients feel degraded and helpless in the process; many teachers teach well but seem unable to help students learn (and there is a difference); school administrators sometimes appear to forget both teaching and learning; counselors sometimes devote enormous energy to describing their clients' problems in terms of some personality model rather than help solve the problems; and some policemen are good at enforcing the law but forget to help and protect the public.

An important difference between recreation and these other fields is the distance between rhetoric and reality. Most doctors know that they are highly trained technician-scientists who can remove your ulcers, prescribe the right antibiotic for your infection, or possibly repair your malfunctioning heart. They do not claim to do more. Recreation is one of the few fields, along with certain branches of mysticism and Sunday-morning evangelism, that claims significant effects on crime reduction; family functioning and unity; social and community development; physical fitness; mental health and therapy; the development of attitudes, values, leadership, and character; psychological and spiritual growth; and "self-actualization."

One wonders how a field can know or do anything about family problems when it seems blissfully unaware that in this explosive, exploratory world there are two-parent families, one-parent families, no-parent families, nuclear families, extended families, childless families, living-together-but unmarried families, married-but-living-apart families, homosexual families, communal families, and probably many more. As for self-actualization, Abraham Maslow's eternal sleep might be fretful indeed, if he knows that the existing practice of recreation is being touted as the pathway to that ultimate state of personality development.

People, especially in America, are today exploring a large variety of lifestyles and leisure pursuits. Much of this is motivated by an urge for creative growth. Some do not participate much in the hub-bub but, instead, observe it, investigate it, try to understand it. Whether as participants or observers, people in other fields appear to be more aware of leisure, its current stirrings, its myths, its possible futures, than many recreation professionals.

In a recent issue of *Psychology Today* a sociologist investigated the rapid growth of around-the-clock activity in American cities.

He showed the banks, supermarkets, garages, restaurants, discotheques, theatres, tour agencies, laundries, and other privately owned facilities were adopting all-night hours to cater to this nocturnal life. No mention was made of public recreation facilities. Are they involved in this latest trend? Many recreation personnel can tell you who won last year's Orange Bowl game and the exact score or the latest attendance figures at the community swimming pool. But do they have a clue, or do they care, what people are seeking by wandering about in the middle of the night?

Economists and other social scientists are investigating possibilities for completely revising the calendar and work-leisure cycles — for instance, a nine-day week with alternating 6 day-3 day, on-off cycles. The way in which we structure and allocate time goes to the heart of what leisure is all about. Yet, where are the recreators — the leisure specialists — in thinking innovatively about this most fundamental commodity?

It is perhaps in the area of research that the reluctance of many recreators to engage in or encourage exploratory behavior is most noticeable. Recreation practitioners often complain of the irrelevance of research, the researcher's apparent lack of concern for "meeting" the practitioner's needs. Despite decades of thought and careful research into the nature of creative thinking, these complainers still are unaware of a fundamental fact: Relevance is not something that is given; it is something that is conceived or created in an individual mind. The internal creative flame often needs external sources of fuel to feed it. But the sources, in themselves, are neither relevant nor irrelevant. It is an exploratory attitude and behavior that make them so.

After these critiques, it is appropriate to acknowledge that there are some changes, which perhaps signify exploratory thinking, in the recreation field. There is a growing emphasis on the leisure problems of special populations that are not in the mainstream of American or Canadian life; there is increasing recognition of the importance of personality, the individuality of leisure, and the possible need for individual lifestyle counselling; in a few communities, recreation departments are "opening up" facilities to multiple and unusual uses, dictated by the felt needs, or whims, of the participants. These approaches had to grow out of some exploratory thinking, because they show a recognition of the idiosyncrasies of human needs — those that cannot be handled by the standardized operating procedure given by organizational charts and activity schedules. In a field that claims to deal in a quality, leisure, that represents freedom from constraints and uniformity, these kinds of approaches should be the rule, not the exception.

REFERENCES

1. The part of this paper that describes the model of play and creative growth originally appeared in Jeanrenaud, Claudine and Bishop, Doyle. "Road Blocks to Creativity Through Play." In Wilkinson, Paul (Ed.) *Play in Human Settlements*, London: Croom and Helm, Ltd., 1979. We gratefully acknowledge the cooperation of Paul Wilkinson and Croom and Helm, Ltd. in allowing a different and expanded version of our original paper to appear here.
2. Hutt, Corine. "Exploration and Play in Children." In *Symposium of the Zoological Society of London,* 18, (1966). pp. 61-81.
3. Linford, Anthony G. and Jeanrenaud, Claudine. "A Behavioral Model for a Four-Stage Play Theory." In Kenyon, G.S. (Ed.) *Contemporary Psychology of Sports.* Chicago: Athletic Institute, Chicago, 1970. pp. 446-450.
4. Hull, C.L., *Essentials of Behavior.* New Haven: Yale University, 1951.
5. Skinner, B. F., *Science and Human Behavior.* New York: McMillan, 1953.
6. Berlyne, D. E., *Conflict, Arousal and Curiosity.* New York: McGraw-Hill, 1960.
7. Fiske, David W. and Maddi, Salvador. *Functions of Varied Experience.* Homewood: Dorsey Press, 1961.
8. Piaget, Jean., *Play, Dreams and Imitation in Childhood.* London: Routledge and Kegan Ltd., 1951.
9. Harvey, O. J., Hunt, D. E. and Schroder, H. M., *Conceptual Systems and Personality Organization,* New York: Wiley, 1961.
10. Eysenck, Hans J., *The Biological Basis of Personality.* Springfield, Illinois: Charles C. Thomas, 1967.
11. Torrance, E. P., "Education and Creativity." In C. W. Taylor (Ed.), *Creativity: Progress and Potential.* New York: McGraw-Hill, 1964. pp. 49-128.
12. Lieberman, J. Nina. "Playfulness and Divergent Thinking: An Investigation of Their Relationship at the Kindergarden Level." *Journal of Genetic Psychology,* 107: (1965). pp. 219-224.
13. Sutton-Smith, Brian. "The Role of Play in Cognitive Development." *Young Children,* 22: (1967). pp. 361-370.
14. Bishop, Doyle and Chace, C., "Parental Conceptual Systems, Home Play Environment and Potential Creativity in Children," *Journal of Experimental Child Psychology.* 12(2), (1973), 212-232.
15. Harvey, et. al., *Op. Cit.*
16. *Ibid.*

Chapter Eight
Conceptualizing Leisure: Making the Abstract Concrete

Peter A. Witt and Gary D. Ellis

What is leisure? The question is simple enough but the answer is complex. In the preceding chapters, a variety of philosophies and definitions have been offered. But are we any closer to knowing what constitutes leisure? Why is deriving a definitive definition of leisure critical in the first place? Is definitional precision a necessity when we all "know" what the term means anyway? If we have a ballpark notion of what constitutes leisure, isn't that enough?

Achieving definitional understanding and agreement would be nothing more than an intellectual exercise to be pursued by University professors if definitional clarity didn't ultimately relate directly to how public and private recreation services are justified, planned and evaluated. Just as medical services are dependent on whether health is defined as the "absence of illness" or in terms of quality of life, leisure services will be fundamentally different in purpose and provision depending on how leisure is defined. To better understand the impact of definitions on service delivery, it is first necessary to delineate several different approaches that have been taken to defining leisure.

TRADITIONAL APPROACHES

Definitions of leisure have been generally categorized into three groups: time, activity and state of mind. Neulinger[1] labels the first two approaches "objective" in the sense that criteria external to the experience of the individual can be derived for discerning what is and is not leisure. The state of mind approach is labeled as "subjective" because it largely depends on the perceptions of the individual that the activity undertaken is leisure. On the surface this dichotomy seems clear enough but, in reality, the distinction between objective and subjective approaches, as discussed below, is not quite so clear.

Under the *time* view, leisure is conceptualized as time left over after the necessities of life have been taken care of. Work, household chores and other obligations are usually included under the heading of necessities. In this sense, the time approach is a "freedom from" definition. One is free from necessity or obligation. The definition, of course, is full of problems. What is obligation or necessity to one person may not be to another. Thus, rather than being objective, the definition is subjective since it is based on an individual perception of what constitutes necessity. Of course, individual perceptions could be ignored and a societal definition of what constitutes obligation and necessity derived. Thus, there would exist a shared, and in that sense objective, understanding of leisure as time left over after work and other obligations have been completed.

Leisure defined as *activity* has also been a popular approach to cutting through the definitional morass. Use of a period of time would be considered leisure if the activity undertaken appeared in an agreed upon list of leisure activities. On the surface, this seems easy and objective. If asked, we would probably all include baseball, quilting, and painting on the list. But what if one plays baseball for pay, quilts to create warm clothing for the family, and paints the house so that the exterior surfaces do not deteriorate? Would card playing be included on the list by everyone or does that depend? Would sex be included if it involved adultery, or would that, too, depend?

According to some definitional schemes that take the leisure-as-activity approach, to be considered leisure the activity must be moral, wholesome, and contribute to the betterment and welfare of the individual. The morass thickens. Clearly each of these criteria involves a series of judgements about what is moral or wholesome, etc. It is easy to see why there is so little agreement on what constitutes leisure. In the final analysis, the activity approach also seems to be largely based on a subjective perception of moral, wholesome betterment and a host of other equally difficult to define criteria. This approach may be comforting but it is hardly objective.

The *subjective or state of mind* approach defines leisure as:

a person's own perception and inference of quantity and quality of activities. Therefore, leisure becomes subjective perception of an actual or imagined activity a person participates in at a given time.[2]

Perceiving oneself as "free" from necessity is more important than actually being free. An activity is leisure if it is perceived as leisure by the individual participant. Thus, leisure has more to do with personal than societal perceptions, although the latter can have a large influence on the former.

While the state of mind approach is appealing, it too is not without its problems. How are work — non-work distinctions to be handled? Can leisure be experienced at work? Iso-Ahola, for example, argues that leisure, however subjectively defined, can only occur during non-work, i.e. free, time.[3] Are there, then, any commonalities in subjective experiences across individuals or are definitions of leisure completely individual? For example, is the perception of freedom and being intrinsically motivated necessary for most people to experience leisure and if so, what does perception of freedom mean?

Besides providing interesting dialogue in undergraduate leisure studies courses, what does it matter that differing approaches have been taken to defining leisure? As noted previously, do the definitions impact on how services are actually conceptualized and carried out? The answer is, inevitably, "yes." In brief, the presumably objective views of leisure mean that we are largely in the free-time activity business. Public or private agencies would be responsible for planning activities that are defined as leisure during non-work, non-obligated periods of time. On the other hand, if leisure is subjectively defined, we need to know more about what is perceived as leisure by each potential participant. The objective approach lends itself nicely to counting how many people show up at a given activity, for leisure is seen in terms of participation in given activities during free time. The subjective approach necessitates our asking what motivates people to participate in an activity and what does each person experience during participation. Success is determined by the individual participant.

While definitions of what constitutes leisure have important implications for the actual delivery of leisure services, only recently have steps been taken to bring a degree of precision to our definitions such that the service delivery implications could be fully realized. Whether approaches to defining leisure have been from an objective, subjective or combined perspective, earlier approaches have been based on what Hollander has referred to as *social philosophy*.[4] Approaching the understanding of leisure from a social philosophy perspective means that we have relied primarily on ideas independent of testable data. We have concerned ourselves with what "should be," resulting in endless debates and conjecture. This approach has proven to be frustrating in an environment that demands a greater degree of objectivity (i.e. based on "hard" data or evidence) than found in philosophic discussion. All of the perspectives described earlier, (time, activity and state of mind) have, until recently, been approached from primarily a philosophic perspective. Thus, we have argued that leisure is time free from obligation or participation in an "approved" activity. We have only recently embraced what Hollander refers to as social empiricism or social analysis in our attempts to understand leisure.

Social empiricism goes beyond speculation and conjecture. While *social philosophy* deals in what should be, social empiricism focuses on understanding what is. Thus, as noted by Iso-Ahola,[5] in the 1960's the study of leisure began to include time budget studies, attitude and interest surveys, and other means to identify *what* people did in free time or what kind of leisure services were desired.

The *social analysis* approach to understanding leisure has been far less prevalent. Social analysis focuses on *why* people do what they do. It results in theory testing and the verification of hypothesized relationships between variables. It is dependent on "operationalizing" variables such that measurement is facilitated and comparison with other studies made possible. A social analysis approach allows us to more definitively answer questions such as: is there a relationship between perceived freedom and leisure?; does leisure contribute to health and well-being?; is a particular leisure service effective in meeting stated objectives?

We are faced with a growing need to provide evidence that our services achieve what they are designed to achieve. To this end, it is not enough to simply assume that either leisure is a necessity in the lives of people or that provided services facilitate people achieving benefits from leisure. Accountability concerns alone necessitate our moving beyond this social philosophy approach to service provision that is based on social analysis. Although progress has been made in this regard, our literature is still woefully weak in taking this approach. Michael Ellis' landmark book, *Why People Play,*[6] and the research of his colleagues at the University of Illinois in the late 1960's and early 1970's, was perhaps the first systematic attempt to take a social analysis approach to the study of leisure (although Ellis focused upon play, which is another issue).

In order to determine the extent of progress the recreation and leisure studies field has made toward moving into the empirically based social analysis stage of its development, it is necessary to examine those lines of inquiry which have included both a conceptualization of leisure and methods of measuring leisure based on that conceptualization. Four major lines of inquiry which include both of these components are M. J. Ellis' optimal arousal explanation of play; Csikszentmahalyi's peak experience, or "flow" model; Neulinger's leisure paradigm; the perceived freedom conceptualization of leisure used by Witt, G. Ellis and their colleagues in the development of the Leisure Diagnostic Battery.

THE OPTIMAL AROUSAL EXPLANATION
OF PLAY

One of the most widely known conceptualizations of a leisure related phenomena which included a measurement component is Michael Ellis' explanation of play as arousal regulating behavior. In *Why People Play,* M. J. Ellis reviewed such early theories of play as the recapitulation theory, the relaxation theory, the surplus energy theory, learning theory, and the compensation theory.[7] Ellis' thorough review of these "classical" and "recent" theories clearly showed their inadequacy as explanations for the very complex phenomenon of play. This led Ellis to propose a "modern" theory of play, based on the work of such "arousal" theorists as Berlyne, Hebb, Duffy, Lindsley, and Malmo.

Application of the arousal seeking theory to play behavior led Ellis to the position that play is caused by a constant, physiological need for individuals to maintain an optimal level of interest or alertness. This optimal level of arousal may be maintained by adjusting the novelty and complexity of input from the environment. Thus, a child needing to heighten his/her level of arousal to the optimal might think of new uses for an old toy (increase novelty and complexity) and a frightened youngster during his/her first visit to the dentist might reduce a too high level of arousal by playing with a familiar toy (reduce novelty) which an insightful parent encouraged him/her to bring. Play, therefore, becomes a mechanism by which individuals regulate their level of arousal.

Measurement
The application of the arousal seeking theory to the study of play was a significant departure from earlier efforts because arousal is a measurable, physiological phenomenon. Unfortunately, early play researchers found the measurement of arousal to be quite complex. Three studies in which play researchers sought to ". . . observe the arousal mechanism in action"[8,9,10] led to the conclusion that "new and more robust measures" were needed before meaningful studies could be conducted on play as arousal regulating behavior.[11]

The absence of related follow-up studies suggests that play researchers have not actively pursued "new and more robust" measures of arousal. Within the last few years, psychologists, spurred by low intercorrelations between different measures of arousal, have begun to distinguish between different *forms* of arousal. Rather than assuming the existence of a strong arousal "common factor" affecting various systems equally and simultaneously as the studies of play assumed, psychologists are beginning to adopt the position that arousal may be described by a number of unique factors, each associated with a different aspect of the nervous system. Measurement of the impact of each of these unique factors may be more meaningful than an attempt to measure a single common factor. Measures of arousal within the autonomic nervous system, for example, include heart rate, blood pressure, and skin conductance. Central nervous system arousal can be measured with an electroencephograph (EES), and an electromyograph (EMG) can be used to measure arousal within the somatic nervous system. Arousal, obviously, is a very complex phenomenon. Any explanation of play based on arousal theory must take into account its various dimensions. Although the methods of measurement within different dimensions of arousal are relatively well established, considerable updating is needed on the conceptualization of play as arousal regulating behavior.

PEAK EXPERIENCES: THE FLOW MODEL

A second model of a leisure related phenomenon which includes both conceptualization and measurement components is Csikszentmihalyi's "flow" model.[12] In developing this model, Csikszentmihalyi conducted several studies with individuals who participated regularly in activities demanding intense involvement and optimal challenge. Individuals studied included surgeons, chess players, rock climbers, and dancers.

Through discussions with these individuals, Csikszentmihalyi was able to develop a description of what we call the "flow" state. A typical description of flow was provided by a rock climber:

> Your concentration is very complete. Your mind isn't wandering, you are not thinking of something else; you are totally involved in what you are doing. Your body feels good. Your energy is flowing very smoothly, you feel relaxed, comfortable, and energetic.[13]

Six characteristics of flow which Csikszentmihalyi derived from such descriptions were as follows:

1. A merging of action and awareness;

2. A centering of attention;

3. Loss of self consciousness;

4. Perception of great power and control;

5. Noncontradicting demands for action and clear, unambiguous feedback concerning the person's actions;

6. The absence of a need for external rewards.[14]

This "flow state" is assumed to result from a balance between the challenges of the activity and the skills of the participant. When the demands of the activity outweigh the individual's skill, anxiety is present. When the individual's level of skill outweighs the demands of the activity, boredom occurs. When the demands of the activity match the skills of the participant, an individual may experience a state of "flow."

Measurement
Like the arousal theory explanation of play, Csikszentmihalyi's flow model includes a measurement component. Using the Flow Model, Csikszentmihalyi and his colleagues have conducted experiential studies in formal and informal sports settings and have found the model to be useful in the prediction of adults' subjective perception of well-being.[15,16,17] Eight components of the flow model were assessed: self-consciousness, skills, challenges, mood, motivation, sense of control, how much is at stake, and difficulty in concentrating.

With the exception of mood, each is measured with single items with each rated on a 10 point scale. The self-consciousness item, for example, is "How self conscious were you (during the activity)?" "Not at all" is rated zero, while "very" is scored as a ten. The "mood" component has two parts: affect and activation. Affect is measured with four bipolar adjectives, on a seven point scale: happy-sad, irritable-cheerful, angry-friendly, and lonely-sociable. The activation component is similar, but includes five adjective pairs: alert-drowsy, strong-weak, active-passive, involved-detached, and excited-bored.

This approach to measurement of flow has worked quite well in studies of experiential states. As leisure research continues the quest for antecedents and outcomes of leisure experiences, this model serves to reinforce the position that what happens to people *during* an activity is also of great interest and concern.

NEULINGER'S PARADIGM OF LEISURE

A third model which includes both a conceptualization of leisure and a measurement component is Neulinger's paradigm of Leisure.[18] That model is an attempt to categorize states of mind which produce leisure and states of mind which produce non-leisure conditions. This categorization scheme is based on two variables: perceived freedom and motivation.

In his paradigm, Neulinger considers perceived freedom to be the "one and only" essential criterion for a leisure experience to occur.[19] Further, perceived freedom is seen as a transitory state which varies from setting to setting and activity to activity. Neulinger explains that perceived freedom is ". . . a state in which the person feels that what he/she is doing is done by choice and because one wants to do it."[20] He also points out that perceived freedom is a matter of personal interpretation rather than objective reality. An individual in a highly structured environment can experience a leisure state if he/she maintains a sense (or an illusion) of freedom.

The second variable in Neulinger's paradigm is motivation. Three types of motivational settings are considered: settings in which the primary motivation is either extrinsic or intrinsic; settings in which both intrinsic and extrinsic motivation are present. The distinction between the types of motivation is in the reward a participant seeks to attain from involvement. If no reward other than satisfaction associated with participation in the activity is present, the activity is considered to be intrinsically motivated. When some external pressure or pay-off is the individual's primary reason for participation, the activity is considered to be extrinsically motivated. Many activities in which an individual becomes involved include both intrinsic and extrinsic motivation.

The paradigm is presented in Figure 1. Three leisure and three non-leisure states of mind are presented. Each of these is associated with a unique combination of the perceived freedom and motivation categories. "Pure leisure," for example, occurs under conditions of perceived freedom and intrinsic motivation. Its polar opposite, the "pure job" state of mind, occurs under conditions of perceived constraint and extrinsic motivation. Neulinger makes it very clear, however, that these discrete categories are intended to serve a heuristic purpose only. Because perceived freedom and motivation are continuous variables, various states of mind within each category also exist.

Neulinger's paradigm of leisure is a major step toward identifying the conditions under which leisure can occur. It falls short, however, of describing the characteristics of the actual experiential state which is associated with each major combination of perceived freedom and motivation. That is, unlike the models of Ellis and Csikszentmihalyi, Neulinger's paradigm does not tell us what "pure leisure," "pure work," or "pure job" states of mind "feel like." Further research will be needed to delineate the specific qualities of these experiential states.

Figure 1

NEULINGER'S PARADIGM OF LEISURE[18]

Freedom					
Perceived Freedom			*Perceived Constraint*		
Motivation			Motivation		
Intrinsic	*Intrinsic and Extrinsic*	*Extrinsic*	*Intrinsic*	*Intrinsic and Extrinsic*	*Extrinsic*
(1)	(2)	(3)	(4)	(5)	(6)
Pure Leisure	Leisure-Work	Leisure-Job	Pure Work	Work-Job	Pure Job
Leisure			Nonleisure		

◄——————————— State of Mind ———————————►

Measurement

The paradigm of leisure also includes a measurement component. This component, the "What Am I Doing" (WAID) scale, is designed to measure the extent to which people experience the conditions under which leisure can occur. The WAID takes a time budget approach to the assessment of these conditions. Over a twenty-four hour period, individuals keep track of their activities at thirty minute intervals. Information concerning the nature of the activity (including duration, timing, sequential order, location, and social nature) is recorded, along with information about choice (perceived freedom) and reasons for participating (motivation).

The WAID has been successfully used in a number of studies of leisure. Neulinger has suggested that although the WAID was primarily designed as a research instrument, its application may extend to leisure counseling and leisure education efforts as well. Neulinger's approach to conceptualization and measurement of leisure, at this point, looks quite promising.

THE LEISURE DIAGNOSTIC BATTERY

The previous models focus on leisure as a transitory state, which may vary with such factors as novelty, complexity, demands of the activity, skills of the participants, perceived freedom, and motivation. The Leisure Diagnostic Battery (LDB) conceptualization takes a different approach. It assumes the existence of a relatively stable perception of self which is maintained over time and which predisposes an individual to experience the leisure state. The "perceived freedom" concept, which is the focus of the LDB conceptualization, therefore, is quite different from the situationally specific and transitory "perceived freedom" concept which is the focus of Neulinger's Paradigm of Leisure.

The LDB defines perceived freedom as a unitary concept, consisting of perceived leisure competence, perceived leisure control, ability to satisfy leisure needs through participation in recreation, ability to achieve depth of involvement in activities, and playfulness. Individuals who are high in perceived freedom are assumed to have a high degree of self sufficiency in leisure. Most of their leisure activities are intrinsically motivated. They have a high propensity to experience the "flow state," they feel comfortable with their level of skill and involvement in recreation activities, and they exhibit a high degree of satisfaction with their leisure. Individuals who are low in perceived freedom, on the other hand, are assumed to perceive a sense of helplessness in leisure. Their leisure involvements are generally extrinsically motivated, they lack confidence in their ability to successfully participate in recreation activities, and they are unhappy with their leisure.

Attribution theory has been used to explain the process by which this relatively stable sense of perceived freedom is established and maintained. [21] Attribution theory, applied in this conceptualization, refers to the causes to which people ascribe success and failure in their lives. Following a win in an athletic contest, for example, an athlete might attribute success to his/her skill, effort, an over-matched opponent (task difficulty), and/or to luck.

The LDB conceptualization asserts that certain patterns of attributions determine an individual's perceived freedom. Individuals who are high in perceived freedom attribute success to such internal factors as skill and effort. "The painting is beautiful because I am a good artist," an artist high in perceived freedom might conclude following completion of a work of art. Failures of individuals who are high in perceived freedom are attributed to such external and unstable causes as bad luck and/or not enough effort. "I lost because of bad luck," an athlete who is high in perceived freedom might conclude. This attributional pattern is assumed to protect the individual's sense of perceived freedom in leisure.

Individuals who are low in perceived freedom, on the other hand, are assumed to adopt an attributional pattern which reinforces their low perceived freedom. Successes are attributed to luck or to an easy task and failures are attributed to a lack of ability. This pattern is assumed to reinforce the individual's perception of lack of freedom in leisure.

Readers familiar with attribution theory will recognize the above conceptualization as the familiar "self serving" attribution hypothesis. That hypothesis has been the subject of numerous studies and conflicting results have been obtained. Some studies have provided evidence of the phenomenon and other studies have provided no support. One of the important issues facing the further development of the LDB conceptualization, therefore, is the validation of an attributional explanation of perceived freedom.

Measurement
Although conflicting results bring to question the validity of the attributional explanation of perceived freedom, considerable evidence exists concerning the validity of the LDB as a tool for the measurement of perceived freedom. Two forms of this tool exist. One form is a ninety-five item summative rating scale which was originally designed for use in the assessment of the leisure functioning of adolescents with disabilities. The second form of the LDB is a twenty-five item short form which was derived from the original version.

Several studies have suggested that the LDB provides a valid measure of perceived freedom in leisure for different populations.[22,23] Populations with which the LDB has been used include 9-14 year-old junior high school students, teenage deaf individuals, substance abusers, elderly individuals, participants in a summer playground program, and college students. Studies involving these groups have produced significant correlations with such theoretically related variables as self concept, self-esteem, life satisfaction, and lack of perceived barriers to leisure involvement. In addition, the hypothesis of a unitary concept has been supported through factor analysis.[24] Thus, the most pressing need in LDB research seems to be the attributional explanation of how perceived freedom is established and maintained, not the measurement of the perceived freedom concept itself.

CAN LEISURE BE MEASURED?

The four conceptualizations and operationalizations described above suggest that progress has been made in moving our understanding of leisure from a social philosophy and social empiricism to social analysis. The described approaches differ from what Ellis has termed the "classical" or "recent" theories because they are more universally applicable, lend themselves more easily to operationalization, and to date have led to instruments that produce more reliable and valid data.

The four approaches have also produced instrumentation that has potential for helping to determine the effectiveness of public and private agency leisure services. Instrumentation that is capable of measuring the leisure state of mind of participants prior to, during or after participation could help supply more effective measures of program success than attendance counts. Although these approaches and methods are still of the "first generation" variety, they do show much potential. They enable us to move far beyond attitude and interest inventories or philosophic pronouncements about the avowed benefits of the leisure experience.

Our task in the future is to continue to sharpen our conceptualization of leisure followed by even more sophisticated attempts to operationalize developed theory. Until the concept of leisure is brought into sharper focus and sufficiently operationalized so as to provide reliable and valid measurement tools, our ability to understand the central phenomenon we are dealing with, and our ability to ascertain if leisure is the benefit that we presume it to be, will be severely impaired.

REFERENCES

1. Neulinger, J. *The Psychology of Leisure*. Springfield, Ill.: Charles C. Thomas, Publisher, 1974.
2. Iso-Ahola, S. E. "On The Theoretical Link Between Personality and Leisure." *Psychological Reports*. 1976, 39, 3-10.
3. Iso-Ahola, S. E. *The Social Psychology of Leisure*. Dubuque, Iowa: Wm. C. Brown Company, 1980.
4. Hollander, E. P. *Principles and Methods of Social Psychology*. (2nd Edition) New York: Oxford University Press, 1971.
5. Iso-Ahola, *op. cit.*, 1980.
6. Ellis, M. J. *Why People Play*. Englewood Cliffs, N.J.: Prentice-Hall, Inc., 1973.
7. *Ibid.*
8. Ellis, M. J., Barnett, L. A., and Korb, R. J. "Psychophysiological Correlates of Play." *Annual Report of the Motor Performance and Play Research Laboratory*. Champaign, Ill.: Children's Research Center, 1973.
9. Barnett, L. A. "An Information Processing Model of Children's Play." Unpublished Thesis, University of Illinois, 1974.
10. Barnett, L. A., Ellis, M. J., and Korb, R. J. "Arousal Modulation as a Function of Visual Complexity." *Annual Report of the Motor Performance and Play Research Laboratory*. Champaign, Ill.: Children's Research Center, 1974.
11. Ellis, M. J. and Scholtz, B. J. L. *Activity and Play of Children*. Englewood Cliffs, N.J.: Prentice-Hall, 1978.
12. Csikszentmihalyi, M. *Beyond Boredom and Anxiety*. San Francisco: Josey-Bass, 1975.
13. *Ibid.*
14. *Ibid.*
15. Gianinno, S. M., Graef, R. and Csikszentmihalyi, M. "Wellbeing and the Perceived Balance Between Opportunities and Capabilities." Paper presented at the 87th Annual Convention of the American Psychological Association, New York.
16. Csikszentmihalyi, M. "Toward a Psychology of Optimal Experience." In Wheller, C. (Ed.) *Annual Review of Personality and Social Psychology*. 1982, 3, 13-36.
17. Chalip. L., Csikszentmihalyi, M., Kleiber, D., and Larson, R. "Variations of Experience in Formal and Informal Sport." *Research Quarterly for Exercise and Sport,* 1984, 55, 109-116.
18. Neulinger, J. *The Psychology of Leisure*. (2nd Edition). Springfield, Ill.: Charles C. Thomas, Publisher, 1981.
19. *Ibid.* page 14.
20. *Ibid.* page 14.
21. LDB Project. *The Leisure Diagnostic Battery: Background, Conceptualization and Structure*. Denton, Tx.: North Texas State University, 1982.
22. Ellis, G. D. and Witt, P. A. "The Measurement of Perceived Freedom in Leisure." *Journal of Leisure Research*. 1984, 16, p. 2.
23. Witt, P. A. and Ellis, G. D. "Development of the Perceived Freedom in Leisure Short Form." Unpublished paper. 1984.
24. Ellis, G. D. and Witt, P. A. *Op. Cit.*

117

Chapter Nine

The "Psychologization" – of Leisure Services

Roger C. Mannell

Today we are often exhorted to think of leisure as a state of mind or as a subjective experience. Unfortunately clear and unambiguous descriptions of this state or experience are all but non-existent. Most of us would be unable to say with conviction whether or not we had encountered one of these mysterious experiences. While "experts" have dodged describing the characteristics of the leisure experience, some view it as being achievable by only a select few,[2] yet others consider it approachable by anyone at almost anytime.[3] Most agree that it is *pleasurable*, yet criteria have not been forthcoming to allow us to distinguish between leisure and non-leisure states.[4] Are religious, mystical, aesthetic, amusement, intense competitive sport, and experiences during altered states of consciousness leisure experiences? With these questions unanswered it is not surprising then, that leisure services have not developed planning strategies specifically to encourage and promote experiencing during leisure or developed evaluation techniques to assess the success of such efforts. Similarly, leisure research, until quite recently, has all but ignored examining the factors which affect the experiential component of leisure.[5]

Now we find ourselves on the threshold of an *experience revolution* — a revolution for which our leisure service delivery systems may be unprepared. Numerous Canadian studies by futurists predict that we will devote increasing amounts of time and energy to creative activity, personal growth and self-actualization endeavors.[6] Over the last few years there has developed a tremendous interest in esoteric eastern philosophies and psychologies western psychotherapies and personal development programs on the one hand, and high risk outdoor pursuits and the hunt for fantasy and amusement experiences on the other. These trends, if they continue, may mean an increase in the search for and collection of exotic, novel and exciting blends of experiences. This experience revolution has many potentially positive aspects, yet like the failure of increases in discretionary time and affluence to lead inevitably to a leisure society, the emerging experience revolution may bring us no closer to achieving leisure lifestyles or self-development.

We must, then, explore the notion of an experience revolution and some of its implications for the delivery of leisure services. And we must look critically at the notion of an ideal human condition or personality and the "experience vendors" who are emerging to meet the demand for experiences that will lead to this state of development. Should leisure services become experiential and compete with the private entrepreneur for their share of the "experience" market? Is there another role that leisure services can play? Will the current interest and efforts in a psychology of leisure result in information that will serve as a basis for some form of "leisure experience engineering" to support leisure services in providing experience oriented (psychologized) services?

DO WE NEED A MAN-OF-LEISURE PROTOTYPE?

In more optimistic times, times pre-dating the energy crisis and the appearance of ecological and environmental concerns, the eventuality of a leisure society seemed assured. Though the details of the nature of such a society have always been obscure, the need to do little or no work, accompanied by abundant amounts of discretionary time and resources to pursue a wide variety of interests seem to characterize this vision. The psychological, economic, political and social changes necessary to support leisure lifestyles for our citizens have not been considered comprehensively other than through the occasional writer's literary construction of a utopian community or society. Similarly the phrase "leisure lifestyle," so frequently used these days, has not been defined, or the types of activities or behaviors comprising this mode of living agreed upon.

During the last decade there has emerged a growing concern that the movement toward a workless society has not resulted in a shift to a leisure society. Increases in discretionary time and affluence have not guaranteed the adoption of leisure lifestyles whatever they are! Some social critics have argued that one of the major barriers to the achievement of a leisure ethic, besides a lingering work ethic, has been its subversion by the consumer ethic.[7] The consumer ethic, a refinement of Veblen's notion of conspicuous consumption, suggests that we have not become leisurely but rather have used increases in discretionary time and resources to purchase and expend more. This consumption oriented lifestyle supposedly allows us to "shore up" our personal identities and establish our social status on the basis of what we spend rather than on the basis of our work. The achievement of a "true" leisure lifestyle would seem to infer that social status needs are to be abandoned and self-esteem result from the personal development allowed one in a leisure society.

More recently there has even been a loss of optimism that we can sustain a continued movement away from a work society, with the appearance of energy crises, population pressures and economic competition with newly developing nations. Yet, in spite of these problems and the spectre of economic collapse the consensus of futurists is that developments in Canada for the next 20 years still hold the possibility of a society with a substantial amount of leisure. Fewer young people, smaller families, shorter working hours, increases in discretionary time are familiar predictions that continue to be made. However, the authors of these reports hasten to caution us that prosperity is not assured, and that our consumption patterns must be made a little more modest since we may be obligated to redefine our concept of prosperity.

Of particular interest is the apparent consensus in the predictions of changes in our values:

"New values will gradually take over as the dominant, decision-making values of our society. There will be a decline in values associated with materialism, private ownership, capitalism and unqualified economic growth. Increasing emphasis will be placed on concepts such as the quality of life, self-actualization, creativity, individualism and humanitarism."[8]

The one recurring theme of most futurist predictions is that there will be an increasing demand or need for opportunities to be more creative and self-actualized, that is, for opportunities for personal development. Apparently then, it is still possible that if man fails to "cremate himself equal" in a nuclear holocaust or crowd himself off the earth, he may be condemned to the horrible fate of a workless society — the victim of automation. What type of person shall inherit this leisure world? Will the survivors possess a huge arsenal of recreation skills and the surviving society be one populated with Renaissance men — the ultimate recreators? Is there a suitable prototype for all members of a leisure society? Is a life based on intellectual and rational pursuits, as well as the pursuit of the cultural arts and recreation able to sustain the total population or only a small elite segment of the population?

We have a need for a "man-of-leisure" prototype, and for a clearer notion of the types of activities and experiences that will sustain this individual and contribute to a meaningful lifestyle. Is this to be a leisure lifestyle? Leisure service professionals are being urged to devote more organizational time to leisure counseling and education which are espoused as suitable mechanisms for shaping the prototype man of the future. What are the features, options and capabilities of this new model of man? What exotic blend of experiences will be needed to "power" leisure man in his search for happiness and self-development?

Today we encounter a variety of competing views regarding the appropriate model for living. These views have been at various times stated in terms such as oneness with the universe, Christian virtue, manhood, proper taste, or self-actualization.

Ideas about the *ideal person* and how he should relate to his world come from many sources. In Western society Christianity contributed to the ideal of *Spiritual Man* whose present life is a preparation for an afterlife where people are to be free and equal. With the European Renaissance the ideal of *Intellectual Man* evolved with the belief that our salvation was to be found in this world and achieved through the application of human intelligence to our problems. The extension of this belief into the political sphere fostered the ideal of a *Political Man* who was to be actively involved in modifying the political institutions of his society to further the quality of life. With the industrial revolution the image of *Economic Man* evolved with the belief that man would achieve the good life through his contributions to economic growth and development.[9] Of course, during this evolution of various notions of the ideal man the development of the scientific method and science contributed to the belief that man could solve all his problems with an objective, rational, and scientific approach. Most recently it has been suggested that a new ideal of *Psychological Man* has emerged with the belief that we are moving into an era in which we are achieving a clearer understanding of human needs and will more completely meet them.[10] Psychological Man is contemporary man with a developed self-awareness who has shifted his attention from the external world to his own nature. Much has been written over the last thirty years concerning the barriers preventing contemporary man from achieving a "free," "self-actualized," and "happy" existence. Numerous models of the ideal orientation to life and means to self-development have been suggested, supposedly based on modern psychological principles.

Other models for the ideal person also exist: the hero/intellectual, the artist, the mystic, the saint and the prophet. These models all suggest different emphases on what are desirable or ideal human traits. While most models of man recognize the need for some kind of psychological growth, there is no universal view of the ideal human condition.[11]

Unfortunately, we are faced with a bewildering array of models of the ideal person which does not help us decide what prototype we should be encouraging in leisure counseling and education. We are not even sure that a society in which most persons did not have to work would be a society where man could survive and adapt in such a way that his life would be perceived by himself as happy and fulfilled. Is a man-of-leisure prototype suitable for all persons, only for an elite, or for no one? Implicit in many of our activities and thinking is the assumption that man — the masses — can be counseled or educated into adopting a leisure lifestyle which will sustain him, provide meaning and purpose in his life, prevent him from becoming a social nuisance, and he and his fellows collectively from becoming a social problem.

The essence of a *leisure problem* would seem to be a question: can man, when biological survival is no longer problematic, adjust his goals and find activity in which to engage that allows him to perceive himself as happy. When work and consuming no longer preoccupy us, we may finally have to personally confront the purpose of our lives. What new goals shall we seek? Can man convince himself that the exploration of his own psyche, the search for self-actualization or personal development is sufficient to provide direction, meaning and importance for his life? How are leisure services evolving to provide for these needs of Psychological Man?

THE EXPERIENCE INDUSTRIES AND THE PSYCHOLOGIZATION OF LEISURE SERVICES

Critics have been pointing out the need to focus a concern not on how much we consume or participate but on the quality of our experiences. As a result leisure is currently viewed by those in the "know" as a state of mind or a subjective experience. Pessimism has been expressed about the possibility of the masses being able to achieve this state. More optimistic futurists predict that the future will see an increasing concern for personal development. Toffler, writing before the appearance of the energy crisis, predicted an experience revolution. He was optimistic that the current preoccupation with acquiring goods and material possessions as an avenue to happiness would pass as merely a stage in the adaptation of man to an affluent society where his needs were readily met.

> As rising affluence and transience ruthlessly undercut the old urge to possess, consumers begin to collect experience as consciously and passionately as they once collected things.[12]

Toffler predicted that the manufacturing sector would direct more resources into the conscious design of "psychological distinctions and gratifications" with the development of experiential industries which would also keep the economy growing as the production of goods went beyond our material needs. "We are moving from a 'gut' economy to a 'psyche' economy because there is only so much gut to be satisfied."[13] The term "psychologization" coined by Toffler, labels this predicted shift from providing goods and services simply to meet functional needs to also generating experiences:

> We shall go far beyond any "functional" necessity, turning the service, whether it is shopping, dining, or having one's hair cut, into a pre-fabricated experience.[14]

Writing before the advent of the energy crisis and our current economic difficulties, Toffler's predictions are still relevant. We will need to focus more and more on psychological or psychic gratifications (experience) because excess materialism beyond a "comfortable" level will be wasteful and costly in a world of scarce resources and large populations.

Will the shift from the acquisition of material goods mean that suddenly we are going to achieve a happy and satisfying life as a society? Toffler, himself, wondered what would happen when industry began to produce experiences for their own sake that ". . . blur the distinction between the vicarious and the non-vicarious, the simulated and the real?"[15] As well, we may give up our need to possess more and more material goods only to replace them by a similar fascination with collecting experiences. One would expect that the simple clamoring after experience does not mean that the road to self-development will be better guaranteed.

THE SEARCH FOR EXPERIENCE

What is the nature of a lifestyle that is centered around the pursuit of experience? Are we now not continually experiencing our surroundings every waking minute? To say there will be an experience revolution seems to suggest that greater concern will be given to "engineering" our experiences and the situations which give rise to them. The purpose of this "experience engineering" would be to create experiences that are somehow of greater quality than in the past, that are perhaps more memorable, that give greater satisfaction, and that perhaps lead to a fuller life or more complete personal development. What types of experiences are likely to attract man if he is given the opportunity to pursue experience for its own sake?

Education and the Search for Knowledge
The formal education institutions of the West have not fostered the "development of the mind " through intense and exotic experiences. Personal development has been based on the slow and gradual acquisition of factual information and the development of intellectual, rational and scientific modes of thought. The education system has been very work oriented. Unfortunately, universities have backed themselves into a corner by stressing their ability to place graduates in jobs instead of the less fashionable and tangible ideals of a liberal education. They are now scrambling to develop and market continuing education programs as self-development opportunities to meet the problems of shrinking enrollments as the number of young people in our population decreases, and, also, they avoid the university since its brand of experience no longer guarantees jobs.

Experience Seeking: Growth or Addiction
A current psychological view of man is that he is constantly motivated to maintain an optimal level of arousal. That is, man attempts to maintain enough change or novelty in his life to avoid boredom or anxiety from too little or too much change respectively. When the challenge of survival is no longer available to provide this arousal as would be the case in a leisure society, man will play or leisure to maintain the optimal level of arousal.[16] When this physiological model is translated into subjective or experiential terms the conditions providing for an optimal level of arousal often lead the human organism to experience "flow" or a peak-like experience which is pleasurable and highly involving.[17] In a workless society many people are likely to search out situations which will provide this type of experience. What role do these types of experiences play in the development of psychological well-being and personal development? For example, the pursuit of high risk activities appears to generate intense and highly involving experiences. Contemporary psychological theory has generally viewed this type of behavior as negative or abnormal, particularly the behavior of those who devote a whole life to its pursuit. Is this merely a hold-over from the protestant work ethic?

If one engages in activities in which one's skills develop so as to make that activity less challenging or novel, then higher risks or novel forms of the activity must be found. In the case of high risk sports this cycle has been seen as addictive:

Stimulus addiction implies the derived need to expose oneself repeatedly to situations where the balance among fear, danger and anxiety remain within the boundaries of personal control. The cyclical need to extend oneself to the absolute physical, emotional and even intellectual limits is the quest to escape from bland tensionless states associated with everyday living.[18]

We might expect increasing numbers of people when freed from the constraints of work and thoughts of survival, no matter how indirect, turning to a more immediate and direct flirtation with survival. Experiences derived from balancing on the edge of survival/non-survival may produce an intoxication that cannot be provided by any other type of activity. The removal of the need to work for one's living or survival, no matter how indirect the connection in our society, may lead us to erect artificial barriers which we then challenge in the face of fear. This activity must take a form that is accepted by society such as play and sport. The endless search for novelty and experience is already underway.

There is a whole set of leisure environments that are becoming a part of American life. These "ultra mod" settings include: electronic game parlors; computer games in people's homes; amusement parks which offer the latest in simulation and fantasy; and lazer light and music entertainment centers.[19]

The Mind Field or the Consciousness Technologies
While our educational institutions have stressed the rational, intellectual and logical approaches to understanding, there has been a trend to seek experiences which provide for self-development and knowledge through more intuitive and experiential modes. Many persons in our society in the search for this self-development are sampling western psycho-therapies and encounter groups as well as various degenerate forms of the esoteric eastern psychologies currently being marketed. We have embraced transcendental meditation, astrology, biofeedback, gurus and trantrum yogas. The need to explore the intuitive side of our natures has caused many ". . . to flock, unthinkingly, to rudimentary spiritual sideshows, which are quick, cheap, and often flashy"[20] . . . and an earnest individual ". . . encounters innumerable freaky, peaky psychologies and associations, advertisements in the Sunday newspapers for courses in instant self-improvement . . . and tiresome loonies of almost every persuasion."[21] While the types of experiences provided by these "growth" fads are undoubtedly self-indulgent and sensational, recent physiological and psychological research on brain function and human cognitive capabilities suggest that man has two modes of thinking or knowing, and a variety of techniques that have evolved in many esoteric eastern psychologies may allow

us to explore one of these ways of knowing.[22] As a nonverbal, nonlinear, nonintellectual approach to knowing ourselves and the world, this mode sharply contrasts with the usual Western approach which utilizes rational, intellectual and verbal modes of thought. Is the search for mystical, religious and peak experiences synonymous with the search for leisure experience? What role will leisure services provide to potential consumers?

LEISURE EXPERIENCE ENGINEERING

Toffler has argued that the psychologization of services will mean that ". . . no important service will be offered to the consumer before it has been analyzed by teams of behavioral engineers to improve its psychic loading."[23] Psychological research on leisure is only now beginning to study mental experience during leisure. The field of psychology abandoned the study of consciousness early in its own history and has only recently begun to consider these processes as legitimate areas of inquiry. The small amount of leisure research done has focused on the motives or needs for leisure and recreation preferences, while leisure experiences have been overlooked. This view of leisure as a state of mind or experience has made it difficult to study from the perspective of the social sciences with their emphasis on the collection of objective data. A handful of studies though, have emerged over the last several years attempting to measure leisure experiences themselves. Several studies have measured recreators' moods over the course of a recreation engagement using measures of the changes in positive and negative moods as unidimensional indicators of leisure experience. In my own research I have attempted to develop several parallel measures of leisure experience. By monitoring changes in subjects' moods, time perception and awareness of their surroundings, I and my colleagues have been able to monitor the impact of environmental factors, such as the degree of freedom to participate and the level of competition in the setting, on experiences during leisure. As well, the effect of personal characteristics on one's leisure response to these environmental factors can be examined.
    . . . the identification and monitoring of these experiences (leisure) will hopefully lend itself to a systematic effort to discover those features of situations, activities, and persons which inhibit or enhance the experience of leisure. The impact on leisure experiences of such factors as freedom of choice, intrinsic and extrinsic motivations, work and leisure attitudes, personality, and man-made and natural environments could be tested experimentally.[24]

Unfortunately or perhaps fortunately, the research output is far behind any attempt to formalize scientific planning and design principles which could provide the tools for leisure service professionals to become "leisure experience engineers."

THE ROLE OF LEISURE SERVICES IN THE EXPERIENCE REVOLUTION

Is there a role for public leisure service agencies in a society in which experiences and consciousness technologies are marketed and sold? Should public leisure services jump into the race and compete for a "piece of the experience market"? Perhaps the private sector should be allowed to evolve unimpeded to meet these experience needs. Public leisure service agencies are unlikely to have the investment monies needed to pioneer the development of the facilities and programs that will be demanded to provide exotic experience opportunities. Perhaps public leisure service agencies should become monitoring and consumer protection bodies to ensure that the experiences entering the market are "safe," "sanitary" and "enriched." We will then need to have knowledge concerning what experience contribute to growth states and consciousness raising and to discern leisure from non-leisure states. We will have to establish criteria for what are "good" experiences and develop standards. A complementary role to the consumer protection and product monitoring role would be to take responsibility for leisure counseling and public education to ensure that people become wise "experience consumers."

Our professional preparation programs in the universities and colleges would have to adapt to these changes. What skills should our students depart with, and where will our students find jobs? Should we be training "leisure experience engineers" able to apply leisure experience principles that have been developed by researchers in the social sciences concerned with human experience and leisure? If we are to take this route there is a need to train some of our students to be behavioral and experiential researchers. Also the majority of the jobs for our students, certainly the most exciting jobs, will be in the private sector, therefore we should better train them to operate and function in the commercial sector both as innovative inventors of experiences and as knowledgeable private entrepreneurs. To ensure the quality of commercial leisure services and the availability of jobs for our graduates, we should press the government to pass legislation requiring the licensing of leisure experience engineers. It would be expected that the designer of a leisure experience would be suitably trained as would be the designer of a bridge. Commercial leisure service firms would, as a matter of course, hire our "engineering" students. There also would be positions in government. Leisure experience inspectors would be needed to police and monitor existing services and new varieties of experience introduced to the market. The experience revolution will mean a whole new role for leisure service professionals and leisure services as they are psychologized.

REFERENCES

1. Toffler, Alvin. *Future Shock*, New York: Random House, 1970. p. 188. Toffler coined the term "psychologization."
2. deGrazia, Sebastian. *Of Time, Work, and Leisure*. New York: Twentieth Century Fund, 1962.
3. Gordon, C., Gaity, C., and Scott, J. "Leisure and Lives: Personal Expressivity Across the Life Span." In: Binstok, R., and Shanas, E. (Eds.), *The Handbook of Aging and the Social Sciences*. New York: Van Nostrand Reinhold, 1976.
4. Mannell, Roger. "A Conceptual and Experimental Basis for Research in the Psychology of Leisure." *Society and Leisure/Loisir et Societe*, 1979, 2, 179-196.
5. Mannell, Roger. "Social Psychological Techniques and Strategies for Studying Leisure Experiences." In Iso-Ahola, S., (Ed.), *Social Psychological Perspectives of Leisure and Recreation*. New York: Charles C. Thomas, 1980.
6. Balmer, Ken. *The Elora Prescription: A Future for Recreation*. Toronto: Ontario Ministry of Culture and Recreation, 1979.
7. Kando, Thomas. *Leisure and Popular Culture in Transition*. Saint Louis: Mosby Co., 1975.
8. Balmer, *Op. Cit.*, pp. 9-11.
9. Drucker, Peter. The End of Economic Man: *A Study of the New Totalitarianism*. New York: John Day, 1939.
10. Tolman, Edward. *Behavior and Psychological Man: Essays in Motivation and Learning*. Berkeley: University of California Press, 1951.
11. Coan, Richard, *Hero, Artist, Sage, or Saint?* New York: Columbia University Press, 1977.
12. Toffler, *Op. Cit.*, p. 193.
13. *Ibid.*, p. 201.
14. *Ibid.*, p. 192.
15. *Ibid.*, p. 201.
16. Ellis, Michael. *Why People Play*. Englewood Cliffs, New Jersey: Prentice-Hall, Inc., 1973.
17. Csikszentmihalyi, Mihalyi. *Beyond Boredom and Anxiety*. Washington, D.C.: Jossey-Bass, 1975.
18. Ogilvie, Bruce. "The Stimulus-Addicts, A Psychosocial Paradox." In: Schwank, W. (Ed.), *The Winning Edge*. Washington, D.C.: American Association for Health, Physical Education and Recreation, 1974, pp. 49-50.
19. Fridgen, Joseph. "Leisure Behavior: An Environmental Perspective." *Leisure Information Newsletter*, 5:4 (Spring, 1979). pp. 6-9.
20. Ornstein, Robert. *The Mind Field*. New York: Pocket Books, 1976. p. 11.

21. *Ibid.,* p. 20.
22. Ornstein, Robert. *The Psychology of Consciousness.* Markham, Ontario: Penguin Books Ltd., 1972.
23. Toffler, *Op. Cit.,* p. 209.
24. Mannell, "Social Psychological...," *Op. Cit.*

SECTION TWO

Changing Services and Resources: Doing More With Less

INTRODUCTION X

The end of World War II marked the beginning of three decades of unprecedented growth and affluence. Not unexpectedly — hindsight the aid that it is — the period was also characterized by turmoil: civil rights activists and campus radicals; moral crusades to end wars and conscription and then to save the environment. But through the same period public education, particularly post-secondary education, grew dramatically. So, too, did the provision of public recreation programs, facilities, and services.

The past decade or so, the harbinger being the formation of the OPEC cartel, has seen gradual but accelerating shifts, including economics characterized by large government deficits, high rates of both inflation and unemployment, and growth rates lower than those of the 1950's and 60's. Liberal governments of two decades ago have been replaced by conservative governments: from Kennedy to Reagan in the United States; Wilson to Thatcher in England; Pearson and then Trudeau to Mulroney in Canada.

These political, economic and social developments have already had significant impacts on public park, recreation and leisure services (and also universities) and appear destined to have even more in the years to come. We are faced, then, with tighter limits and tougher choices. We are faced with the task of doing more, better, and different than what has been done in the past and this must be done with fewer of the resources, especially financial, that we have relied upon for so long.

In the chapters comprising this section, "Changing Services and Resources," the need to change, and sometimes also the desire to change, is paramount. The section opens with Gold's (10) broad brush painting of the background of change which encompasses our field. He speaks of frugality, self-sufficiency and an era of limits which we can no longer fail to recognize. Godbey (11) paints some of the detail, noting a number of "sins" of omission or commission. These have often been the result of governments' well intentioned interventions, growth in agencies leading to specialization and often splintering, and of the sense of complacency into which many were lulled by years of expansion and affluence. Gold

131

ends calling for new activities, institutions, concepts and agendas. Similarly, Godbey concludes his chapter with a major challenge, the result of people having accepted the meaning and significance of leisure in their lives, leaving many leisure service workers and agencies proselytizing each other.

Bannon (12) notes that change is a constant and that a better understanding of history would give us a better understanding of change in our time. He also notes that plentitude, not as past reality but as an enduring attitude, can only magnify the difficulty of change, and he appeals for an ecological perspective akin to the environmental ethic so widely discussed in the 1960's and early 70's. In fact ethics weave throughout his exploration of the administrator's milieu, changed as it has due to accelerated technologies, gender equality in the work force and family, deteriorating environments and the like.

Like Gold (10) and Godbey (11), Bannon encourages imagination and innovation, and also a broad intellectuality and humanistic approach to one's work in the field. He also makes a number of suggestions for administrators, including the use of modern management tools and the encouragement and use of research.

One such tool, which Crompton (13), almost single-handedly, has introduced to the public park and recreation field is marketing. Here, Crompton deals with some causes of resistance public service administrators often demonstrate toward the marketing concept, despite the fact that it involves much more than promotional activities. Recognizing its sometimes unsavory history, Crompton argues that marketing is "Neither Snake-Oil nor Panacea" but a useful tool for administrators.

While Crompton notes that marketing is not, per se, a mechanism for raising revenues and does not necessarily lead to distorting priorities, Goodale (14) is even more emphatic about preserving the public service mandate under which public park and recreation agencies operate. He argues that the talk of "smaller" government is simplistic but also a seductive cover for political, economic and social values reminiscent of those holding sway a century ago. The increased emphasis on costs, revenues, efficiency, effectiveness, and on public, private and merit goods may result in gradually bending the mandate in directions dictated by the current winds of change.

An important example of the use of research which Bannon (12) called for is Kelly's (15) summary of years of research attempts to understand such a complex phenomenon as recreation. As he notes, our attempts to catagorize activities and predict them according to socio-economic and demographic influences have not been especially fruitful. Kelly suggests what may be a more useful perspective, with core activities centering around home, family and informal social relations plus other, different activities serving to provide balance according to the individual's needs and interests at a particular but changing stage during the course of a lifetime.

Kelly also notes that rather than the activity, i.e. what an individual does, we should consider style, i.e. how an individual goes about what he or she does. Matters of style and role recall the major challenge Godbey (11) introduced and also provide a good introduction to Sessoms' (16) elaboration of the concepts of lifestyle and lifecycle. After discussing the historical antecedents of our current understanding of recreation programming concepts (constructive activities for children: a variety of physical, social and cultural activities for everyone), Sessoms argues that those concepts are too confining given the great diversity of recreational pursuits. In the life of individuals as well as societies, change and development are constant and concepts of stage, style, role, identity and image provide a more contemporary base for thinking about programs and services.

Sessoms and Kelly particularly, but also all the authors represented in this section, speak of a pluralistic society and culture. Godbey (17) focuses on the concept of pluralism with reference not only to behaviors but also to values. In this quotable chapter, Godbey contrasts single and plural culture societies to help point out their differences and the implications those differences have for planning. In so doing, Godbey is critical of the emergence of experience consumers seeking a pound of experience for an ounce of investment. So he speaks of planning services to which people must make a commitment and for which something else must be sacrificed, a cold shower, perhaps, for those for whom "me" and "now" have become the criteria of daily life.

Irene Spry's discussion of "The Prospects for Leisure in a Conserver Society" (18) reinforces Godbey's (17) concern about our breakneck speed to consume time as well as material things. Spry's chapter is particularly interesting as she is a resource economist who has been extensively involved in multi-agency, multi-disciplinary studies of the future. She is clearly hopeful that the recognition of limits will result in conserving resources and environmental quality by limiting consumptive and destructive pursuits. In their place will (hopefully) emerge activities which are not only parsimonius but also characterized by intellect and imagination, beauty and good taste, social esteem and self-respect, all based on a life that has significance.

The chapters in this section are similar in that the necessity for and inevitability of change underlies each. Just as the future is uncertain, the outcome of change, whether chosen and pursued or coerced and resisted, is also uncertain. And that is a source, however great or little, of anxiety for us all. In the concluding chapter of this section, Goodale (19) notes that it is easier to anticipate and discuss change than it is to experience it — much less instigate it. But it seems clear that the reality of social, economic and political forces point in the same directions as the emerging, more humanistic philosophy of recreation and leisure service. He argues that the burden of change and the responsibility for it ultimately rest with each individual. Obstacles and opportunities abound, as is evident throughout the chapters in this and other sections. It is also evident that within the recreation movement or (arguably) profession, much re-thinking is underway and much is needed.

TLG
PAW

Chapter Ten
Future Leisure Environments in Cities

Seymour M. Gold

It is time for great optimism in the field of parks and recreation because, after years of romanticism, professionals are beginning to cope with reality. Changing values, technology, the energy crisis and inflation are forcing cities to do out of necessity what they might have done by choice. The traditional approach to providing open space and leisure services, long dominated by the use of arbitrary standards, outmoded concepts and conventional wisdom is being challenged as never before in the literature and in practice.

A new generation of recreation spaces and programs is evolving that presents some hopeful alternatives. These alternatives are based on the ideas of a small group of professionals who have been: (1) calling for a redefinition of leisure services in cities, (2) describing the phenomenon of nonuse of local parks, (3) alerting us to a *cost-revenue crisis* in government, (4) urging realistic citizen participation in the planning and decision process for urban parks, (5) pleading for more research and demonstration programs in park planning and management, and (6) suggesting it is not how much, but how good urban parks are. These people have been telling us the major problem in this field has been, and will be, coping with *change*.

REALITY CHECKS ON THE PRESENT

A critical review of the literature and practice yields these reality checks on the present:

Recreation Planning
The current state of the art is characterized by tradition. Recreation planning and design has been dominated by the use of arbitrary standards, and irrelevant concepts. Most of the ideas in current use are premised on 1930's thinking about recreation and open space preservation in cities.

Most recreation plans still assume an emphasis on youth, unlimited growth, increasing personal income and mobility, cheap energy and unlimited public budgets. They project a past and present that may not be realistic in light of current trends toward an

135

aging society, growth management, decreasing real income and a growing energy crisis.

Problem-Solving
The park and recreation field is essentially retrospective and romantic in the way it approaches problem-solving. Most recreation plans do not acknowledge or accommodate significant changes or trends in leisure lifestyles, legislation, technology or values.

Demonstration and innovation are the exception in most communities. Studies of user behavior are not evident in most recreation plans. Parks and recreation is still not considered an experimental field with credible solutions, measures or a theoretical foundation. It has not applied sophisticated planning or management techniques such as: systems analysis, performance budgeting, critical path method or gaming simulation to assess the future impact of options or programs on people, cities or the profession.

People Orientation
The objectives of many public park and recreation systems better accommodate the needs of the supplier than the user. Public participation in the planning process is still viewed with professional skepticism and given token attention. Nonuse, especially of neighborhood parks, is common in most communities because these spaces do not accommodate the recreational needs of people.

Advocacy and pluralism are becoming accepted dimensions of the planning and decision-making process. It is no longer enough for government to do things for some people. It must do things for and with all people and be able to rationalize this effort in human terms. The needs of specials populations, e.g., racial and ethnic minorities, senior citizens, the poor, physically handicapped and mentally retarded, have not been met in most communities that have yet to meet the needs of the general population.

FUTURE TRENDS AND EVENTS

Philosophical and pragmatic changes in American society, the recreation movement and evolving public policy reveal these changing perspectives, trends and events which will have a significant impact on urban parks and recreation and open space.

Lifestyle
A cultural revolution is taking place in thought about environment, leisure, work and sense of community. It is concerned with the con-

sumer, physical health and the quality of life. Translated into space or services, this revolution demands a more enlightened view of the way people use leisure time and space in cities. It implies rethinking our conceptual distinctions between space and services, public and private opportunities or indoor and outdoor spaces.

The idea that urban parks are for all people and established for the pleasurable use of leisure time is in contradiction with the lifestyles and leisure behavior of a growing number of people. Many types of leisure behavior are labeled as "deviant" because of outmoded laws, arbitrary policies and conventional thinking. Urban parks are one reflection of reality in an increasingly plastic world. The notion that they should be used by only "normal" people for the "constructive" use of their leisure time may be in violation of human rights.

Professionals have begun to redefine recreation in terms of human development. In the emerging view, it is not activities, facilities or programs that are central, it is what happens to people. Recreation is not a specific event, point in time or space. It is a dimension of self-development that has little to do with activity.

Self-Sufficiency

A new spirit of self help, volunteerism and community involvement is emerging in many places. This spirit recognizes the limits of government in solving many human problems. It senses a degree of commitment, responsibility and resourcefulness that can be used by people to help design, develop and maintain urban parks. The ideas of self-generated and self-maintained urban parks have yet to be tested in most communities. The expectation of professionals or government doing everything may be passe, fiscally impossible or not serve the best interests of people.

The logic of voluntary simplicity, self-sufficiency and self-directed leisure is the wave of the future. This idea, coupled with the philosophy of alternative, noncompetitive recreation programs such as "New Games," implies drastic changes in our approach to program leadership. It casts the professional as an enabler or resource person and the citizen as a volunteer leader.

Frugality and Austerity

Taxpayers, faced with a decline in real income, are not likely to approve bond issues or tax increases for local parks. They are developing a serious interest in the effectiveness of leisure services to obtain the best value for their dollar. Parks and recreation must now compete as never before for budget. The days of rationalizing public budgets with rhetoric instead of facts are gone.

Local governments are experiencing a cost-revenue crisis that will not diminish in a steady state economy coupled with rapid inflation, high levels of unemployment and a federal policy of indifference to the critical problems of American cities. Cities cannot expect needed financial help from the states or counties for the same reasons. Drastic cuts in municipal services will be necessary just to keep pace with inflation.

The existing system of recreation spaces in most communities will be all they can afford to operate and maintain. Funds will not be available for new spaces which implies making the best use of existing spaces that need renewal. *Recycling* urban parks in the same way we recycle newspaper or glass is the only strategy for many communities, and it makes good sense.

The traditional priorities of land acquisition, development and programs are being reversed in some cities that are beginning to sense the entire city as a recreation place in which voluntary program leadership in private or quasi-public spaces are more effective than extensive public investments in land and facilities.

Consolidation and Integration

A consolidation of government services is rapidly combining the park and recreation department with other social or environmental services. In both cases, the traditional "fun and games" or "housekeeper" images of these departments is dramatically broadened toward human development and environmental management.

The "withering of city hall" and "strategy for attrition" of local govenment is an irreversible trend in the 1980's. Park and recreation agencies that cannot justify cost-effective leisure services will be replaced with private contractors. Many professionals will shift from the public to the private sector, if they wish to stay in this field. Public leisure services that are not self-supporting or subsidized by charitable donations or voluntary efforts will become endangered species.

Limits

An "era of limits" is being defined in politics, science, government, and industry that says small is beautiful, less is more, that we have reached the limits of unqualified growth and must make more rational use of existing resources. In a materialistic society, it is "Economics as if People Mattered" based on a lower set of expectations and conservation of human and natural resources.

The energy crisis is real and beginning to show an impact on disposable income, mobility patterns, and lifestyles. The choice of work or leisure places is being conditioned by the price of fuel. The increased cost of gasoline or the prospect of fuel rationing may force many people to drastically change their priorities and seek energy conserving ways to spend their leisure time in or near cities. The option of personal transportation will be replaced with mass transit alternatives or bicycle or pedestrian access to local recreation opportunities.

Municipal austerity programs have had a profound effect on the maintenance, development and redevelopment of urban parks. These park systems would be unable to accommodate the sustained levels of increased use which could result from a prolonged energy crisis without substantial increases in funding. At the very time urban parks are needed to provide energy conserving leisure options for many people, these systems are in jeopardy. The "energy connection" represents the last best hope to justify a significant federal and state commitment to the direct support of urban park systems.

These future trends will have a significant and sustained impact on the nature of urban leisure patterns, public services and the profession. However, there are several current conditions which may have an even greater impact on the future. These conditions should influence our thoughts, plans and actions. They represent restraints and opportunities for coping with change and reality. For example, these items can have profound implications on future leisure environments in cities:

1. People's trust in institutions is at an all time low. Most people do not trust authority. The credibility of government and professionals is being questioned as never before. At the very time we need credibility, it would seem few people are listening. The legacy of Viet Nam, Watergate and a host of events such as the Three-Mile Island nuclear accident or DC-10 engine mountings failure have eroded public confidence in authority.

2. The taxpayers' revolt is real. There is widespread overt and latent national support for balanced budgets from both political parties. People have embraced this as a new cause or religion. They are angry at big government, excessive tax burdens and waste. Their mood is reactionary and uses the only initiative left which is to cut public budgets or remove politicians who will not do so. Public agencies that cannot justify their existence in credible human terms that have political support have dim prospects of survival in an era of scarce resources and competing needs.

3. Society is aging. The post-war baby boom of the 1950's has become the baby bust of the 1980's. The "Greening of America"[2] has changed to the "Graying of America." Surplus schools are being turned into nursing homes as the youth culture fades. The median age will pass 30 in 1981, reach 35 by the year 2000 and approach 40 by 2030. During this period, the number of people over 65 will more than double to 52 million, one out of every six Americans. The demographic facts are irrefutable.

4. Working wives, moonlighting and late retirement as a way to cope with inflation or declining family income are causing significant changes in leisure patterns. Many people have less leisure time or flexibility which implies peak use of limited facilities or use rationing. The recreation demand projections of the 1980's based on increasing levels of leisure time may not reflect the work and leisure of the 1980's. For most people, the recreation use patterns of the 1980's may, of necessity, parallel the patterns of the 1880's with weekends and holidays being the major source of leisure time.

5. Individual and family income is declining in terms of purchasing power. The gap between the rich and poor is widening. Many people will have less disposable income for leisure services at the same time most communities are considering significant increases in fees and charges to make these services self-supporting. A severe economic recession is likely. The length and depth of this recession will depend on this country's ability to become more self-sufficient and energy conserving which has a direct relationship to the way we use leisure time and space in cities.

These perspectives call for drastic changes in the current approach to urban recreation and suggest a radical departure from the traditional approach of applying arbitrary standards to the past or present recreation activities of a mythical population to rationalize the allocation of recreation space or services. They imply a sophisticated understanding of urban living, leisure, behavior and the future not common in this field.

In a planning context, these changes imply it is necessary to move beyond a narrow focus on recreation activities, buildings and parks toward a mission of improving the quality of life and environment. At the policy or operational level of local government, these concepts place park and recreation services in the broader context of a social service delivery system which emphasizes a humanistic approach to problem solving. They recognize the interrelation of recreation and park services to the social and physical environment of cities.

This emphasis on cities, people and the future will require the bold vision and sense of social purpose which characterized the early years of the park and recreation movement. It will also require a commitment to research and demonstration to find new ways to think about leisure in cities. Most important, an emphasis on the future will require an understanding of social or technological change and innovation.

CHANGE AND INNOVATION

If change were to take place with equal force or speed, it might allow projection or, at least, prediction. But now change is uneven and subject to great forward leaps. A breakthrough in one area can have profound impact in other areas. Who anticipated the consequences of these items we now take for granted: automobiles, space flights, income taxes, billboards, air conditioning, frozen foods, computers, penicillin, hydrogen bombs, Kentucky Fried Chicken, paper wedding dresses, dune buggies, neon lights, disposable diapers, color television, collective bargaining, credit cards, nuclear power, affirmative action, social security, vending machines, mobile homes, supermarkets, jumbo jets, detergents, tranquilizers, revenue sharing, shopping centers and suburbia?

Each item has had some influence on urban life. Combined, they have created a need for people to adapt to or cope with change which is the fundamental cause of most issues or problems. Some of these problems include: an energy crisis, racial polarization, juvenile delinquency, traffic congestion, water and air pollution, urban blight, inflation, diminishing open space, crime, flight to the suburbs, water shortages, inadequate schools, bankrupt cities and slums.

Beyond the present is an uncertain future where innovation and technology may solve some problems, but create still more. Who is considering the future impact on leisure patterns of: increased lifespan, disease eradication, psychedelic drugs, weather control, cybernation, guaranteed minimum wage, and flextime work schedules?

In the context of urban parks and recreation just 10 years ago, who envisioned: skateboard parks, racquetball centers, mainstreaming the handicapped, unisex toilets, inflatable buildings, water scooters, giant slides, electronic games, hang gliders, roller skates, astro turf, surf machines, and solar heated pools?

Most important, who is thinking about the possible impacts on the park and recreation experience or agency of: legalization of marijuana, nude beaches, an aging society, social impact reports, surplus schools, television games, growth management, mopeds, a major recession, a sustained energy crisis and zero-based budgeting?

SCENARIOS OF THE FUTURE

One way to focus on the possible implications of change and innovation is with four scenarios of the future that can be translated into two options for people and professionals to consider. For example, these scenarios of the future seem possible:

Traditional View
The traditional view projects trends which may no longer be true.[3] For example, by the year 2000 population density, mobility and personal income will double, the work week will decline and people will retire at 60. An energy crisis and economic depression will not occur. Growth and affluence will continue with an unlimited consumption of resources. Simple forms of outdoor recreation will continue, but more specialized and expensive activities will gain mass appeal. The work ethic will prevail and leisure time will be used to escape from cities to the country.

Humanistic View
The humanistic view envisions a future where there is little distinction between work and leisure.[4] Work in an affluent society may become a privilege for a few and mass leisure will be socially acceptable. Work will become people-oriented instead of object-oriented. The emphasis of society will be on human services instead of things. Education systems will prepare people for a life of leisure instead of work. A leisure ethic will replace the work ethic and humanism will replace materialism. The question will no longer be the production of wealth, but the fair distribution of wealth. Open space will be a public trust for future generations instead of a speculative commodity to be exploited for profit.

Pessimistic View
The pessimistic view sees the future as one of complexity, scarcity and turmoil with mass leisure as a problem in an industrialized

world with diminishing resources and competing needs.[5] Technology, combined with an accelerating pace of change, will subject recreation to "Future Shock."[6] Our relationship with things will become more temporary and the throwaway culture and transience described by Toffler will become a way of life for many. His descriptions of items like: portable playgrounds, modular fun palaces, experience-makers, life environments, fun specialists and leisure-based subcults would boggle the minds of most park and recreation commissions. Open space preservation will be an opportunity foregone or a luxury beyond the reach of most communities.

Optimistic View

New work attitudes, lifestyles and ethics will shape our leisure patterns. Three-day work weeks and flextime schedules will level peak use. Work sharing, extended vacations, sabbaticals and early retirement will allow extensive travel and participation in local recreation programs. Work will be done at home or workers will live close to where they work in new or recycled cities. Cottage industries will bring work and leisure environments together again. Gasoline shortages will force people to rediscover urban parks. Inflation and declining real income will force people to discover simple activities. Managed open space will create the environmental framework and social focus of cities. Open space and parks will be considered an essential of urban living to be provided by community action and sophisticated long range planning.

These views imply significant changes in our mission, meaning and nature of urban parks. They require a critical evaluation of existing policies, acknowledgement of reality and radical changes which will not be easy to initiate or accept. These changes can be described with two coping strategies:

Urban Parks (Status Quo)

A business-as-usual attitude of delay and obfuscation of the real facts and issues. Tokenism and attempts to solve problems by treating the symptoms or effects instead of the causes. Bureaucratic finger-pointing and prolonged studies to evade the questions of responsibility. A naive hope and idealism that urban parks are a necessary "good" to be justified on their own merits. A posture of status quo, defensiveness to criticism, and assumption that the current and future changes or challenges will magically vanish with time.

Urban Parks II (Survival)

An attempt to change the situation based on the real facts and issues. Bold innovation, demonstration, and full commitment to solve problems by treating the causes. Bureaucratic honesty and immediate or interim policy statements to fix the questions of responsibility. Sober reflection and reexamination of the role and value of urban parks as they relate to other public services. A posture of reasoned change, humility instead of arrogance, and conviction that the current and future changes or challenges will accelerate with time.

The predictable result of strategy I is the demise or deterioration of existing urban parks. The impact of this scenario is unthinkable to many who have long considered this public service or institution impregnable. The result in human and economic terms seem catastrophic for this field which has never experienced public censure or had its professional survival threatened. This scenario is tragic and needless. Its impact on urban America would be profound and regretful.

The predictable result of strategy II is the survival and improvement of urban parks. The impact of this scenario would be to sustain, strengthen, and justify the provision of leisure services as a vital American institution. The potential results in human and economic terms seem impressive, considering the level of investment already in public open space. Most important, the potential of parks and recreation to contribute to the quality of urban life and the urban environment could be realized. The impact of this scenario on urban America would be dramatic and hopeful.

NEW DIMENSIONS OF RECREATION

Regardless of which events or scenarios occur in the long range future, a spectrum of new activities, institutions and concepts is evolving that should be considered now in the preparation of recreation plans. These items represent some dramatic alternatives for the provision of leisure opportunities in cities. They illustrate what is needed and possible.

New Activities

A new generation of activities will become common in or near cities. These activities will require new spaces, management techniques and sophisticated leadership. Many of these activities will be self-directed, noncompetitive and energy conserving in the use of land or facilities. They will symbolize dramatic changes in lifestyle, ethics or attitudes toward people and the environment. A sampling of these new activities includes: ballooning, ski-touring, windsurfing, put/take fishing, land sailing, psychodrama, PONG, turf-skiing, spinnaker flying, New Games, water-walking, ski-bobbing, hot tubbing, flingbee, snurfing, spelunking, para-sailing, camera hunting, par-course fitness, yoga, Rolfing, wind skating, flicker-ball, disco skating, and swing-ball tennis.

New Institutions
A new type of institution will develop to accommodate the lifestyles and leisure needs of the future. Human development and environmental management will become the expanded focus of public parks and recreation agencies. The arts, culture and education will be closely coordinated in departments of life enrichment. Among the new or expanded institutions of the future will be:

1. Public Utilities — To provide leisure services in the same way as gas, water, electricity and mail are delivered to local communities.

2. Recreation Franchises — Private contractors will provide revenue producing services, e.g., tennis, golf or marinas.

3. Contract Services — Private contractors will provide many of the planning, design, management, maintenance and program services now provided by the public sector in most communities.

4. Commercial Enterprises — Private concessionaires will provide community and regional theme or amusement parks on public land.

5. Company Resorts — Private corporations will provide special park and recreation opportunities for their employees in or near cities.

6. Leisure Cooperatives — Individuals, neighborhoods and organizations or social groups will join together to provide specialized leisure opportunities or equipment for their members, e.g., sailboats or swimming pools.

7. Leisure Counselors — Public and private specialists will advise people on alternative ways and places to use their time budgets in the same manner as investment counselors now advise people on how to spend their discretionary money.

8. Day Care Centers — Public and private places to provide supervised care for children while parents are participating in recreational activities will become common at the neighborhood level.

9. Community Colleges — Local colleges will assume a dominant role in providing arts, cultural and human development programs for adults. Their facilities will be integrated with park and recreation facilities to serve the entire community.

New Concepts

We need new ways to think about leisure in cities. For example, we have traditionally considered only public land and water for outdoor recreation, but new or expanded use of approaches to design, management and program offer these exciting possibilities:

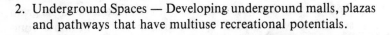

1. Air Rights — Using space over public and private urban development for leisure opportunities. We can deck over freeways, railroad yards, warehouses and parking lots for recreational use.

2. Underground Spaces — Developing underground malls, plazas and pathways that have multiuse recreational potentials.

3. Risk Recreation — Providing activities and places that encourage physical and mental challenge or self-confidence.[7]

4. Self-programmed Recreation — Encouraging simple, energy-conserving, noncompetitive activities such as New Games[8] or Parcouse fitness.

5. Recycling Existing Parks — Renewing existing parks that no longer meet the needs of users to include a major emphasis on adventure playgrounds, community gardens, and water or energy conserving landscapes.

6. Reuse of Existing Buildings — Converting abandoned or obsolete buildings to public or private recreational uses, e.g., theaters, schools, factories, or supermarkets.

7. Self-generated Parks — Encouraging residents to help design, develop and maintain neighborhood parks.

8. Rooftop Spaces — Making intensive use of rooftops for public and private recreational opportunities.

146

9. Recreational Retailing — Combining amusement parks with shopping centers.

10. Reuse of Cemeteries — Redeveloping or opening cemeteries for passive recreational use, arboretums and wildlife preserves.

11. Urban Campgrounds — Providing campgrounds in urban parks for tourists.

12. High Rise Recreation Structures — Building or redeveloping high rise structures for recreational use, e.g., tennis clubs, hostels or play areas.

13. Pneumatic Structures — Providing large air supported structures for special events or temporary facilities in changing neighborhoods.

14. Joint Use of Facilities — Using private clubs, marinas, golf courses, shopping centers and industrial parks for public programs.

15. Public/Private Opportunities — Considering the entire city as a recreation place to include places such as streets, theaters, bars, restaurants, libraries, museums, historic districts, private plazas and flea markets where people can experience diversity, pleasure or enrichment.

We can build cities in parks instead of parks in cities. The idea of parks or recreation as an isolated set of spaces or experiences in cities is passe. Past distinctions between indoor and outdoor spaces and public vs. private opportunities are fading with new concepts that integrate space and service to serve the needs of people at the lowest possible cost.

A NEW AGENDA

It is time to rethink the future of urban parks. A new agenda is necessary to cope with the present and shape the future. This agenda will require an unparalleled sense of urgency, innovation and professional sophistication. There is no substitute for these ingredients. The positive or negative results of our actions or indifference are predicatable on the quality of urban life and environment.

There has never been a better time for innovation and demonstration in the parks and recreation field, if we will try to understand and shape the future. There is much to be done. Here are some places to begin:

1. Study the future as well as the past and present to see if we are thinking boldly enough about current issues and trends. We teach courses in the history of recreation, why not the future?

2. Develop a more humanistic or people-serving concept of urban parks and recreation. It is time to balance our emphasis on the resource with a serious concern for the user.

3. Broaden our interpretation of urban recreation in time, space and attitude. There is no rule that says parks must be public, square, horizontal, and dull places that do not relate to people.

4. Encourage the private sector to provide high quality services. Government cannot and will not do the whole job.

5. Consider parks and recreation an experimental field with a major emphasis on research, demonstration and innovation to develop new products and services. It took thousands of experiments to develop birth control pills or color television, surely we can find an alternative to competitive sports or traditional play areas.

6. Link our efforts to improve the quality of urban parks to the energy crisis, changing needs, priorities, and lifestyles of people living in cities to include those with the greatest need for leisure services, e.g., the poor, senior citizens, physically handicapped and mentally retarded.

7. Challenge the assumptions, concepts and standards traditionally used to provide leisure opportunities in cities. One mark of professionalism is self-criticism.

8. Understand the best way to preserve wilderness areas from overuse is to improve the quality of life and environment in cities. By placing a priority on urban open space we can solve instead of perpetuating these two problems.

9. Develop objective measures to assess the need for and effectiveness of urban leisure services. It is difficult to do research

or rationalize public funds for the support of parks and recreation without credible measures.

10. Train or retrain a new breed of enlightened professionals in Parks and Recreation to meet the challenges and opportunities of the future.

The impact of a taxpayers' revolt and energy crisis will probably do more to increase the effectiveness and appreciation of urban parks and recreation as a vital public service than the environmental movement and host of federal assistance programs. We have been given a powerful mandate to show the value of urban parks compared to other public services. The park and recreation movement can flourish by using this opportunity to develop a new constituency for urban parks that reflect the diverse populations of urban America.

The situation suggests this agenda: (1) asking the right questions before we seek answers, (2) re-examining the fundamental justification for providing leisure opportunities, (3) developing effective methods of recreation, planning, design and management, (4) applying these experimentally in demonstration areas, and (5) critically evaluating the process and products of this effort. The situation also suggests: (1) treating the causes of problems instead of the effects, (2) sorting out means from ends in the context of public policy, (3) calling problems by their real instead of their reverse labels, (4) humility instead of arrogance in relating to taxpayers, and (5) a dimension of serious thought and bold action uncommon in this field.[9]

This agenda will not be easy, but it is worth the effort if we believe public parks and recreation can make a significant contribution to the quality of urban life and environment. If we do not believe this is possible, it may be time to shift this responsibility to the private sector and accept the consequences or blessings of our action or indifference.

A PROFESSIONAL MANDATE

The personal challenge is to understand the dimensions of change in the future and accept a profession that may be more conditioned by world events and the media than tradition or reason. It is time to be bold and visionary instead of fatalistic. There is much hope; we can begin coping with change by: (1) discarding the romantic myths and conventional wisdom that pervade this field, and (2) turning the changing values, technology, and lifestyle of society into an advantage for this field that has so long stood for human and environmental values. It is time to ask and answer these questions:

1. How can we finance and justify park and recreation systems in an era of limits?

2. How can we build political constituencies for parks and recreation now?

3. If we cannot finance or justify public parks and recreation or build effective political constituencies in the 1980's — what alternatives are possible?

4. How should the profession and each of us respond to these challenges? Can we act instead of react to crisis or do we even believe there is one?

5. Are we part of the problem or part of the solution in terms of our level of commitment to this profession, understanding of reality, and interest in the future?

We have a mandate a few similar professions have faced: to cope with the present and invent the future in an era of limits. The task will not be easy, but it is worth it, if we believe in the values of parks and recreation. We may be witnessing the end of one social order and beginning another, for better or worse. There is little time left for debate. What we do in the next few years will determine the future course of public parks and recreation in this country.

The Park and Recreation Movement and urban parks need not "muddle toward frugality" or become "endangered species" unless we want to. This profession has the guts and brains to cope with change in an era of limits. The essence of the past and hope of the future will not be lost, if we can sense this opportunity and do something about it now.

There is every reason for hope and optimism, if we begin to realize the potentials of living with nature in an era of limits. Of all our resources, the most precious is human awareness. This awareness causes us to re-examine the purpose of life and ask what fulfillment really means. Urban parks, recreation and open-space offer society unique opportunities for this examination. They can provide the time, place and means by which people can achieve self-discovery that leads to self-respect and a better society.

REFERENCES

1. Schumacker, E. F., *Small is Beautiful: Economics as if People Mattered*. New York: Harper and Row, 1973.
2. Reich, Charles A., *The Greening of America*. New York: Random House, 1970.
3. See: United States Department of Interior, Bureau of Outdoor Recreation. *Outdoor Recreation: A Legacy for America*. Washington, D.C.: United States Government Printing Office, 1973.
4. See for example: Kaplan, Max. *Leisure: Theory and Policy*. New York: John Wiley and Sons, 1975.
5. See for example: Michael, Donald N., *The Unprepared Society: Planning for a Precarious Future*. New York: Harper and Row, 1968.
6. Toffler, Alvin. *Future Shock*. New York: Random House, 1970.
7. Dunn, Diana R. and Gulbis, John M., "The Risk Revolution." *Parks and Recreation* (August, 1976), pp. 12-17.
8. Fluegelman, Andrew (Ed.). *The New Games Book*. San Francisco: Headlands Press, 1976.
9. Gold, Seymour. *Recreation Planning and Design*. New York: McGraw-Hill, 1980.

Chapter Eleven

Urban Leisure Services: Reshaping a Good Thing

Geoffrey Godbey

Urban park, recreation, and leisure services have a long and proud history in North America. These services have reflected a range of ideas concerning how urban life could be made better. Basically, the many social and ecological interest groups which have made up the parks, recreation and leisure movements have attempted to bring about reform designed to improve the quality of everyday life for urban residents.[1]

For those interested in a career in urban leisure services, the good news is that urban areas continue to be in need of reform and our planet's inhabitants continue to move inexorably toward cities. Public leisure service agencies have been and continue to be the best value for money that urban government has to offer. For a sum as paltry as $15 per year per resident, a huge range of leisure facilities and programs have been available to the public which, otherwise, would have been out of their reach. At their best, urban leisure services have expanded horizons, promoted a sense of community, and contributed to our physical and emotional fitness.

Urban leisure services have a proud history. Their obvious successes, in the recent as well as distant past, are praiseworthy.[2] There are, however, a number of problems, relatively recent in origin, which need to be addressed and gradually alleviated. In addition, there is one central challenge.

PROBLEMS OF RECENT ORIGIN

Transition to a Close-Ended System

Administrators of public urban leisure services became accustomed to a model of open-ended growth in the 1960's, as did most of society, and became skilled in planning, acquiring, implementing and developing leisure services. They did not, however, get used to maintaining, conserving, incrementally changing, retrenching, protecting, substituting, or optimizing. Now they, like the rest of society, are having to learn. This is a particularly difficult task since federal legislation of the 1960's increased the agencies' hardware and infrastructure with no provision for maintaining it. Today, when maintenance is needed, local governments are often unable to supply the funds and are unwilling to seek more taxes to do so. Legislators will propose laws to establish new parks but not to maintain old ones. At the same time, "demand" for many kinds of leisure services is increasing from a public which is often not willing to either (a) pay more taxes, or (b) do it themselves. What is a poor leisure service administrator to do? The transition from quantitative growth to maintenance and qualitative growth is difficult and involves a change in basic mentality. The official American Prayer Book contains only one word — "more" — and leisure is the altar at which most praying is done.

Location of Park Land
During the last three decades there has been a tremendous acquisition and development of parks at the local, state, and national levels. A number of factors have brought this about, including mandatory dedication laws and state, provincial, and federal legislation providing partial funding for such acquisition. While this process has been, on the average, quite worthwhile, it has resulted in at least three problems: 1. Acquisition of cheap land away from population centers; 2. The dedication of flood plain and other undesirable land for local parks; and 3. Disproportionate development of new parks in affluent areas due to matching fund requirements for cities in federal and state legislation.[3] Many parks in urban areas, therefore, are located on the least desirable land while state or provincial parks are not often accessible to the urban resident. Poor cities have benefitted least from federal and state park acquisition funds since they often could not provide matching dollars. In general, the mentality in regard to acquisition has been to think about how much land, rather than how useful or how beautiful the land was.

Inappropriate Use of Leisure Services to Address Social Problems
Because public leisure services are comparatively inexpensive, and because they can be altered quickly, they have often been used inappropriately by government to address other social problems. Perhaps the most dramatic example of this was during the urban riots of the late 1960's and early 1970's, when the Federal Government suddenly pumped money into the cities for summer recreation for inner-city residents.[4] The fundamental problems of such residents were housing, health care, education, transportation and, of course, employment. Recreation and park departments, however, were often the first to respond — a sometimes reluctant agent of social control.

The same argument can be made for the Comprehensive Education and Training Act and other public employment or so-called "job training" programs. Recreation and park agencies were persuaded to utilize so many of these temporary employees that, by 1975, CETA workers constituted 15 percent of all full-time leisure service employees at the municipal level. Never mind that there was precious little money for training. Let them cut brush. CETA employees sometimes replaced regular staff employees, often with disappointing results.

In less dramatic ways, public leisure services are used as tokens in political wheeling and dealing, particularly when some other requested commodity can not be supplied. While recreation and park administrators have often resisted such efforts, their resistance has frequently been futile.

Assignment of Urban Leisure Concerns
to Federal Land-Managing Agencies
Federal involvement in urban recreation, park and leisure services, such as supplying technical information, administering federal funding programs, developing standards, and providing direct technical assistance has been entrusted largely to land managing agencies such as the United States Forest Service, National Park Service, Army Corps of Engineers, Bureau of Land Management, and others. Even the Bureau of Outdoor Recreation and its successor, the Heritage Conservation and Recreation Service, were staffed primarily by former personnel from federal land-managing agencies. Such staff were often largely ignorant of urban recreation and parks and displayed an anti-urban bias. Their backgrounds in recreation and parks were usually limited to situations in which recreation was the secondary use of large isolated land masses which had some other primary purpose. They were not often interested in the inner city resident, the programmatic use of recreation areas, or establishment of high density recreation areas. Also, they generally did not want to work with other federal agencies (and vice-versa), let alone the private sector. No wonder the redevelopment of urban water fronts has gone on, largely successfully, without them. Their leadership has hindered urban leisure services.

Separation of Design, Program, and Maintenance Functions
within Urban Agencies
One of the unfortunate consequences of attempts at professionalization of urban leisure agencies has been separation of design, programming, and maintenance of recreation areas. Ar-

chitects and landscape architects have often worked in isolation as have recreation programmers and maintenance staff. Maintenance personnel are perhaps the most isolated, often relegated to a separate equipment storage area with a supervisor who occasionally makes trips into the "main office." This method of operation has been a catastrophe. Maintenance, today, is often the number one urban leisure problem and it has to be approached in an integrated manner with the participation of all staff. Designers and programmers of urban park and recreation areas have to understand the maintenance implications of what they do before they do it. While survey after survey shows that the quality of maintenance and safety are the two biggest concerns of urban park users, the process of maintaining areas and facilities is not often systematically reexamined in terms of integration within the agency.

Emphasis on Activity Rather Than Process
Among the most serious kind of cultural lag exhibited by urban leisure service agency staff has been the tendency to think of what they are providing as "activities" or "facilities" rather than to conceive of their role as facilitators of a process which involves an activity or facility. The commercial sector has often understood this much better. "Going swimming" does not only constitute merely getting into a pool and swimming because one likes to swim. It happens for a myriad of reasons: a person is bored, or hot, or a competitive swimmer, or wants to be with girlfriends, or is forced to go by parents, or because there is a snack bar at the pool, or to watch the kids, or practice. The experience of swimming often includes driving an automobile, eating, drinking, sun-bathing, sleeping, reading, standing in water, card games, gossip, flirting, racing, floating, baby-sitting, snorkeling, listening to music, etc. Swimming is many activities done for many reasons and the design of the swimming area and the programming for that area must recognize this, but often such recognition is absent. While the British have begun, for instance, putting day-care facilities, pubs, sauna baths, and other amenities in their sports centers, our public sector has often avoided this approach. Leisure is a process, a complex process, and it must be intelligently thought through, rather than thinking, "Let's dump one more swimming pool in the ground at Location X." What does it mean that many "swimmers" spend more time out of the water than in? What does it mean that many swimmers who are in the water are more likely to be standing and talking than swimming? Leisure service professionals must know what these situations mean from a design, management, programming, and maintenance standpoint — to say nothing of marketing.

Inadequately Prepared Employees

The growth of employment in public leisure services has frequently taken place with little concern for or understanding of what these positions could or should entail. In many cases, no knowledgeable person or organization has "interpreted" such positions to employers. In other cases, employers simply did not care. This situation has resulted in a frequent pattern of employing staff with no appropriate post-secondary education, employing staff with low quality education in recreation or related areas, and employing staff based on partisan political motives. All of these patterns have resulted in problems.

There is a great tendency to think that urban leisure services are staffed by professionals. Such, to a great extent, is not the case. Appointments to urban leisure service departments are often made based upon partisan political motives. A survey of U.S. local recreation, park, and leisure service agencies by Don Henkel and me (1977) found that only 40 percent of full-time staff in local leisure service agencies had post high-school education specializing in recreation and parks or a related area.[5] Appointments to big-city agencies are even more disproportionately made as rewards by elected officials, regardless of the aptitude, educational qualifications or experience of the candidate. This is true in such cities as New York, Boston, and Chicago, and also in smaller communities. Parks and recreation is often the dumping-ground agency for the loyal party member who lasts in the job as long as his or her party is in office.

Civil Service sometimes helps the situation but can make it worse. In many cases, Civil Service exams are selectively administered, subjectively judged, and otherwise used to select the applicant that the political official in question wants.

In spite of problems of patronage, post-secondary education in parks and recreation has increasingly taken on the responsibility for professional preparation. Curricula grew rapidly through the 1960's and 1970's until an estimated 40,000 students were majoring in this academic area in the United States and Canada. Unfortunately, this growth often took place without a corresponding growth of qualified faculty. Universities sometimes viewed recreation and park curricula as an inexpensive program to initiate, which would compensate for declining enrollments in other areas, such as physical education. While the National Recreation and Park Association and Society of Park and Recreation Educators have made valiant efforts to bring about a meaningful accreditation program, to be accredited, a curriculum must have staff which often were graduates of the very second-rate curricula being evaluated. In any event, such accreditation is after the fact. The huge growth in curricula is over and natural market forces are now beginning to bring about declining enrollments.

Many recreation and park curricula have been intellectually sub-par, staffed by professors who have made a career of being "nice folks." It's important to be nice, but it's not enough. Curricular content is often a disgrace, utilizing a small body of knowledge to generate ten or twenty courses where three or four would do. Recreation and park curricula in urban areas have sometimes been diploma mills. Only a handful of curricula have had the desperately needed inter-disciplinary involvement to adequately prepare students.

While increasingly needed, comparatively little continuing education is currently available for personnel of leisure services, and what does exist is often attended by those who need it least. A great flurry of research is underway, but much of it is suspect and almost none of it will be read by or interpreted to practitioners.

THE CENTRAL CHALLENGE

The previous problems, while vexing, are ones upon which we can incrementally improve. One other problem, however — really a challenge — confronts the field. If it is not quickly dealt with, the previously mentioned problems of urban leisure services won't matter much. This problem or challenge is central: to rethink what we are about. To develop a better understanding of how leisure has changed our society and react accordingly. The role of leisure in our society has gone, in many instances, from a search for catharsis to pleasure to meaning. As this has happened, leisure behavior has become of increasing importance to the individual. This seems an obvious point. We spend a higher proportion of our money for leisure than previously, rate it a higher component of life satisfaction, increasingly use it as religious or spiritual expression, and find its contribution to our self definition has grown greatly. Our field has grown so used to proselytizing about the importance of leisure that we seem not to have noticed that the public believes it too, often more than we do. I remember once attending a conference where we all sat in the work-like atmosphere of the meeting room, our name tags in place, listening to one more speaker drone on about the importance of leisure and how we had to educate the public. Outside that room (it was a beautiful day in the city), people were going to a nearby museum, picnicking at a public plaza, sun-bathing, playing tennis, running, talking and flirting in a cocktail lounge, painting a picture of City Hall, sight-seeing, playing an accordian, etc. We sat in our meeting room imploring each other to spread the good news about leisure.

If leisure is of increasing importance, a response is demanded by leisure service agencies and that response is to provide not more, but better. That response is to quit worrying about how many acres can be acquired and see if all of the litter can be removed from what exists; see if the Elms can be saved; see if flowers can be kept in every public place.

That response is to stop sponsoring programs merely because people will participate — people participate more in watching television than any other leisure activity but most don't think it very important. That response is to stop hiring employees just because they have the right degree or will be dependable. In hiring employees, look for vision, ideas, curiosity, and a concern for the lives of other people.

If leisure is important, it will require cutting back some services which can't be done right (and taking the heat for it) and improving what remains. If leisure is important, it will mean that a constant dialogue with the public is necessary whether or not the public is interested in talking.

A new approach must be taken to judging the success of leisure services which allows for judgements about the qualitative aspects of the service by those who have experienced them or could experience them. One example of an approach to doing this is Importance-Performance Analysis, which starts by identifying what features or attributes of the given leisure service are important to an individual, having them rate these features in terms of comparative importance, and then rating them in terms of how well the leisure service "supplied" these features.[6] Such an approach allows the agency to understand what the participant thinks is important and how closely agency provision of the service corresponds to what is important.

It must be said once again that if leisure is important, urban leisure service organizations must play an enabling and facilitating role rather than one of direct service provision. This means, among other things, entering the consciousness of other organizations within the urban community and seeking to coordinate or cooperate with their efforts. The synergetic leisure service, in which many organizations contribute their resources, will have to become commonplace.

If leisure is important, then leisure services must reflect the unique characteristics of the city; no model can be transported. As

Cranz points out in her remarkable book *The Politics of Park Design*, urban parks:

"have been diffused from city to city and region to region through such media as annual reports, congresses, manuals, national professional associations, and universities. The process has led to design criteria with little living relation to particular cultures, climates, or people. Its antithesis, designing with local roots, could introduce regional character into the line of park design options."[7]

An urban park, in other words, doesn't really mean much until you put it into a specific environment. Designing a park is not a matter of technology, but one of cultural discovery. It distresses me to see essentially the same "fitness trail" in Sao Paulo, Brazil, and State College, Pennsylvania; the same playground in Melbourne, Australia, and Philadelphia. If leisure is important, facilities cannot be "tacked on" to the environment.

In every post-industrial society, a decentralizing process is taking place, the nation state is an increasingly obsolete economic, political, and social institution, and a differentiation process is at work in terms of regions and sub-regions of the country. This process has profound implications for urban leisure services. Administrators must work from data concerning their own local area and this information must deal with qualitative aspects of local residents' lives as well as quantitative ones. Leisure services in urban areas are going to have to start from the specifics of people's lives and that means having administrators who understand what everyday life is like in each housing project in their community, understanding why old ladies go to the annual flower show, and what percentage of the "runners" of the city are interested in mini-marathons.

Public leisure services in urban areas can seek to change the small problems they face incrementally. But the big issue, that leisure is now of central importance and that quality of experience is everything, demands an immediate response. In responding, urban leisure services must be recreated — and the process of recreation must be different in each urban area.

REFERENCES

1. See, for instance,

   Cranz, Galen. *The Politics of Park Design — A History of Urban Parks In America.* Cambridge, Mass.: MIT Press, 1982. p. 250.

   Dulles, Foster Rhea. *A History of Recreation.* New York: Appleton-Century-Crofts, 1965.

   Duncan, Mary. "Back to Our Radical Roots." In *Recreation and Leisure: Issues In An Era of Change.* Edited by Thomas Goodale and Peter Witt. State College, Pa.: Venture Publishing, 1980.

   McFarland, Elsie. *The Development of Public Recreation In Canada.* Ottawa: Canadian Parks/Recreation Association. 1970.

2. For an accounting of the benefits of public recreation and parks, see *Winning Support for Parks and Recreation,* by the National Park Service, State College, Pa.: Venture Publishing, 1983.

3. One study which documented this situation in regard to the Land and Water Conservation Fund Act was Burdick, John M. *Recreation in the Cities: Who Gains From Federal Aid?* Washington, D.C., Center for Growth Alternatives, 1975.

4. I remember working as an intern for a large city recreation and parks department which, during the period of the urban riots, had several million dollars almost forced upon it by a federal agency.

5. Henkel, Donald and Geoffrey Godbey. *Parks, Recreation and Leisure Services: Employment In the Public Sector — Status and Trends.* Arlington, Va.: NRPA, 1977.

6. Martilla, J. A. and J. C. James. "Importance-Performance Analysis for Developing Effective Marketing Strategies," *Journal of Marketing,* 4(1), Jan., 1977.

7. Cranz, *op. cit.*

Chapter Twelve

Public Administration: Roots and Implications of Change

Joseph J. Bannon

> Chaos often breeds life,
> when order breeds habit.
>
> Henry Adams[1]

A HISTORY OF CHANGE

In reading the above work, written about the pervasive industrial and technological changes in the nineteenth century, one is freshly reminded how widespread and dynamic were the many social, cultural, and economic transitions of that century. Although we tend to view our own times as the most historically hectic and uncertain, to read any book prior to this modern-day era quickly reminds one that change is endemic to existence; and if one agrees with historian Henry Adams, change is also the basis of vital life itself. It is valuable to read personal reflections on historical transitions — apart from the old belief that one thereby avoids repeating prior mistakes — simply for the clear evidence of repetition and similarities throughout time.

Most of Henry Adams' generation and class were either gainfully unemployed, or employed and enthralled by the railroads. In more recent decades, the technological magnets — attracting an entire generation or more — are computers and other advanced, automated systems. The impact remains similar nonetheless, as we respond to change, resist it, or, more problematically, ignore it. The value of historical perspective cannot be overstated, though ironically the tempo of education, and the process of change itself, often preclude or retard the opportunities for any worthwhile historical assessments. Americans have been called "the most electric of people" (Englishman, John Cowper Powys), a trait indicating our lack of in-depth reflection in the face of change. Furthermore, change in our society is often compounded by a national tendency to hurtle through time, devour contemporary events and transitions without mindful consideration, and emerge frequently puzzled or out of focus as a result. Americans are timeless in some ways, having undoubtedly one of the poorest and shortest historical memories of note. It is not only the complexity of events that evades us, but also their sheer number, exacerbated by media that lead Americans (as a contemporary French journalist said) to be overinformed and underreflective about national and world events. Obtaining a background on change, therefore, is not an assimilation of facts or events but rather a perceptual skill, a broad-based knowledge of the past, an ability to assess that past, as well a desire to comprehend events rather than be at their mercy, or at the mercy of inertia (doing nothing) for that matter.

Historically, public administrators have been bureaucrats, which essentially means they are more likely to be reactive rather than causative agents in the course of events. I see no likelihood of that tendency changing, no matter the tempo of socio-economic developments. In fact, many bureaucrats lead a dual existence, or have split perceptions, being comprehensively aware of change while at the same time pragmatically or politically passive. They are also taxpayers who may harbor ambivalence about funding social services! When funds are abundant or at least available, public administrators are not so much daring as expansive in their expenditures. The inverse requires, of course, the opposite — shrinkage or elimination — though that is naturally more difficult, especially if imposed on an administrator rather than by choice. Since leisure services are relatively recent in the public domain, the parks and recreation profession has not encountered or endured expansion and contraction very often. Thus, in the ups and downs of institutional survival we are relative novices. We have not amassed the expertise for dealing with these cycles or fluctuations as have older bureaucracies that have endured them. We tend, rather, to be over-anxious, aggravating an historically poor social memory even further.

At one extreme, the postwar world economic system is dramatically changing or failing: at the other, local taxpayers will no longer fund human and social services with unquestioned fidelity and generosity. Whatever perspective is used, recreation and leisure services, since these are invariably viewed as communal amenities, will experience resource cutbacks sooner and more drastically than most other social/human services. For those who came of age after World War II, and especially those who are even younger (notably the readers of this text), American middle-class affluence has been generally continuous and unparalleled throughout our relatively short history. The terms "forthcoming" or "available" were often used to describe the resources to meet our needs, with more land or other resources apparently infinite. Waste has been a constant variable of our history, from the earliest settlements in New England until the last decade or two. Therefore, when the elimination of waste, or the depletion of resources, was suddenly called shortages or cutbacks, this was often interpreted as a tempory constraint:

> Although we often tend to associate ecological changes primarily with the cities and factories of the nineteenth and twentieth centuries, it should by now be clear that changes with similar roots took place just as profoundly in the farms and countrysides of the colonial period. The transition to capitalism alienated the products of the land as much as the products of human labor, and so transformed natural communities as profoundly as it did human ones. By integrating New England ecosystems into an ultimately global capitalist economy, colonists and Indians together began a dynamic and unstable process of ecological change which had in no way ended by 1800. *We live with their legacy today.* When the geographer Carl Sauer wrote . . . that Americans had not yet learned the difference between yield and loot, he was describing one of the most longstanding tendencies of their way of life. Ecological abundance and ecological prodigality went hand in hand: the people of plenty were a people of waste.[2] (Ital. added)

I have resorted to an ecological perspective for two reasons, and not simply for analogy. Firstly, an ecological framework, for the analysis of any finite system, is the broadest one can use; thus, it is intellectually and ethically useful for discussion. Secondly, our profession is considered one of the prime providers, guardians and users of these natural resources, without which the cultural component of organized recreation would be drastically curtailed or even eliminated. It, therefore, behooves us to review more traditional concepts of shortage and waste, realigning ourselves with an ethic (long in development) in which a reverence toward resources prevails. It is important, that is, to avoid nostalgia for any golden age of public leisure services — or of this country's destiny for that matter — coming to terms instead with a honing of activities and resources that respects the actual state of national and global resources. I have also intentionally simplified this discussion, in line with ethical or moral precepts, to avoid any discussion of political strategies or realities, since an ecological framework presupposes a communal world view, where each special-interest group might seek to serve some goal broader than itself. A cubbyhole or myopic approach to change is destined to fail, or at best delay the social mechanisms that have begun to redefine our scope of action, narrower certainly, but perhaps more meaningfully. The challenge, as always, remains ours.

MAJOR CHALLENGES

The size of state and local government as a percentage of the gross national product has started to shrink. In 1980, state and local government employment grew at a slower rate than the U.S. population for the first time since the end of World War II. In 1981, the numbers showed an absolute drop . . . 'The tax revolt has stopped state and local spending dead in its tracks and is now actually bending it backwards.'[3]

The most publicized constraints public (and private) administrators face are, first, financial, then (and this is far less flexible) the depletion or deterioration of most natural resources. Since both these limitations dramatically affect the provision of leisure services, perhaps more than for any of the other human services, it is important to view these changes as an overall pattern, a matrix of several factors impinging, interacting or competing with each other. Thus, there are several urgent areas of concern that affect public agency administrators. Many of these are problems that the postwar generation did not have to contend with or could easily ignore. Although these challenges are burdensome, in that one is rarely prepared for change, they are a relief in one respect, since they put an end to some of the irrational expansiveness of hectic postwar development. In many ways, the generation that is being trained to eventually guide this profession (and country) has been forced to come to terms with limitations, realigning the profligate atmosphere of the past four decades (indeed of U.S. history itself) with unavoidable global and planetary realities.

Ecological and Environmental Deterioration

By far, the most pervasive change is ecological and environmental deterioration. This is not simply one aspect of change among others, but forms the very basis, or is the precipitator, of all transformations, and is thus the foundation for any social indicators discussed. There has been an abundance of data and warnings on ecological/environmental matters published in the past twenty years that it is difficult to be thoroughly conversant with even small sub-areas of concentration. But, fortunately, expertise is not as essential as the awareness that, indeed, there is a widespread problem. Ecosystems, from the minute to the major are no longer to be unquestioningly manipulated, though it surprises me how many public administrators still attempt to avoid this universal constraint, assuming their little drop in the bucket will not poison the well.

It is ironic, for instance, that leisure service professionals often have little knowledge of or control over the natural resources under their jurisdiction. That is, we hold or exercise little control ourselves over questionable manipulations of these resources. It is essential we go beyond being merely custodians of natural resources and seek to be guardians as well. As guardians, we would then be obliged to better understand the scientific and legal aspects of resource use (and abuse) as well as demonstrate an ecological perspective in all our professional activities. This control should not be forfeited to other professionals. We might use them as consultants or co-adjudicators, but we would direct rather than follow.

While much control over natural resources rests with various governmental units, we should seek to influence their policies and decisions, instead of observing or unquestioningly implementing them. Otherwise, we conspire in the accelerating destruction of the natural resources so essential to our profession. One must become either part of the solution or remain a part of the problem itself.

What we also lack as a profession, and more so as a society, is an ethic of responsibility about individual actions, especially their impact on larger systems or communities. The roots of this carelessness, or ignorance, are deep in our economic and social history, which makes it difficult for individuals to affect larger systems in unselfish ways. Everyone for themselves has disastrous consequences when viewed socially or ecologically, as these past decades of formidable deterioration have shown. We must rid ourselves of knee-jerk reactions to Big Brother or totalitarianism, and realize that many actions are not private, especially when enacted in the public sphere. As public administrators, we can begin to outwardly portray less the behaviors of the rugged individual and more the qualities of the conscious ecologist. Since our profession is responsible for or guardians of many natural and cultural resources, we are in an excellent position to slow the pace of change (often for its own sake) and, frequently, deterioration.

Financial Limits
Although often receiving more fanfare and publicity than ecological/environmental constraints, the financial limitations encountered in the past ten to fifteen years are definitely secondary. Money has symbolic value only, serving as a medium of exchange,

whereas natural resources are actual, and in many instances not renewable or replaceable. Thus, when we speak of financial limitations, we must examine what is behind the money, what it symbolically represents. Invariably, it is ecological constraints we encounter again, as the cost of most goods and services continue to rise. An ecological-economics is more to the point, where the roots of financial insolvency or revolt can be traced to the international scope of resource demands and availability.

Most economic predictors indicate a slowed rate of economic growth for the rest of the century, while political activity presages a continued taxpayer refusal to fund social and human services as these have been funded during the past decades. A combination of slowed economic growth, and the passage in nearly all states of tax- or budget-limiting legislation, places leisure services in an unprecedented financial and political bind. And the situation is likely to worsen. The slow-down in economic growth is not in and of itself likely to affect per capita income because of a concomitant reduction in population growth and an increase in two-income families. It is the pressure of inflation, and the undeniable political hostility toward "free handouts" that seriously threaten the viability of leisure services in the future.

It is, therefore, important that public administrators avoid the wishful thinking that more money would cure our problems, or that a disproportionate amount of energy devoted to obtaining funds other than property taxes might be the solution. The solution, or certainly a goodly portion of it, is in conservation. Since our profession strives to encourage conservation, or support conservationists' efforts, it is time to apply this ideal to ourselves. The loss of public funding from property taxes, or at least its drastic decrease this past decade, is a long-needed reform, despite the immediate hardship or threat this imposes to leisure services. At such times, the habit of historical perspective is valuable, not only in the sense of weathering a storm, but in comprehending the roots of socio-economic change, its inevitability, and where we might best concentrate our energies and the resources that remain.

Civil Rights and Gender Equality

Although economic constraints might be expected to retard the momentum of other social changes, it is historically significant that the pressure for rights and gender equality continues unabated, not dampened in the least by the loss of funds. The greater the financial and ecological constraints, the more minority groups and women seek an expanded role in social and economic decisionmaking. For the first time, these groups will not recede in the face of any "larger" crisis, since many believe the roots of such crises lie with those who are presently in power at all levels of society.

I recall the prediction of the American Indian sage, who said his people would regain their land once the white man had fouled his nest sufficiently to make it uninhabitable for himself. Their historic patience is based on a faith in natural justice, in retributive justice actually: that their due would become more evident through time. Their expulsion from positions of power and influence, and that of women and other minority groups as well, is reflected in the impoverished destiny of this naturally rich continent. The viewpoints of these apparent outsiders or incompetents are essential to our well-being. Any public administrator would be committing professional suicide to pretend otherwise.

During the 1960's, we were often criticized for failing to serve all groups equally. We were also questioned about the lack of minorities and women on our staff or in leadership positions in the profession. Without governmental demands for affirmative action, our employment record would be even worse. Sexual, racial, and ethnic groups must be represented in our organizations in comparable proportions to their numbers in society. Though many object to quotas, there is no surer way of assuring an equal and just number of minorities in the leisure services.

We must also give up the belief that minorities will automatically share and assimilate our goals and values. As businesses diversify their product mix to make themselves less vulnerable to market fluctuations, we must diversify our staff and leadership to make ourselves more responsive to the actual conditions in which we live and work. Perhaps the most important impact on our organization and values will be the influence of women. There are few women filling leisure service positions presently, though this is a career that attracts many women to university study, and a profession that serves females in abundance. Not only must we actively recruit women for leadership positions, we must overcome any deep-seated male attitudes of superiority.

Labor Force Changes
Related to the ongoing struggle for civil rights and gender equality are the ongoing *changes in the American labor force* — its number, composition, values, and aspirations, including the shift in unionization from blue-collar to white- and pink-collar workers. A major challenge for many organizations, public or private, lies in their relationship with and responsiveness to employees at all levels. In addition to client satisfaction, leisure service administrators must now concern themselves with employee satisfaction as well.

Employees are composite people; they bring their values, aspirations, and problems to work. Organizations have increasingly begun to contend with these aspects of worker demands, from the executive suite to the mailroom. At all levels of the organization, administrators are encountering new work values, as dissatisfaction with tradition or with hierarchical relationships increases.

This change is basically a generational effect, although the influence of women and ethnic values are involved as well. While the growth rate of the overall labor force is slowing, those with these new work values are peaking in numbers: Workers in the 25 to 44 year-old age group are anticipated to double in number by the 1990's. In addition to sheer numbers, this generation is also considered the best educated workforce in world history. While education certainly constitutes a great asset, it also poses an enormous challenge and threat to entrenched hierarchies.

Employee dissatisfaction is no longer confined to blue-collar workers. In increasing numbers, groups of nontraditional workers form or join white-collar unions. This is one of the most important organizational realities of this decade. The response of leisure service administrators must be toward increased organizational democracy and harmony if they are to avoid a degree of resistance unknown in U.S. labor history.

Expanded, Accelerated Technology
Interconnected with the impact of ecological and economic constraints is the impact of an expanded, accelerated technology. This major factor embraces as well the responsiveness (or lack of it) of technological inventions to human needs, the protection (or invasion) of individual privacy, and other impacts of technology on human lives, communities, and natural systems.

The new technologies, like all technologies, are morally neutral. Whether their advent makes the world a better place or not depends on the uses to which they are put. And that, in turn, depends upon the decisions of many people, especially of politicians, managers, trade union leaders, engineers and scientists. The new technologies, cheap, flexible, dependent on knowledge and information as their main input, can free human beings from many of their current constraints, for instance constraints of resources, geography and location. But the new technologies could also enable those with power to control their fellow-citizens more effectively than in even the most efficient dictatorships of the past. They could impoverish large sections of the community by destroying jobs. The information society will make colossal demands on our imagination and ingenuity and on the capacity of our institutions to respond to new challenges.[4]

168

The purpose of this discussion is not to emphasize hardware, or job displacement statistics, but to describe the parameters of the controversy and impact of technology, so that park and recreation administrators are not carried away by seemingly inevitable technological pressures and demands. Technology does not arise in a vacuum, but is encouraged, subsidized and supported by governments and business: the day of the disinterested, solitary inventor is quickly passing. Science and technology are in profound acceleration now, and are predicted to become more so throughout the remainder of this century, in response to challenges of worldwide economic and military competition.

The impoverishment of communities, which Shirley Williams warns of, has already occurred, a notable example being Youngstown, Ohio, a community that the auto industry (by closing its plant in 1980) threw away as if "an orange peel."[5] This discarding and impoverishing of a community, when no longer profitable to an industry, is perceived as inevitable if the United States is to remain industrially proficient in a post-industrial global society! Automation and technology are not always threats in themselves, but are harmful and potentially destructive when used to displace workers and threaten community survival for purposes of retaining or regaining a questionable economic superiority (e.g., substantial profits). Workers are often told that automated computers and robots can ease and simplify their lifestyle, granting greater leisure, while at the same time these mechanical inventions take away jobs and threaten communities. Ease and leisure then become meaningless and bitter compensations for such losses. These losses are not a likelihood, but a daily reality in this country. The explanations offered are that inflation and reduced productivity have caused these grave problems, with companies helplessly at the mercy of an all-powerful economy.

Technological Impact and Shared Power
The positions are clear, then, between those who seek to rely on advanced technologies in the quest of a competitive edge commercially, despite the cost to individuals and communities, and those who wish to minimize the impact of displacement technologies through compromise, modernization of existing plants, decentralization, shared decision-making, reduced work-time, as well as shared power and profits in the operation of businesses and institutions. To know that eventually most offices and factories will be highly automated is not to accede to that probability, since alternative futures exist if enough citizens consider hegemony (either domestically or internationally) as too socially and humanly expensive to obtain. The "new workers," especially, are potentially more

169

resistant to these changes because of their generally higher level of education, and the comparative leisure that permits them to think and confer, enabling them to perceive and comprehend the forces that contend in reshaping a post-industrial society. In essence, the struggle is whether we are to be economically successful (money-makers), or whether we desire a more authentic, enriched existence, where machines are not dominant.

Finally, there are two aspects of technology that will likely continue as challenges for the remainder of this century: the relationship of technological change and innovation to human needs, and the impact of technology on natural systems. Experience with computers or telecommunications systems ranges from exceptional convenience to the invasion of privacy. If we object to the invasion of privacy, which the computer certainly facilitates, we must more directly object to the agency behind the equipment, rather than attack technology per se. Technology reflects the people who use it, for better or worse. Human error or myopia in the use of any technology pose grave threats to our natural environment as well as our psychological and physical well-being. Since people control technology, the responsibility is ours to safely and humanely use such unprecedented technical resources.

Ethics And Behavior
Finally, there is increased public concern with ethics and behavior in business and the professions, including the quality, necessity, and cost of goods and services, as well as what some consider a decrease in productivity. Private and public organizations operate far more in the public eye than ever before and are increasingly accountable for their products, decisions, services, and behavior. It is becoming more difficult, especially for public organizations, to ignore the demand for accountability and evaluation. Although as a profession we have a good image and reputation among lawmakers and citizens, this reputation may suffer as pressures mount, or as we are tempted to cut corners and make deals to ensure our survival. There is a behavioral "bottom line" to be avoided and a "high road" to be sought.

Since we are integrated with other social and human services, we must never deny these connections to win favor for ourselves. Our ethical position must be that the mix of social and human services presently available is essential in any advanced, civilized society. It is difficult to walk the line between political awareness and involvement, seriously depleted resources, and the maintenance of high operational standards. Whether we deserve public mistrust or not, we will be sure to earn it for any flaw during these times of various governmental scandals. Thus, an ethical standard should be explicit and instinctual in all our professional behavior.

ADMINISTRATORS' RESPONSES

Leisure services administrators must be able to withstand enormous conflicts and pressures. This prospect poses more than a dilemma for managers; it represents the ongoing reality of managing infinite uncertainty. Apart from cataclysms, the next few decades will undoubtedly see the culmination of many issues raised in recent decades, as well as the emergence of other issues barely evident now. Those issues will affect park and recreation administrators, just as they affect other organizations and institutions, public and private. The provision of leisure services, generally considered a positive cultural component in an advanced society, in no way frees our profession from the confusion of social, political, technological, and ethical pressures brought to bear on most organizations these days. It is naive to believe that a public agency can avoid the political and monetary pressures private enterprise faces. In many ways, our direct accountability to taxpayers puts us continually in the limelight.

Change is common to people, particularly in industrialized, competitive societies. The above challenges have been with us for decades, and the leadership qualities needed to manage organizations in transition must include at least comprehension of these broad issues. To successfully administer an organization, an administrator must possess the following attributes:

— Excel in organizational and interpersonal communications, reflecting a humanistic approach to administration. The scope of these skills includes the necessity for creating workplaces that stimulate individual motivation. It is a waste of an administrator's time to ceaselessly motivate others. Through effective, empathetic communication skills, an administrator should counsel, coach, and inspire others to undertake their own self-development, as well as ensure a work environment that in no way opposes or contradicts more humanistic values.

— Be a scientific administrator, using accountability systems such as PERT, Management-by-Objective, Zero-Based Budgeting, systems analysis, or other managerial models and programs. These management and accountability systems are integrated with and rely on computers and other automated devices. Parks and recreation professionals should not avoid these systems on the assumption that our organizations are too simple or small. In a time of increased accountability, the more sophisticated and accurate our planning and record-keeping systems, the greater the chances for improved performance in the face of reduced resources.

— Possess a broad, eclectic intellectuality, not simply technical or administrative. Although technology and automated systems are important, administrators should avoid becoming enamored of hardware. An administrator should obtain an overall knowledge of equipment and systems in an organization without gaining a specialist's or technician's comprehension of these technologies. The tendency to become an administrative technician should be avoided, as knowledge of machines often draws one away from concern with people, a prime administrative task.

— Recognize that what was once considered a long range must be treated in shorter segments. There is nothing sacred about a 20-year-span, especially when a few years can dramatically undermine any analysis with unexpected change. If forecasting is to be more meaningful, administrators must limit their time horizons, while at the same time expanding their imaginative and speculative viewpoints.

— Be proficient in the use of evaluation techniques for staff and service performance, which are necessary for accountability and productivity assessments. The literature on evaluation research methods has grown steadily during the past 20 years, offering administrators systematic programs for appraising an organization's internal and external performance. An administrator need no longer rely on intuition or personal judgment in measuring an employee's ability or a service. Such personal assessments are both arbitrary and subject to poor judgment. They are also subject to challenge, legally and otherwise. Evaluation and accountability, especially in public organizations, go hand in hand. The more select and controlled the evaluation methods, the more likely administrators will avoid conflict with any emergent new work values, or a quality-conscious, resource-limiting public.

— Contribute to and encourage original research in leisure behavior, reducing conflicts between theory and practice in parks and recreation. For the most part, recreation and parks literature is derivative or secondary, drawing on sociology, psychology, business administration, information science, economics, and marketing. While secondary data are not, in themselves, second-rate, there is a clear need for encouraging intellectual leadership and creativity in leisure research.

The logical focus for such research is within the profession, itself, drawing on rather than relying so heavily on other disciplines. To bridge the gap between academics and practitioners, we need skillful and tactful interpreters of research. The snobbery of the intellectual and the myopia of the hands-on practitioner have no place in a progressive organization.

As opportunities for leisure grow, our profession will be called upon to assess the phenomenon of people's diverse responses to more discretionary time. Currently we follow rather than lead in the analyses of leisure behavior. For instance, the popular press is ahead of us in such analyses, whereas in most other disciplines, popularization of ideas follows rigorous research and experience.

The most necessary skills during any transitional period are adaptive behavior and innovation. During these years of resource constraint, what is immeasurably important as everything shrinks is that our imaginations expand. While there are limited funds for traditional services and programs, it is surprising how much money is available to support new and innovative approaches. Unfortunately, many of these ideas and proposals are coming from private businesses and private contracts, or from administrators and employees who desert public agencies for the more lucrative atmosphere of private enterprise. Thus, the need for imagination and innovation in the face of change cannot be over-stressed.

For this purpose, an historical and intellectual perspective are both essential for effective, adaptive behavior. To understand what is happening at any point in time, one has to comprehend what has happened before, what has led up to, brought about, or even caused circumstances to change or evolve. Comprehension is an intellectual habit, best acquired in youth, and invaluable in an administrator. Nothing happens in a vacuum, but is related and inter-related to a variety of factors and circumstances that must be intellectually and personally perceived. It is not enough to accept what others posit as causes, as much as to determine these for oneself, or at least to go beyond the rhetoric of simplistic analyses or rationales that might be forthcoming. Although political realities are unavoidable, the larger constraint that parks and recreation faces as a profession is broader than politics, involving an ecological and ethical framework that takes us beyond self-interest and reactionary fear, that seeks to avoid anxiety, defensiveness or political conservatism. Change is inevitable, a form of temporal evolution essential to any vital existence. We should not regret what time has brought to bear, but rather confront the realities of the present day with the weight of history ever in mind, an inspiring burden in many ways if one has taken a proper measure of the centuries; taken the time, that is, to comprehend the forces of change in one's own time.

REFERENCES

1. Adams, Henry. *The Education of Henry Adams: An Autobiography*. Boston: Houghton-Mifflin Co., 1918, p. 249.
2. Cronon, William. *Changes in the Land: Indians, Colonists, and the Ecology of New England* (New York: Hill and Wang — a division of Farrar, Straus & Giroux, 1983, p. 170).
3. Carlson, Eugene. "Drive to Cut Local Tax Rates Thriving Despite Challenges," *The Wall Street Journal*, August 24, 1982, p. 33.
4. Williams, Shirley, *Politics is For People* (Cambridge, Mass.: Harvard University Press, 1981), reprinted in *Across the Board* (July/August 1981), p. 14.
5. Lynd, Staughton. "Reindustrialization: Brownfield or Greenfield?" *Democracy*, vol. 1, no. 3 (July 1981), pp. 22-36.

Chapter Thirteen

Marketing: Neither Snake Oil Nor Panacea

John L. Crompton

An increasing number of managers in recreation and leisure settings are recognizing that marketing offers a useful framework for explaining and integrating many of the decisions involved in the delivery of services. However, few have had formal training in marketing with the result that there is a lack of insight and understanding of marketing principles and techniques. The simplicity of the marketing paradigm has a beguiling attraction. But beneath this attractive veneer there is a complex web of issues which require much greater consideration, knowledge, and understanding than they are generally accorded. Marketing is often presented as nirvana, a cure-all and solution to all management problems. However, much of what is currently applied under the name of marketing in this field is snake oil with minimal redeeming qualities.

This article discusses four common conceptual fallacies. They represent misapplications of marketing principles or techniques which are widely found in the field. These usually occur because the principles have been gleaned from a *superficial* awareness of what has been done successfully by others either elsewhere in the public sector or in the private sector. In some instances the principles are deemed to have failed because either the expectations associated with them were unrealistic, or because there was a failure to recognize the differences between the objectives and operating environments of public leisure agencies and the commercial sector. After discussion of the conceptual fallacies, the article concludes with two common failings of implementation. In these instances, there may be a good understanding of marketing principles, but lack of experience in implementing them has led to relatively disappointing results.

FALLACY #1: MARKETING IS A EUPHEMISM FOR HUCKSTERISM

Although recreation and park professionals would be indignant at any suggestion that they were hucksters, many of them have unwittingly adopted the approach of the huckster in their efforts to engage in marketing. Marketing is two things. First, it is a philosophy, an attitude, or a perspective. Second, it is a set of activities used to implement that philosophy. Many recreation and park personnel, like the huckster, embrace neither the philosophy nor the full set of marketing activities when they try to engage in marketing.

Acceptance of the philosophy is a prerequisite for successful implementation of the set of marketing activities. The philosophy of marketing is simple and intuitively appealing. It is a philosophy which states that the social and economic justification for an agency's existence is the satisfaction of customer wants. It entails establishing a way for an agency to learn about customer wants, and use that information internally to create marketing programs that will satisfy targeted clienteles.

This philosophy has evolved over time as the understanding of marketing has passed through various stages in recreation and parks field. These stages may usefully be labeled the product era, the sales era, and the marketing era. Although these three eras evolved sequentially, all three orientations still exist in the field today.

Before the mid 1970's, public leisure agencies typically practiced what might be called "minimal marketing." They assumed that demand for a service would grow simply because they were offering it well. Thus, they did not consciously perform marketing functions. Their thinking was, "why should we have to sell a worthwhile service?" Agency personnel were *product oriented*. That is, they were primarily concerned with producing more of what they produced, rather than with selling the services they produced, or trying to learn what clients wanted them to produce.

Many recreation and park agencies are still product oriented. They regard their primary task as providing the facilities, services, and programs which they consider to be the most appropriate, as efficiently as they are able, within the resources that they have available. Their orientation is inward looking, dominated by programs, presumptions and processes. There is a presumption that it is "our agency" rather than a recognition that it is the residents' agency. The extent to which a service meets people's needs is not carefully considered. Such agencies feel they have fulfilled their obligation by simply making the facilities, services, and programs available.

A product-oriented agency decides what it can do best, or what it wants to do, and then offers internally designed programs and services to the public. Such agencies hope that the public accepts the programs and services and uses them. Services are offered on a "take it or leave it" basis. If there is no response to an offering, these agencies are likely to conclude "the citizens missed a fine opportunity: we did our best."

The following are typical manifestations of a product-oriented agency:

— Day camp or summer programs which operate 9:00 a.m.-4:00 p.m. This gives the program staff who come in at 8:00 a.m. an hour to organize their program materials and equipment before the children arrive. Similarly, they have an hour at the end to tidy up after the programs before they leave at 5:00 p.m. These hours are convenient for the staff but very inconvenient for client families in which both parents work 8:00 a.m.-5:00 p.m.

— A swimming pool at which loud, "heavy metal" pop music was played over the speakers. The pool was a small, shallow neighborhood pool used exclusively by parents and their young children. Teenagers went to larger more exciting pools elsewhere in the city. When asked, "why is pop music being played?", the response was "Because the teenage lifeguards like it." The musical preferences of the users were not considered.

In the late 1970's the situation changed for many agencies. When resources were no longer as plentiful, economic necessity forced them to go beyond the prevailing product orientation. There was a growing awareness of the need to adopt a more aggressive posture and persuade clients to use services in order for agencies to develop a constituency which would oppose budget cuts. The primary emphasis shifted from a product orientation to a *selling orientation*. However, emphasis was still on the service being sold rather than on the benefits that clients wanted to receive.

Agencies adopting a selling orientation decide what programs should be offered and make an effort to aggressively sell and promote them to potential users. Instead of merely offering programs and services on a take it or leave it basis, selling-oriented agencies attempt to convince prospective clients that they should participate in the program or use the service.

It is at this stage, when agencies ask "What do we want to offer that we must convince clients to support?", that similarities with the huckster emerge. There are three primary characteristics of a huckster. These are:

1. Hucksters will sell anything they can, irrespective of whether or not it satisfies a client's wants or needs. They think of what the sale will do for them and their agency, rather than what it will do for their clients.

2. Hucksters focus on the immediate sale. They do not think about repeat business from their clients.

3. Hucksters will use intensive promotion in an effort to persuade a client to use a service, even if it is not to the client's advantage to do so.

In the 1980's some agencies recognized the limitations of this selling orientation and moved one step higher up the evolutionary ladder to embrace a *marketing orientation*. There was a recognition that what an agency thinks it produces is not of primary importance to its success. What a client thinks he or she is buying determines what an agency is, what it produces, and whether or not it will prosper. Success is not determined by the producer, but by the consumer.

Central to the concept of marketing is the attitude, "produce what you should sell," rather than, "sell what you can produce." Thus, an agency is more likely to succeed if it tries to understand people on their own terms, "looks through its clients' eyes," identifies what the client wants, and then provides it. A well-known marketing aphorism states: "To sell Jack Jones what Jack Jones buys, you have to see through Jack Jones' eyes." This increased responsiveness to the client has led to the emergence of the marketing or consumer-service orientation in a few recreation and park agencies.

Embracing the marketing concept requires agency personnel to determine what client groups want, and then to provide services that meet those wants. Consider the question, "how do you get street kids into recreation centers?'' This is a selling orientation which is doomed to failure. The marketing answer to this question is, "You don't: you get street kids into street programs." Whereas selling and hucksterism focus on the needs of the seller, marketing focuses on the needs of the buyer.

The aim of marketing is to make selling superfluous. The aim of marketing is to know and understand the consumer so well that the product or service fits him and sells itself. Ideally, marketing should result in a customer who is ready to buy. All that should be needed then is to make the product available, i.e., logistics rather than salesmanship, and statistical distribution rather than promotion.[1]

Hucksters seek to achieve their sale through intensive promotion activities. In contrast, marketers recognize that promotion is only one of six primary marketing activities (Figure 1). It is the tip of the iceberg, the most visible marketing activity and the one which arouses public attention. The marketer recognizes that each of the other five, which are below the surface and not as visible, are just as important as promotion.

Figure 1

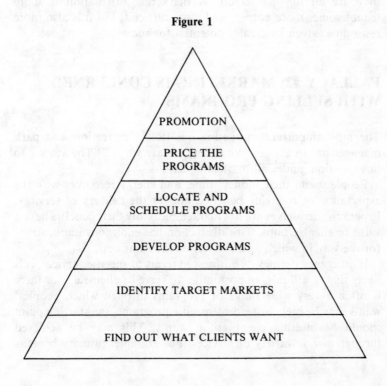

PROMOTION

PRICE THE PROGRAMS

LOCATE AND SCHEDULE PROGRAMS

DEVELOP PROGRAMS

IDENTIFY TARGET MARKETS

FIND OUT WHAT CLIENTS WANT

Two key questions provide insight into the extent to which an agency and its personnel are marketing oriented. The first question is: "why do we do what we do today?" The answer should be, "Because our clients want these services and regard them as high priorities." Unfortunately, the real reason frequently is product oriented: because the agency has always offered this service, or because it is what the staff have been trained to do and they feel comfortable doing it.

The second question is: "What are we doing differently than we were doing five years ago?" If the answer is "not much," then the agency is probably product or selling oriented because citizen needs and priorities are likely to have changed in the last five years.

A marketing orientation may appear to be expensive because it requires an investment of time, money, and personnel to find out what a clientele wants. However, a marketing orientation is, in the long run, likely to be less expensive than a product or selling orientation because it enables an agency to act responsively and minimize ineffective allocation of resources. The failures of an agency can usually be traced to its neglect of the basic wants and desires of its potential clients. As Aldous Huxley is alleged to have pointed out, it is not very difficult to persuade people to do what they are all longing to do. A marketing orientation is more troublesome, more bother, and more difficult, but it is also more rewarding, given its greater potential for success.

FALLACY #2: MARKETING IS CONCERNED WITH SELLING PROGRAMS

The most important marketing question a recreation and park manager has to ask is "What business are we in?" The answer to this question guides all marketing actions.

People spend their money, time, and energy resources with the expectation of receiving benefits, not for the delivery of services. Programs themselves are not marketable. Only their benefits have a value to client groups. This distinction has enormous implications for the way in which agencies define their business.

If an agency defines its business in terms of specific services, it is likely that it will miss opportunities to serve its clientele, for there is often a very wide range of programs through which peoples' wants may be met. Instead of specific programs, the starting point should be meeting client group wants. This may be achieved through a wide variety of services. For example, primary benefits people seek from using libraries are specific information, entertainment, and general-knowledge. These benefits can be facilitated through a wide variety of programs and services including books, movies, lectures, discussion groups, and trips. It is not the book that is important, rather it is the information, entertainment, or general-knowledge benefit derived from reading that the consumer seeks. By offering other services in addition to books, libraries are able to reach more citizens and to better satisfy their existing clientele.

Those agencies and personnel who think of their job in programmatic rather than benefit terms are vulnerable to being afflicted by marketing myopia.[2] Too often public leisure personnel define their business in product terms such as athletics, aquatics, parks, or arts. These are programs and the marketing concept implies that our business should be defined in terms of the consumers' wants.

Charles Revson, who was responsible for building Revlon cosmetics into the thriving enterprise it is today, is reputed to have said, "In the factory we make cosmetics. In the store we sell hope." Women use cosmetics but they do not buy them; they buy hope. In a like manner the recreation and park agency develops and offers services and programs. Participants purchase benefits; the programs are simply a means to an end. These benefits may include such things as social interaction, prestige, relaxation or escape.

Taking a benefits approach helps us to understand that different people may participate in the same program but they will often be seeking different benefits. Similarly, people may be able to derive similar benefits from very different programs. Thus, instead of specific programs, the starting point should be meeting client group wants.

At a recent workshop, aquatic personnel were faced with a problem: attendance at the city pools had declined substantially in the past three years. The workshop participants identified their primary market as teenagers and, after discussion, determined that the primary benefit which teenagers sought at the pools was socialization. The workshop participants divided into groups for a brainstorming session in which they were asked to list all the program ideas they could think of which would facilitate socialization for teenagers in a swimming pool. After the 30 minute brainstorming session, 142 different program ideas emerged. The participants were surprised and elated at the result. Many of the ideas were new, exciting and feasible. Once they had moved away from defining their business in such product-oriented terms as "managing an aquatic facility" toward the marketing-oriented definition "facilitating socialization opportunities for teenagers," a new range of programs emerged which offered potential for reversing the attendance decline.

While the definition of an agency's business should be sufficiently broad to provide room for growth to respond to the changing environment, at the same time it should be narrow enough to give specific direction to the agency. If the definition is too broad, then it may not be useful for giving direction. For example, little useful guidance is likely to be gained by a manufacturer of lead pencils defining his or her company as being in the "communications business.". There must be a common thread linking existing offerings and proposed new services. Expansion into service areas outside the leisure field for which the agency has no "feel" and no management expertise is unlikely to lead to client satisfaction or to enhance the agency's reputation.

In defining the business we are in, the key question is not, "What is the best way that benefits can be facilitated through the traditional leisure services we have offered given the resources available?" That would be a myopic approach. Rather the appropriate question to ask is, "What is the best way that sought benefits can be facilitated, given the resources available?"

All services are likely to decline over time, no matter how vigorous their present growth. In the present environment, a leisure agency's interpretation of the business it is in is not likely to be useful for longer than five to seven years. Changes may occur either because client group wants and the benefits they seek change, or because competitors offer more effective programs for servicing those wants. If the agency does not change by reexamining its business definition and adjusting its program offerings accordingly, that agency is also likely to decline. In asking "What is our business?" agencies also need to add "And what will it be in five to seven years time, given the changes in the environment we can presently discern?"

Answering the question "What business are we in?" in terms of the benefits rather than programs or services has at least four important advantages:

— It ensures that an agency retains its focus on client groups and does not become preoccupied with programs, services, or the agency's internal needs.

— It encourages innovation and creativity of programs and services by suggesting that there are many ways to service similar client group wants.

— It stimulates an awareness of changes in client group wants as they occur, and hence services are more likely to remain relevant.

— It will probably lead to a broader definition of the role of the agency and thus contribute toward keeping its services abreast of society's wants.

FALLACY #3: MARKETING IS PRIMARILY AIMED AT GENERATING REVENUES

To many public recreation and park people, the term "marketing" is anathema because they perceive it to entail a shift away from the primary mission of encouraging human growth, toward a focus on generating revenues. Marketing frequently connotes an activity associated with the commercial sector's goal of maximizing revenue. Certainly, the crisis which stimulated an interest in marketing by many public leisure agencies was a reduction in operating revenues from tax sources which became prevalent in the late 1970's. It is no coincidence that at this time most of the agencies which are seriously committed to adopting marketing concepts and tools are located in those areas of the country which have been most subjected to financial constraints.

Many recreation and park managers have no formal training in marketing but they are aware that it is considered to be a key ingredient by commercial organizations in their efforts to generate a profit. Thus, marketing frequently is perceived as a promising approach for increasing revenues. However, the equation "marketing = more revenues" is overly simplistic and misses the point. Marketing offers a philosophy and a set of neutral tools which can be used to contribute to the attainment of desired objectives.

In the private sector, the desired objective is profit. However, in the public sector there are other equally important objectives. The "marketing = more revenues" equation is often inappropriate because public agencies are not commercial businesses. Their primary reason for being is not to generate revenue. They are social service agencies which are searching for new tools so they can be more efficient (or "business-like") in achieving their goals.

In the late 1960's and early 1970's considerable controversy was engendered in the marketing literature by the initial suggestion that marketing principles and techniques were appropriate for use by public agencies. Critics argued that marketing should be confined to market transactions characterized by the sale and purchase of goods and services by private sector firms.[3]

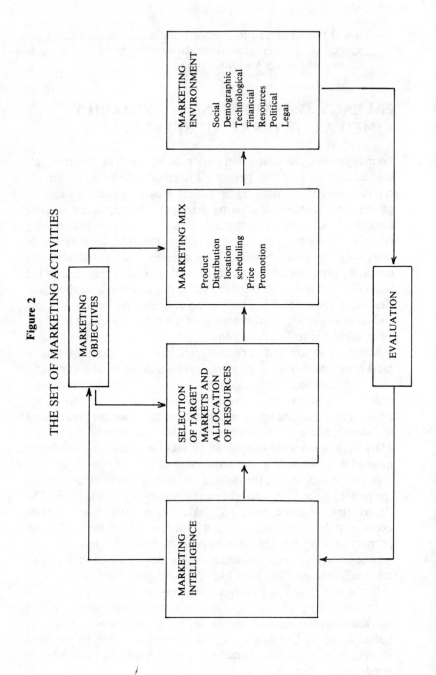

Figure 2

THE SET OF MARKETING ACTIVITIES

MARKETING OBJECTIVES

MARKETING ENVIRONMENT

Social
Demographic
Technological
Financial
Resources
Political
Legal

MARKETING MIX

Product
Distribution
location
scheduling
Price
Promotion

SELECTION OF TARGET MARKETS AND ALLOCATION OF RESOURCES

EVALUATION

MARKETING INTELLIGENCE

Over time it was realized that the set of marketing activities are neutral tools which can be used to assist an agency to achieve whatever objectives it establishes. It is this characteristic which makes their application as appropriate for use by public leisure agencies as in commercial enterprises. Marketing is a process concerned with maximizing the use of scarce resources to achieve whatever objectives a community seeks. The interrelationship of the set of marketing activities is shown in Figure 2 and this model can be applied equally well in a public agency program which yields zero revenue, as it can in Disney World. For example, the market research or intelligence may reveal a need for wellness opportunities for senior citizens.

— The target market is senior citizens and this may be defined more narrowly using descriptors such as age (e.g. under 70 and over 70), income, ethnicity, singles and couples, etc.

— The program may involve physical recreation, mental health, financial planning, nutrition, counselling, or any other subject that contributes to wellness.

— Distribution involves decisions about where the programs should be offered and when they should be scheduled.

— Promotion involves communicating details of the program to senior citizens. How can seniors be effectively contacted? What media should be used? How should the content of the message be structured?

— Finally, price decisions have to be made. The decision may be to charge nothing. However, participants are still faced with a series of other costs they have to pay to use the program. These may include travel costs, the opportunity cost of their time, embarrassment costs associated with difficulties in interacting with others, and the physical effort or personal energy costs expended in getting to the program.

After these decisions have been made, the program is provided and its success is monitored. Feedback serves as market intelligence which may be used to adjust the product, distribution, promotion or price if the service is not as successful as had been anticipated.

The perception of marketing as focusing a department's attention on revenue production rather than human growth reflects a misunderstanding of its potential. Since discovering the marketing paradigm and potential (around the late 1950's), the private sector has been the primary and most visible implementer of marketing the tools used to maximize revenue. Much of the resistance to marketing by recreation and parks practitioners would dissipate if there was an understanding of this. In 25 years time the connotations of marketing reflecting revenue production will probably no longer be paramount.

FALLACY #4: MARKETING IGNORES EQUITY

This issue is related to the misplaced tendency to focus on revenue generation when an agency initiates a marketing program. Most recreation and park professionals have failed to understand the important role of equity in implementing a marketing effort. All organizations strive to be efficient, effective and accountable, but in addition public agencies have to be equitable. There is often a conflict between efficiency and equity that is overlooked. The two concepts are defined in the following paragraphs.

Efficiency
Because efficiency is relatively well understood and has been discussed at length in the literature, it will only be briefly defined here.[4] Efficiency measures the amount of effort and expense involved in offering a service and is concerned with the question, "To what extent does the agency produce the output as inexpensively as it could?" It is measured in such terms as attendance days per dollars expended, subsidy per person in a program, acres maintained per dollars expended, or number of hours of operation per dollars expended.

Equity
The concept of equity has been explored in detail elsewhere,[5] but it has received relatively little attention in the recreation and parks literature. For this reason, a more extensive exposition is provided here.

In every resource-allocation decision there are winners and losers. Equity addresses this issue by asking the question, "Who gets what?" Because subjective, normative judgements are involved. There probably cannot be any "right" or "wrong" concept of equity. Indeed, three fundamentally different models of equity are commonly recognized. These are equal opportunity, compensatory equity and market equity.

Equal Opportunity is the most widely accepted model of equity. Its wide acceptance is probably a reflection of traditional values which recognize equal protection under the law. Equal opportunity entails allocating equal amounts of services to all citizens, regardless of need or the amount of taxes paid.

Compensatory Equity involves allocation of services so that disadvantaged groups, individuals or areas receive extra increments of resources. The operational objective of this equity model is to increase the compensatory role of public leisure services so opportunities for the underprivileged are improved. This requires that resources be allocated in proportion to the intensity of the need for them.

Market Equity entails allocating services to groups or neighborhoods in proportion to the tax or fee revenues that they produce. Market equity draws from the prevalent allocation model used in the private sector. Full commitment to this equity model would mean accepting the principle that citizens are not entitled to equal access to outlets, and that citizens' needs are not relevant unless they are backed up by dollar votes in the marketplace.

Demand Is An Inadequate Surrogate: it is not an equity model. However, it is included in this discussion since it is used extensively as a surrogate in lieu of a real equity model. The demand approach allocates resources on the basis of consumption and/or vociferous advocacy or complaints. It cannot serve to guide the allocation of services in a predetermined, agreed direction. Rather it is a complicating factor — a pragmatic, reactive approach to which agency personnel and elected officials frequently resort because it is administratively convenient. Its use is likely to result in an unpredictable and inconsistent set of winners and losers. Demand may lead to adoption of a pattern of services reflecting any of the three conceptual alternatives discussed previously, or it may fluctuate inconsistently among them.

The Dilemma

Traditionally, most recreation and park agencies have adopted either the compensatory or equal-opportunity equity models. However, as part of efforts to be better marketers, and the assumption that marketing implies increased revenues, many agencies are adopting higher prices. In so doing they are moving away from the two traditional models toward the market-equity model. The market-equity model enhances efficiency and responsiveness of resource allocation. Citizens do not receive services they do not want, nor are they required to pay through the tax system for what other citizens use.

This approach offers the most efficient use of resources but it ignores the social benefits associated with compensatory equity and equal opportunity. If market equity was completely adopted, then individuals and groups deprived by the operation of the private sector would be disadvantaged by the public sector as well. Adoption of this model would mean that, over time, recreation and park services would be substantially reallocated from poor neighborhoods to wealthier neighborhoods and directed exclusively at those client groups that can afford to pay.

The basic question is "What is our mission and whom should we be serving?" In the private sector, organizations usually give priority to developing target markets most likely to be responsive to particular offerings. However, park and recreation agencies seeking to service multiple potential markets face a dilemma. Potential client groups have differing abilities to pay and each market segment is likely to have a different price elasticity of demand. This means that when a price increase is imposed, it has a different impact on the quantity of demand from each group.

Which potential target markets should be given service priority? Is the agency to act like a private organization and ignore those segments likely to be less responsive to service offerings if prices are raised? If the role of the public agency is to facilitate delivery of a particular service to as many constituents as possible, and to complement the private sector, then public-sector agencies should be concentrating efforts on these less-responsive segments, leaving the more responsive segments to the private sector.

The development of marketing efforts aimed at relatively unresponsive target markets is a problem unique to marketers in public agencies. Indeed, the most critical question facing park and recreation agencies often is not how to develop marketing efforts to optimally service relatively responsive target markets, but rather what strategies are most useful for attracting those who are apathetic, disinterested, or reluctant to use service offerings.

Although many recreation and park services are initially justified on the basis of their compensatory contribution, their relative success often has been evaluated not in equity terms, but rather in terms of their efficiency and to a lesser extent their effectiveness. Two reasons have contributed to this inappropriate evaluation priorization. First, because efficiency measures are more readily available than equity measures, it is expedient to measure recreation and park service delivery only in terms of efficiency. Second, budgetary constraints have forced agency managers to increasingly focus upon efficiency. The situation was summed up by one agency in these terms, "We do not render services to collect money. However, it is now necessary for us to collect money in order to render service." In time of financial scarcity it is relatively easy to secure increases in cost efficiency by changing from a compensatory to a market-equity prospective.

Park and recreation agencies have limited financial resources, which means that they are required to address the dilemma of who should be given priority in service delivery. The resolution of the dilemma is dependent upon how an agency interprets what constitutes a fair or equitable allocation of resources.

It is not sufficient to evaluate services only in terms of efficiency because this may result in an equity model deemed to be inconsistent with an agency's mission. Thus, although it is likely that an additional number of dollars may generate more recreation attendance at a program, and hence be more efficient if invested in one neighborhood, greater equality of opportunity or greater compensatory results to disadvantaged groups may be produced if it were spent in a different neighborhood.

Consider the case of a large traditional outdoor swimming area in a major metropolitan area operated by a public agency. Annual attendance was 120,000 visits. There was an admission charge of 50 cents and the facility was a break-even proposition over the course of a season. The agency then leased out the facility to an operator who transformed it into an aquatic theme park. The admission charge was increased to $8.50. In its first year 400,000 visits were recorded and the agency received $330,000 from the lease arrangements. This was cited by the agency as a good example of the results of its marketing effort. But is it?

In terms of efficiency the agency has made a quantum step forward since the facility accommodated many more visits and net revenue increased by $330,000. But what about equity? Has there been some displacement? Are the users the same people who used it before the lease or have those people been squeezed out by the new high prices? If there has been displacement is the efficiency/equity trade-off justified? There may be other inexpensive aquatic opportunities offered by the agency in close proximity to which displaced clients may gravitate. Further, the $330,000 revenue increase may enable new services to be developed for low-income groups for which previously there was no funding.

If efficiency/equity trade-offs such as this swimming pool situation are to be rationally addressed, three steps must be taken. First, an agency must determine what business it is in and adopt a statement of mission and objectives which will serve as the guiding criterion for all subsequent efficiency/equity trade-off decisions. Second, the impact of price on equity needs to be assessed by conducting surveys which monitor changes in user characteristics when price increases are implemented. Third, accurate cost-accounting data are required to measure the relative efficiency of delivering a service by identifying all costs associated with it.

Public-sector marketing is concerned not only with efficiency but also with equity, and it is this latter concern which is the primary characteristic distinguishing it from marketing in the private sector. Many public leisure agencies are rushing into marketing and seeking greater efficiency, but they are ignoring equity implications. This is not consistent with the mission of public agencies.

IMPLEMENTATION FAILINGS

In some instances there may be a good understanding of marketing principles, but lack of experience in implementation may lead to relatively disappointing results. Two such implementation failings concern the role of marketing specialists and the use of needs assessments.

There is often a belief that to have a successful marketing program an agency must have marketing specialists who are charged with the task of marketing the agency's offerings. Such specialists are likely to be helpful but it is important that they continue to engender awareness of the basic principles of marketing among all staff as well as to undertake specific assigned project responsibilities. If this general education function does not occur, then the hiring of a marketing specialist may be a step backwards rather than the anticipated quantum leap forward in the marketing effort.

The establishment of a marketing division may be an immediate signal to all other personnel that marketing is no longer their problem or responsibility. Thus, two percent of agency personnel have a marketing title and a marketing function, while 98 percent may comfortably return to being product oriented.

The attitude and actions of all personnel must be marketing oriented. A single employee may be the only contact a particular client has with an agency. Hence, in that client's mind, the employee is representative of the agency. A single person who is not client oriented can totally undermine the efforts of a marketing specialist. For example, if the person answering the telephone is abrupt or discourteous, that contact is taken by the client as being representative of the agency's orientation.

Figure 3

Letter to *The Miami Herald* 6-30-83

DESTROYING CASTLES IN THE SAND

It was a Saturday afternoon on the beach in Larry and Penny Thompson Recreational Park. My wife, my daughter, my toys, and my sunburn were on the sand amid a crowd of children and parents.

First, came the lifeguard — you always feel the presence of a lifeguard there because every 10 seconds you hear his whistle or megaphone making the beach sound like Victoria Station in England. But people do not mind; they seem to like being bossed around on the beach.

The lifequard asked me to destroy the sand castle that my daughter and I were building: "It is not allowed on this beach" he said seriously. My sand castle was nowhere near or in front of a lifeguard station.

Then two park rangers came and again asked me to destroy my sand castle. I told the rangers that I didn't believe there was such a rule. If there is such a rule, no sign said anything about it; therefore the public has not been properly warned. They threatened to put me under arrest.

Imagine the headlines: "Man Arrested for Building Sand Castle." The tourists will eat it up, one wonderful season after another.

So I asked the rangers to destroy the sand castle themselves — if they really believed in the rule. Without really knowing it, I challenged them to make absolute jackasses out of themselves, and they did. Yes, one ranger destroyed my sand castle in front of my daughter.

After a confused conversation with the rangers, the manager of the place, and others, no one had succeeded to give me a rational reason why sand castles are not allowed on the beach. I detected a fear of possible legal problems, but not a word of reason.

The saddest part of this already-sad story was the apathy of the public around me. It was the look of giving up, the expression of silent fear; fear to say "no" to authority; to say "enough."

This is a rule that is ridiculously stupid, yet you have hundreds of people lying there, taking it quietly, defenseless, beaten.

Consider the lifeguard's actions described in Figure 3. The lifeguard was intent upon enforcing an ordinance which prohibited excavation of county property. He interpreted this ordinance to include building sand castles at the water's edge. Clearly, the lifeguard was more concerned with enforcing the regulations than with sensitively responding to a client's needs.

Those staff members who deal face-to-face with client groups are likely to be the first to learn about changes in client wants and to be most responsive to them. They provide key feedback. If they are not client oriented and sensitive to the implementation of the set of marketing activities, it is unlikely that the agency's marketing efforts will be successful no matter how many marketing specialists are hired.

Needs assessments is a second area in which there is frequent implementation failure. They have too often been perceived as the panacea for answering all questions which confront an agency. Although there is general agreement that needs assessments should form the starting point of a marketing effort (Figure 2), it is important to emphasize that needs assessments cannot replace professional judgement; they are an aid to it. Indeed, it is a dangerous fallacy to suppose that the answer to every marketing problem is more or better information.

Not all new service offerings, for example, ought to originate in response to a stated or obvious need, because needs are likely to be at least partially defined by citizens' knowledge of the availability of services. There was no recognized need by consumers for powdered potatoes, xerography, computers, or windsurfing until they were available.

Preferences articulated by client groups must be mediated by sound professional judgment as to how sought benefits may be facilitated. The consumer is *not* king. If consumers were kings (or queens) they would know exactly what they wanted and demand it. However, we are all prisoners of our experiences. There is a well-known adage which suggests that "people don't know what they want — they only want what they know." Consumers have a limited set of experiences and are unlikely to assertively request anything beyond those experiences because they are not aware of benefits which may accrue from other potential offerings. For example, before the automobile was invented people knew they wanted transportation but could not articulate these sought benefits in terms of a motorized vehicle. The introduction of various outreach programs such as meals-on-wheels and home health services probably resulted from client groups identifying needs and professionals developing the services which met those needs.

Consider the following example:

If symphony orchestras always played what a majority of audiences requested, then Beethoven's Fifth Symphony and Tchaikovsky's *1812* Overture could well be played every week! If the audience were to be given exclusive decision rights as to what is performed, then there is a danger that the classical music repertoire would be relatively narrow and sterile. However, human beings seek optimal arousal. They respond positively to new stimuli which avert boredom. Thus, there is likely to be a positive response to new artistic experiences of which audiences were previously aware.[6]

Complete disregard of the potential for professional insight to improve service delivery options means a very substantial resource in which the public has invested would be ignored. The distinction is subtle between a product orientation and discounting overt popular preference in favor of professional judgment. The essential difference is that the latter approach focuses on the long-term needs of the consumer, while the former approach exhibits no genuine effort to be responsive to consumers' behavior or needs.

Interpreting the numerical responses to needs assessment surveys requires considerable skill, experience and judgement. For example, if 70 percent of citizens prefer project A compared to 30 percent who prefer project B, does that mean project A should be given highest priority? If A is a swimming pool and there are several already in the city, whereas B is an ice-rink of which there are presently none, then a decision to proceed with the rink rather than the pool may be the right decision in order to provide a balance of leisure opportunities. A public agency has to serve pluralities and not yield to the tyranny of the majority, which is what happens if needs assessment numbers make the decision rather than professional judgement.

The challenge is to study client groups, listen to them, observe them, and then to *interpret* their input and behavior. It is inappropriate to implement what consumers ask for on every occasion, because this usurps the opportunity to take advantage of professional expertise.

Needs assessments are valuable tools for gathering information which should lead to better decision making. They offer illumination and insights but they do not make decisions. Some administrators see needs assessments as a costly and time-consuming process that does not produce benefits sufficient to justify their expense. This is an inappropriate generalization often made by managers who believe that experience and intuition are the only tools useful for decision making. Both are necessary. While it is true that needs assessments cannot eliminate uncertainty, it is equally true that they can substantially reduce uncertainty. Failure to do market research of this type will lead to managers remaining "permanently superficial" about the client groups they seek to serve.

FINAL THOUGHTS

The philosophy and set of tools which comprise marketing having proved to be an effective framework for the delivery of commercial sector services. Interest in their use in the public sector emerged only in the late 1970s. Marketing is in its formative years in the recreation and parks field. It suffers from frequent inaccurate conceptualization and inexperienced implementation. Marketing is in the early introduction stage of its life cycle. Trial and error and fine tuning are normal manifestations when launching any unfamiliar tool or product.

Marketing emerged in the commercial sector in the late 1950s and it is only in recent years that it has been widely understood. Given this experience, it seems reasonable to hypothesize that the widespread diffusion of a real understanding of marketing in the public recreation and parks field may take another decade. As the concept diffuses, we can look forward to a consistent rise in the quality of the performance of recreation and park agencies.

REFERENCES

1. Drucker, Peter F. *Management: Tasks, Responsibilities, Practices*. New York: Harper and Row Inc., p. 64.
2. Levitt, Theodore N. "Marketing Myopia," *Harvard Business Review*, July-August 1960, pp. 45-56.
3. See for example Luck, David J. "Broadening the Concept of Marketing Too Far" *Journal of Marketing*, Volume 33, July 1969, pp. 53-55.
4. See for example Hatry, Harry P., et.al. *How Effective Are Your Community Services?* Washington D.C. The Urban Institute, 1977, p. 217, and James M. Buchanan, *The Public Finances*, Homewood, Illinois: Irwin, 1970, pp. 452-453.
5. Crompton, John L. and Charles W. Lamb, "The Importance of the Equity Concept in the Allocation of Public Services," *Journal of Macromarketing*, Vol 3, No. 1, Spring 1983, and Crompton, John L., "Are Your Leisure Services Distributed Equitably? Leisure Today," *Journal of Physical Education and Recreation*, April 1982.
6. Searles, David P. "Marketing Principles and the Arts", in Mokwa, Michael P., Dawson, William M. and Prieve, E. Arthur (eds.), *Marketing the Arts*. New York: Praeger Publishers, 1980, p. 69.

Chapter Fourteen
Prevailing Winds and Bending Mandates
Tom Goodale

> Who has seen the wind?
> Neither you nor I.
> But when the trees bow down their heads
> The wind is passing by.
>
> > Christina Rosseti

How frequently we allude to natural forces when referring to human affairs. We speak, for example, about political or social climate and we speak about the winds of change. We even offer each other prayers: "may the wind be always at your back." If, like a weather vane, one turns with the wind, it will always be at your back. It will also always dictate the direction in which you point.

The thesis here is a simple one. In adjusting to the prevailing winds, the park and recreation movement appears to be changing course. There is a need, then, to renew the dialogue of mandate and purpose; that is a dialogue of bearing, course, and heading. That is particularly needed with reference to public park, recreation and leisure services since they reflect our collective judgement and perhaps our collective purpose. A useful start would be to cut through the fog and haze of argument and rationale which has come to cloud our vision.

WHAT GOVERNMENT IS BEST?

"That government is best," said Thomas Paine, "that governs least." Modern reactionaries, parading slogans such as "getting government off our backs and out of our pockets," are rather fond of what Paine said, or at least that part of what he said that points downwind. The upwind part is more to the point. "Government, like dress, is a badge of lost innocence." Since that statement tells us more about ourselves than we care to know, we turn our backs on it. Innocence is pretty shaky ground for most of us to stand on. In the absence of evidence of recaptured innocence, the reactionary stance is hopelessly naive and wrong-headed. There is, in fact, much evidence suggesting we will have more government rather than less.

Pluralism or Nihilism

One principal reason is that the value concensus, which makes the social order self-regulating, is breaking down. We have prided ourselves on the emergence of pluralism by which we mean people derive their values from a variety of sources. The sources are human institutions such as the family, community, religion and education. But since these institutions have lost much of their influence, our value sources are not so much pluralistic as atomistic. There may already be too many value orientations, which is very much like having no value orientation at all. That is the inconvenient part. Similarly, we have come to pride ourselves for our tolerance which may be the convenient term for indifference. There is as much evidence of the one as of the other.

We seem to be experiencing what Geoffrey Vickers, in a seminal article, referred to as moral inversion and ethical nihilism, which he summarizes in these words:

> Moral criticism of human institutions is frequent: the acceptance of social constraints by the free individual is rare. This moral inversion is inconsistent with the survival of an increasingly interdependent society. Statements of human rights must be replaced by statements of human responsibility if we are to make the world viable.[1]

Over 50 years ago, Will Durant also noted the serious sociopolitical hazards when individuals are content merely with freedom in their gonads and in their cups.[2]

Legitimate Needs

The second reason why we may have more government rather than less is that there are needs to be met and they are costly ones. For example, the population aged 65 and over, now about 9% of the population, consumes about 35% of the cost of our health care system. Soon that population will be 12%, absorbing about 50% of the costs of health care. And the costs of that system are increasing dramatically. Similarly, the demographic forces of a baby boom followed by a sharply reduced birth rate means serious problems with our pension system around the year 2010 as the first of "the big generation" reaches 60 years of age. Currently, about six workers contribute to public and private pension plans for each person drawing from them. Soon, that ratio will be three to one.

196

Other major problems include the imperatives of international economic competition and the temptation to replace labor with technology, adding to the problem of income distribution. Too, a slowly growing economy will not produce enough "new money" to meet growing needs. Thus, existing financial resources will have to be redistributed, a task which seems beyond our present government.[3]

For cities, the gap between needs and resources is growing steadily. Long standing problems such as stable or shrinking tax bases and limitations on taxing powers remain, and despite all efforts to broaden the tax base, property taxes still provide the same proportion of municipal revenue as they did 80 years ago. Further, we are now painfully aware of the vast sums needed to repair and replace the aging infrastructure of most of our older cities: as much as 60 billion dollars during the next 10 years for New York City alone. Finally, the withdrawal of grants by senior levels of government raises serious problems. A number of students of the distribution of local government services have noted that without grants and transfers, services for the poor, including parks, recreation, cultural facilities and libraries, will be seriously curtailed.[4] Kenneth Boulding suggested that grants were either gifts motivated by love or tributes motivated by fear.[5] In that light, limiting or ending grants for such reasons as restraint or local autonomy sounds hollow. It has its convenient side — not paying tributes out of fear — and its inconvenient side.

Institutional Inertia

A third reason why we may have more rather than less government is that individuals and agencies involved in the provision and distribution of public services are not immune from the penchant for ideas and courses of action which are convenient. Nathan Glazer has noted that our intended services objectives may be distorted not only by the search for revenue but also by the search for "a comfortable, secure and well paid position with government."[6]

It is often noted that collective life, that is life in organizations, is conservative and bent on maintenance of the status quo. The present order, even if it doesn't work, is preferred to the potential disorder which often, perhaps necessarily, accompanies change.

The normal state of an organization, therefore, as observers everywhere testify, is caution. It gets along by doing what it has always done. Before it does more, its bureaucrats, like other rational people, want to know whether they will benefit. Organizations exist to benefit their members. They have come to terms with their environment, terms that reflect existing relationships, not future ones. So they deal with the presenting problems, as social workers say, and do not go looking for trouble.[7]

Blame it on the Economy
This is one of our most convenient rationalizations. Just as individuals often use lack of time as the reason (read rationalization) why they do not participate in this or that activity, so agency personnel use lack of money as the reason for not providing this or that service. Even in the most vibrant economy, no government, agency, or individual can do everything. So the issue is not financial resource limits but rather priorities: the issue is not economics but political and social values. One must view with equanimity any claim of financial limits in a world in which 1.5 billion dollars *per day* is spent on the ability to make war — all for the purpose of not having one.

No doubt there is an economic limit to the total amount of goods and services that can be produced. But within that limit, social and political values determine what is produced and who gets it. A budget, therefore, is an allocation based not on dollars but values: it converts resources into human purposes. By using the economy as a scapegoat, we avoid the central question of human purpose, including the purpose of government involvement in service provision.

Lacking a self-regulating social order which is the only real alternative to government regulation and control; confronted with growing needs to be met now and well into the future; unable to shake our penchant for the convenient, our inertia and our scapegoating, we have arrived at the point where the purpose, rationale, and mandate of public services may be bending. Perhaps that has already begun; certainly there is much potential for it.

GRADUALLY BENDING

That becomes evident when we examine the concepts and processes which shape the provision and distribution of local park, recreation and leisure services. These include concepts such as equity, merit goods and efficiency and activities such as reducing costs and increasing revenues. Though treated separately here, it is clear that these concepts and activities are inter-related. The starting point should be the concept of equity since a principal function of government is the allocation of resources. Private, market mechanisms do not always result in "fair" resource allocations. Public recreation services began for the purpose of making resources, thus opportunities, available in forms not otherwise provided and for people who would not otherwise have access. This is the fundamental rationale for public involvement in this field.

Equity
Equity can be conceived in several ways and there are different views about which type of equity measure to use. Still, some types are considered clearly inadequate by most. Five types can be identified and arrayed along a continuum according to the extent of resource reallocation resulting from each. From least to most redistribution they are: market equity; demand; equal input; equal opportunity; equal result.

Market equity is the receipt of goods and services exactly in proportion to the amount paid. It accomplishes no redistribution. Since those who can afford good services get them, the affluent benefit and the poor remain poor. Most students of government reject this criteria.[8] Yet in establishing fees and charges, the cost of comparable services provided by the private sector is one of the guides we use.

The second criteria, demand, is usually rejected, too. It is a pragmatic but often inappropriate criteria as it tends to be reactive and to favor those who are comparatively well-off: reactive since agencies react to demands placed upon them; favoring the comparatively well-off since they are the ones who know how to extract benefits from the agency.

Equal input, which is sometimes mistakenly taken to mean equal opportunity, is perhaps the most frequently used criteria for assessing the equity of service distribution. While it assures more of a redistributive effect than market or demand criteria, it is regarded as inadequate by some. According to Lineberry and Sharkansky, "Money spent is a commonplace, but not very good, index of service quality or productivity."[9] Wolman is even more emphatic, arguing that, "input equality is a ridiculous standard."[10]

Market equity and demand as criteria for service distribution are rejected in principle by nearly everyone although there is evidence, though perhaps not awareness, of their informal application in practice. These criteria are measurable although that is never easy. Equal input is also, with difficulty, measurable and is for many an acceptable limit to income transfers and redistribution efforts. Yet it is apparent that to equalize opportunity for many segments of the population a more than equal share of resources may be required. Opportunities for the poor, the handicapped and other sub-groups of the population may become equal only with a greater than equal share of resources.

Equal outcome or result is recognized as being unachievable and undesirable. On the other hand, there is a need to realize positive results from the public provision of services. As with any intervention, if it doesn't make any difference, why bother? There are some persuasive arguments for equity criteria which include measures of opportunity but also measures of results in desired directons.[11] The problems we confront in pursuing these equity objectives are two.

The great difficulties we have in measuring opportunity and result is one about which several writers on the subject comment along with the consternation of not being able to detect results from increases in inputs. The second difficulty with opportunity and result measures of equity is that additional resources are required. Disparities in opportunity and result cannot be reduced by lowering the top but by bringing up the bottom; a leveling up rather than down. The criteria of opportunity and some indication of positive effect are the appropriate ones. But given the problems of measurement and cost, along with the real possibility that many service providers do not accept these criteria, equity is often judged from the standpoint of input, or worse, demand and market criteria.

Cost Reduction

Among the principal cost reduction strategies has been the adoption of means to save time and energy. Saving is realized with, for example, increasing use of computers to handle a variety of administrative and clerical functions; changing maintenance schedules; conserving gas, oil and electricity via design, monitoring, automated controls and the like.

A second principal cost reduction strategy is the increasing use of volunteers. There are, of course, other desirable objectives realized through the use of volunteers but philosophy and necessity are conveniently wedded here. To some extent we have come to incorporate self-service in the notion of volunteerism, in contrast to the traditional meaning of service to others.

A third principal strategy, an extension of volunteerism in some respects, is privatization of service delivery and contracting for service. Unquestionably, some local services can be delivered more economically this way. In the park and recreation field, some services have been effectively privatized. In Ottawa, Canada, for example, grants to neighborhood groups for the maintenance of natural ice skating rinks saves the city an estimated half-million dollars annually with no apparent decrement in service. But unlike other cost reduction strategies, privatization of recreation services is a contentious issue, however widespread the practice.[12]

Those opposed to privatization often base their opposition on such grounds as decreased service quality or at least decreased control over service quality. But another concern is that not only control but also public resources are turned over to those groups and agencies who already possess the resources, including organizational and administrative skills, with which to provide service. Too, privatized service is typically self-service, which is good. But services for those without resources must be assured somehow and that is a collective responsiblity.

Efficiency

Cost reduction is one way of increasing efficiency as long as the quantity and quality of services available is not also reduced. One cannot be opposed to that. Still the efficiency criteria may result in distorting objectives. Often, efficiency is mistakenly accepted as a measure of effectiveness, perhaps in part due to the lack of effectiveness measures. Efficiency and effectiveness should not be confused. Efficiency tells us if we are doing things right: effectiveness tells us if we are doing the right things.

Attendance, for example, is often used as a measure of effectiveness. In fact it is a measure of efficiency in that user days or hours is part of the equation by which unit costs (such as cost per hour of participation) and efficiency criteria are calculated. Where unit costs are low, fees and charges can also be low and still realize significant cost recovery or revenue generation. The consequence of such decision making for the sake of efficiency results in agencies concentrating energy on doing what is easiest. Consequently, ease rather than need comes to shape service provision. Such an outcome, however unintended, seems quite contrary to the objectives of public service.

While efficiency is a means of increasing production, it is not, or at least should not be, a criteria for determining what is to be produced. Further, production must be thought of as separate from, even if simultaneous with, distribution since the amount produced is independent of who receives it.

Where people are involved, one should not worship too long at the altar of efficiency. The work force was sometimes sacrificed at that altar, first by exploitation and more recently by displacement. Dictatorships are more efficient than democracies. And where leisure and recreation are concerned, efficient time use may simply mean we are all more harried. Something important may be lost in playing the Minute Waltz in thirty-seconds, or speed reading the novels of Mark Twain in a single evening — without laughing once.[13]

Merit Goods

The concept of merit goods provides the rationale for establishing fees and charges and, presumably, the amount charged. Briefly, there is no charge for public goods (available equally and indivisibly to everyone) and the charge for private goods (individuals benefit in proportion to amount paid) should cover the full cost. Unfortunately, despite the wide gamut of recreation and park services with which local government agencies are involved, there are very few services for which benefits are purely public or purely private. Most are "merit" goods which convey some public benefit and some private, but the task of determining how much is which is a very difficult one.[14]

It is generally recognized that in the provision of park and recreation services a minimum level of service quantity and quality should be available to all constituents. This, in a sense, is the level of service provision that would be considered public goods. Presumably, there would be no charge for such services. After such provision has been assured, merit goods can be provided and fees and charges established to recover the private goods portion as opposed to the portion which benefits the public and thus deserving public tax support. Obviously, the greater the private goods portion, the greater the revenue that can be generated and the greater the distortion of the public service objective. Until the basic level of service has been defined and opportunity to avail oneself of it assured to all constituents, merit and private goods, thus fees and charges, are premature.

Valuable as is the merit goods concept, there are other problems with it which are not always evident in the parks and recreation literature. One problem is that the merit goods argument is as valid for the private sector as for the public sector. There is some public benefit in people having recreational experiences regardless of the agency involved in its provision: fitness maintained at a private facility yields as much public benefit as that maintained at a public facility. In addition, the public benefit which merits support is, presumably, the same whether the individuals supported are rich or poor. The problem, of course, is that the public receives no benefit — the merit goods portion — from anyone who cannot pay the fees and charges for the private benefit portion. The situation is not unlike that of matching grants; the amount of the fee or charge being the portion which qualifies the grantee to receive support. So the rich get richer.

A third problem with the merit goods concept results from the difficulty of determining the public and private portion of a good. Consequently, the amount of fee or charge imposed depends on

202

criteria other than merit, such as whether or not the fee is politically palatable, is appropriate vis-a-vis private sector pricing, is not so high as to result in lost revenue, and is not based on full cost because of the difficulty of determining full cost. So fees and charges are based neither upon merit nor cost. Consequently, we don't really know how equitably public resources are distributed though it is apparent that market and demand criteria are used in establishing fees and charges.

Increasing Revenues

Since tax support for park and recreation services is not expected to meet much more than inflation induced cost increases and sometimes not even that, increases in financial resources must come from contributions of various kinds or from revenue generated by services provided; that is, fees and charges. Contributions can come in the form of transfers or grants from a myriad of government and non-government sources, and increased efforts have been devoted to tapping those resources. More is being done to secure commercial and other sponsorships, local foundations to support park and recreational services are pursued more aggressively, and many other initiatives have been taken to secure additional financial support.

However, the principal source of increased revenue remains fees and charges. For several decades, this has been a contentious issue in the field of parks and recreation. In recent years, however, philosophy and necessity have shifted the issue from whether or not to charge to how much to charge. The other side of that coin is determining the level to which tax revenue should subsidize activities for which charges are made.

With any fee there will be some who do not have the ability to pay and who, therefore, will be excluded from the opportunity unless some special provision is made for them. In virtually every quarter, some kind of provision is made for at least some services, if not all. Passes, sponsorships, free periods, reduced fees and other provisions are made to provide access and, hopefully, if not always successfully, avoid stigmatization. Sometimes the poor pay in time (or inconvenience) while others pay in price.[15] Others note the utility of varying fees according to site quality or desirability as a means of distributing demand.[16] Thus both convenience and quality are trade-offs for ability to pay. They also argue that fees may work in favor of the poor for services to which the poor do not have access anyway. But they do not make clear what services the poor do have access to.

It has also been argued that discrimination does not result from user fees based on a study in which attendance at a park did not decrease as a result of establishing a modest parking fee.[17] The study did not address the question of discrimination, however, as the title and text presume. In the main, the fee successfully dislocated a use considered undesirable as the park was used as "a late night hangout for youthful beer parties (sic)." Again, there is no mention of what became of those youth. Clearly, there is no intention to discriminate and every intention to make provision for those lacking the ability to pay the fees and charges imposed. Discriminatory effects result nonetheless.

Virtually all fees and charges revenues come from two sources; participation in programs and use of facilities. Certainly programs and facilities are important agency products, but there are at least two others. One such product is information, including but not limited to agency provided opportunity, along with leisure education and perhaps counselling. A second product is community development, including all those activities described as enabling and facilitating, support services and the like. Much of the professional literature of the past several years has been devoted to the development of these two service products as opposed to direct provision of programs and facilities. By the very nature of information, education and community development services, fees and charges are seldom appropriate and unlikely to produce much revenue in any case. Consequently, perhaps inevitably, fees and charges push us back in the direction of direct provision of programs and facilities.

Among workers in the park, recreation and leisure service field and among the general public, there is widespread agreement on two types of direct provision by the local government agency. One is the provision of parks and open space. The other is the provision of programs and services for those with special needs. A system of parks and open spaces is perhaps the best example we have of a public good provided by park and recreation agencies. Further, those with special needs quite often are those with least ability to pay. The likelihood of subsisting near or below the poverty level increases if one is elderly, non-white, in a female headed service provision may be distorted in the direction of direct services which convey private benefits for those who have the ability to pay.

WHO GETS WHAT?

In the determination of who gets what services, agencies engage in activities which either meet demand or, on a routine basis, attempt to discover needs. Agencies are judged to be reactive according to their demand, in contrast to need, orientation. Pro active agencies are most persistently engaged in searching out needs. Resources for doing so are, of course, necessary. When resources are limited, search activities are too readily abandoned and demand rather than need come to dominate service distribution and delivery decision making. The result has been referred to as "Adam Smith" agencies. Thomas Paine, writing without the encumbrance of Smith's invisible hand, would have called them by another name.

Revenue generation, efficiency, merit goods and related criteria may not only distort agency service objectives but in fact counter them. That is recognized in the literature but sometimes that recognition is unquestioned. According to one recently published textbook, programs which do not at least break even "will not be tolerated; in other words, the 'social welfare' approach to programming is rapidly being replaced by a capitalistic approach."[18] If so, there is no rationale for public sector involvement in park, recreation and leisure services. Similarly, it has been noted that with increasing wealth, the equity standards for service shifts away from market equity and toward the criteria of equal result.[19] The economy of the past several years has resulted in a shift toward market equity; a private enterprise rather than public service approach.

These trends are much in evidence. But trends are not laws, and social realities are not unalterable facts but products of political and social values. In light of these trends and what appears to be too ready accession to them, there is a need to renew the dialogue of purposes and objectives. As Poole writes:

> Rather than engaging in fruitless nickel and diming with local bureaucrats, we ought to raise a more fundamental question: why is local government providing a particular good in the first place?[20]

Answers to that question appear in a number of related phrases like distributive justice, equal opportunity, meeting needs, creating desirable outcomes, serving all constituents, providing public goods, and the welfare of people and community. They provide the rationale for local government services, park and recreation services significant among them.

Nearly a century ago, a void was created in a society dominated by Social Darwinists, Robber Barons, and the leisure class so deftly ridiculed by Veblen.[21] That void was filled by the reformers and radicals who founded the movement which has become public parks, recreation and leisure services. The playgrounds of Boston and Halifax and the community centers of Chicago and Winnipeg may not have recaptured our innocence but they reminded us of our neglect and our obligations to our children, our immigrants, and our poor. Amidst the clamor for smaller and less costly government, we shouldn't forget our origins or the rationale for public service provision. If we want less government, we must have more community. Clamoring won't help; commitment will.

The preservation of endangered species, fragile habitats and magnificent land and seascapes is a human responsibility. These are also public goods, even if the vast majority of people never experience them directly. The human spirit is recreated by the knowledge that we have shared in assuring that that is done. Similarly, as a measure of the quality and effectiveness of parks, recreation, and leisure services, perhaps we should make certain that the last person in our community, the one facing the greatest obstacles and handicaps with the fewest resources, has a good opportunity of having a good day. There is public good in the knowledge that we have shared in providing that opportunity. The welfare of the community is at stake, not simply the welfare of the individual.

> When the Stranger says:
> "What is the meaning of this city?
> Do you huddle close together
> because you love each other?"
> What will you answer?
> "We all dwell together
> To make money from each other?" or
> "This is a community?"[22]

REFERENCES

1. Vickers, Geoffrey. "The Future of Morality." *Futures,* VII:5 (October, 1979), p. 371.
2. Durant, Will. *The Pleasures of Philosophy.* New York: Simon and Schuster, 1953. Chapter XVII.
3. Thurow, Lester. *The Zero Sum Society.* New York: Basic Books, 1980.
4. c.f. Levy, F., Meltsner, J. and Wildawsky, A. *Urban Outcomes.* Berkeley, Cal.: University of California Press, 1974. Mladenka, K. and Hill, K. "The Distribution of Benefits in an Urban Environment: Parks and Libraries in Houston," *Urban Affairs Quarterly,* 13:1 (September) 1977, pp. 73-94. Farnham, P. "Measuring the Change in Urban Recreation Service Distribution.: The Case of Oakland, California." *Journal of Leisure Research,* 13:4, 1981. pp. 353-364.
5. Boulding, Kenneth. *The Economy of Love and Fear.* Belmon, Cal.: Wadsworth, 1973.

6. Glazer, Nathan. "Toward a Self-Service Society." *The Public Interest,* 70 (Winter), 1983. pp. 66-90.
7. Levy, F. et. al., *op. cit.,* p. 229.
8. Crompton, John. "Are Your Leisure Services Distributed Equitably?" *Journal of Physical Education, Recreation, and Dance,* 53:4 (April), 1982. pp. 67-70.
9. Lineberry, R. and Sharkansky, I. *Urban Politics and Public Policy* (3rd Edition). New York: Harper and Row, 1978. p. 265.
10. Wolman, H. "Urban Public Benefits and Fiscal Retrenchment: The Distributional Impacts of Municipal Expenditure Reductions." In: Rich, R. *The Politics of Urban Public Services.* Lexington, Mass.: D.C. Heath, 1982, p. 123.
11. Levy, F. et. al., *op. cit.*
12. Contracting Out. *Recreation Canada* (Special Issue), 4:1 (February), 1984.
13. William Baumol's suggestion of the thirty-second waltz is well known. The example of speed-reading Mark Twain was Carl Tucker's in "Racy Reading." *Saturday Review,* March 18, 1978. p. 72.
14. For a useful summary, see: Crompton, John. "How to Find the Price That's Right." *Parks and Recreation,* 16:3 (March), 1981. pp. 32-40.
15. Becker, B. "The Pricing of Education — Recreation Facilities: An Administrative Dilemma." *Journal of Leisure Research,* 7:2, 1975. pp. 86-94.
16. Manning, R., Calliman, E., Echelberger, H., Koenemann, E. and McEwen, D. "Differential Fees: Raising Revenue, Distributing Demand." *Journal of Park and Recreation Administration,* 2:1 (January) 1984. pp. 2-32.
17. Manning, R. and Barker, S. "Discrimination Through User Fees: Fact or Fiction?" *Parks and Recreation,* 16:9 (September) 1981. pp. 70-74.
18. Edginton, C., Compton, D., and Hanson, C. *Recreation and Leisure Programming: A Guide for the Professional.* Philadelphia: Saunders College Pub., 1980. p. 18.
19. Crompton, J., 1982, *op. cit.*
20. Poole, R. "Objectives to Privatization." *Policy Review,* 24 (Spring) 1983. p. 105.
21. Veblen, Thorstein. *The Theory of The Leisure Class.* New York: Macmillan, 1899.
22. Eliot, T.S. "Choruses from 'The Rock'." *The Complete Poems and Plays: 1909-1950.* New York: Harcourt, Brace and World, 1971. p. 103.

Chapter Fifteen

Sources of Leisure Styles

John R. Kelly

The observable diversity in leisure is almost beyond description. Let your imagination roam freely enough to picture some of the variety.

— There are countless environments for leisure: natural and constructed, open and confining, quiet and clamorous, inviting and forbidding . . .

— There are the social contexts of leisure: solitary and intensely interactive, silent and communicative, unstructured and rule-intensive, cooperative and competitive, exploratory and role-rigid, strange and familiar, comfortable and threatening, mass and intimate . . .

— There are the mental states of leisure: relaxed and tense, detached and intensely involved, preoccupied and exhibitionistic, free and conforming, excited and bored, seeking novelty or defensive, sensual or rational . . .

And there are the activities themselves: from daydreaming to drag-racing, running to reading, contemplation to conversation, gardening to grappling, painting to parading, and devotion to drinking.

However, much more significant are the orientations of engagement. Exactly the same activity may have different meanings for participants of the same age depending on how they define themselves. For example, a teen may drink decorously in anticipation of adult status-group behavior or rebelliously in defiance of both law and parental preferences. A woman in mid-life may take an evening class as a pastime, an exploration of her potential to begin a career, or hoping to meet interesting others. Retirement men and women may have a familial style of nonwork life or be seeking new investments in personal development. The real issue of style is not what people do, but how they do it.

All this suggests that the variety in leisure styles may be even greater than is palpably observable. Not only are there thousands of activities that may be leisure, but there are the different meanings, intensities of engagement, and intentions for any activity. Leisure is "existential" as decision inaugurates action that creates at least part of its own meaning. It is also social in both its aims and its resource contexts.

This chapter will explore the seeming endless diversity of activities that may be leisure, and the different meanings, intensities of engagement and intentions for any activity. Three models depicting ways of viewing people's activity patterns will be explored as a way of bringing some order to the diversity noted above. This search for order in what people do will be followed by a discussion of why people undertake specific activities or a particular activity in a particular way and what may account for changing patterns over the lifespan. A role-identity model will be used to show that leisure may vary in meanings and environments, in intentions and intensity. And the self we present or hope to become may vary from one context to another. Leisure with its existential element of relative freedom may be that social space for *becoming*, for developing and establishing our personal and social identities. Whether an event or interstitial in a routine of obligations leisure has meanings and consequences that are more than the filling of leftover time.

THREE MODELS OF LEISURE STYLES

The "how" of leisure engagement, the style of participation, may be approached in a number of ways. Three basic approaches have emerged in the literature. Each has some basis in research, but each also has the potential to be deceptive and misleading.

The Stereotypes Model

Stereotypes are a form of convenient classification, based on attaching a label according to some simple and generally observable factor. Leisure stereotypes presuppose that individuals are essentially monothematic in their leisure. A leisure style may be multidimensional, but a stereotype is reduced to a single dimension.

The stereotype of the blue-collar male is that he is so stifled by his work routinization that he seeks only escape in the relatively undemanding leisure of drinking with male companions, watching television (especially contact sports), and occasional masculine excursions into the back country armed to the teeth to slaughter some small animal. The stereotype of the history professor is that he drinks a dry white wine, reads thin books of poetry, listens to string quartets, and carries an umbrella when the sky is clear. Stereotypes of adolescent males focus on sports and sexual aggression; of older widows on loneliness and soap operas; of young mothers on discussing toilet training with other young mothers; and of urban singles on specialized bars and one-night stands.

Of course, we seldom know anyone who fits the stereotype. Further, the support seemingly given by research in the 1960s has largely evaporated. Multi-variate analyses of national samples in North America now report that very little variation in frequency of participation in kinds of activities can be accounted for by discriminating variables of sex, age, income, occupation, education, and race.[1] Once the threshold of real poverty is crossed, remaining correlations are largely limited to the masculine dominance of team sports and drinking in bars, decreases in active sport participation with age, a female reluctance to go hunting, and a relationship between education level and certain elite arts interests.

A major justification for presuming the existence of leisure stereotypes has been on-site observation. However, seeing 1000 teens on a beach does not tell us where the other 100,000 are at the same time. Knowing that 50,000 went to a rock concert on Friday does not tell us what they will do on Saturday. Most of leisure is not that observable, and the stereotypes tend to be based on the very biased evidence of impressions gained at public events.

However, more recently a particular data-reduction method seemed to promise a sophisticated basis for typologies. "Factor analysis" has been employed to group activities or participants based on commonalities in participation. Early results seemed to indicate that participation classifications such as "active-diversionary," "status-based," "sports," "water-based," "backwoods," and even "fast living" might characterize the leisure of identifiable aggregates of people.

However, a number of difficulties soon emerged. Sample differences produced different factors.[2] Heterogeneous lists of activities did not produce the same neat categories as more limited sets.[3] In fact, too often, the same activities were in different factors from one sample to another. Stable factors and consequently valid stereotypes were just not found.

Several reasons may account for the failure to find clear typologies or stereotypes via factor analytic procedures. First, factor analytic results may in fact be misinterpreted. A given individual has a pattern across factors. Thus, stereotyping an individual based on a high score on a single factor is inappropriate. Second, numerous activities don't seem to enter into the factors at all. Many of these activities are among the most informal and accessible for both students and adults. This would suggest a core of leisure experiences that cut across society generally with individual differences in meaning appearing as an overlay or refinement.

This does not mean that there are no single-minded individuals who pursue a "high-risk" sport, fine arts production, or some social group to the exclusion of almost all else. Nor does it mean that there are no significant differences in leisure styles, in *how* people do what they do. But for most of the population, stereotypes are blurred by the commonalities of leisure as well as by the relative diversity of interests and commitments.

The Balance Model
The second model is based on the evident variety of leisure common to most individuals and on the multiplicity of meanings that they find in their activities. The same activity generally has more than one meaning. Those meanings shift from one occurrence to another depending on a number of social and environmental factors as well as the predisposition of the actor. Further, anticipations and satisfactions often change for the same activity as we move through our life course.

Nor do most persons engage in only one kind of activity. Rather, we do a variety of things seeking many different outcomes. We seek to make new friends and deepen ongoing intimacies, to learn new skills and enhance old competencies, to relax and discover excitement, to gain interpersonal acceptance and self-development, to express our individuality and strengthen role relationships, to discipline our bodies and free our imaginations, to think quietly and subject our minds to maximum stress, to risk uncertainty and enjoy comfort and security. In our leisure histories, we have found that certain activities, locales, and social contexts are most likely to produce certain combinations of outcomes for us. So we return to such opportunities when we seek the outcomes.

The balance we seek may change through the life course. Opportunity structures are different for children, students, establishment adults, and so on. We are likely to seek to explore sexuality in adolescence, develop intimacy in early adulthood, enhance the nuclear family in childrearing years, seek personal re-integration in midlife, provide a context for social integration in later years, and employ leisure to begin again when life is disrupted by trauma.

In the balance model, leisure *style* is not a monothematic stereotype. Style is the combination of activities and contexts through which we seek to work out the hierarchy of meanings for leisure at that time in the life course. Leisure style is a pattern, not a label; the shape of a process, not a caricature. Style is the set of investments with the personal and social meanings they have for us.

A leisure style may not be a perfect balance. At a given time, it may tilt toward personal expressivity, family solidarity, physical development, or affective involvement. Thus, according to the balance model, style is multi-dimensioned and changing, with contrast and complexity rather than a single color of unrelieved hue and intensity.

The Core Model

The balance model is a significant step beyond stereotypes. However, there are strong grounds for adding to it. The core model does not deny the diversity and richness of the balance mode. Rather, it adds one simple element: the considerable commonality of adult leisure.

In a national sample surveyed in the United States, 91% read for pleasure, 58% walked for pleasure, 48% swam, 88% watched television, 62% listened to the radio, 83% spent evenings with relatives regularly, and 65-75% engaged in sexual interaction.[4] The point is simply that there are a number of relatively accessible, low-cost, and often home-based activities that most people do a lot. Some involve the media, especially reading and television. Many are social, informal interaction with intimates who most often are those living in the same household. Some are found in the midst of nonleisure settings, a bit of fooling around at work or school or task-inattention almost anywhere.

The best-supported model, then, is probably the "core plus balance" model. The core tends to cross social lines, partly because so much is available and resource-free. It continues in some form through most of the life course. As a consequence, comprehensive participation studies do not locate the marked differences in style we think we observe.

The balance part of the model is most likely to change through the life course. As opportunities, developmental orientations, and social roles change, we seek somewhat different satisfactions in our leisure. Further, that balance is not just the same for everyone. I may not be able to imagine my own life without both music and strenuous physical activity. However, the contexts of sport and arts investments have both changed considerably in the last ten years; and no doubt will change again.

THE LIFE COURSE

Having searched for an explanation of common themes in leisure involvements, further explorations are necessary to account for the changes through the life-course. How are the core and balance affected through the life course? The core may be more stable than the balance for most persons, but neither is untouched by either the passing years of our lives nor by alterations in our social institutions. Leisure must change as our identities and roles change. Leisure in which intimacy is developed and expressed undergoes transitions as we mature, leave the parental home, marry, divorce, become parents, see our children gain their own independence, and either die or are widowed. The social identities accepted and reinforced in our cultures change in relation to age. Insofar as leisure is a major social space for the expression and exploration of who we are, then it must change with age. Here a few examples will have to serve to suggest that complex process.

Social Role Change
The life course involves major changes in all our institutional roles. Only leisure totally segregated from the rest of life can fail to be influenced by our role transitions. In the preparation period of life, we are primarily students rather than producers, dependent members of a family of orientation, and engaged in a number of developmental tasks related to gaining autonomy and independence, establishing personal and sexual identities, and learning the modes of acceptable personal and social interaction. The environments of our lives move from home and neighborhood outward to incorporate school and community. The playyard is augmented by the playing field, the home by other homes, and the neighborhood by the shopping center and other meetingplaces.

The transition to early establishment involves shifts in aims as well as opportunities for leisure. On school-leaving the locales of leisure shift from school facilities and commercial locales to the residence augmented by special events in exterior locations. Companions narrow to intimate dyads in many cases and then expand back to inter- and intra-familial groups. Leisure is more tied to the establishment of institutional roles for those in the early stages of employment and to inaugurating a family. There is a concerted effort to retain and develop some leisure that contributes to personal growth and expression, some leisure that individuals claim as really their own.

Middle years may include a number of traumas and transitions. The traumas include mental and physical health problems for the self or significant others, the death of intimates, disruption of primary relationships in marriage, work crises from disallusionment to unemployment, and geographical relocations. These impact the opportunities, social contexts, and often personal resources for leisure. In turn, a major leisure investment of the self can influence decisions and resource allocation for home, family, and work. The diminution in salience of any one role can lead to concentration on another. Failure in family or work may turn us to a leisure investment for fulfillment and meaning. Loss of a leisure resource, on the other hand, may cause us to reinvest in our families.

The later years of life, a time of culmination and integration for many, may also encompass a loss of leisure resources — financial, social, and personal. Yet leisure and leisure contexts of social interaction may at the same time become more important to our schedules, priorities, and self-concepts. As provider and caretaker roles recede, leisure and intimacy take on even greater significance. The loss of work schedules that have given shape to the week, reductions in income, possible health impairments, and eventual loss of the primary leisure companion for the marital survivors all require reorientations of leisure contexts, resources, associations, and even aims.

Developmental Changes
However, shifts in roles are not the only changes important to understanding leisure styles through the life course. A major contribution of Rhona and Robert Rapoport in the past decade was to begin to combine attention to leisure with both human development and social roles.[5] In our life journeys, we change not only externally, in our roles and environments, but internally in our selfhood. We respond to the social and biological timetables that call for us to change in what we are able to do, how we act and enact our roles, and how we define ourselves.

Some examples have already been introduced. In early adolescence, the child has to learn to define him or herself as a sexual and sexually-identified being, to become a man among both men and women or a woman among significant same and other-sex others. Later retirement years usually entail defining the self as one who *was* a contributing worker and who now finds meaning and identity without that ongoing role.

Other illustrations abound: What about the home and family-invested woman who finds herself without a life companion? How does she redefine herself when so much had been invested in being a supportive homemaker? What about the woman who chooses to make a work identity primary in her life? What about the man who is told that his skills are redundant in the labor market, the youth who can no longer explain himself as still getting ready for some unspecified future, the professional who "burns out" in his or her vocation, and so on?

We are not just units being processed by the computer of life, bytes of information to be sorted by the great machine. We are reflexive, thinking and self-conscious animals who try to make sense of who we are and what we may become. We are always in the process of becoming. That process involves not only social negotiation over who we are; it involves a process of self-definition and development that is never finally fixed. We are always at work on ourselves, on how we can conceive of ourselves, our competencies, our limitations, and our gifts.

The Career of Leisure
Leisure, then, has a career. Like work and family, there is a line of behaviors and actions undertaken primarily for their own sake that we call "leisure." In this career, there is both change and continuity. There are evident changes in opportunities and competencies through the years. There are less-evident shifts in intentions and identities, in the aims of our lines of action and how we define ourselves within them.

In this career of leisure that intersects with our other life careers, style is not static — learned once in the familial culture and retained rigidly ever after. Leisure careers are not isolated, but develop in our "social convoy" — the cohorts who make the life journey through the same historical events and social changes that impact our lives. Further, there are culture-specific attitudes, values, modes of communication, and learned behaviors that make up part of our life and leisure styles. How we present ourselves to others, communicate who we are, would like to be received, and generally negotiate who we are among others — that is, our public leisure styles — are learned in our social convoy and culture. As a consequence, our leisure styles are not quite like those of any other age group when they were or will become our age; just as our own styles change through our life journeys.

A PLURALISTIC APPROACH TO LEISURE

In brief, this means that leisure is neither separate from its historical, social, and cultural contexts; nor is it wholly determined by them. Leisure is both social and existential. We do choose something of the shape and content of our leisure styles, but we choose out of the times and places through which we make our way.

From a pluralistic perspective, there are multiple and interrelated sources of leisure styles. Leisure is always *of* the culture, ethnic. It is developed in a social context and responsive to the social structures and role norms of the system. It takes place in varied environments and is influenced by their location, size, shape, and quality. On the other hand, the variety of leisure cannot be explained in any deterministic model. It is not simply the result of one or two variables — social class, status forces, market provisions, marketing, mass media, or childhood socialization. Identifying sources of leisure styles does not lead to the further step of labelling "determinants" of leisure.

The two dimensions of leisure, the social and the existential, are also the two polarities in the dynamic of leisure styles. If leisure is neither totally segmented and separated from other roles and relationships nor fully determined by them, then some sort of dynamic relationship is implied. This relationship may be conceptualized as a dialectic in which the social and the existential in tension, with both synergy and conflict, produce actual leisure choices and investments. The sources of leisure styles are in this dynamic interplay between the structures of society and the existential self-creation of the individual (Kelly, 1981).

Socialization into Leisure
From the social side of the dialectic, leisure is viewed as learned behavior. We learn not only how to engage in activities and interact with others in leisure settings, but we learn culture-specific values and orientations for our leisure. The ethnicity of leisure is evident in its aims as well as contents.

In a differentiated social system, divided by cultural identification as well as by economic position, we make our life journeys with different sets of opportunities for leisure. Further, we do not all learn the same expectations for our roles. What it means to be a father or mother, son or daughter, student or worker, neighbor and citizen all vary according to just where we are in the society. We learn the same roles in different ways. Insofar as leisure is connected with those roles, then we can be expected to vary in our leisure behavior. We may party, drink, compete and travel; but in different ways. We may argue, flirt, play games, inaugurate friendships, and demonstrate our gender identities; but quite different vocabularies, symbol systems, and presentations. We do not all play our parts in our social dramas alike; and, to a large extent, the differences have been learned in our socialization histories.

Nor do we cease learning at some magic point in our development. Leisure style may be changed, both because of how others define and respond to us and because of how we have come to understand ourselves. Further, what is available to us changes and we learn to adapt to our opportunities.

The Existential Element

Such learning does not negate the existential element in leisure. There is always the "not yet" of life, a looking forward to what we might become. We seldom see ourselves as completed products with nothing more in life than to finish out what is settled and unchangeable. We are always in a process of "becoming," of dreaming, planning and deciding how we may enact our roles in ways that alter and enhance what we may be in the future. We develop lines of action with at least a direction, if not a clearcut plan and final goal.

Leisure may, in some periods in the life course, provide the fullest space for such existential operation. If leisure is the most free of life's spaces, the least determined by necessity and structure, then we may use our leisure opportunities, activities, and relationships to explore the potential of tomorrow. In the interplay between what is and what we might become, we try out new portrayals and new parts. We may explore the possibilities of change. In the relative freedom of leisure, we take the first steps toward selfhood and contexts for living that are not quite like the present. Leisure, despite the centrality of the present experience, may also have a decisive openness to the future.

THE ROLE-IDENTITY MODEL

The crucial issue is just how we bring together these seemingly disparate elements in leisure — the social and the existential, socialization and becoming. What I propose is an approach that combines each side of the dialectic in a "role-identity model." If style refers to *how* we enact our roles, then we need both the role context and the decisive element of enactment in the model. Role identity combines the social context with our self-definition of who we are in taking a role and how we choose to enact it.[7,8] Style, then becomes a melding of role content and enactment a bringing together in the decision process of what we have learned and what we seek to become.

Rather than belabor definitions, we may advance the argument best with three analytical examples:

(1) The party: If a party can be considered a leisure event, then its taken-for-granted and agreed-on expectations for behavior can be assumed to be leisure roles. Depending on the complexity of the party, there may be roles of being host and hostess, intimate helper, familiar friend, official guest, companion of guest, guest of honor, stranger and so on. The interaction patterns, self-presentations,

physical gestures, degree of cooperation, self-placement in a central or peripheral position, and other elements of action are role-related.

However, an individual may be in multiple role relationship with others at the party — spouse to one, boss or employee to another, colleague, partner, neighbor, schoolmate, lover, political opponent, parent, and others. The reciprocal expectations and mutual histories cause the ways party roles are enacted to change from one grouping to another. We may be in several roles at any given time as people move through our milieu.

As if that were not complex enough, each actor may define him or herself somewhat differently in each of the roles. Therefore, in a given conversation, there is the delicate negotiation of presenting an identity that is not inconsistent for those familiar with any of the roles and yet furthers the line of action desired at that time and place. We may present a self that is not too assertive for a work superior, affectionate enough for an intimate, aggressive enough to secure a place in the interaction, and reserved enough to allow for redirection. Every shift in composition of our conversation group slightly alters how we play our roles. The process of the interaction may even cause us to redirect our self-portrayal as our identity takes shape in the event. We may become funnier, quieter, more poised, or less passive. We may play scholar in one episode, good old chap in another, sensitive listener in a third, and aloof superior in a fourth. In the role mix, we retune our presentations to offer identities — role portrayals — that fit our aims in that particular situation. As a consequence, the party becomes the social context for an endless variety of role-identity offerings. In fact, the real content of the leisure event is the negotiation of such role-identities.

(2) Swimming: As another illustration of how role-identities give insight into leisure styles, take the common leisure activity of swimming in a public pool. The various styles of behavior — from lounging near the fence and maintaining consistent distance from the water to exhibitionist diving, a boisterous ball game, or solitary swimming of fifty laps — are more than preferences for different degrees of physical education. Rather, they reflect how identities are presented in that leisure context. Further, the behavior may change if only one new person arrives on the scene. The sequence of life-course roles and related identities is demonstrated by the quite different behaviors exhibited by frolicking children, self-conscious and posing teens, caretaking young mothers, cardplaying students, and disciplined length-counting later-life men and women. The leisure environment, the pool, provides a social context for demonstrating and trying out a wide variety of portrayals that are the basis for the different styles.

(3) Day-dreaming: Even in the movement-free leisure of day-dreaming, we try out identities. We may enter a normally inaccessible environment, acquire previously unattainable skills, and interact with formerly-distant others. The leisure of day-dreaming may leap all kinds of barriers. However, we are still ourselves in some recognizable form. Even more, we transcend some of our normal limitations to try out identities outside our normal reach, relate to others actually continents away, and develop interaction sequences that may never come to pass. Yet, in all this we are still acting out who we would like to be — on the stage of the imagination. And often the portrayal is that of a wished-for leisure style and competence.

THE CENTRALITY OF LEISURE

How does all this come together? We began with the variety of leisure. Stereotyping approaches were rejected in favor of a combination of core and balance that together make up an individual's leisure style. The core of accessible and informal engagements seems to change somewhat less than the balance through the life course. However, both are affected by role shifts and developmental needs. Leisure was then analyzed as a pluralistic phenomenon, neither separate from our institutional roles and cultures nor wholly determined by them. Leisure is both social and existential, shaped by socialization and yet encompassing future-oriented decision. Leisure is experience, with intrinsic meanings rather than productivity aims; yet it is also a social space in which we may work out meanings of selfhood that are crucial to our identities and our primary relationships.

Leisure styles, then, are not the result of some simple set of determinants that can be run through a computer to produce a profile of predicted styles. Again, style is more a matter of how than what, or who we are than what we do. All approaches and models are faulty when they begin with the assumption that leisure is somehow residual, leftover in time and always secondary in meaning. Leisure may indeed be simple rest, a change from duty and a recuperation from strain. But leisure may at some times and places be at the absolute center of our lives, exactly where we develop our most significant relationships, express our most profound emotions and desires, and portray our most crucial identities.

Leisure, then, requires an existential element, that dimension of freedom that enables us to choose — at least within limits — the contexts of our role portrayals. This relative freedom makes possible the investment of self that leads to the fullest development of ourselves, the richest expression of who we want to become, and the deepest experience of fulfillment. This freedom to choose also enables us to relate most fully and expressively to those intimate others central to our lives, to develop trust and communication, to experience histories of enjoyment, and to weave color and texture into our ongoing relationships. Leisure is freedom — sometimes freedom to fill time aimlessly and retreat from ourselves and others; but also to invest ourselves most fully, to seek to become something more than we have yet become, and to add the reality of joy to our bonds of intimacy.

REFERENCES

1. Kelly, John R. 1980. Outdoor Recreation Participation: a Comparative Analysis. *Leisure Sciences*. 3:129-154.
2. Schmitz-Scherzer, R. et al. 1974. Notes on a Factor Analysis Comparative Study of the Structure of Leisure Activities in Four Different Samples. *Journal of Leisure Research,* 6:77-83.
3. Kelly, John R. 1983a. Leisure Styles: A Hidden Core. *Leisure Sciences,* 5:321-338.
4. Kelly, John R. 1983. *Leisure Identities and Interactions.* London: George Allen and Unwin.
5. Rapoport, Rhona and Robert. 1975. *Leisure and the Family Life Cycle.* London: Routledge and Kegan Paul.
6. Kelly, John R. 1981. *Leisure Interaction and the Social Dialectic. Social Forces,* 60:304-332.
7. McCall, George and J. Simmons. 1978. *Identities and Interactions,* 2nd edition. New York: Free Press.
8. Kelly, John E. 1982. *Leisure.* Englewood Cliffs, NJ: Prentice-Hall.

Chapter Sixteen
Lifestyles and Life Cycles:
A Conceptual Programming Approach

H. Douglas Sessoms

The activities and services offered by various park and recreation systems today are not too different from those provided a half century ago. Granted there have been some innovations in the delivery of services and the content of programs but, for the most part, recreation and park agencies continue to do what they have done in the past. The innovations which have occurred have been largely in response to modifications in financial realities rather than resulting from the profession's insight, the changing nature of expressed public demands, or the role park and recreation agencies must play in the post-industrial world.

In many communities it seems the public and the recreation profession have accepted a limited role set for the organized recreation movement, a very traditional and static approach to the provision of activities and services and one not too satisfying for those who subscribe to the humanistic perspective.[1] In others, programming is still an open issue: who to serve, how to serve them, and how much service to provide? May the debate continue, for it bears the seeds of change and may help the profession to further define its role and function.

Much of our professional literature on programming and the delivery of recreation services still deals with the "hows" and "whats" (content and techniques), not with the "whys" (conceptual basis) of our services. Little is said about the assumptions we make about human behavior and the role recreation experiences play in each stage of life. It largely focuses upon the activities of children and youth, the importance of diversionary activity, techniques for improving physical fitness, and the necessity of providing spaces for recreation. More often than not the literature is a discussion of the techniques used by a particular recreation agency in promoting and sponsoring a given program, rather than a discussion of the agency's rationale for the provision of that service or set of activities.

The one major exception to this has been the question posed by some professionals as to whether recreation's primary responsibility is to be that of a facilitator (one who uses resources to assist others to achieve their program goals and activities) or to be a direct provider of services (one who offers activities and programs based upon the professional's perception of need and wants). This choice will have much to do with determining the future directions of the movement and our profession.

If our role in meeting the leisure interests of the public has been limited, it is probably because of the conceptual bases which we have accepted for the services and activities we provide. If our programs are static, consisting largely of the same kinds of activities, and attract primarily the same individuals year after year, we must ask why is that so? Activities are like the tip of an iceberg; they are what we see, but the real determinants of the program are invisible. They are our concepts and assumptions about our services — who we serve, what we serve, and why we serve them.

HISTORICAL PRECEDENTS

To a great extent the organized park and recreation movement evolved out of society's need in the late 19th century to socialize its youth, particularly the children of immigrants, into an urban way of life.[2] Recreation settings and activities were viewed as means to an end — the development of character and the instilling of the "American way of life." It was generally assumed, as reflected in the writings of Lee, Gulick, Curtis and others, that there were inherent values in recreation and play activities. Play was deemed as a natural process and, through the playing of "proper games," children grew and developed into socially useful adults. They assumed the values of society and became "law-abiding citizens." The misuse of leisure and/or the pursuit of "sinful" activities was felt to bring about social and personal problems.

Play as School
Since many of the early activity leaders were teachers, it is not surprising that recreation programs took on a school-like quality. Activities were scheduled in much the same way as teachers scheduled academic subjects. This was especially true at camp or on the playground. The sequence of activities offered each day reflected a logical functionalism. The more energetic sports programs were scheduled for the early and mid-morning hours or in the late afternoon, periods when the sun was least hot. Storytelling and arts and crafts, the more sedentary activities, were programmed in the middle of the day during the periods of intense heat. Children were moved from one activity to another according to a time schedule.

There was little choice in all of this. It was assumed by those in positions of responsibility that they knew more about the consequence of participation than did the participants. Since there were limited opportunities for alternative play activities and since the efficiency of the activity approach did maximize the utilization of limited play spaces, the organized recreation movement accepted this approach as sound and appropriate; so did its sponsors and its participants.

As is often the case, approaches that are found to be functional for one time period become institutionalized and are continued even though the reasons for their original function may no longer exist. When this occurs, the institutions supporting those patterns of behavior develop new rationalizations for their continuance rather than discarding them. It is much easier to justify why something is being done than it is to discontinue the "proven practice" and begin anew. This seems to have happened with the organized recreation movement. Although society's ability to control its environment through the use of artificial lights and air-conditioning negated the rationale for many of the traditional program schedules and activities offered by recreation agencies, it did not radically alter their approach or the content of their service. The playground approach remained even though the playground movement was dead. The same may be said about the profession's understanding of play, its motives and the forms it takes throughout one's life.

To justify our earlier program thrusts, two popular rationales were developed. Both were couched in the "need" theories developed by psychologists and sociologists in the mid 1930's and early 1940's. They have had tremendous impact on present day thinking and programming and merit a quick review.

Programming Based on Satisfying Needs
The first approach held that recreation programs should provide the needed balance between active and passive forms of expression. Interestingly, the emphasis was nearly always on the physical aspects of activity, not its psychological or emotional components. Passivity was always defined in terms of physical inactivity, never discussed from a psychological perspective. Since it was assumed that most workers and children were physically passive in their daily routines of factory and school work, participation in vigorous sport should be encouraged. Artistic and other more passive forms of physical expression were to be promoted for those who expended considerable labor in the performance of their daily work. However, since most organized recreation agencies programmed

primarily for children, few recreation services assumed any responsibility for promoting adult programs, especially those of a non-sports nature. This void was partially filled through the establishment of community theaters and allied art centers, services administratively separate from recreation and parks, thereby limiting the focus of recreation and park agencies. Recreators were supposed to be concerned with youth, sports, and diversionary activities, not with the arts or adult interests nor with those experiences which might be emotionally taxing or psychologically demanding. No one seemed to challenge the definition of active play, to see it in dimensions other than its physical component.

To deal with the issue of program thrust, and to make sure there were a variety of experiences provided within a community, an activity typology based primarily on the major focus of the activity was developed. It was assumed by its advocates that all activities could be grouped under one of four major need headings: physical, emotional, cultural, and social. Furthermore, it was believed that a balanced recreation program should include activities from each of these four types since it was unrealistic to expect any one activity to meet all four "needs." How could participation in tennis, a physical activity, provide cerebral and social satisfaction? Likewise, how could a cultural activity, such as dramatics, accommodate one's physical and intellectual needs? No recognition of the complexity of an activity or experience was apparent; those who supported this approach were only concerned with the major structure of the activity. The simplicity of the approach allowed for its immediate implementation. Programmers could quickly categorize their activities and events and could readily report if they had achieved complete coverage of activities from the four program groupings.

The Balanced Diet Approach
The second major approach to classifying activities was similar to the one just described. It focused on the form the activity took. Activities were viewed as being either sports and games, nature and outings, dance, music, dramatics, social, literary, or arts and crafts. Activities could be placed in any one of these eight types according to the activity's structure or the setting in which the activity occurred. Proponents of this approach acknowledged the potential of any activity to meet various needs such as physical, emotional, cultural and social expressions. However, they assumed that the "complete individual" should participate in activities from each of these categories in much the same way that nutrition experts assume each meal should contain foods from each of the major

food groups. Some writers have coined this classification and program approach as the "balanced diet" approach to recreation services.

According to the supporters of this theory, the benefits derived from any one activity were not as important as the need to participate in a wide range of activities. Although not stated, one of the underlying assumptions of this theory was that balanced growth and development (a socialization ideal) could only occur when individuals experienced and participated in a wide range of activities. Specialization or concentration on one activity or activity group would result in inadequate development — a narrow personality. Though this approach was more holistic than the other — accepting that multiple satisfactions could be derived from one activity — it was no more humanistic. It, too, ignored the theory which holds that leisure expressions are an extension of personality, that the forces which motivate and shape other behaviors are the same which trigger our interest in a specific recreational activity, that individuals do not consciously attempt to balance interests and pursuits but respond to their own psychological gyroscope. The focus was on the activity, not the individual. Scheduling was still more important than were the motives, interests, and judgements of the participants.

For the most part the recreation professionals advocating these classification systems were value-oriented. They believed certain activities were inherently more valuable than others; they relied heavily upon the child development and play theories of their day. They even went so far as to develop hierarchies of activities based upon their perceptions of the ability of each activity to meet specific needs and add to the quality of the individual's experience. J. B. Nash was one of the leading proponents of this hierarchical approach.[3] Nash valued creative expression and thought participation in physical activity was a high form of creativity, much better for one than merely being a spectator, a role couched in his concept of physical passivity. He discounted the emotional and psychological involvement one can experience as a spectator; watching others play rather than playing yourself was almost a "sin." To Nash and those who subscribed to the "activity" school of thought, physical activity was one of the more highly desirable forms of recreation expression. Their influence on recreation programming was significant; their philosophy reinforced the importance of sports as a major program component. Furthermore, their view of the role of the recreation agency further reinforced the public's perception of recreation and sports as synonymous activities.

The late Charles K. Brightbill was an advocate of the balanced diet approach.[4] He strongly urged public recreation departments to provide "cafeterias of activity and services" so individual freedom of choice could be promoted. Brightbill felt recreators should not impose their values on the participant but should encourage participants to develop a wide range of expression so they could "choose" their activities. He held freedom of choice was essential to leisure; the more knowledgeable the individual, the more skills he possessed, the greater range of choices he/she had. The provision of facilities, the offering of instructional programs, the scheduling of activities and events — all of these were important in assuring the public a wide range of opportunities for expression. He felt agencies should offer activities from each of the eight activity groups and should encourage participants to develop skills which would allow them to participate in as many of the activity groups as possible.

Merging Parks and Recreation
These views of programming dominated the thinking of park and recreation professionals during the middle decades of the 20th century. They might have continued to be the dominant view of the profession had it not been for the emergence of outdoor recreation interests in the late 1950's and the merging of the park movement and recreation movement into one in 1965. The amalgamation of parks and recreation, functioning as a single administrative unit at the local and state/provincial level, had tremendous impact on the recreation programming philosophy. Interest in selecting activities according to their major form or primary focus gave way to concerns for the resource in which people engaged in their preferred leisure activities. The critical program issue became one of determining which activities were appropriate for which environments. Interest in the proper sequencing of activities on a playground or community building faded somewhat as recreation and park professionals turned their attention to the carrying capacity and design of recreation spaces. New classification systems such as the one developed by the Bureau of Outdoor Recreation (later the Heritage Conservation and Recreation Service) became the yardstick for measuring program balance. Questions such as "does the park and recreation system have adequate balance of recreation spaces for each of the six BOR categories?"[5] replaced the older one of "does the recreation agency offer activities from each of the eight activity families?"

Concomitant with the merging of park and recreation programs into one administrative unit was the public's general rejection of having its free time expressions highly structured. Its dependency upon public recreation and park services to provide adults and children with opportunities for play declined although its interest in recreation activity increased. In response to these changes the leisure service delivery system grew in complexity as commercial and private recreation interests developed their constituencies. The role of recreation and park agencies was affected by the presence of these "new" elements. To compete, public playground and community building programs had to change; they could no longer rely upon the fixed schedule approach and the program rationales of the past regardless of which classification system was employed. New patterns of life were emerging. New approaches for the provision of services were expected. America was in ferment — student revolts, civil rights marches, anti-establishment protests — its people and its delivery systems were undergoing change.

RECENT EVENTS

In response to these changes and demands for change, the park and recreation profession sought a new direction. In the 60's and 70's writers, such as David Gray, Seymour Greben, and James Murphy, called for a humanistic programming approach. According to them, the recreation interests and behaviors of the public should not be programmed independently of the clients' need for other services; a holistic approach had to be established. Recreation activities and services must be consistent with the lifestyles and the resources of the people involved; no single program approach or planning design could possibly meet the needs of a highly diverse population with its many ethnic and cultural sub-groups. Concerns for process replaced concern for content and structure. What was left was the need for a theory which could give direction, suggest strategies, and assist programmers in making choices about who to serve and in what ways.

In addition to these more dramatic social revolutions, America was also experiencing some basic shifts in its industrial and technological base. These, coupled with two other fundamental but less obvious changes at the time, were ultimately to alter our way of doing business. The latter two dealt with our demographic patterns and social values; all are interrelated and their consequence has been significant.

Changing Demographics

Rather than the United States being a nation of the young as it had been in the 1960's, America in the 70's was becoming a society of adults. Demographers were projecting that the median age in the United States in 1985 would be 32 years of age; more than two-thirds of the population would be over the age of 21.[6] Further projections held that the declining rate of birth which had been recorded since 1957, along with increased longevity, would result in a shift of services. With potentially one-fifth of the population being over the age of 65 in 2033, the need for services for adults and older adults would relegate programs and services for youth to a second class status. Could those approaches and philosophies developed by the park and recreation profession in response to the needs to socialize the young be modified and made appropriate when applied to adults?

Changes in political and social values were also occurring. America was becoming more politically and socially conservative. Rather than depending upon government to provide many of its social programs, Americans were forming mutual aid and self-help groups to provide those services, privately, within their own neighborhood structures. There was a revolt against big government and governmental spending as exemplified by the enactment of Proposition 13 in California in 1978. There was also a growing belief that groups should take care of their own, that big government was incapable of responding to the needs of individuals.[7]

This phenomenon of decentralization has been well documented by such popular writers as Toffler,[8] Naisbitt,[9] and Peters and Waterman.[10] It is behavior characteristic of adults, of interdependent communities and groups. Private entrepreneurs responded to these shifts in behavior, including those of a recreational nature, by offering new opportunities and an alternative to the public sector for the delivery of these services. There was no lessening of interest in recreation pursuits, only a change in the type of pursuits and the management which offered the opportunity. The public was exercising its right to make decisions and if the public park and recreation movement was to remain vital, new theories and explanations of programming and new structures for delivering services had to emerge.

The more successful recreation and park agencies quickly found that if their approach to services was multi-dimensional, and if they served more than one segment of the population, they were in a stronger position for political and economic support. They began to discover the mosaic of lifestyles and life stages which exist in every community, that no one set of services or approach to services could meet the needs of all. This pragmatism may eventually lend itself to the acceptance of a new theory base, one which emphasizes the developmental aspects of adulthood as well as childhood, one which explains diversity and the need for a decentralized approach. It has already encouraged recreators to take a longitudinal view of leisure behavior, to see it in an experiential and qualitative context. The notions of lifestyles and life stages stimulate a holistic and integrated view of people and their behavior.

As stated previously, the park and recreation movement has been largely concerned with the activities of youth and children. Children were perceived to "need" organized play and although there were variations in the play patterns of different groups according to their social class and residence (urban/rural), the pattern was much the same. Young boys were expected to participate in athletics; adolescent girls were to be majorettes, cheerleaders, and good dancers. Racial and sexual stereotypes abounded.

Beyond Rigidity

The services approach was equally rigid. People were expected to come to the recreation centers and parks for their "recreation," to participate in the activities offered by the park and recreation professionals. Recreation and park departments tended to program only those activities and services which were "acceptable" to the larger society. Those exhibiting a lifestyle pattern contrary to the accepted mode were discouraged from participating in many of our public park and recreation programs or, if they did, they were expected to give up their "offensive" style. Park and recreation agencies had been established to aid in the socialization process, not to accommodate those who deviated from the norm.

In general, society has been very optimistic about its ability to shape and modify the behavior of people, especially its young. It assumes that children and adolescents are immature and therefore need direction; adults are presumed to be socialized and are thus able to function on their own, to organize their own associations and groups. Society has relied heavily upon the theories of child growth and development to undergird its approaches to the delivery of services, even those offered adults. Top down structures, highly organized and centralized, characterize most of our public agencies. It is not surprising therefore that very few adults participate in the programs offered by park and recreation agencies other than those, such as athletics and various instructional classes, which lend themselves to these structures. The major exception to all of this has been the public's use of its outdoor recreation resources which, by their very nature, have allowed individuals to utilize the resource without the direct supervision of the park and recreation professional. The social gerontologists and developmental psychologists now tell us that adults, too, need socialization throughout life. The need to adapt to new roles and status are ever present. Each life stage requires adaptation; the findings of both the Rapoports[11] and Max Kaplan[12] dealt with this phenomenon. In their works the Rapoports emphasized the relationship between leisure behaviors and the various cycles through which families move while Kaplan concentrated more on the effects of various external (cultural and environmental) forces upon individual behavior throughout one's lifetime. These and other studies conclude that there is a potential role for recreation and park agencies in the ongoing socialization of adults.

SOME NEW CONCEPTS

It is imperative for the profession to develop program strategies which allow it to work with all segments of the population, adults as well as children. The concepts of lifestyle and life stage have application to those strategies.

Lifestyle Defined
The term *lifestyle* has become popular in recent years. Prior to the counter-cultural movement in the mid 1960's, it was a nice sociological term, used primarily in the classroom. Now, it is viewed as an essential concept for the planning and expediting of various human services, recreation included. In many instances, it is a misused term, a popular catch-all phrase used to explain the significance of behaviors which we do not understand or with which we are not familiar.

Essentially, one's lifestyle is his/her mode of expression. When sociologists speak of lifestyle, they are really describing the behaviors and attitudes that characterize one's existence. It is the way one lives. An individual's behavior is determined by the unique configuration of social values and personal experiences which influence behavior and cause him or her to identify with those who also share those behaviors. The outward manifestation of one's lifestyle includes such items as dress, speech patterns, language, activity selection, living arrangements. Most sociologists agree that there is an integrated core of activities associated with each dominant lifestyle. Lifestyle behaviors result from the interaction of the means by which we fulfill our needs (personality development) and the experiences which reinforce those behaviors (our socialization). Those who share a similar lifestyle tend to form sub-groups which constantly reinforce their individual choices and set their behavioral priorities. These patterns are strengthened by the skills and self-concept which one develops in order to express and benefit from the chosen lifestyle. All of life's experiences are influenced by these learnings, attitudes and personality expressions.

Generally speaking, there is also a dominant force at the center of one's lifestyle. For example, drugs dictate the behavior and social relationships of the drug user. Likewise, dress and appearance dominate the thinking and behavior of those "into" fashion. For the avid camper, camping and camping concerns shape his associations and actions. The books and magazines one reads, the friends one chooses, the priorities one sets are determined by the central focus of the lifestyle. In a work oriented society one's occupation and job dominate; all relationships and activities result from or are affected by it and the status assigned work. In a leisure oriented society, it is one's recreation activities which tend to set the lifestyle patterns. Lifestyles may also center around religion, politics, social relationships or some other potentially all-consuming activity.

Lifestyles are dynamic; one may exhibit various lifestyles during a lifetime. Some lifestyles, such as that of the college student, are characteristic of specific life stages while others, such as those associated with religion or one's ethnic or racial background, may cut across many age groups or life stages. Even within a dominant lifestyle, such as that of a college student, there are sub-lifestyles. The lifestyle of the fraternity/sorority member and that of the athlete may be similar, since both share the common experience of being a college student, yet each may be quite different in its own way. Each has the potential of becoming the all-consuming set of values and behaviors.

Lifestyles also determine how one processes or seeks experiences as well as what one does. For example, if one's central interest is gourmet cooking, it is highly unlikely he/she would turn to a public agency for support of this interest. One would seek out that network which "feeds" his/her interest. One would turn to those private clubs, gourmet shops, restaurants, and the like for information, cooking classes and well-prepared meals. On the other hand, if one's activity, say choral singing, is largely supported by the actions of government or some membership body, options would be largely determined by others: the facilities they provide, the leadership they employ and the schedule they create. One would expect the agency to provide the service whereas the gourmet would not have the same expectations.

Life Span and Life Stage Defined

The concept of lifespan implies that life is a series of connected stages (life stages), each influencing one another but being distinctive. Each life stage is characterized by a unique configuration of roles and dominant activities which seem to be related to some biological and/or psychological (developmental) change. The developmental psychologists have spent considerable time and energy in explaining the progression of lifes stages, particularly those of youth. Less work has been done on young adults, adults and the elderly, although popular writings such as *Passages,*[13] which describe some of the emotional and sexual modifications one experiences as he/she goes through a separation, divorce or remarriage, have been developed. In all, there seems to be well-defined developmental patterns which we all go through throughout life.

Each stage of life is characterized by certain "expected" behaviors. Consequently, as one moves from one life stage to the next, role modifications occur; new role sets emerge as we respond to both our own and society's perception of what is proper at any given stage. What may be an engrossing recreation activity or approach for the provision of services at one stage of life may be dropped or only tolerated in a later stage.

There seems to be a physiological readiness for specific roles and the activities which characterize each stage. What does trigger or initiate shifts in roles? Are these changes biological in origin or do they result from social expectation and experiences or a combination of these? Witt and Goodale suggest there are barriers which prohibit leisure enjoyment and serve as a possible explanation for discontinuance.[14] Many of the barriers they identified were related to the physical changes we experience as we age as well as the social and economic changes which occur throughout life. The interaction between all of these forces, these triggers and barriers, is dynamic and complex.

Unfortunately, simplistic explanations abound for our observed behavior. When we see an eighteen year old fraternizing with a member of the opposite sex, we say "that's adolescent;" we expect teenagers to interact with members of the opposite sex, and they do. Is it because of the development of their biological sexuality or is it a socially expected behavior of eighteen year olds? More likely it is a combination of both. If we see the same kind of behavior among members of the opposite sex when both participants are married and not with their spouse, we describe the fraternizing in other terms. We may talk about philandering or an affair. On the other hand, if this behavior occurs publicly, say in an office party or at a class reunion, it may be dismissed as "they've had too much to drink." When we observe young married couples going to the movies less frequently than they did while courting, we may attribute it to a "change of interest" when, in fact, it may be the direct result of some barrier such as financial cost, which has triggered the change. These perceptions have great significance for recreation and park programmers since we, too, are "victims" of the propensity to stereotype. And, in our haste to help individuals adapt to a new life stage, we may actually discourage participation in some activity which they enjoy but which seems to be related to a previous life stage. Similarly, we may encourage and even force participants into new activities, assuming they are the proper involvements for that stage of life.

There are certain roles, such as parenthood, which do occur in a specific life stage which tend to dominate that phase of life. Much of the Rapoports' work dealt with that phenomenon.[15] In the case of parenthood, the triggering mechanism is biological; in the case of recently married young adults, the role shift may be culturally determined. The move from one life stage to the next appears to be developmental rather than hierarchical. No one stage is more or less than another, only different. These differences take one of two forms: behavior, what we do; and process, how we act. In other words, changes in the way we behave and expect others to respond to our behavior are equally as significant in each life stage as are the changes in what we do. As a teenager we may expect others (the school, park and recreation agencies, parents) to provide and financially support many of our play experiences. As adults, we assume that the provision of these services is our own responsibility so we join a health spa, hire a tennis professional to give us lessons, or join with our neighbors in developing a community swim club.

LIFELONG INTERESTS

Our expectations of what we should do in a specific stage of life are conditioned by the attitudes and values of the larger society. The specific forms by which these expectations are manifested are determined by the values of those who share our lifestyle. We tend to do only those things which are socially approved by those we respect. It is unrealistic for recreation and park professionals to expect those whose lifestyle is centered in literary and antiquity interests to join in recreation programs designed for the sports enthusiasts.

Likewise, it is unrealistic to think that recreation and park departments will be effective in attracting to their programs members of a given neighborhood if those person's friends dislike the recreation program — its offerings and leadership — or if the people in that community tend to believe that organized recreation programs are the responsibility of the private sector. The same holds true for those in a specific life stage.

I remember when our youngest son finished the sixth grade and was promoted to the seventh. During the spring he played dodge ball daily as did most of the older elementary school children. It was the activity of the sixth grader. Three months later, when he entered junior high, he lost interest in dodge ball; junior high students did not play it. His personality and biological self had not changed to any great extent in that three month period but his perception of the role of a junior high student — a new life stage for him — and the activities they pursued prevented him from playing dodge ball, even though he dearly loved it. Occasionally he would "fall off the wagon" and would play with some of the neighborhood elementary school children who still thought of it as a good sport, but he did not let his junior high friends know of his transgressions. His behavior reinforced what we know to be an operational fact; what we do at any stage of life depends more upon what our peers do and their perceptions than do the activity skills we have learned. Both Unkel[16] and Edwards[17] cited this fact.

In her study of the relationship between leisure styles and one's race and residence, Edwards suggests that ethnicity was a major factor in determining the leisure activities of blacks when they lived in a black neighborhood. However, when they lived in an integrated or predominately white neighborhood, blacks tended to adopt the dominant pattern of their neighbors. In other words, they tended to be like those around them, in part as a function of resources available, but also because of their anticipated socialization into the larger culture.

Unkel wrote about the effects of sex stereotyping on the forms of physical recreation participation of males and females during various adult life cycles. According to her, there were marked changes in participation from team to individual and dual sports as one moves from young adulthood to middle adulthood, especially among females. She concluded that role expectations seem to be more critical in effecting these changes than did the loss of physical skills or the lack of opportunity to play. Social expectations and social pressures can be powerful forces available to recreation programmers when they are sensitive to the role played by life stages and lifestyles.

Childhood experiences are important primarily as antecedent conditions in the selection of our lifestyle expressions. To illustrate the point, let us turn our attention to the promotion of lifetime sports and the athletic pursuits of children. For many recreators, being physically active is a highly desirable way of life. But not everyone is interested in being physically active, at least not in the sense of playing sports and games. To them, to be physically active may mean hiking or working in the garden. Sports are not a part of their priority system even though physical fitness may be an essential element of their lifestyle. To assume that everyone should participate in sports because sports are a good way to keep fit, is to ignore the realities of a population with diverse lifestyles.

It is hypothesized that the adult lifestyle which has sports as a part of it could have been predicted by earlier activity behavior of its members. Children who play sports and get positive reinforcement from them generally continue to participate in sports as adults and select friends who also engage in them. The motivation is not necessarily for physical fitness; sports has become an integral part of their reward system. Their earlier behavior did not determine their later recreation interests and experiences, only forecast it. The selective process was already in operation. For those who are not inclined toward physical activity or who are physical but not sports oriented, introducing them to sporting contests or suggesting that they should play sports rather than hike or play the piano is like washing dirty clothes without soap; it accomplishes little. This is true for both youth and adults.

There also appears to be a readiness for participation in specific activities and that readiness is tied to one's life stage and lifestyle. For urban, inner-city youth, basketball seems to be an important activity. To suggest to these children that they should be playing tennis or golf because they can continue them in their adult years makes little sense to them. The reinforcers are not there. It is difficult to convince most eleven year olds they should be learning the skills and activities they will enjoy in the future when their present social environment says they should be playing team sports. The same holds true when introducing music appreciation or teaching someone to play an instrument. What the child wants to play and hear is what his peers want to play and hear. At best we can develop an individual's sensitivity or receptiveness to participation in the so-called "lifetime activities" when he/she reaches the appropriate stage in life to enjoy them. Whether he/she does engage in them as an adult depends upon a host of variables over which we have little control. Recognition of this fact should not deter professional program planners from introducing new activities to their constituents but it does demand a more careful reading of how those experiences are introduced and what the expected results may be.

Style and Stage Choices
Our lifestyle and stage of life serve as our antennae. We only pick up those vibrations which are in tune with our receiving units. Our psychological readiness is directly related to our life stage and our willingness to participate is a function of our lifestyle. True, without exposure to a variety of activities there would be no knowledge of what might be acceptable and therefore little diversity in lifestyles. However, exposure does not determine choice; it only makes choice possible. Attention must be equally given to those attitudes, values and motivations which provide the capacity to choose as is given to those forces or barriers (time, money and opportunity) which prevent the exercise of choice.[18]

In her work on development and perspectives of aging, Bernice Neugarten vividly described and documented the life selecting process.

Life is essentially a two-stage phenomenon in which the first stage is devoted to the development of abilities, skills, and mechanisms for dealing with the world and with one's self. It is an expansive stage. The second stage or phase of life involves the reorganization and evaluation of behaviors. Changes in the quality of social interaction and a growing concern for the inner life are its major components. The maintaining of one's self and one's interests becomes paramount.[19]

The first stage is quantitative; the second, qualitative. Youth is characterized by growth, skill development, exploration and expansion as a part of the growing process. Learning requires a wide range of experiences; from them, a variety of lifestyles evolve. This is an important understanding for those who see leisure education and leisure counseling as responsibilities of the park and recreation professional. They need to know the origin of various lifestyles and the relationship of those behaviors to specific life stages.

The adult stage of life is characterized by selectivity. Having experienced the expansiveness of youth, adults tend to sort out activities and channel their energies. These characteristics are typical in the mature state where one seeks to maintain and stabilize preferred behaviors rather than continue to be explorative. Of course, exploration occurs in all stages of life as does maintenance behavior; it is really a matter of degree.

The number of activities in which we engage during our discretionary time is somewhat reflective of our life stage. During the expansive period, we participate in a greater variety and number of activites. As we age, we modify this pattern; we participate in fewer activities and tend to select those of a less physical nature (Unkel, 1981). Breadth of experiences seem to give way to depth of experiences. We come to understand that life is an integrated process with satisfactions being derived from a variety of expressions, recreation pursuits being only one of them.[20]

Some adults tend to have a low activity profile when their recreational behavior is measured by our more conventional recreation activity inventory schedules. This fact, alone, should not bother us. As youth, they probably did not play many of the playground games, choosing other activities as their means of satisfaction. The services of recreation departments may have been rarely used. As adults, they probably continued to "tune out" the offerings of the recreation agencies and thus, do not appear as a part of our constituency. Also, they may seem to engage in fewer activities. But, do not be misled. The number of activities engaged in is not directly related to the quality of involvement. The more complex the activity, the more absorbing it is in terms of lifestyle development, the less need there is for diversity of activity in order to "meet needs." To the dog fancier, raising and showing canines is "all there is." It provides social interaction, a sense of purpose and achievement, travel, new experiences — all the elements of satisfying lifestyle, of a satisfying recreation lifestyle. As programmers, what we need to be sure of is that the offerings and approaches we develop and use do not encourage dependency, that they increase, not decrease, one's sense of freedom and choice. Yet, some of our efforts and many of the offerings of commercial amusements do encourage a reliance on others for entertainment.

Most recreation and park professionals would argue vehemently that their program approaches do not encourage dependency. Recreators like to believe in their ability to move people to self-directed behaviors. If this goal is achieved, however, the likelihood of the participant returning to the recreation professional for direction and support of his interest may be minimized. The recreator is in the same position as the teacher. If he/she does the job well, the service may no longer be needed; the client now knows how to learn, how to process experiences, how to problem-solve, and, hopefully, how to have a more meaningful and satisfying life. Fortunately for recreators, fostering independence and autonomy are not incompatible with our mission. As individuals develop these qualities, their need for services continues, but the type of services required may change. Park and recreation programs must be able to respond to those changes.

Recreators must also overcome the fallacious belief that people only recreate when they go to recreation centers. Only a small percentage of one's free-time is spent in a designated "recreation" area or participating in a recreation "activity." It is unrealistic to think that those who do not come to organized recreation and park facilities or to programs sponsored by recreation and park departments are recreationally illiterate or not engaging in satisfying experiences. Self-directed adults frequently reject the services of park and recreation agencies when they perceive these approaches as inappropriate to their life stage or lifestyle. Again, the means by which we do things are as important as are the offerings we provide. Therefore, we need to make sure that our program concepts are broadly based and take into account the developmental sequences which occur as we move through various life stages; also, that our approaches and the content of services take into account the expectations of those we serve and accommodate.

Theory of Continuity/Discontinuity
Besides the work on life stages and life cycles, there are additional research findings from gerontology which have meaning to recreation professionals. Among them are those related to the theory of continuity, an approach which might aid us in predicting the future recreation behavior of an individual. The theory holds that if the activities of youth are known, a person's general patterns, throughout life, can be predicted, that people tend to continue in the same general mode throughout their lives although there are patterns of discontinuity. The discontinuity concept states that when a lifestyle pattern changes as a result of an accident, a crisis or some other unexpected event, the person involved generally reacquires an interest and a lifestyle he has known in the past but discontinued as a result of his/her concentration on those activities which were more consistent with the lifestyle he/she was developing. For example, the theory of continuity would say that those interested in the out-of-doors will pursue activities related to that dominant interest and lifestyle throughout each stage of life. If, however, something prevented the individual from participating in those activities, he/she would drop back to an earlier stage of interest and pursue an activity of earlier years, say crafts, which had been enjoyed but had been discontinued.

The theory of continuity assumes an integrated and holistic approach, an evolutionary process, which moves people from one stage of life to the next with no radical departure from their previous activity patterns. The implications of the theories of continuity and discontinuity for therapeutic recreation are enormous.

If the theories are valid, they suggest to therapeutic recreation specialists that they should determine the past preferences and behaviors of a client to see if there might be a discontinued set of activities or lifestyles which could be reestablished. This is a current strategy of those working with alcoholics and drug addicts. What were the leisure behaviors dropped when alcohol or drugs become the dominant life interests? Could they be reacquired or do the expectations and demands of each life stage, the barriers which alter or limit choices, and the demands of a specific lifestyle preempt their pursuit? Which would be more expedient — the development of new skills and essential interests or the resumption of a discontinued activity pattern? Would it be easier for the client to develop a new set of relationships to support new interests or should the reinforcers come from earlier associations? For those patients who do not need to modify their current life behaviors, the theory of continuity has relevance. Activities should be selected which are consistent with one's lifestyle and stage. They should be an extension of the present behavior and in the direction in which the personality (lifestage/lifestyle) is developing.

There are some research findings which suggest that the activity level of childhood directly influences the adult activity level and that there is a direct relationship between one's social class and one's lifestyle. Yoesting and Burkhead[21] reported the first observation; Havighurst and Feigenbaum[22] contributed the second finding. Both observations support the theory of continuity. They say nothing about the "healthiness" of high activity participation, only that our previous experiences are correlated with our present activity patterns and that one's social class and expected role configurations are more involved with what one does than with the satisfaction derived from the activity *per se*. As suggested previously, the number of activities engaged in (high activity patterns) is not necessarily correlated with leisure satisfactions. It is the quality, not the number of experiences, which determines satisfactions. Being highly active, both in terms of the variety of activities engaged in and the amount of physical exertion required, is not a prerequisite for a satisfying leisure lifestyle although there is some evidence that those who are active do have a more satisfying leisure lifestyle.[23]

Finally, the fear of failure seems to be a major determinant in the continuation of previous activity patterns. Loofts reported that the fear of failure is a major problem in adult socialization.[24] With experience, "historical time" is developed; one comes to know the results of failure. To avoid it, we continue those patterns we know. Possibly this is why life span patterns are so predictable for a given individual. The lifestyle remains the same, being comprised of experiences which are understood and which provide satisfaction. We adapt to the expected role patterns of each stage, fearing to deviate from the expected since we know the potential consequence of failure.

IMPLICATIONS FOR PROGRAMMING

The implications of the concepts of lifestyle, life stages, continuity/discontinuity, holism and adult socialization are critical to the future programming efforts of park and recreation professionals. They are useful concepts in developing leisure counseling strategies, in selecting approaches and activities for a constituency which is growing older, for broadening our professional sphere of influence and acceptance, and for the maintenance of the vitality of the park and recreation movement. The content of our delivery system as well as the means by which we offer services and programs should reflect our understanding of these concepts which take into account the interaction that exists between various psychological, sociological, and physiological factors. If the park and recreation profession chooses only one mode of programming or plans only for one lifestyle and/or life stage, its offerings and impact will be limited and its public support minimal.

There are a variety of program actions the profession can take to assure broad public support and valid programs. The usefulness of the concepts described in this chapter does not require a rejection of previous explanations for recreative behavior. Earlier classification systems and explanations of recreation activity are still useful but the more contemporary explanations acknowledge the interactional dynamics of behavior which were ignored in the profession's earlier attempts to explain the need for activity, as justification for the services and programs we offered. Contemporary life requires a multi-faceted approach to recreation programming; a new set of actions to assure its success.

The first step necessary in the implementation of this approach is the recognition of the target groups to be served. Different lifestyles and different life stages require different programs and program approaches. For some segments of the population, the scheduling of activities and events and the supervising of recreation experiences is suggested. This may be the most appropriate approach for the young, the inexperienced and the economically and socially dependent. It may be totally unacceptable for the mature or the self-reliant. For them, another strategy is indicated.

The provision of recreation spaces — areas and facilities — is a program approach in its own way. The providing of places where people can go to enjoy themselves in self-directed activity may be all that's required for some individuals and groups. Occasionally, these areas must be reserved for specific activities and events, such as athletic contests, in order to accommodate large numbers of participants but, in general, their near availability and proper maintenance is enough. The actors turn the stage into a theatre.

A third program approach involves the amassing and dissemination of information and knowledge about activities and services offered. This approach embraces the concepts of leisure counseling and leisure consulting, including the offering of technical assistance to self-help groups. When recreation and park professionals share their knowledge about the recreation opportunities and processes available in the community, regardless of who sponsors or offers them, or influences behavior through leisure counseling and consulting, they are providing a program service. They are aiding the citizenry to engage in meaningful recreation experiences just as much as they do when they provide facilities or supervise activity. Some constituents only want or need this level of service. Once they know what is available (leisure information) or how to prepare their equipment (technical assistance) or what are the costs involved in developing different hobbies upon retirement (leisure counseling), they can act accordingly. Adults are certainly more likely to seek out leisure counseling services than are youth; the same may be said in terms of those who ask for technical assistance services. They want the recreation and park agency to respond to their request for aid rather than their being dependent upon the department's schedule and activity offerings for some of their recreation experiences.

The fourth and final program thrust involves learning. Interpretive services, activity instruction and skill development classes are examples of educational program efforts. Like the information approach, the end result of this element of programming is the freeing of the participant, making him/her more knowledgable and self-reliant about his/her leisure. Although appropriate for all lifestyles and life stages, the means by which instruction and learning occur should vary. Certain methods are more appropriate for specific lifestyles than they are for others; then, too, certain techniques are more appropriate for those in one life stage than they are for those in another stage.

The more diverse the populations served, the more diverse the program approach and program structure must be. If the recreation and park movement is to develop its own body of knowledge and maintain its viability as a profession, it must integrate contemporary theories of sociology and developmental psychology into its methods and techniques of programming. The organized park and recreation profession exists to provide a service so that people might have more meaningful leisure expression. To measure against this objective recreation and park professionals must recognize the diversity of interests, lifestyles, and age groups (life stages) they serve and program accordingly.

REFERENCES

1. Gray, David and Seymour Greben. "Future Perspectives," *Parks and Recreation*, Vol. 9, No. 7, 1974, p. 49.
2. Cheek, Neil H., Jr. and William R. Burch, Jr. *The Social Organization of Leisure in Human Society*. New York: Harper and Row, 1976, 283 pp.
3. Nash, Jay B. *Philosophy of Recreation and Leisure*. St. Louis: The C. V. Mosby Company, 1953, 222 pp.
4. Brightbill, Charles K. *Man and Leisure*. Englewood Cliffs, N.J.: Prentice-Hall, 1961, 292 pp.
5. The Bureau of Outdoor Recreation classification system is based upon expected behavior patterns and physical resource characteristics. The six BOR classes are: I — High Density Recreation Area; II — General Outdoor Recreation Areas; III — Natural Environment Areas; IV — Unique Natural Areas; V — Primitive Areas; and VI — Historic and Cultural Sites.
6. U. S. Department of Interior. *The Third Nationwide Outdoor Recreation Plan (The Assessment)*. Washington: U. S. Government Printing Office, 1979, 264 pp.
7. Naisbitt, John. *Megatrends*. New York: Warner Books, Inc., 1982, 290 pp.
8. Toffler, Alvin. *The Third Wave*. New York: Morrow, Inc., 1980.
9. Nasibitt, *op. cit.*
10. Peters, Thomas J. and Robert H. Waterman, Jr. *In Search of Excellence*. New York: Warner Books, Inc., 1982, 360 pp.
11. Rapoport, R. and R. N. Rapoport. *Leisure and the Family Life Cycle*. London: Routledge and Kegan Paul, 1975.
12. Kaplan, Max. *Leisure: Lifestyle and Lifespan*. Philadelphia: W. B. Saunders Company, 1979, 286 pp.
13. Sheehy, Gail. *Passages*. New York: Bantam Books, 1977, 559 pp.
14. Witt, Peter A. and Thomas L. Goodale. "The Relationship Between Barriers to Leisure Enjoyment and Family Stage," *Leisure Sciences*, Vol. 4, No. 1, 1981, p. 29.
15. Rapoport, R., and Rapoport, R.N. *op. cit.*
16. Unkel, Margot B. "Physical Recreation Participation of Females and Males During Adult Life Cycle," *Leisure Sciences*, Vol. 4, No. 1, 1981, p. 1.
17. Edwards, Patricia Klohes. "Race, Residence and Leisure Style: Some Policy Implications." *Leisure Services*, Vol. 4, No. 2, 1981, p. 95.
18. Witt, P. A., and Goodale, T. L., *op. cit.*
19. Neugarten, Bernice L. "Developmental Perspective," *Reading in Gerontology* by V. M. Brantl and St. M. R. Brown. St. Louis: The C. V. Mosby Company, 1973, p. 33.
20. Ragheb, Mounier G. and Charles A. Griffith. "The Contribution of Leisure Participation and Leisure Satisfactory to Life Satisfaction of Older Persons," *Journal of Leisure Research*, Vol. 14, No. 4, 1982, p. 295.

21. Yoesting, Dean R. and Dan L. Burkhead. "Significance of Childhood Recreation Experiences on Adult Leisure Behavior: An Exploratory Analysis," *Journal of Leisure Research*, Vol. 5, No. 1, 1973, pp. 25-26.
22. Havighurst, R. J. and Feigenbaum, K. "Leisure and Life Style," *American Journal of Sociology*, Vol. 64, 1959, pp. 396-404.
23. Ragheb, M. G., and Griffith, C. A., *op. cit.*
24. Loofts, William R. "Socialization in a Life-Span Perspective: White Elephants, Worms and Will-O-the-Wisps." *The Gerontologist*, Vol. 13, No. 4, 1973.

Chapter Seventeen
Planning for Leisure in a
Pluralistic Society
Geoffrey Godbey

Leisure, in the sense of being free of the struggle for existence, is the oldest dream of mankind. To exist on one's own terms, to pass time in voluntary, pleasurable ways has been the ultimate transition hoped for by individuals in many cultures and the ultimate test of the few who partially achieved these conditions.

The situations which constrain leisure and those which shape it have varied historically among cultures. These different life situations, in large part, have been responsible for differing conceptualizations of leisure; different notions of what is meant to be free.

DETERMINANTS OF LEISURE

This chapter will examine some factors of our own society which are believed to be of great importance in shaping our potential for leisure, both at an individual and group level. Rather than defining leisure, a definition will be implied from examining its determinants. Particular attention will be given to implications for organized leisure services.

Work
Quantitatively, a higher percentage of the population now works for pay compared to the 1940's, because of both more female and more teenage employment. Additionally, a greater percentage of our population desires to work in some capacity. This trend, combined with rapid changes in the kinds of work available in our society and the educational requirements for such work, has brought about a break-up of the "linear life cycle" in which one received full-time formal education for one period of life, then pursued one career throughout his working life, and then retired.[1] Today, people starting second and third careers in midstream, taking an early retirement, returning to education in their middle-age, or switching from homemaking to part or full-time employment are redefining traditional patterns of work.

The content of our work has also shifted so that more people are involved in the production of services than the production of goods, and service occupations are devourers of time because service workers tend to be less efficient, live performance and personal contact are involved and capital cannot be substituted for labor. Thus, it is not surprising that the average workweek for the full-time employee has remained relatively constant since World War II.

The increases in leisure which are occurring are due to increases in large blocks of time such as vacations and holidays. There is evidence that workers prefer that any future increases in leisure come in large blocks rather than slight decreases in the total workweek. Three current trends constrain opportunities for us to increase our leisure: inflation, an aging population, and the energy crisis. As inflation continues, many people must work longer hours or have less material welfare. While some people will choose to do without, many will choose to work longer hours.

Increased leisure will additionally be constrained by the age characteristics of our population. While today one retired worker on social security is supported by almost five workers, that ratio may shrink to one to three or even one to two within the next hundred years. Rather than take the severe tax bite, retirees, teenagers, and housewives are likely to enter the job market, forcing wages down further.

While there is every reason to believe that alternative fuel sources will be found to solve the energy crisis, the transition period from fossil fuels will involve some temporary scarcities. These scarcities will further increase the cost of virtually all material things since the cost of making them and transporting them to the marketplace will be increased.

While these situations may help correct the overemphasis upon material things in our society, they will hardly contribute to increasing leisure in the short term.

Basic Values

When planners try to plan for leisure in our society, their focus must be on the total human experience. Vast changes have occurred in our techniques and meaning of work and there is increased unwillingness in much of the western world to accept the concept of fate.

In the last 300 years within the western world there has been increasingly less economic constraint on human behavior and yet an increasing inability of man to develop a meaningful reintegration with the rest of the living world. Our increased social and economic freedoms have been purchased at the cost of isolation and alienation from those systems which allow this world to survive and function. Our notion of God and theology have become increasingly vague yet people still long for the simple faith and answers of former times. Our machines have shown us the uninhabited heavens while parting the angelless clouds. At the same time, another part of our collective mind begins to see what we could do to become God by controlling nature. We can unlock knowledge by which we can live like a logical extension of the Earth. With such aspirations, it is perhaps natural that what we do or what we achieve is dominant over what we are. Our ascribed statuses: gender, race, age, religion, etc. are used less and less to convey who we are to other people. Instead, we become virtual composites of what we do, and it is doing something that keeps us from being nothing.

The rush to experience, particularly among those with high levels of education and income in advanced industrial societies, has led to "time deepening."[2] Time deepening occurs when the individual seeks to undertake more activity than can be accommodated with existing economic and educational resources. In other words, the more activities people undertake, the more they desire to undertake. Time deepening has three primary consequences for planners: (1) people do more and more activities in less and less time, e.g., eat lunch in ten minutes or get strenuous exercise in less than an hour with a game of racquetball; (2) people increasingly have the desire and ability to do more than one thing at the same time, e.g., to watch television while eating dinner or to listen to music while talking with a friend and reading the newspaper; and (3) people increasingly have the desire and ability to deal with more precise units of time, e.g., to schedule meetings at 10:36 a.m. rather than 10:30 or know within fifteen minutes how long a 300 mile drive will take. Time deepening is caused by and in turn facilitates experientialism, and it means that most of us approach both leisure and work activities within the same set of values and attitudes. These values and attitudes reflect our seriousness, rationality, hurried pace and lack of playfulness. They also reflect our doubt as to whether we belong in this world.

Democracy
Leisure has always been closely interwoven with political belief and shaped by political systems. The systems by which humans exercise power directly influences the quantity and quality of our leisure experience. The original notion of leisure, born in the Golden Age of Greece, was directly shaped by a political system in which only a minority of its residents enjoyed citizenship. Participation in the decision-making process was mandatory. The ideal of cultivation

of self was more fully realized through the existence of an extensive slave system which freed the citizen from mundane work.

Unlike that of the ancient Greeks, our own democracy has been built around two key ideas: individual freedom and equality under the law. Over one hundred years ago de Tocqueville observed:

"When men living in a democratic state of society are enlightened, they readily discover that they are not confined and fixed by any limits which constrain them to take up with their present fortune. They all, therefore, conceive the idea of increasing it — if they are free, they will attempt; but all do not succeed in the same manner."

Thus, differences in well being were closely linked to one's personal efforts, to one's ability to compete, to one's level of aspiration, need or greed. Among those things early Americans pursued competitively was "happiness." Today happiness can be pursued by the acquisition of experiences as well as the acquisition of things. The struggle for the acquisition of material goods is more successfully undertaken by most people and the pursuit of happiness is today more a matter of individual self-expression than instrumental activities.

The combination of individual freedom of choice, voluntary action and technological capitalism have emphasized maximizing profit and production divorced from identified need. These have combined to change our notion of what is "voluntary" or "freely chosen." Since leisure is usually thought of as freely-chosen activity, this change of notion is important. "Voluntary" formerly meant a choice from among many alternatives which was freely and agreeably made by the individual, not externally constrained. Choice meant foregoing several attractive alternatives in order to gain the most satisfying one. In short, pleasure involved sacrifice.

People today are more nearly able to avoid sacrifice, seeking instead to experience all choices, do it all, see it all, and do it and see it now. In the 1977 Nationwide Outdoor Recreation Survey (undertaken by the U.S. Heritage Conservation and Recreation Service), respondents listed "time" more frequently than anything else as a factor limiting their participation in outdoor recreation.[4] Not money, or transportation, or crowding or health problems, but time. This could be taken as a statement of our system's success. Imagine a former generation saying that the main limitation on their leisure was neither capital nor technology but merely enough time to use them. In *How Americans Use Time*, Robinson found that one of four American adults said they *always* felt rushed.[5] This rush to experience, in one sense, indicates people have more democracy to do more and more chosen activities.

The lack of willingness to sacrifice one desirable activity in order to undertake another, however, suggests a new way of attempting to deal with our mortality: to deal with our greatest enemy, time, by doing more and more within a given period of time. Democracy has always dealt in finite terms, allowing us to choose either A or B. For a democratic government to work, people must be able to choose and accept, for example, either a clean environment or reduced taxes, either better health care for the aged or an alternative use of funds such as space exploration, either a president or prime minister with one set of beliefs (and faults) or another. Democracy involves sacrificing that which is potentially good for that which is potentially better. When we are no longer willing or capable of doing that or no longer allowed to, democracy will no longer function and we will enslave ourselves for one more utopian dream of life without limitation.

Cultural Pluralism
Our cultural pluralism also shapes our leisure behavior and values. The many ethnic, religious and political minorities who maintain their identity rather than completely assimilating further the process of pluralism. The United States has historically represented a model of cultural pluralism due not only to its historic ties with Britain, Europe, Spain and Africa, but also due to immigration policies which continued the immigration of new groups. Canada has also experienced a more pluralistic culture during the last few decades as immigrants from Europe, Asia, the Caribbean Islands and the United States transform the country from one which was dominated by the French and English to a multicultural nation.

The effects of cultural pluralism on the leisure behavior of a post-industrial society are illustrated in the following table. The table attempts to identify the features of cultural pluralism in a mass culture which moves toward having even more things in common, primarily due to the pervasiveness of the mass media. Mass culture has been defined as:

> "Elements of culture that develop in a large, heterogenous society as a result of common exposure to and experience of the mass media . . . The emergence of mass culture is a part of the process of the development of common unifying cultural values and attitudes in the new and vast population of modern national social units."[6]

248

Table One

Leisure in Singular and Plural Cultural Societies

	Plural Culture Society	Single Culture Society
Concept	Leisure is anything the individual chooses to do which he finds pleasurable. Leisure is unlimited. An end in itself.	Leisure is a set of identifiable experiences which the individual is taught to enjoy. Leisure is limited. A means to an end.
Variation in Behavior	Range of acceptable behavior wide.	Range of acceptable behavior narrow.
Standards to Judge Behavior	Laws set limits. No universally accepted mores by which to judge leisure behavior.	Mores and folkways set limits of behavior. Universal standards for leisure based upon perceived cultural necessity.
Role	Individual and sub-cultural identity linked to leisure behavior.	National identity linked to leisure behavior.
Role Problems	Difficult to judge leisure ethically. Dispute over leisure values. Lack of meaning.	Lack of experimentation or alternatives. Persecution of that which is foreign. Easy to use leisure as a means of social control.
Government's Role	Identification of recreation needs difficult. May provide only selected kinds of services or serve certain sub-cultures or groups disproportionately.	Identification of recreation needs easy. May provide services which serve as a common denominator.
Commercial Organization's Role	Commercial sector has more diverse opportunities. Can cater to individual or subculture's tastes. Easier to create needs.	Commercial sector has more limited opportunities. More difficult to create needs or cater to individual or sub-culture's tastes.
Mass Media's Role	Limited in its ability to reflect culture. Diversion and entertainment function.	Less limited in its ability to reflect culture. Transmission of culture function.

Cultural pluralism emphasizes the role of leisure as anything the individual chooses to do for pleasure. The limits of such behavior are defined only by laws, with activity representing an expression of personal interest or "lifestyle" rather than one's culture. The social pressure resulting from fads and created leisure needs stimulates further innovation and a speeding up of the consumption of leisure experience. One solution to the accompanying uncertainty over what is worth doing is to do nothing, but a more prevalent reaction is to try to do or experience everything.

Self-Consciousness

Social psychologists claim that consciousness of self is what distinguishes us from other animals. Self-awareness is necessary and worthwhile for humans, but only within limits. Perhaps no society has been more self-conscious than our own. Our physical selves are seen instantly by cameras, we see ourselves dancing on our mirrored dancefloors or on the moon, and we receive advice concerning how to change ourselves for the better from a myriad of sources. We see and adjust ourselves daily in test scores, in beauty contests, in TV instant replays, in tape recordings, in factor analyses, in insurance company predictions and equations concerning our death, in newspapers, in sociograms, and, of course, in advertising. Advertising teaches us to be self-conscious. Am I succeeding? Am I having fun? Reaching for all the gusto? Am I in command?

Heightened self-consciousness shapes our leisure. It may limit our playfulness. Play is outside ordinary life, limited in time and space, and surrounded by an air of mystery. Self-consciousness allows us to dismiss mystery, to take the element of surprise out of ordinary life. We may actually take leisure counselors seriously, shy away from singing in public or reciting limericks to strangers, seek to rig our competition in advance or analyze why we like music. Thus, while leisure and play allow us to "get lost" in what we are doing, it becomes increasingly hard to get lost. Our heightened self-consciousness undoubtedly prevents us from doing some things in our leisure which would surprise or harm us. Additionally, it may make it more difficult to have fun. Fun, as Huizenga pointed out, is an irreducible category.[7] You cannot successfully analyze fun and break it down into component parts, although a number of social scientists are now trying. When you try too hard to analyze fun, it disappears.

Post-Industrial Capitalism

Daniel Bell has characterized post-industrial society not so much by the absence of certain traditional forms of material scarcities such as food and shelter, but by the development of new forms of scarcity.[8] Such new costs or scarcities include the cost of information, the cost of coordination, and the cost of time.

Information is mandatory in our society, and the rate at which we are bombarded with information increases daily. Every new social or political movement seeks to "educate the people." Thus, consumer activists want to provide more and more accurate information to the consumer to insure logical choice. This movement's success, however, is predicated upon individuals digesting large amounts of information, processing decisions, not unlike a computer. To buy the best tennis racquet requires extensive data not only concerning comparative price, but also on durability, flexibility of head, throat, and shaft; weight and weight distribution; head shape; size of "sweet spot"; racquet head torque; vibration; stringing pattern; grip composition; string type; string composition; and so forth. Such an approach assures that the individual pays for the racquet not only with money, but with his time, energy, and added complexity to his life. Here the consumer movement becomes an apology for materialism, not usually questioning the need for products, just instructing the potential buyer on how best to choose among alternatives.

Similarly, our society is characterized by new costs of coordination. A more complex society means more interdependence and as our ability to interfere or do harm to each other increases, planning and regulating our society becomes more important and more complex. The necessity of interacting with increasing numbers of people and a greater number of social situations involves more travel. Such coordination is not just the prerogative of elites, but necessary for everyone to minimize the possibility of killing ourselves with our own cars, chemicals or radioactive wastes.

Both the need for information and coordination help create a third scarcity — time: the ultimate scarcity for those who wish to consume and experience at an historically unprecedented rate. Those who wish to achieve or conquer in such fashion have a problem which is, in many ways, a luxury to have: not enough time to do all the things they want to do.

The desire to experience all things pleasurable, to be needed and involved in as many sets of human experience as possible, is, in many respects, the ultimate greed. Two things must be said about this greed for experience. First, it springs directly from the processes and mentality of economic capitalism, where competition for goods and the production process is divorced from need. It is natural that this progression has taken place. Much as the capitalist accumulates and invests money, we can see that the investment of time by individuals in diverse, pleasurable activity is a capitalist form of self-actualization: a competition with time as the scarce resource to find out who we are by literally recreating ourselves experientially.

Capitalism also sowed the seeds of experientialism by saturating us with unneeded material objects. As the ability of our economic system continually to create needs for new material products begins to find limits, these needs are transferred to leisure experiences. People are sold the experience of gambling, traveling through

Europe, viewing other people's sexual activities, going down a wild river on a raft, learning tennis from a Zen Buddhist perspective, changing personal relationships through a multitude of therapies, making wine, and any other experience they will buy. What is produced is a wanderlust, not for other places but for other lives.

THE EMERGING LEISURE SERVICE PROFESSION

The industrial revolution was responsible for an increasing collectivization of work, concentration of power and the increasing organization of many aspects of our lives. The recreation and park movements in both the United States and Canada have historically represented an attempt to counter the negative effects of industrialization: the growth of urban areas without provision for children's play, the decreased contact of people with the natural environment, and the insidiousness of commercial recreation. Thus, it was a movement to reform, and reform takes organization. Yet a classic negative consequence was inevitable: in order to fight for their beliefs, those in the recreation and park movements were often forced to adopt the tactics and mentality of the system which produced the situations they were fighting to correct. To counter those who wished to plan, acquire and develop land for financial profit, parks people have had to maneuver in the same political arena with similar tactics to plan, acquire and develop land for the purpose of leisure. Rather than preserving leisure as it had been in pre-industrial society, it became more organized, more specialized, more scheduled in accordance with the demands of mass production, more influenced by consumerism and the increasing ability of the economy to produce "things" to play with, more fadlike, and so forth.

The movements for public recreation and parks, then, were not centered on freedom of leisure expression but with improved opportunity for participation in several forms of activity, such as outdoor recreation, sports and supervised play which were believed to be superior to the alternatives provided by the urban environment. The movement's founders were missionaries, seeking to convert people to forms of leisure expression they believed to be superior. Informed, rational choice, they believed, would lead people to the activities they advocated. The problems they fought against were real: children left with only the dangerous streets for playgrounds, men and women in the grim factories cut off from nature, the lack of recreation resources among the poor, and urbanites badly in need of exercise.

As these movements became institutionalized, recreation and parks became separate, then a combined function of local government. Both world wars, the depression, and the urban riots of the 1960's all served to heighten the growth of such agencies. Growth has brought a corresponding push for professionalization of employees, including specialized higher education curricula, attempts at certification of practitioners, professional societies and a specialized literature. Such professionalization has tended to minimize the advocacy role of most practitioners, and led to a posture where the recreation and park (leisure service) professional seeks to assume a role of only passively reacting to recreation need or demand, serving all people "equally" and reacting to rather than initiating societal change.

At the same time this professionalization is taking place, there is evidence that the growth of leisure service agencies in the public sector has largely halted or even been reversed, after a decade of growth.[9] This trend appears to be most pronounced at the local level, where the bulk of such services take place. Responding to such constraints will require new ways of proceeding, some of which may not be in keeping with "professionalism."

PLANNING FUTURE LEISURE SERVICES

How can the emerging leisure service profession respond to these complex situations? While the question is complicated, leisure planners will not have to invent things for people to do. They should provide a mechanism to encourage people to do things which are necessary for society but unfunded. In concert with the emerging deurbanization or atomization of our society, public leisure service planners must abandon the large scale planning mentality which has ignored the quality of neighborhood life and substituted standardization, formality, efficiency and bigness. The leisure service professional is no longer viewed as a public servant, but as a bureaucrat lacking respect for variation in life style and particularly leisure life style. Public leisure services, in short, must reflect rather than create culture.

Each of the previously outlined situations call for some redefinition of leisure services. With regard to work trends, for example, as a higher percentage of our population becomes involved in part-time employment, as the linear life cycle of education, single career and retirement ends, and a leisure or non-work time becomes available in large blocks of time, the purposes or satisfactions from leisure activity may have less to do with refreshment or diversion from work and more to do with activity which is considered worthwhile or satisfying on its own merits. Relations between work and leisure may become far less systematic. The common work leisure cycle may become increasingly differentiated. For the leisure planner, services can no longer be confined to a few common periods of time such as weekday evenings, weekend holidays, and summer vacations.

While the relation of leisure services to work may in some ways be diminished, the impact of continuing inflation will be such that leisure service agencies will have to sponsor more activities which provide a useful end product as well as the pleasure of doing them. Gardening, cooking, crafts with useful end products such as furniture reupholstering will all increase in popularity as will voluntary activities which provide a useful end product for the community and a worthwhile experience for the participant.

The rush to experience in our society which has brought about time deepening, and the attendant diminished spirituality must be countered by the provision of leisure experiences which require commitment, sacrifice and a progression of skills. Timelessness, simplicity, joy and celebration are leisure values which must be promoted in such activities if leisure planners are to actually serve as advocates of leisure. Public leisure service, in short, should be concerned not only with "the pursuit of happiness" but also with "insuring domestic tranquility." Remember those phrases?

Our pluralistic culture makes it difficult for leisure service agencies to "create" culture. Rather, they must reflect the many cultures around them. This cannot be done without intensifying efforts to involve citizens in decision-making using a diversity of formats. This is not to say that the agency should be culturally neutral, having no values other than those interjected by various public lobbies and pressure groups. Rather, the agency cannot afford to be ignorant of public opinion and diversity of opinion among subcultures. Maintaining cultural pluralism requires that a delicate balance be maintained between ignoring differences in culture to the extent that those within specific sub-cultures are either alienated or surrender their identity and recognizing such differences to the extent that members of society have little in common. Leisure service agencies must seek this balance.

Our heightened self-consciousness may indicate a greater need for opportunities for individuals to lose themselves in play and in service to others. While facilitating service to others may mean serving as a clearinghouse for voluntary action, promoting play will require much effort including redesigning many physical environments so as to encourage it.

In the future many unconventional types of property will be valued for their potential as a leisure resource. Cemeteries, for instance, are already undergoing a transformation from a burial place to one in which people may play. A spokesman for the archdiocese of Chicago said, "The trend is clear. Cemeteries will increasingly have more than one use. They have to. It's just good citizenship. In many areas the cemetery is about the last open green space left."[10] Churches, schools, museums, shopping centers, and private organizations are increasingly providing recreation and leisure services, and leisure service planners must be aware of them in the planning process.

Streets also have a leisure potential which planners must seek to recognize, particularly in the urban areas. The Chief of Comprehensive Planning of Baltimore City Department of Planning recently pointed out that the conversion of streets into public play areas sometimes appears to be an ideal solution but in doing so the system of space management that exists is disrupted.[11] Since many urban residents, however, center their leisure activity around the sidewalk and street in front of their houses, he suggests the following:

> "Sidewalks should be widened, traffic lanes should be reduced and traffic speed cut done by using such devices as bumps in the road bed. Suitable space should be provided for sitting, playing games, congregating around activity nodes such as bookmobile stops, places for vendors of fruit, fish, vegetables, ice cream. These spaces should be suitably paved, well lighted, equipped with mailboxes, telephone booths, trash containers. They should have trees or some other shading devices."[12]

Additionally, he suggests the demolition of old buildings in such areas, that windows be introduced into any standing blind walls, that playground equipment should *not* be introduced but that street furniture should be provided so that it can serve a recreation function. Steps should be wide enough for comfortable sitting and playing step ball, fire hydrants should be made suitable for leap frog, paving surfaces should be useable by residents, adjoining residents should be encouraged to exercise surveillance over neighborhood playgrounds. Undertaking such steps would represent a revolution in thinking on the part of leisure service planners because it would be, in effect, creating a new leisure environment, rather than dropping a few pieces of playground equipment into a decaying environment and then expressing surprise when such equipment is not used or misused.

In all these undertakings, leisure services must help us to be humble; take ourselves less seriously. Help us attain a new tranquility which can come only with the sense of wholeness, the holiness, of this world. Those leisure services which are of greatest benefit to our world and for which we must plan will be those which help us see why it makes sense to celebrate this world and our very lives.

REFERENCES

1. See, for instance, Best, Fred, Bosserman, Phillip and Stern, Barry. *Changing Values Toward Material Wealth and Leisure in the United States,* Washington, D.C.: NEW, January, 1976.
2. See, for instance, Scheuch, Erwin, "The Time Budget Interview." In: Alexander Szalai, ed., *The Use of Time — Daily Activities of Urban and Suburban Populations.* The Hague, Netherlands, 1972. p. 77.
3. de Tocqueville, Alexis. *Democracy in America.* New York: Mentor Books, 1956. p. 161.
4. Piney, John, Godbey, Geoffrey and Robinson, John. *A Survey of Outdoor Recreation in America — Summary.* Washington, D.C.: Heritage, Conservation and Recreation Service, 1979.
5. Robinson, John, *Leisure and Our Changing Use of Time,* College of HPER Colloquium, The Pennsylvania State University, University Park, Pennsylvania. (November 13) 1976.
6. Theodorson, George A. and Achilles G. *Modern Dictionary of Sociology,* New York: Thomas Y. Crowell, 1969. p. 246.
7. Huizinga, Johan. *Homo Ludens: A Study of the Play Element in Culture.* Boston: The Beacon Press, 1950.
8. Bell, Daniel, "The End of Scarcity." *Saturday Review of the Society,* (May) 1973. pp. 49-52.
9. See, for instance, Kraus, Richard. *Urban Parks and Recreation: Challenge of the 1970's.* New York: Community Council of Greater New York, 1972.
10. "Cemeteries Opening Gates for Recreation." *The New York Times,* (December 10), 1972. pp. 1, 76.
11. Brower, S.N. and Williamson, P., "Outdoor Recreation as a Function of the Urban Housing Environment," *Environment and Behavior,* (September) 1974. pp. 342-3.
12. *Ibid.,* p. 343.

Chapter Eighteen

The Prospects for Leisure in a Conserver Society

Irene M. Spry

Since Adam and Eve left the Garden of Eden human beings have dreamed of a life free from drudgery. In the last century in affluent western countries, the burden of incessant toil has largely been lifted from human shoulders. When the Toronto typographers, who in 1872 had won the right to organize a union, struck for a nine-hour day, the employers would not even meet them to discuss the matter.[1] Since then, the work week in Canada, as in the United States, has contracted progressively. Average hours in manufacturing fell from 59 a week in 1890 to just over 40 hours a week in 1960.[2] Unions have fought long and hard for an eight-hour day,[2] and today a seven-hour day is not uncommon. A five-day work week is normal and experiments are being made with a four- and even a three-day work week. Besides longer week ends, most Canadians have ten or more paid holidays a year with two weeks or more paid vacation time. Pension plans have made possible retirement at an earlier age and the young stay longer at school and university before entering the work force. Besides, the unemployed have unwanted free time on their hands.

Side by side with this increase in time off from earning a living, there has been a reduction in the hours that must be spent on household chores. Washing machines and spin-dryers, mechanical ironers and electric and steam irons, vacuum cleaners and electric polishers, microwave ovens, juicers and blenders, kleenex and throw-away diapers — a whole array of devices offer possibilities of cutting down the time and effort that must be spent keeping homes and their inmates clean and tidy and providing meals. Eating out at the local branch of a fast food chain, or buying ready-cooked fried chicken, pizza, or Chinese dishes make possible a further escape from housework.

Whether there has been a proportionate increase in time that is free to be spent as individuals choose is by no means clear. Many put in far more hours earning a living than the average work week, especially those who are self-employed, while women who combine work outside the home with household duties commonly have little if any spare time. Hours spent commuting and waiting in line-ups at the supermarket cash register and the like also erode leisure time.[3]

Whether the trend to shorter income-earning hours and reduction in the time that must be spent on household and personal maintenance will continue in the future is even more uncertain. If we are approaching limits to the growth of an energy-intensive way of life and, if the price of electricity and gasoline goes up still further, we may find that we must go back to using more human effort and more time in industrial, agricultural, and commercial activities as well as in household chores. It may be, however, that new discoveries of fossil fuels and new technologies, especially electronic devices, will, for a time at least, allow still further expansion in free time. This would intensify the already critical problems of the role of leisure in human happiness and of demands made by leisure time activities on material resources and on the environment.

SPARE TIME ACTIVITIES

Nearly all Canadians spend at least some of their time watching television, while some 15 per cent of us spend a massive 30 hours or more a week in front of our TV sets. A large majority of us spend some time listening to radio each week, and nearly half of us listen to records, tapes, or cassettes, though, no doubt, many of us do other things at the same time as we look and listen. Nearly two-thirds of us read newspapers and magazines, but only about one-sixth of us spend seven or more hours a week reading books as a leisure time occupation.

Only a small proportion of Canadians go to the theatre, opera, ballet or concerts, but more than a third of us go to the movies. Similarly only a few of us visit museums, art galleries and historic sites, but nearly a quarter of us spend at least some time attending sports events, some of us as regular spectators.

How many of us spend time wandering round the stores does not seem to be recorded, but this is undoubtedly one of the major diversions of the crowds that throng shopping malls and department stores, window shopping and "just looking." Eating out may be necessary at school or at work, it may be a quickie substitute for a meal at home, or it may be — and seems increasingly to be — a leisure activity, along with drinking.

Travel and tourism, ranging from Sunday driving and holiday camping trips to tours of Europe, and escape to sunny climes by refugees from a harsh winter, are becoming more and more important in our affluent and increasingly leisured lives. Some two-thirds of all Canadians indulge in recreational driving, while we spend billions of dollars in travel abroad.

A different type of leisure time occupation involves arts, crafts, music and hobby activities. A quarter of all Canadians spend some time, effort and imagination each week on such creative activities, though this estimate is uncertain as it is difficult to draw the line between such occupations as dress-making undertaken as a pleasing activity, for the fun of it, or as a necessary household chore. Twelve per cent of us spend some time on hobbies, but only half as many of us give fifteen hours or more a week to those hobbies.

Substantially more than half of all Canadians spend at least a little while in sports and physical activities, a few in organized sports events and many of us in swimming (apparently the most common type of exercise right across Canada), jogging, hiking, and doing exercises, ice-skating, skiing, playing tennis and badminton or golf and other games.

Besides card games, chess, bingo and electronic games, there are other ways of spending free time, such as entertaining and socializing, lazing in the sun, indulging in more sleep than is physiologically essential to maintain health and strength, or just sitting around, like the old lady in Vermont who said, "Sometimes I sits and thinks and sometimes I just sits."

THE COST OF SPARE TIME ACTIVITIES

Of all these varied ways of putting in leisure time, some entail very heavy demands on material and environmental resources. Travel means jet planes, the fuel they use, and the cloud cover they create. Automobiles mean using up metals and gasoline and creating smog. Television means cameras and kleig lights, congested air waves, production studios, elaborate transmitting and receiving equipment, including satellites and other apparatus of space technology. Movies mean cameras, sound recording equipment, filmstock, sets and costumes, cutting rooms, theatres and projection apparatus, to say nothing of the extravagances of the glamour industry. The record industry has similar requirements as does sport, both professional and amateur, organized as entertainment. International competitive sport has escalated jet set glamour and the kind of emulation that gives rise to Olympic extravaganzas. Even unassuming, personal participation in sport has become the raison d'etre for promoting sales of elaborate equipment and clothing, while the record industry and night club dancing have become multi-billion dollar businesses.

Underlying the expansion of the mass media — TV, radio, records, computers, the press and periodicals — and their role in leisure time, is the proliferation of sales promotion and advertising. Shopping as a pastime simply adds to the perpetual pressure to buy more, have more, and consume more.[4] Increasing leisure time has become a market to be exploited through the ruthless promotion of the idea that more and ever more elaborate possessions and expenditure will add immensely to the satisfaction that can be won from leisure time. Power boats and snowmobiles, ten-speed bicycles and fancy skis, stereo-phonic record players and computers are becoming widespread items of household equipment, besides TV sets, radios, telephones and cars.[5] Emphasis is given increasingly to the apparatus used in leisure time activities. This is generally true of affluent societies. A recent publication, *Leisure Markets in Europe*, was announced with the statement that:

Leisure goods and services absorb more than one fifth of total consumer spending in Europe. That makes leisure very big business.

Leisure markets are expected to grow faster than all consumer spending in the 1980's with an average growth for Europe as a whole of around 5% a year at constant prices.[6]

Should leisure time continue to expand in the future as it has expanded in the recent past, and should emphasis persist on leisure as big business, leisure time activities will undoubtedly play a part in the continued expansion of our mass consumption economy. Increasing spare time may well become the focus of intensified consumption and sales in the entertainment industry, the travel and tourist industry, and the sports equipment industry. Even jogging and cross-country skiing are now the target for sales of special clothing, special footwear, and special equipment.

Paradoxically, increasing leisure time creates a need for so much increased expenditure that it induces people to undertake more income-earning activity, moonlighting or mothers going out to work to procure the income to buy skates, skis, cameras and the like, or to pay the installments due on a color televison set or a car, or even on the labor saving equipment that is designed to increase leisure time. The choice does not seem to be a choice between more consumption and more leisure time, but between more consumption for leisure time activities and more consumption of other sorts.

Does this mean that more and more leisure time will inevitably reinforce other pressures in the direction of continued economic growth? Does the novel expansion of substantial leisure time to an increasingly wide range of classes make the possibility of a conserver society increasingly difficult to achieve? Is the transition from an economic system based on a high rate of material growth to a slow-growth economy, or even a stable economy,[7] all the more unlikely by reason of the growing demands of the expanding leisure market? The answer depends on the forces which shape our preferences and choices as to how we spend our leisure time.

LOW COST POSSIBILITIES

The TGIF ("Thank God It's Friday") view of the working week suggests that few of us get much satisfaction out of what we do to earn a living. In that case we must depend on what we do in our leisure time to give us a satisfying life. This raises the question whether modern conveyor-belt workers, either in a factory or in an office, when they finish a shift — even a short shift — of mind deadening work have enough energy and initiative, enough resilience, to launch into any mind or muscle stretching activity, even though they may have time to spare. Is there any impetus in their environment to stimulate them to creative effort? Do the mass media and the conservation of their associates suggest any possibilities other than seeking diversion and excitement from television, and spending more and consuming more? Ideas as to the good life absorbed from television programs and advertisements combined with conspicuous consumption to keep up with the Joneses mean continued, open-ended increases in consumption that bring very little satisfaction to the consumers. Thorstein Veblen's *Theory of the Leisure Class* is as relevant today as it was when he wrote it in 1899. Contemporary economists, notably Fred Hirsch and William Leiss, have developed the same theme.[8] One-up-manship means bigger and faster cars, more lavish household furnishings and equipment, up-to-the-minute power boats and snowmobiles, as well as travel to more remote and unusual places than those which neighbors and work-mates have visited. Emulation in consumption satisfies no one and there is no limit to the burden which it imposes on scarce environmental and material resources.

There are, however, a few straws in what may be a wind of change. The popularity of jogging, of trail skiing, and of cycling suggests that simple activities, without a great elaboration of apparatus, are coming into their own. Yoga and meditation, similarly, make very little demand on material support systems. Gardening, crafts, carpentry, and all sorts of do-it-yourself activities, ranging from home dress-making to household repairs, may actually conserve material and environmental resources, since they combine recycling of materials with satisfaction of the instinct of workmanship. Leisure time pursuits should be undertaken, not in the hope of winning Oscars or Olympic gold medals, but for their own sake, because they are fun or interesting, or because they contribute to a cause that is considered to be useful or worthwhile. Participation in the work of public interest groups intent on achieving desirable social objectives is an example of an activity that can give great satisfaction while making few demands on material or environmental resources.

Would a shift to such low consumption leisure time occupations mean serious losses in leisure time satisfaction? The answer seems to be that there is wide scope for increased leisure time activities of a type that would not increase consumption expenditures and might actually decrease demands on the resources of the bio-sphere, while contributing more to human happiness then do many of today's high consumption activities and entertainments. More and more satisfying leisure need not mean more expenditure; it might well mean less.

The most obvious use of leisure time is to give respite from stress, rest and relaxation, "re-creation" in the literal sense of restoration of depleted energies. More important, in a world of mass production conformity and monotony, leisure gives people a chance to exercise their own initiative, to follow their own inclination, to "do their own thing" in their own way. It is an opportunity for personal choice and self-expression, for the development of individuality, for exploring and cultivating the full richness of human diversity. In leisure time people can exercise cramped and atrophied bodies; exercise and develop powers of intellect and imagination and of independence of thought and character. In their time off from earning an income and doing necessary chores, they may cultivate the taste and sensibility which will allow them to enjoy the beauties of nature, and the glories of great art and architecture, the splendor of music, the bouquets of fine wines, or the nuances of cordon bleu cookery. They may themselves experience the joy of creative activities. It is on leisure time occupations that most of us have to depend for the stimulus and excitement that human nature needs for fulfillment, and to leisure time encounters that we must look for "laughter and the love of friends," for chances to meet satisfying sexual partners, and for the satisfaction of working with close colleagues to achieve a shared objective. In our leisure time we may do things that engage our abilities to their full capacity, we may contribute something of importance to the community of which we are part, so earning the social esteem and self-respect which can come only from lives that have some significance.

CONSUMPTION VERSUS SATISFACTION

Few of us are lucky enough to find in our working lives opportunities for all these varied satisfactions. Do we find them in our leisure time? Might we do so? How heavy would be the burden of such human fulfillment on the material and environmental resources of our space-ship planet?

Rest and Relaxation

For rest and relaxation we need some degree of comfort, tranquility, agreeable surroundings, and unexacting diversion. Many people, whose living conditions do not provide these requisites, escape into the image world of television, a world in which they may effortlessly join the jet set in gracious living. It is not a world that gives relaxed contentment; rather it generates restless discontent. It is a world in which the importance of having more and more consumer goods is relentlessly driven home, a world in which the emphasis is constantly on the apparatus of living, not on the quality of life itself.

Initiative and Individuality

Watching TV may open new worlds to the viewer, the world of ballet, of opera or of wildlife in the unspoiled wilderness of the far north, of the sweeping Pacific beaches, or of Newfoundland's cliffs and bays, but the message of the medium is more commonly that a finer car is essential, or a shinier floor polish or a zestier beer to ensure a good life. The emphasis is persistently on *having* things — the things that everyone else has — not on *doing* the things that interest you as a unique human being, nor on *being* that individual to the utmost limit of your powers. In the barrage of advertising, in the flood of thrillers and "sit coms" and "shows," is there any spark that would fire individual enthusiasm for striking out on some personal line of activity, for following some special interest?

Bodies and Beer

TV programs certainly foster admiration of physical prowess. The hockey or football star, the Olympic gold medalist is idolized, but what has the Stanley Cup play-off to do with the ordinary citizen's need for a stimulus to exercise neglected bodies? Hockey Night in Canada and Saturday afternoon sports programs are more likely to promote passive viewing, beer in hand, than physical activity. It is true that an occasional "Participaction" advertisement may exhort the viewer to keep fit by taking to some form of exercise, but the insistent model is that of a car-borne, candy and beer consuming way of life which is the antithesis of a way of life in which leisure is used to build bodily health and strength.

Despite the huge disparity between the number of Canadians who watch television and the number who engage at least occasionally in some exercise or sport, there does seem to be a new interest in getting fit and keeping fit. More and more Canadians "run for their lives" when they take to jogging but the figures for participation in swimming, skating, skiing, tennis, golf and other physical activities suggest that there is still plenty of room for higher standards of activity.

Intellect and Imagination

Some programs on television or radio provide food for thought and stimulate the mind and the imagination, evoking a creative response from viewers and listeners. For the most part, though, viewers and listeners are merely passive spectators or auditors whose minds and imagination are neither challenged nor stimulated by what they see and hear.

The much smaller number of people who go to live theatre, concerts, ballet and opera have more chance of a stimulating experience that requires an active contribution of thought and sensitive imagination. Visits to art galleries, museums, and historic sites also are likely to stimulate both mind and imagination. Continuing education plays its part in developing intellectual muscle and opening opportunities for creative experience, as may also be the case with some formal education. The activities of public interest groups and voluntary organizations, ranging from tenants' associations to Women's Institutes, stimulate thought and imagination, widen horizons, and offer opportunities for creative experience.

Taste and Beauty

Music on radio and television, ballet, and some dramatic performance present beautiful sounds and sights for those that have ears to hear and eyes to see. Some wilderness programs may allow city dwellers hemmed in by walls and concrete to experience in some small degree the delights of natural beauty. Sights and sounds which are lovely to some people, however, may give little pleasure or even be distasteful to others. Their enjoyment requires not only the time that must be spent in looking and listening, but, as well, time and experience are needed to cultivate the taste which will give the viewer or hearer the capacity to delight in them, just as an educated palate is necessary for enjoyment of subtle sauces and exquisite wines. Enjoyment of beauty involves a learning process that goes on through a lifetime of leisure experience. Only if a person seeking satisfaction can contribute sensitive perception can the full possibilities of the enjoyment of beauty be realized.

Creative Experience
The active enjoyment of beauty is a creative, not a passive, experience. The creation of beauty may give a still richer satisfaction, the satisfaction attained by a quarter of all Canadians, who take part in some kind of art, craft or musical activity. Playing a musical instrument, singing in a choir, drawing or painting what they see in the world around them, fashioning a carving or a sculpture, expressing their insights and ideas in poetry or prose, taking part in a play, or at a more practical level, making a lovely quilt or a handsome piece of furniture, growing a glorious garden, or baking a splendid cake, they need never be dull; there is always something exciting and rewarding waiting to be done. Such leisure time arts and crafts may give outlets for the instinct of workmanship if earning a living fails, as it often does, to satisfy this deep human need.

Stimulus and Excitement
Since jobs may be repetitive and deadening, it is leisure activities that must fill yet another fundamental human need: the need for stimulation and excitement. We no longer face the daily challenge of escaping from sabre-toothed tigers or of running buffalo. It is true that driving a car or merely crossing busy streets gives some spice of adventure to our lives, but many of us seek an escape from boredom in purchasing every novelty that comes onto the market and acquiring a vast variety of consumer goods.[9] Such attempts to maintain an interest in life require continual escalation. The need for stimulus grows as it is satisfied. Similarly, neither television violence nor entertainment-sport can perpetually arouse interest and excitement without novel features and intensification of sensationalism. The only way in which we can hope to achieve a crescendo of interest, stimulation and excitement throughout a lifetime is in pursuing some unfolding interest, achieving new skills, discovering new creative possibilities, exploring new ideas and widening horizons, developing a more and more lively creative imagination.

Arts, crafts, and musical activities can give such stimulation, such unflagging and developing interest; so can a variety of hobbies which lead the enthusiast on from one level of attainment to another, unendingly. In the last analysis it is not outside stimuli that can solve the problem of boredom; each individual must generate his or her own interest and excitement in life through activities that hold the possibility of progressive achievement, deeper perception, new invention and discovery. Competitive sports and the excitement of watching one's team win a contest give an ephemeral stimulus, but only playing a game oneself, one's own creative activities, one's own physical, intellectual and imaginative development will sustain interest and excitement that time and use will not dim, but constantly intensify. The solution lies not in a multiplication of consumer goods, or increasing indulgence, but in the development of human skills and non-material interests and activities.

Friendship and Team Work
Some people are so fortunate as to earn their living working with colleagues who are friends, with whom they can co-operate wholeheartedly. For many, if not most of us, this rewarding experience is more likely to be attained in activities undertaken in time off work, perhaps in sport, or in voluntary activities with a church organization, political party or other public interest group, or in a choir, an orchestra or band, or in a dramatic group. We have very little information as yet on how much time and energy is spent in spare time team work in such shared endeavours. That contact with other people is important for most of us, we do know, since more than three quarters of us spend part of our leisure time visiting friends and relatives. Apart from the cost of establishing and maintaining contact with voluntary colleagues and friends, telephone service, postage, travel, and the like, and perhaps the consumption of food and drink that ordinarily takes place on social occasions, such sociability and cooperation does not seem to require any extensive material support. The potlatch type of formal entertainment may be necessary to ensure social esteem, but it probably contributes little otherwise to human happiness except insofar as it is the occasion for agreeable indulgences.

Social Esteem and Self-Respect
Social contacts may, however, mean conspicuous leisure, conspicuous consumption, and rivalry in lavish entertainment. All these have played a part in patterns of spending and patterns of leisure time activities. They have all been important as evidence of social status. They have all contributed to the association of leisure with lavish spending. Perhaps, as the idea of a conserver society spreads, other criteria of social worth and social respect may begin to make headway against competitive consumption. Just as concern is growing for the quality of life that cannot be measured in Gross National Product figures, so may concern be growing for human quality that is not demonstrated by lavish expenditures and an elaborate apparatus of spare time enjoyment. If ways can be

found of gauging the character and caliber of what individuals and groups contribute to the community in creative stimulus, artistic achievement, constructive intelligence, and the assumption of social responsibility, there may be hope that, in the time in which people are free to do what they like, what they like to do will prove to be what will earn them the respect and esteem of their community. Such esteem is an essential element of a good life; even more important is the individual's own sense of contributing something of significance. If what one does to earn a living seems trivial, this vital sense of significance must be won in leisure time pursuits that are considered to be important in themselves or in the social results that may be expected from them.

A recent estimate puts average expenditure on recreation in Canada at some ten per cent of total personal expenditure. If one adds to that expenditure by governments at all levels on recreational services and facilities, to say nothing of the share of the cost of public goods (highways, waterways, education, communication and transport systems and the like) that is put to recreational use, the total becomes one of considerable significance. In addition, some family expenditures that are classified as expenditures on clothing and shelter, household operation, furnishings and equipment, and travel and transportation are probably related to recreational activities. What happens to leisure time and to leisure expenditures will, therefore, have an important part to play in future trends in consumer expenditure. Increasing emphasis on leisure time as an opportunity for the enhancement of human quality and the enrichment of creative experience, rather than as an opportunity for the elaboration of entertainment, escalation of self-indulgence, and multiplication of apparatus, would reconcile a trend to more leisure with a need for and the possibility of less spending.

CONSERVING THE SELF AND THE SURROUNDINGS

Pierre Falcon composed his ballads without any equipment other than his mind, his voice, and his enthusiasm for the feats of his compatriots, "ces braves Brois-Brulés." Shakespeare and his actors performed plays that have lasted through the centuries with little costuming and less scenery. They depended for success not on super-colossal spectacles but on splendor of language and perception of human problems. The winner of a recent contest (that elicited 10,000 entries) needed only a pen (or, perhaps, a typewriter) and some paper and a sensitive mind to produce her poem. One of the finest performances of *Hamlet* given in recent years was the work of amateurs in a chapel in off-hours with only one "prop," a bean bag, and one item of costume, a cloak made from a table cloth. An Inuit theatre group from Greenland, using masks and costumes but neither scenery nor stage, created a deeply moving theatrical experience. A single flower can give enjoyment more exquisite than a mass of bloom. A family can have as much fun playing scramble-demon with old packs of cards as it might get out of a sophisticated electronic game. Spillikins or tiddly-winks can give more scope to precision of eye and delicacy of touch — and at least as much excitement — as playing a "one-armed bandit." Watching one live bird in the back yard can give more delight than watching an army of exotic creatures on the TV screen.

Leisure time activities stressing human perception and creative imagination and human thought and skill, put material accessories in their proper place as simply the instruments of human experience and human creativity. If this shift in emphasis is supplemented by a shift from stress on competition to cooperation, the pressure for ever more and more elaborate equipment would be still further reduced. Leisure occupations might then play a significant part in a movement towards a conserver society.

There will, of course, be enormous difficulties, difficulties in overcoming ingrained pecuniary canons of taste and tests of achievement; difficulties in breaking through barriers of lethargy to open up to everybody the excitements and rewards of do-it-yourself leisure activities; difficulties of dislocations in the business world and in the labor market, to say nothing of the unsolved problem of how to turn persistent unemployment into real leisure.

Perhaps the greatest difficulty of all, and one which is not just a problem of transition from a high consumption to a high activity leisure lifestyle, is the twin problem of space and of natural beauty. More and more space will certainly be needed for any massive expansion in creative activities. At the receiving end, all you need for TV viewing is somewhere to sit and a TV set. To act a play, to sing in a choir or play in an orchestra, to paint or sculpt, you need suitable space, and a good deal of it. For outdoor recreation you need playing fields, ski-slopes and beaches, lakes and rivers. For camping, wild river canoeing, mountain climbing, or bird watching you need unspoiled wilderness. When these delights become a wider part of the leisure life of growing urban populations with increasing free time, and, especially, bigger blocks of free time (three days at work, four days on the ski slopes), how can sufficient wilderness be made available to meet the demands that will be made on it? Here is a dilemma: Of all leisure time activities, experience of nature may be the most truly recreation, the most rewarding, and the most health-giving to mind and body. The need is evident but how can it be met? Throngs bent on wilderness experience destroy the wilderness. (The same problem already exists in the enjoyment of art and ancient buildings, as is illustrated in the congested condition of Florence and its galleries.) Perhaps, though, an end to high consumption life styles may release more wilderness for recreation by reducing the threat of destruction of wilderness beauty by hydro-electric development, lumbering or open pit mining.

Being and doing, not having; using only what is needed to realize human values, instead of consuming conspicuously; these are surely the keys to the future. They may prove the keys even to preserving unspoiled wilderness, our cultural heritage, finite resources, and, above all, personal and collective sanity.

REFERENCES

1. Innis, H. A. and Betty Ratz. "Labour," Encyclopedia of Canada, Vol. III. W. Stewart Wallace (ed.), Toronto: University Associates of Canada, 1936.
2. Ostry, Sylvia and H. D. Woods. *Labour Policy and Labour Economies in Canada.* Toronto: Macmillan of Canada, 1962. pp. 335-336.
3. Perspectives Canada II. Ottawa: Statistics Canada (Catalogue No. 11-508, 1977). p. 133.
4. Cordell, Arthur. "Bye Bye to Buy Buy," *Conserver Society Notes*, 11:3 (Summer, 1977). pp. 5-18.
5. Household Facilities and Equipment. Ottawa: Statistics Canada (Catalogue No. 64-202.).
6. Martin, William H. and Sandra Mason. *Leisure Markets in Europe.* London: Financial Times Business Publishing Division, 1978.
7. See, for instance, Daley, Herman (ed.) *Toward A Steady State Economy.* San Francisco: W. H. Freeman and Company, 1973; and Stapenhurst, Frederic. "Some Implications of a Conserver Society," *Labour Gazette* (November, 1977). pp. 511-513.
8. See, for instance, Hirsch, Fred. *The Social Limits to Growth.* Cambridge, Mass.: Harvard University Press, 1979; and Leiss, William *The Limits to Satisfaction.* Toronto: University of Toronto Press, 1976.
9. Scitovsky, Tibor. *The Joyless Economy.* Oxford: Oxford University Press, 1976.

Chapter Nineteen
Of Godots and Goodbars:
On Waiting and Looking For Change

Thomas L. Goodale

An often repeated short dialogue may be a useful beginning. It's a brief exchange between a native and a missionary.

> Native: "If I didn't know about God and sin, would I go to hell?"
> Missionary: "If you didn't know . . . well, no you wouldn't go to hell."
> Native: "Then why are you telling me these things?"

There is little doubt, anymore, that during the closing years of this century we will experience change; perhaps as rapid, pervasive, and dramatic as at any time in our history. And there is no doubt about which shoulders the burden of change rests upon, ..."the cutting edge of social change works at the level of the individual. Social change is change in an aggregate of individuals.'"[1] For a number of reasons, those working in the field of recreation, especially those employed by government at the municipal level, will be "front and center" through these years of change and will bear their share and more of the burden.

WE SHOULD CHANGE

First, even in a welfare state, the direct provision of recreation services is a peripheral rather than a central task of government. That does not, in any sense, diminish the importance of recreation or the legitimacy of government involvement. Rather, the nature of government involvement is at issue, as is the nature of recreation. The provision of recreation services through a large and complex organizational and institutional framework may, in fact, be antithetical to the nature of recreation; blocking rather than opening paths to the goals we espouse. This fundamental problem has been addressed by philosophers and utopians — Plato and Mill, Bellamy and Orwell for example — of every age. Bertrand Russell summarized it well more than 60 years ago:

The problem which faces the modern world is the combination of individual initiative with the increase in the scope and size of organizations. Unless it is solved, individuals will grow less and less full of life and vigor, more and more passively submissive to conditions imposed upon them. A society composed of such individuals cannot be progressive or add much to the world's stock of mental and spiritual possessions.[2]

WE MUST CHANGE

The second major reason why recreationists will be shouldering the burden of change is that most of the indicators of the decline (failure, demise, crisis, bankruptcy, etc.) of the present institutional order point to problems to which the recreation movement has always addressed itself. Perhaps the problems would have been worse if the recreation movement had not been concerned about them . And certainly recreation can't be faulted for the world's ills. Still, the problems remain, and remain the concern of recreationists in particular. Among indicators of failure, and consequently the need for dramatic change are, according to one of America's leading futurists, Willis Harman:

decreased sense of community;
increased sense of alienation and purposelessness;
increased frequency of personal disorders and mental illness;
increased rate of violent crime;
increased frequency and severity of social disruptions;
increased use of police to control behavior;
increased public acceptance of hedonistic behavior (particularly sexual), of symbols of degradation, and of lax public morality;
increased interest in non-institutionalized religious practices (e.g. cults, rituals, secret practices);
signs of specific and conscious anxiety about the future;
in some cases, economic inflation.[3]

As has frequently been noted, recreationists have been trying diligently, through organizations and institutions, to forestall or resolve these problems and the recreation movement has been drawn along in the development of a vast, public, social service system during the past several decades. But the problems remain; some suggest that we have made conditions worse through our well intended efforts to make them better. More and better of the same, we now recognize, will not help. What is required is different; not re-doubling our efforts or even reform. What is required is change.

New genres of literature have emerged in the past several years; notably the literature of crisis and transformation. We have, it seems, a population crisis, a food crisis, an economic crisis, an energy crisis, an urban crisis, a government crisis, and an environmental crisis. At the root of all this is said to be a crisis in values. Much recent literature has been devoted to discussions of "old" and "new" values, transforming values, and shifting from these values to those. But another genre of literature has emerged which suggests a crisis related to but perhaps even deeper than the crisis of values. It is a crisis, variously, of spirit, hope, courage, or will evident in the writings of Fromm, Tillich, May, and many others. Unless that crisis is solved, none of the others can be. And without intending "gloom and doom," Alexander Solzhenitsyn, in his widely debated 1978 commencement address at Harvard University, noted that, historically, the loss of spirit marked the beginning of the end.

The difference between a crisis of values and a crisis of spirit, hope, will or courage is important in another respect. The former exists at the social, organizational, institutional level; the latter exists at the individual level. As Kristol writes:

"A crisis in values is something that happens *out there*. It is something you can cope with through rational manipulation of institutions, of beliefs, of ideas. A spiritual crisis is something that happens to *you* — deep·down — and that you have to cope with. Therefore the phrase crisis in values can mislead by emphasizing what is essentially a technological approach to a problem that is not technological; this technological approach asks; how do we look at society; how do we manipulate it; how do we shape it in such a way that we don't have a crisis in values? I don't think that's the way. Real spiritual crises are resolved not by social science but by mysterious cultural processes which somehow reach inside every human being."[4]

Thus the indicators of widespread, systemic failures and the need for change relate particularly, but of course not exclusively, to the recreation field and the burden of change it must bear. And if the most fundamental crisis is not environment or population, or even values, but spirit and hope and courage and will, then the burden rests on the shoulders of individual recreationists and not on our agencies, organizations, or institutions.

Perhaps a brief, practical illustration will clarify the point and show the cutting edge in operation. A few years ago I had the opportunity to converse at length with about 35 recreationists employed in two Ontario municipalities. The informal interviews ranged into the future, dealing with goals, values, aspirations and the like for the society, their respective agencies and themselves. Materialistic and consumptive values and aspirations came under attack many times, and there seemed a longing for a conserver society and simpler and more authentic lifestyles. It was often mentioned, too, although with an air of chagrin, resignation or sometimes anger and frustration, that for the past three or four years, salary increases had been about six percent — significantly below annual increases in the cost-of-living — consequently they were falling further and further behind. Can it be that materialism is an "out there" notion while falling behind in salary is something that reaches deep down?

WE WILL CHANGE

The third reason why the burden of change rests heavily on the field of recreation, on individual recreationists, and particularly on those working in municipal government agencies is that our social-political-economic situation is already bringing about change. Slow growth is the underlying characteristic of our situation now and for the forseeable future. Slow growth in population, especially the decline in birth-rate to below replacement levels in North America and other "advanced" nations, is one element of this situation. The reshaping of age distribution from a pyramid to a diamond has consequences more far reaching than a shift from mainly child and youth oriented recreation services to serving adults and seniors more than previously. The impact on schools, teachers, local taxes, transfers of funds from other governments for education and other consequences is just one, albeit highly visible, example. Slow population growth also contributes to the present and foreseeable future situation of slow economic growth.

Inflation alone results in a smaller economy and at the present time the annual rate of inflation in the U.S. and Canada is about ten percent. Stagflation has recently entered our vocabularies to cover an economic period characterized by high rates of inflation and unemployment, both at the same time. In a global village, every nation's economy is shaped by international economic forces; the cartel of the major oil producing nations and the increasing industrial capacity of developing nations, among them. Slow growth, and perhaps eventually no growth — material growth at least — is the major force already reshaping our present situation and certain to shape our future.

The consequences of these changes in the economy and in the age distribution of the population are already being felt by many. Some examples are widely recognized; affecting the world of work, families, and government, and they apply to recreationists as individuals as well as employees. Work: increased competition for jobs; less job mobility; slower advancement for younger employees; increased frustration with conservative managers and administrators at the top; those with several years in a position "locked in" or "priced out" of other positions; unemployment and underemployment. Families: more two-income families in order to acquire today's standard necessities and modest amenities; more children and teen-agers on their own much of the time; pinched "discretionary" income forcing harder choices; more marital stress related to finances and to child rearing; alternative "family" groupings. Government: increasingly costly government sponsored social welfare programs for children and teens, the unemployed, and the growing number of retired and elderly persons; larger and costlier programs to combat alcoholism and other social problems; higher taxes when there is already widespread public concern with the size and cost of government in relation to its perceived efficiency and effectiveness.

The dilemma confronting government — increasing demands for government sponsored programs and services on one hand, and increasing concern about the present size and cost of government on the other — is a difficult one. "Proposition 13," a phrase understood everywhere in North America and in overseas places as well, had, as one significant consequence, a serious demoralizing effect on the public service in California.[5] Low morale among government employees at all levels seems a universal problem.

The impact of increased demand and increased disenchantment about the size and cost of government is felt most, but not exclusively of course, at the local government level, despite the fact that most people believe the efficiency and effectiveness of local government is greater than that at federal, or state or provincial levels. Diseconomies of scale alone warrant that belief. That the impact is felt most by local government is related to accessibility and familiarity and also to the tax structure. The bulk of local taxes is raised through the property tax, an annual visible bite taken after other taxes (income, sales, etc.) have already been paid. In a sense, property taxes are paid out of "after tax" dollars. Despite the fact that only a small proportion of an individual's or family's total tax burden is for municipal purposes, the impact of taxpayers discontent is felt first, and most, at the local government level.

After two or three decades of successfully competing for local tax dollars and good treatment in the hands of local taxpayers and politicians, "leisure service" expenditures have declined as a proportion of municipal government spending during the past decade or so.[6] It appears, too, that personnel expenditures, while still taking the lion's share, are decreasing as a proportion of leisure service spending. A review of budgets for six cities in Ontario for the years 1974 and 1978 revealed that while the combined budget increases totaled nearly $8,000,000, only 30 new, full-time positions were added. (If the average salary was $14,000, this accounts for only 5 percent of the total increase. Without detailed data, one can still safely guess that the increases must be due to inflation — energy costs and current capital expenditures — and probably debt service, both important budget items after salaries and wages).

What seems clear from all this is that we have created a large and complex array of public agencies and have "institutionalized" recreation as part of the total government social service system. It also seems clear that the recreation institution, if not the whole social service structure, cannot be sustained and we are caught having created demands and expectations that probably can't be met. This point has been argued by many, but perhaps none more cogently than Geoffrey Vickers:

If our world is to survive for another generation in any form which we today should regard as worth striving for, I have no doubt that for everyone, what we expect of ourselves and each other will have to go up and that for most of us in the western world what we expect of the system will have to go down.[7]

WE ESPOUSE CHANGE

The fourth reason recreation and recreationists must bear the burden of change is that for many years now, we have professed to want change. We even prided ourselves on being "change agents." And we have experienced in recent years a period of critical self-analysis, and either evolution or devolution to a philosophy suggesting quite different service modes than those characterized by direct provision of programs and facilities, telling our constituents about ourselves and encouraging them to participate with us.

Like Bertrand Russell, we want people to grow more full of life and vigor; we want to promote individual initiative. Is that not what we mean when we speak of learning, growth, development, positive health, self-actualization? Like Irving Kristol, we are concerned about what happens inside individuals, deep down. Is that not what we mean when we speak of individuation and holism, of qualitative dimensions and experiential qualities and therefore our subjective and intuitive selves? Like Geoffrey Vickers, we want people to rely more on themselves and each other rather than on the institutional complex of leisure services. Is that not what we mean when we speak of citizen participation and involvement and community development, and of self-sufficiency and self-determination? These and so many other voices are not singing a dirge; they're singing our song. That it may sound like a dirge merely illustrates that change is difficult, and sometimes threatening and abrasive. It may mean, too, that recreation is not institutionalized but recreationists are.

The roles and functions we have defined for ourselves during the past several years, and thus a service mode different from programmer and provider are widely accepted, at least among recreationists. So we have come to describe ourselves as educators, advocates, facilitators, enablers, catalysts, animators, encouragers, and developers. Still, this is more the idea than the practice.

WITHOUT GODOT OR GOODBAR

Godot, in the form of organizational or institutional change, is not likely to appear. What we get is reorganization. Petronius Arbiter, in the 210 B.C., noted: "I was to learn late in life that we tend to meet any new situation by reorganizing; and what a wonderful method it can be for creating the illusion of progress while producing confusion, inefficiency, and demoralization." Creative organizations, we have found, tend to be characterized by small size and autonomy.[8] Neither of these conditions obtain in most municipal recreation agencies, and only size may be characteristic of others. Organizational development, however widely touted, may be beyond us. As Donald Michael has noted, this requires years of effort and a champion at the top who can control the organization's resources and boundaries; requirements not found in government. Further:

The personal and interpersonal skills needed to cope with the emotional and intellectual burdens of the changeover and the operating situation far exceed those that most people seem to possess, and certainly exceed those that organizations, particularly public agencies, reward.[9]

Chris Arygris carries the argument further in discussing "Some Limits on Rational Man Organization Theory." He notes a process by which individuals become passive, lose a sense of being an origin or cause, deny or suppress their own self-actualizing needs, and rationalize being passive and controlled by taking it as a measure of loyalty and maturity.[10] Warren Bennis, in exploring reasons why leaders can't lead, notes that all of us conspire in submersing ourselves in routine and formulates Bennis' Law (joining Parkinson and so many others) stating that routine work drives out important work. He, too, notes that change may be possible for small groups given enough truth and trust.[11] In most large organizations accounting to and informing everyone else about virtually everything one does has become a major task and a major source of succumbing to routine. Whatever arguments support this routine, still it a symptom of generalized lack of trust.

Organizational change, like social change, results from change in an aggregate of individuals. Waiting for change is a non-exercise in futility; in the meantime an organizational climate conducive to change may deteriorate as incompatible demands from the outside are felt more and more. Too, the gap between the idea and the reality widens. Similarly, Mr. Goodbar, in the form of answers to questions or solutions to problems, may not be found no matter how harried our search. At issue is the nature of change, organizations, leadership and the like. Without that understanding, we might as well keep working on blue-ribbon task forces, which, Bennis argues, insures the status quo as "their reports get better and better while the problems get worse and worse."[12]

Organizations, anymore, are beleaguered by attempts to provide answers and solve problems. Technique after technique is adopted and soon discarded. Barely was the Management by Objectives technique understood before Management by Results replaced it. After struggling with Program Performance Budgeting Systems, we are now struggling with Zero-Based Budgeting. We have sharpened and flattened pyramids changing steps in the hierarchy and span of control, and developed matrices and ad hocracies. Even if all these techniques contributed enough to off-set the drain from other efforts required in adopting them, the major effect seems still to be on organizational efficiency — an internal, system criteria — rather than on effectiveness — an external, service criteria. Organizational change does not appear to result from technical remedies for internal problems. The cutting edge of change is at the individual level.

SOME OBSTACLES

If the emerging philosophy of recreation service and the emerging social and economic forces point us in the same direction, then smooth and orderly change, and a smooth transition to a new service mode for the future should be expected. But the reality is that each of us resists change; each of us being products of our past; each of us better able to respond to yesterday's situation than tomorrow's. Understanding and managing change as a personal process is a requirement for all of us and there is a rich and growing literature to help meet it.[13] Along with obstacles to change which face everyone, recreationists have others, in addition to those noted or alluded to above, to overcome. A few are noted that seem sufficiently general as to apply to many.

1. Lack of union strength or professional status may result in some anxiety and insecurity. Difficulties in identifying specific and special competencies (a problem now being addressed in several quarters) adds to the problem.

2. Direct provision of programs and services is visible, tangible proof of a service being rendered. The roles attendant on the emerging philosophy — enabling, facilitating, and the like — are much less visible. There is some risk in foregoing visibility, since credit tends to be contingent upon it.

3. The development of successful programs, even if only measured quantitatively, is not always easy. There is an investment and some satisfaction of the need to be needed. The emotional task of letting go is difficult.

4. Recreationists do much simply because it's easier; that is, more efficient. Effectiveness may sometimes require a recreationist to do nothing, a task difficult enough in itself, and exacerbated by pressure from those who appreciate no objective except efficiency.

5. Success as providers, and the resulting dependency of the public on direct services, will be a source of stress and friction.

6. While recreationists are intent on enabling growth, learning, self-determination, development, involvement and the like, increasing stress on members of the public may mean that their primary objective in a recreational pursuit is simply escape.

7. Roles have been identified, however ill-defined, but less progress has been made in identifying goals and objectives and even less in establishing criteria by which to judge the success of the new service mode suggested by philosophy and identified roles.

The last obstacle listed is one which recreationists, as a group, can address so some fairly specific goals and objectives are suggested, not for adoption but for discussion and debate. While the goals and objectives relate to recreation service rather than individual change, they can only be achieved when the aggregate of individuals in their respective agencies, change. Some uncertainty, stress, risk, and failure will likely accompany change since the amount and pace of change is hardly uniform, and since organizations and institutions are not conducive to it. In this process we cannot expect much from our institutions. What we expect of ourselves and each other will have to go up.

SOME ASSUMPTIONS

By way of a summary and to re-set the context in which the suggestions are cast, six assumptions about our present and foreseeable future situation are noted.

1. It is assumed that the foreseeable future will be characterized by a slow growing and smaller economy: slow growing as population growth slows and at some point stabilizes; smaller as a result of inflation, resource shortages and limits and the like.

2. It is assumed that the pressures of increasing demands for service and increasing concern about the size, cost and inefficiency of government will be felt first, and most, at the local government level.

3. It is assumed that what we expect of our institutions must go down and what we expect of ourselves and each other must go up.

4. It is assumed that the cutting edge of change is at the individual level. Institutions and organizations are not going to collapse, as some suggest, nor are they likely to change rapidly or markedly. Social change is the result of change in an aggregate of individuals.

5. It is assumed that there is already much individual stress in the society and that there will be much more. The reconstruction of viable, convivial institutions in family, neighborhood, and community groups and among colleagues will be essential if people are to have the necessary base of support from which to foster and manage change.

6. Finally, the fundamental assumption underlying all of this is that individuals and groups are fully capable, with support as needed, of generating most of their own recreational opportunities, including most of what is now provided by governments. The hesitancy and reluctance born of paternal dependence, thus far agreeable to both the people and the government, is perhaps the overriding obstacle to change consistent with our professed beliefs and contemporary situation.

If the assumptions are not acceptable, then the suggestions certainly won't be because many will be difficult to accept in any situation. Each suggestion leads to many others, some of which may be even more difficult to accept. To suggest, for example, decreased budgets and personnel complements in the public sector is a direct challenge to our thinking about manpower, college and university enrollments and curricula, and a host of related matters.

SOME TASKS

Some objectives and criteria for the new service mode might be:

1. A smaller role for government: reduced program expenditures by government with no reduction in participation; reduction of total man hours of employment in the public sector; wholesale reduction in the number of rules, regulations, policies, and laws.

2. More assistance to others: redistribution of government resources to community groups via grants; sharing space, office supplies and equipment, technical administrative support, and the like; "no strings" support of voluntary, non-profit agencies; more incentives and more cooperation with the private sector.

3. Greater community identity and autonomy: decentralization of decision making authority throughout staff and back to community groups; indices of shifts of power away from government; reemphasis on smaller, decentralized, and community controlled facilities.

4. More public (versus special interest group) service: increased emphasis on geographic community rather than communities of interest; increased shares of resources for the general public rather than special interests; increased integration of age and interest groups.

5. Less structure and rigidity: reduced "red tape" and faster response time; increased flexibility in scheduling; fewer leagues, teams, and classes; increased spontaneous activities and events.

6. More efficiency and (hopefully) effectiveness: improved coordination of current and comprehensive community information for all programs, resources, social services and government affairs; increased coordination of all community programs, facilities and resources; increased use of all facilities in place; reduced debt service and current capital expense.

7. Less political alienation and social anomie: increased political sophistication and participation in the political process; decreased brutal, sensate, and escapist activity; reduced vandalism, alcoholism, and other indices of social malaise.

8. Increased individual assumption of responsibility: growth in volunteer services; increased neighborly sharing and self help; increased family activity; reintegration of the young and old in meaningful community service roles.

MOVING ON

Essential next steps include refining and consolidating appropriate objectives; redefining or "operationalizing" statements into measurable terms; identifying indicators by which progress or its lack can be observed; establishing baseline information. Another critical next step is to educate elected and appointed officials and the public about our situation, philosophy and assumptions about the next decade or so, and thus the efficacy of a different service mode and the objectives being pursued. Again, the service will become lower profile, if not invisible. Too, there is much evidence that the public is happy with the status quo based on direct provision of programs, facilities and services.[14] And if Lasch is correct in his depiction of a narcissistic culture,[15] these steps are very long ones and they're uphill all the way.

None of this will come about by "Waiting for Godot" or "Looking for Mr. Goodbar." Every individual recreationist is responsible for change. There are no easy or universal answers to our questions or solutions to our problems. The circumstances of every muncipality are different. The circumstances, mandates, and resources of every agency are different. Problems and opportunities in one area do not exist in another; an appropriate strategy here would be inappropriate there. If the burden of change finally rests on the shoulders of each individual, then the ubiquitous question of how can only be determined by each individual according to his or her own lights, abilities and limits.

We began with a dialogue and end with one since the question of how we get from where we are to where we would like to go reminds one of the exchange between a tourist and a New York City cab driver.

Tourist: "How do I get to Carnegie Hall?"
Cab driver: "Practice, my friend, practice."

REFERENCES

1. Pizer, Stuart and Travers, Jerry. *Psychology and Social Change.* New York: McGraw-Hill, 1975. p. 11.
2. Russell, Bertrand. "Individual Liberty and Public Control." In Desaulniers, Louise (Ed.), *119 Years of The Atlantic.* The Atlantic Monthly Company, 1977. p. 272.
3. Harman, Willis. "The Coming Transformation." *The Futurist,* 11:2, (April, 1977). p. 107. That these are recreation's tasks see Weiner, Myron E., "A Systems Approach to Leisure Services." In Lutzin, Sidney G. and Storey, Edward H. (Eds.), *Managing Municipal Leisure Services,* Washington, D.C.: International City Management Association, 1973. p. 7.
4. Kristol, Irving. "Values in Contemporary Society." *Working Paper of the Rockefeller Foundation,* (March, 1974). p. 7.
5. From a conversation with Dr. David Gray, Vice President for Administration and Staff Development, California State University at Long Beach, January, 1979.
6. Crompton, John L. and Van Doren, Carlton S. "Changes in the Financial Status of Leisure Services in Thirty Major U.S. Cities, 1964-1974." *Journal of Leisure Research,* 10:1, (1978). pp. 37-46. This is also the case in Ontario cities according to data compiled by James Maxwell for presentation to a meeting of the Ontario Municipal Recreation Association, March, 1979.
7. Vickers, Geoffrey. *Making Institutions Work.* New York: John Wiley and Sons, 1973. p. 15.
8. Steiner, Gary (Ed.). *The Creative Organization.* Chicago: University of Chicago Press. 1965.
9. Michael, Donald. "On the Social Psychology of Organizational Resistances to Long Range Planning." *I.E.E.E. Journal,* SCM2:5, (November, 1972). p. 583.
10. Argyris, Chris. "Some Limits on Rational Man Organization Theory." *Public Administrative Review,* 33:3 (May-June, 1973), pp. 253-267.
11. Bennis, Warren. *The Unconscious Conspiracy: Why Leaders Can't Lead.* New York: Amacom (A Division of the American Management Association), 1976. p. 161-186. As to succumbing to routine, see especially Mintzberg, Henry. *The Nature of Managerial Work.* New York: Harper and Row, 1973.
12. Bennis, *Op. Cit.,* p. 33.

13. See Pizer and Travis, *Op. Cit.* and Adams, John, et. al. *Transition: Understanding and Managing Personal Change.* London: Martin Robertson and Company, 1976.
14. Goodale, Thomas and Witt, Peter A. "Goals for Municipal Recreation in Ontario." *Recreation Research Review.* 7:3 (December, 1979). pp. 17-26.
15. Lasch, Christopher. *The Culture of Narcissism: American Life in an Age of Diminishing Expectations.* New York: W.W. Norton and Company, 1978.

SECTION THREE

Rethinking Professional Status: A Word Of Caution

INTRODUCTION

The first two sections of this book deal with a) the need to clarify the conceptual basis of our field in order to improve our understanding of the phenomena (recreation, leisure, play, etc.) we are dealing with and b) the kinds of service provision changes that are necessary if we are to make the park and recreation movement more responsive to the needs of citizens in the 80's and beyond. The ten articles in this section deal with a variety of issues concerning growing professionalization within the park and recreation movement both in the United States and worldwide.

The articles cover three sub-areas and a "final thought." In the first of these sub-areas, the authors raise issues and questions about the search by and benefits of professional status for workers in the park and recreation movement. Witt (20) critically analyzes the motives for seeking professional status, by asking whether professional recognition is sought to achieve power for professionals or as a means of achieving better service for consumers. Lord, Hutchison, and Van Derbeck (21) examine the impact of professional practice on the needs and goals of consumers. Reynolds (22) challenges us to examine whether our professionalization efforts lead to too much social control over our "clients" by manipulating expectations and values. Witt (23) questions whether our efforts should focus on re-educating consumers about leisure or reforming a service system that does not fully meet people's needs. Together, they ask us to examine whether we inappropriately blame individuals for lack of motivation where in fact inadequate service provision may be equally at fault. They also ask us to determine whether we inadvertently disable individuals via too narrowly defined professional responsibilities, buckpassing, or misguided benevolence.

These first four articles present issues that are too often ignored by those who argue for the necessity of park and recreation workers achieving professional status. In an age where it is not clear whether professionalism implies service or survival, Witt (20), for example, raises questions that must be dealt with before the recreation and park movement rushes headlong into acquiring the trappings of professionalism such as accreditation, certification, registration, licensing, and a code of ethics. In essence, the authors in this sub-section are more concerned with the impact of professionals on people's lives than with the criteria for being a professional.

Woven through these first articles are a series of dilemmas which face any aspiring profession. One series deals with the thin line distinguishing between attempts at helping versus influencing or leading versus directing. Another series deals with means for preserving the delicate balance between independence and dependence of action or intrinsic and extrinsic motivation. In the rush to achieve status and authority, Lord, Hutchison and Van Derbeck (21) ask whether the recreation and park movement has failed to consider whether professionalization is consistent with meeting the needs of the people we intend to serve.

Indeed, as Reynolds (22) and Witt (23) note, it is not clear whether the people we serve are considered clients, recipients, or consumers. Although just labels, each designation has broad implications for determining the source of control, motivation, evaluation, and mandate for services.

Another theme that is touched on by a number of the authors is the growing uneasy feeling, perhaps even malaise, among many professionals that all is not right. Our public selves increasingly seek status, recognition, and security; our private selves wonder whether we are really fulfilling the kind of dream for the recreation and park movement that Duncan (29) sees many of our founding leaders as having. In a field dominated by civil service workers, and given the dilemmas and contradictions that daily haunt our decisions and practices, there is a tendency to ask too few questions. The conspiracy of silence thus threatens to become a pattern of "benign neglect." It is not clear whether the recreation movement as it has emerged in the later half of this century has the philosophic foundation or creative instinct to get beyond muddling through the difficult issues that lie ahead.

Several other aspects of the rush to achieve professional status are raised by the articles in the second sub-area of the section. In general, these chapters deal with the knowledge base on which practice is based and the organizational problems that diverse park and recreation organizations have faced in binding together diverse interests into a movement.

Burdge (24) discusses the struggle to create a viable body of knowledge that would add credibility to the movement's claim for professional status as well as the quest by researchers from a variety of disciplines to find an institutional home for leisure research. Goodale (25) discusses some of the fundamental problems or biases that are inherent in the conceptualization and methodology of leisure research.

Burdge (24) asks whether leisure research can exist within professionally oriented park and recreation departments. He notes the name changes that many of these departments went through in the 70's and early 80's to include the idea of "leisure" and "studies" along with or as a replacement for recreation and parks. Burdge is concerned that more discipline oriented leisure researchers (sociologists, economists etc.) may have difficulty living within the expectation and support systems of these renamed units. More importantly, Burdge is concerned whether leisure research will be supported by the profession. Thus, he sees a growing separation of leisure research from parks and recreation education programs whose central concern is professional training.

Goodale (25) explores some of the underlying issues impinging on the quantity and quality of leisure research. He notes, for example, the problems of aligning discovery with a publish or perish university environment that rewards production. Thus, editors receive more manuscript status inquiries as tenure time approaches and investigators gear research efforts to areas where funding is available as opposed to undertaking a line of inquiry consistent with their own interests. Goodale also points to our rewarding of atomistic approaches as opposed to theory building and overview efforts. Finally, Goodale looks at what we do and do not research. For example, demand and wants seem more prevalently investigated than need. Does this exemplify a society of affluence or is it a result of our inability to operationalize difficult concepts?

Together Burdge (24) and Goodale (25) raise the level of discourse about the purpose and support systems for leisure research. Combined with articles in the first subsection, they expand the debate about whose interests are served by professional status, research undertakings, and professional preparation programs.

Hartsoe (26) discusses the past, present, and future of professional organizations in the park and recreation field with particular reference to the National Recreation and Park Association. Hartsoe traces a past leading to the merger of diverse organizations into NRPA in 1965 and a future that may see the re-emergence of diverse state and national organizations representing a variety of sub or regional interests. He also discusses the inherent structural problems of NRPA in its uneasy marriage of professional and lay interests.

While a body of knowledge, research efforts, and some kind of organizational structure are considered essential to the development and legitimacy of a profession, Burdge, Goodale and Hartsoe all point to the dilemmas and contradictions in creating processes, symbols and substance. The diversity of matters is clear and the complexity of alternatives overwhelming. Consensus as to purpose and methods, in the final analysis, may be an illusion.

Westland (27, 28) provides two chapters that constitute a third sub-area of this section. Westland (27) helps us to avoid a myopic view of recreation and leisure services as well as emerging professionalization by discussing developments in other countries. In particular he notes the resentment of the export of the North American post-industrial recreation services model in emerging or industrial nations. Ironically, he points to the re-emergence of the belief in the individual as his/her best leisure resource in highly industrialized regions of the world at a time when developing nations with strong central governments are showing a strong tendency towards state intervention. Westland wonders if the North American experience needs to be studied and its strengths adopted while avoiding the pitfalls of direct implantation of philosophies and methods created for another culture.

Westland's second paper (28) leads directly from the first. Here he discusses alternatives in developing national recreation policies. Governments may take an integrated, sectorial or no-policy approach to planning. While he argues for the former, he clearly shows the advantages and disadvantages of each. In doing so he reiterates a central theme developed in the first four chapters in this section: that individuals, not governments must ultimately be responsible for their own leisure. He also directs us to rethink the meaning of leisure as a prelude to developing policy.

Section three and the book conclude with Duncan's (29) persuasive reminder of our roots and their implications for our present and future. The park and recreation movement had as its founders people who even today would be considered radicals and reformers. Gulick, Addams, Olmsted, Riis and Lee would feel comfortable with the discussions of purpose and concerns with professionalization contained throughout the book. Their focus was on people, needs (not wants), and means (not ends). Duncan's radicals would feel at home with Westland's (29) call for a society where "to be", "to produce", and "to participate" are valued more than "to have," "to consume" and "to withdraw."

T.L.G.
P.A.W.

Chapter Twenty
Gaining Professional Status: Who Benefits?

Peter A. Witt

Is there any documented correlation between possession of a recreation degree and innovative leadership within the profession and community served? Are there any concrete data which demonstrate that recreators who have degrees in social work, teaching, psychology, or even English are less effective than those with degrees in recreation?[1]

Since the merger that formed the National Recreation and Park Association (NRPA) in 1965, achieving full professional status for workers in the park and recreation field has been a steadfast goal. However, concern within the field for instituting accreditation and certification goes back to the 1930's and 1950's respectively. In the 1980's, NRPA and the American Alliance of Leisure and Recreation (AALR) are close to achieving procedures in these areas. Along with defining a body of knowledge, establishing a code of ethics, and achieving other trappings of a profession, these efforts have been hailed by workers in the field as giving them the status and recognition they feel they deserve in addition to potentially protecting the public via improved quality of service delivery.

While acquisition of the accoutrements of professionalization has been a central goal of the park and recreation field, professional status, power and the ability to provide service to consumers is being increasingly questioned in a variety of other fields. Although park and recreation workers are basking in their new found status, it seems appropriate to examine why there is increasing agreement with George Bernard Shaw's observation that "professions are a conspiracy against the laity." While continued efforts to professionalize the field are inevitable, understanding the increasing concern over the power and status of professions may help the park and recreation field achieve the advantages of professionalization while avoiding some of the pitfalls.

COMPETING EXPLANATIONS

While there has always been a bit of suspicion of the power and prestige held by professionals, societies (especially western) have fostered the growth of professions despite Shaw's warning. In most instances the public has been willing to grant special power and privilege to specific occupational groups in exchange for dedicated service. Larsen notes that:

> Society grants these rewards because professions have special competence in esoteric bodies of knowledge linked to central needs and values of social systems, and because professions are devoted to the service of the public, above and beyond incentives.[2]

This view is similar to what Cullen labels the "exchange-structural" explanation for why occupations develop professional elements. Exchange-structuralists argue that accomplishing intellectually complex tasks in occupations centered on working with people "necessitates occupations having features such as long training, ethical codes, licensure, high income and high prestige."[3] Thus, granting professional status is a bargain struck between society and a given occupation by which individuals agree to acquire the knowledge and education necessary to perform a complex task in exchange for power and privileges. Society gives professions the right to monitor their members' performance and prescribe educational curricula and standards. Professions, in return, give dedicated, quality service.[4]

An opposing view of professions to that of the exchange-structuralists is the "power orientation" perspective. This orientation questions the underlying motivation of occupational groups in their quest to be recognized as professions. Power and prestige rather than quality of service are viewed as the major motivation for development of a profession. While the exchange-structuralist view implies a free market system of rational exchange of status for quality service, the power orientation views professions as monopolies based on self-interest.

> Consistent with their critical position, the power theorists are quick to argue that many of the occupations considered as non professions are qualitatively no different than the accepted professions — yet, because they lack the necessary resources and power, these non-professions are not successful in convincing society of their needs for autonomy.[5]

While the exchange perspective views professionalism as a means, the power perspective sees professionalism as an end.[6]

The difference between these two views of why professional status is sought or granted can help us understand why professionalization is viewed as a direct benefit to society by some and as a conspiracy by others. The exchange view sees the trade off value of what professionals receive in return for service while the power theorists are suspicious that status and prestige have been usurped under false pretenses primarily for reasons of self-interest.

Cullen offers further contrasts between how the exchange and power perspectives approach certain criteria used to define a profession. Three are discussed here in order to more fully understand the differing approaches: the code of ethics, long formal training, and licensure or credentialing.[7]

Criteria Defining Professions: Two Views
In the exchange view, a code of ethics is the "institutionalized manifestation of the service ideal and colleague control."[8] The need for a code of ethics arises due to the competency gap between clients and professionals. Only fellow colleagues are thus thought to be able to monitor the performance of their professional peers. A code of ethics also promotes the interests of the client by specifying criteria for judging service delivery and quality.

Power theorists argue, on the other hand, that a code of ethics is simply a public relations tool. Friedson has noted that:

a code of ethics may be seen as one of many methods an occupation may use to induce general belief in the ethicality of its members, without *necessarily* bearing directly on individual ethicality.[9]

In the case of long formal training, exchange theorists believe that the complexity of professional work necessitates this commitment. On the other hand, power theorists contend that the presumed necessity of long formal training is just another smoke screen or attempt to sell the earned nature of power and prestige to the public. Power theorists point to studies showing the lack of a direct relationship between length of formal education and actual job performance.

Similar contrasts can be made between the exchange and power perspective on licensure and credentialing. Exchange theorists view the license or credential as a method of the profession and a mandate by the society for establishing standards that limit entry to professional practice to only those individuals with the capability of serving the public interest. Federal and State regulatory agencies assess whether or not such a mandate should be extended to a given occupational group. In essence, these regulatory bodies do not establish standards. In most cases they give the profession the right to judge, for example, whether an individual possesses sufficient knowledge or expertise to be credentialed or licensed. What constitutes sufficiency or expertise is also usually left to the profession to decide.

Noting both the competence gap associated with highly professionalized occupations as well as the 'institutionalized altruism' (Merton, 1975) built into the ethical code and other norms of professional behavior, exchange-structuralists see autonomous self-control as necessary for the professions because they believe it is a viable mechanism by which society can be protected from dangerous exchange relationships with 'quacks.'[10]

On the other hand, power theorists see potential for abuse in a system that can be utilized to monopolize the job market by using licensure and credentialing as means to decrease the supply of practitioners and increase occupational rewards. Because education is often used as the standard for defining whether an individual is qualified to be credentialed, licensing laws can specify strict accreditation and educational standards that limit enrollment or the number of graduates. While these laws may seem on the surface to be aimed at protecting the public by promoting quality education and in turn improved practice, power theorists are again suspicious that the implied monopoly may encourage abuses and laxness based on self-interest.

As a result of acquiring this highly specialized knowledge, professions demand autonomy and independence for their actions. They demand immunity from the consequences which result from intervention (except by peer evaluation). In a sense, professions which are accorded [this status] are removed from the competitive marketplace . . . . Once an occupation is able to subordinate the consumers' freedom of choice, it has monopolized services.[11]

The resulting monopoly may create a situation, for example, where salaries are artificially inflated because demand for workers outstrips the sanctioned supply and where quality of service is controlled by occupational standards as opposed to consumer criteria. Often this means that the profession, rather than the consumer, controls the basis, rationale, and mechanics of service delivery. Professional control of entry, knowledge to be acquired, and standards of practice may give it undue autonomy and powers of self-regulation.

Power or Exchange

Cullen has conducted an exploratory, yet complex, study designed to ascertain whether either the exchange or power perspective is supported by available data concerning the relative impact of both power-related and exchange-structuralist determinants of professionalism. While no formal theory was tested, Cullen's findings led him to several propositional conclusions. In essence, Cullen concluded that in most professions functional reciprocity (exchange) and power act concurrently. He noted that a) "occupational task-complexity and intellectual sophistication are the major determinants of professionalism's characteristics" (ex. educational requirements) and b) "to the degree that professionalism's characteristics are not determined by task complexity/intellectual sophistication, they are determined by the occupational group's power."[12]

Cullen's propositions do not indicate that task-complexity and intellectual sophistication are necessary for an occupation to achieve status. Indeed, occupational groups involved in work requiring lower levels of task-complexity and intellectual sophistication may be able to achieve designation as a profession via increased use of power (ex. influence or use of the financial resources of the national association). Power alone, however, in absence of perceived task complexity and intellectual sophistication of the role requirements, may be insufficient for achieving professional status. Regulatory bodies and public suspicion probably will prevent creating a profession based purely on the use of influence or organizational resources.

From the foregoing discussion, it should be clear that there is probably no such thing as a pure profession or only one route by which an occupation becomes recognized as a profession. Listing a set of characteristics that typify a profession and checking off how many of these elements a given occupation possesses fails to take into account which characteristics are the most critical under the law (i.e. laws that grant rights to license or accredit) or in the eyes of the public. In point of fact, many occupations possess some elements that have been used to designate a profession. The label "profession" may be in fact misleading and subject to abuse.

It is also necessary to keep in mind that occupational groups seek professional status for differing reasons (i.e. exchange or power). Thus, a discussion of the role, value and legitimacy of a given occupation's claim to professional status should be based on an assessment of the motives of the occupational group, benefits of the perceived status to society *and* the occupational group, and also the costs or negative consequences of granting such status.

LEGITIMATE PURSUIT?

Do current efforts to achieve the professional designation for the park and recreation field arise out of the belief that the occupational tasks involved are *complex* and the knowledge base for practice characterized by *intellectual sophistication?* Or, do efforts at achieving professional status depend primarily on the use of influence and organizational resources (such as NRPA's staff and the hard work of members)? Or, as noted by Cullen, are there elements of exchange *and* power at work in the field's quest to be designated as a profession?

There is little hard evidence to support the contention that exchange or power alone or some combination of the two motivations are driving current efforts at professionalization. My own view is that some combination of exchange and power are motivating the efforts being made to achieve recognition of the AALR-NRPA accreditation process by the Council on Professional Accreditation, the national body responsible for legitimizing a given occupation's desire to accredit educational programs. Elements of exchange and power also seem to be the motivation for establishing certification procedures, a recognized code of ethics, parameters for defining a body of knowledge and other elements that are considered essential to defining an occupation as a profession.

While my own inclination is to agree with Shaw's conspiracy view of professions, it is also easy to understand why the park and recreation field would seek professional status from an exchange perspective as well as self protective reasons independent of exchange.

Increasingly, achieving designation as a profession is seen as one way of defining job specificity, legitimizing control over working conditions, and meeting the needs of society for quality performance. While this may sound like a restatement of the power view, it is more a recognition of the degree of status and prestige accorded to recognized professions and the desire of a wider group of occupations to achieve the resulting rewards. Successful democratization of access to status and rewards in the last 20 years will probably only lead to redefinition of criteria for determining acceptance and designation of a given occupation as a profession. But, for the time being, it appears that many occupational groups involved in work without evidence of task-complexity or intellectual sophistication are seeking professional designation.

On the sole basis of "keeping up with the Jones," the park and recreation field probably has good reason to seek professional status. If we believe remuneration is too limited and differentiation of occupations on the basis of professional recognition is an important determinant of remuneration, self protection in an age of specialization seems mandatory. Of course we should not delude ourselves as to our motivation by believing our own pronouncements on the irreparable societal consequences of failing to grant the park and recreation field the status of a profession. While we may need to develop an elaborate "story" to sell our claim we should be cognizant of the impact of the game on the quality of service we may ultimately render to the public. In other words, whether professional status is achieved as the result of exchange or power, or as requisite to occupational survival, we need to ask the more fundamental question: are the needs of consumers ultimately served? The following section will briefly discuss several consequences of professional status that may be potentially detrimental to the consumer and in some cases even the professional. These consequences include: a) inappropriate socialization of potential workers and b) failure to meet consumer needs.

THE SOCIALIZATION PROCESS

One of the potentially negative consequences of the accreditation/certification/licensure process is the establishment of a process of socialization that individuals must go through to gain the right to practice. Thus, individuals are selectively admitted to degree granting programs, educated with regard to a particular body of knowledge, taught accepted skills and techniques, and reinforced for absorbing a prescribed set of occupational values and attitudes. The more rigid the accreditation (what can be taught) and certification/licensure (what should be learned) processes, the more rigid will be this socialization process.

It has been observed in the literature dealing with a variety of professions that each profession tends to develop a paradigm based upon:

a taken-for-granted conception of what the issue is, and how it is solvable. Each profession tends to see the world in terms of its own characteristic conception of problems and solutions . . .[13]

Thus, professions tend to become like social movements.

They recruit only certain types of persons, they develop highly elaborate ideologies and supra-individual values, they have their own mechanisms of socialization and they often attempt to proselytize and bring new members into the fold.[14]

Implicit in these statements is the danger that the paradigm may cloud professionals' perceptions of consumers' problems and needs and thereby diminish the prospect of successful service delivery. Two major sources have been identified to account for the development of a professional paradigm: 1) the personality and other characteristics of individuals who self-select or are chosen to enter a particular profession; and 2) the training and socialization process that individuals go through prior to and during their professional careers. Both of these sources have the potential of developing filters or biases concerning the problems a particular profession chooses to address and the solutions adopted for dealing with the perceived problems.

Bishop, et. al. found significant differences in selected personality traits and achievement measures between students in recreation and those in other university departments.[15] Of particular interest was that recreation students were shown to be exceptionally high in extroversion when compared to students in other departments or to general population norms. Based on these results and on similar test results involving recreation students at four other universities, along with Eysenck's[16] theory of extroversion-introversion and its behavioral implications, Bishop observed that:

Many recreation students (and in our judgment many recreation professionals) tend to be socially oriented and dependent, somewhat conventional, need fairly large amounts of temporal variation or change, tend to prefer action over thinking . . . . All of these characteristics cannot be explained by extroversion. They do suggest a consistent recreology character or type, however, of which extroverted tendencies appear to be an important part.[17]

Added to Bishop's results are observations that recreation students tend to have a significant history of recreational involvements through which they developed the requisite skills to participate and the motivation for continued involvement. Many of these interests are in physical activities although recreation students currently seem to have more diversified interests than previously, when recreation was largely associated with physical education and a "jock" mentality. In addition, most students entering the recreation field have had significant contact with some form of recreation service agency through part-time work.

The socialization and training process that potential professionals are subjected to via educational experiences prior to entering the field and on an ongoing basis via inservice training and contact with fellow workers, exposure to a common group of educational and professional materials and so on, also has a significant impact on the development of a paradigm.[18] These experiences are usually endorsed by educators and practitioners alike as necessary to successful professional development and socialization.[19] There is a tendency to adopt a fairly consistent in-group philosophy of the need for recreation services, the benefits of participation and the best means of organizing recreational opportunities. Many of these perceptions will be "correct," i.e., they will prove useful in meeting needs as defined by consumers. However, in some cases professionals seem to develop a paradigm either for the rationale or the methods of offering services that differ dramatically from citizens' perceptions of what needs to be done. As Hughes notes, "Professions profess. They profess to know better than their clients what ails them or their affairs."[20]

Most people feel the need to identify with some group. Combining this need with the tendency of the in-group to preserve itself via subtle pressure to conform to ideas and working practices may lead workers in most professional areas through an acculturation process wherein the social values, behavioral norms, and symbols of the occupational group are internalized.[13] In this way, the philosophy and practices of a given profession are institutionalized and protected from erosion from outside influences. Most professions tend more toward the status quo led by an old guard that depends heavily on tradition and years of experience rather than an ongoing process of questioning of assumptions and practices as a basis for future services. Of course, every profession also has its "black sheep" and its radicals, those who resist the acculturation process. They, in fact, play a valuable role by questioning underlying assumptions and providing a basis for innovation and change.

There are some other potential costs in the accreditation/certification/professionalization process. Standardization of practice and knowledge, for example, can be good but it can also squelch innovation, experimentation, etc. One wonders whether, if people in Columbus's day had had a professional body to adhere to, we still might think the world was flat and rests on the backs of a group of turtles.

I am also concerned that we will make the entire focus on university education to get a job, i.e. to prepare students to enter a profession. This refocusing of *higher* education on *hire* education and job training violates the basic tenets of being an educated person. While a liberal arts education may also be abused, there are advantages to understanding the world in which we live in more general terms than professional education will allow.

RISING CONSUMERISM

As a result of the socialization process, recreation professionals may develop and protect assumptions about consumer needs that do not match consumers' perceptions of their own needs. Thus, professionals may over- or under-estimate the extent to which particular barriers such as lack of time, money, or equipment, are problematic for consumers. For example, recreation professionals may see lack of motivation, inability to maintain commitments, or even lack of physical fitness, as problems of greater magnitude than they actually are. Such "conclusions" may be self-serving in that they can be used to justify the development of services to overcome professionally perceived barriers. Service professions need people who need services.

Another example of where professionals and consumers may differ is over how to define what is a "wholesome" leisure activity.

Obviously, it can be viewed differently by the provider of park and recreation services and the consumer. Therefore, the critical question becomes this: who is to determine what is wholesome, the consumer or the professional? Should the profession impose its values upon the consumer or should the consumer exercise control over the profession . . .?[20]

It should be noted that professional "biases" may actually be based on facts or knowledge not available to or ignored by consumers such as the relationship between fitness and health and the demonstrated low level of fitness in the populace. On the other hand, it could be argued that citizens are as fit as they want to be, are aware of the implications of fitness for health, and do not share the profession's concern with developing a fit society. Who is "right" raises numerous questions for professionals, such as whether to be proactive or reactive or adopt a leadership as compared to a followership posture. Who has the right to make decisions is another issue; professionals have the responsibility to do so. The biases upon which professionals make those decisions is at issue.

One result of the growth of professionalism and the tendency toward developing professional paradigms has been a corresponding emergence of consumerism. Consumerism involves an attempt to insure that the type, quantity, and quality of goods and services provided are in keeping with needs and standards as defined by the ultimate user as opposed to the supplier. As professionals have moved toward increasing autonomy and control, consumers have fought back by demanding greater involvement in all aspects of the planning and provision of needed goods and services. Thus, for example, the delivery of park and recreation services is being increasingly affected by the emerging awareness, sophistication, and competency of consumers. As consumer involvement in decision making processes affecting the delivery of services increases, a clearer understanding of the relationship between the rights, needs and obligations of consumers and providers must be established.

One result of emerging consumerism is an increasing responsibility to clearly identify the source and validity of professional assumptions and practices. Constant attention needs to be given to sorting out whose interests are served by service provision efforts. Professionals need to avoid self-serving ideologies that preserve the status quo in the face of evidence that those ideologies are inappropriate. On the other hand, professionals should avoid seeking change simply because it avoids routine or appears progressive.

Thus, ways need to be found to overcome professionals' perceptions based on personal needs or orientations of the provider and to adopt outlooks that give more credence to consumer generated perceptions of needs, problems, and solutions. Ways need to be found to return control over service conceptualization and delivery to those whom the services are designed to benefit. This will help avoid the dependency that professionalism often entails. It will also help overcome the mentality that professionals' views take precedence because of the supposed advantage accruing to those who have studied in a given area or devoted their working lives to solving a particular problem or issue. We must overcome the mentality that the capacity for solving problems is narrowly distributed within the society, existing only in the realm of the profession. Recognizing that being certified and graduating from an accredited school guarantees access to a job but not necessarily the ability to do the job may help alleviate some of this problem. Where is the evidence that degrees, certificates, and titles assure expertise and competence?

Raising consumer expectations and worker obligations (and perhaps expectations) is another of the undesirable and potentially dangerous side effects of accreditation, certification, and licensure. These practices create an aura of knowledge and infallibility which may, in turn, lead to dependence and unfounded expectations of success. The medical and legal fields are replete with stories of clients who grow to expect too much from professionals rather than being taught how to do for themselves.

TOWARD INCREASED COLLABORATION

In the final analysis what is needed is a renewed spirit of collaboration between professionals and consumers. While professionals may have specific interests in gaining a personal measure of status, authority, and autonomy, it should not be accomplished at the expense of consumer needs or rights. Expertise has its place but professionals need to recognize that they serve at the behest of consumers and not in opposition. The granting of special powers and privileges through processes such as accreditation, certification, and licensing should only be done to the extent that tangible benefits to consumers can be shown. In the case of the park and recreation field, we need to ascertain more clearly the unique knowledge or skills that recreation professionals possess that would justify certification or licensing or the unique roles played by park and recreation curricula that would justify accreditation.

Ultimately, recreation workers may be simply playing a game within a structure established by perceived necessity and reality. However, to confuse economics, job protection, and liability limitation concerns with actions which purport to protect the interests of consumers is misleading and potentially dangerous. Creating a union, while less glamorous, may be more appropriate.

REFERENCES

1. Yale, D.R. "Certification and Registration: A Mistake." *Parks and Recreation.* 1975, 10, 24-25.
2. Larsen, M.S. *The Rise of Professionalism: A Sociological Analysis.* Berkeley: University of California Press, 1977. p.x.
3. Cullen, J.B. *The Structure of Professionalism: A Quantitative Examination.* New York: Petiocelli Books, Inc., 1978, p. 2.
4. *Ibid.* pp. 48-57.
5. *Ibid.* p. 67.
6. *Ibid.* pp. 58-64.
7. *Ibid.* pp. 64-70.
8. *Ibid.* p. 65.
9. Friedson, E. *Profession of Medicine.* New York: Dodd, Mead and Company, 1970. p. 187. Quoted in Cullen, *op. cit.,* p. 66.
10. Cullen *op. cit.,* p. 68.
11. Edginton, Christopher R. "Consumerism and Professionalization," *Parks and Recreation.* 11 (9), 1976. p. 42.
12. Cullen. *op. cit.,* p. 204.
13. Friedson, Eliot. *The Professions and Their Prospects.* Beverly Hills: Sage Publications, 1973. p. 31.
14. Denzin. N. K. "Pharmacy: Incomplete Socialization." *Social Forces.* 46 (3), 1968. p. 376.

15. Bishop, Doyle W. *In Investigation of Some Temperament and Ability Differences Among Advanced Undergraduates of Selected Departments at the University of Ottawa.* Mimeo paper, 1979.
16. Eysenck, H. *The Bilogical Basis of Personality.* Springfield, Illinois: Charles C. Thomas, 1967
17. Bishop, Doyle W. *op. cit.* p. 29-30.
18. Pavalko, P. M. *Sociology of Occupation and Professions.* Itasca, Illinois: Peacock, 1971
19. McChesney, James C. *Professional Development and Involvement of Recreation and Park Students.* Unpublished Doctoral Dissertation, Indiana University, 1974.
20. Hughes, F. C. "Professions". *Daedalus.* 92, 1963. p. 67
21. Edginton, Christopher R. *op. cit.* p. 84

Chapter Twenty-One

Narrowing the Options: The Power of Professionalism in Daily Life and Leisure

John Lord, Peggy Hutchison, and Fred Van Derbeck

Choice, risk, and involvement are vital elements in growth and development and human experience. In our society, however, adults have become less playful and more security-oriented. Many of our institutions are dominant and unresponsive, making it difficult for people to feel a sense of purpose and control in their daily lives. To regain a willingness to risk and change, we need to increase the options in our lives, beginning at the personal level and moving to community and social system levels. So it is necessary to examine the inter-relationships between our creative, playful selves and the systems of professional dominance which narrow our options. It is timely to analyze this process in the field of leisure services because of the current thrust toward certification, standardization and professionalization. An exploration of the power of professionalism in daily life and leisure will help us to clarify the relevant issues and to come to an understanding of our role in creating more options for ourselves and our communities.

NEGATING PLAY THROUGH PROFESSIONALISM

Professionals often destroy or exclude play and playfulness by disregarding and institutionalizing the central elements of play. Spontaneity and exploration are obliterated by a preoccupation with teaching and structure. Internal motivation is weakened by imposing rewards and external controls. We become dependent upon professionals, rather than relying on ourselves and our community of friends.

We have become serious about ourselves and our work, unable to be playful, and unable to recognize opportunities for play. Most of us probably smile when we observe children laughing, sharing, creating, and exploring at play. But do we smile only because we fondly remember how important play was to us? In other words, is children's play an external event to us, rather than something in which we feel comfortable joining?[1]

Perhaps some of us wonder why we have lost our ability to play and self-generate. One possibility is that professions which dominate our lives lower people's trust in themselves to generate energy, ideas, and alternatives. Our lives are permeated by services which create dependency on the part of both the client and the professional. Dependency for the client means that the capacity for self-development is narrowed to the choices offered by the experts in a particular field. Dependency for the professional means that his or her actions become nearly synonymous with the profession's need to help and to create needs.

Play is also negated or destroyed by control and fragmentation, two characteristics of professionalism. Both these elements have had an impact on children by the time they are six years old. Children at school soon learn that play is relatively unimportant and that the only valuable knowledge is formal knowledge which is acquired primarily from professionals. It is in this sense that professionals and institutions control the lives of children and adults. As several researchers and social critics have emphasized, children's sport and recreation programs reflect the dominant social values, as indicated by competition, leader-directed activity and exclusion.[2,3]

Beliefs which permit professionalism to dominate and control our lives lead people to separate their work and play. This kind of fragmentation makes it difficult for people to have meaning and understanding in an increasingly complex world. Many people with whom we have spoken see their lives as routine and unconnected. The way we separate our lives into units for leisure, work, family, and sleep are disabling, particularly as recreation and leisure become residual events in our lives. Play is no longer a space for exploration and learning but becomes a space, like work, for the accomplishment of narrowly defined tasks. The negation of play by professionalism, then, is a serious paradox for recreationists, since play and professionalism have become fundamentally antithetical practices.

THE GROWTH OF PROFESSIONALISM

Two important historical periods have been identified with the rise of professionalism in western culture. The first took place in the middle of the last century with the development of cities and a corresponding rise in commerce. From these influences, a middle class emerged which resulted in increased inequalities of wealth distribution.[4] The idea of individual career patterns and upward mobility, in contrast to community sharing as a way of meeting human needs, became important. This historical perspective remains relevant today since most professionals continue to support inequality and social hierarchies. Consider how human service workers at the direct programming level are devalued, both in terms of social status and financial remuneration.

The second period associated with the rise of professionalism was the middle part of this century when professions became more dominant in people's lives by acquiring authority and control.[5] This period was in contrast to earlier times when professionals had a more benevolent role. For example, a medical practitioner made home visits, diagnosed sickness, and recommended a variety of prepared and home remedies. In contrast, the medical profession today controls health-related matters and provides impersonal service.[6] It has been suggested that medical practices themselves stimulate further problems by focusing on illness rather than health and prevention.[7] Doctoring today is thus an industry, not a service. A second example concerns recreationists who, in the past, cooperated with citizens' groups in order to provide a variety of formal and informal leisure opportunities for the community. Again, this is in sharp contrast to many current recreation professionals who feel they need to institutionalize our leisure and organize our time. Have you ever tried to go skating in a municipal rink more than once or twice a week? Schedules, leagues, and narrow age groupings for organized sport dominate most hours of the day and night.

THE MAKING OF A PROFESSIONAL

In our society the professional occupies a privileged position. S/he did not get there because of innate individual characteristics, but rather because of our particular societal organization. However, the power of the person who is a professional is also dependent upon the willingness of that person to conform to the standards created by his/her profession.[8] Professionals view themselves as owners of their area of expertise and as custodians who have the right and responsibility to control access to that occupation. The definition of a profession, then, is largely determined by:

> the professional's authority to define a person, as client, to determine that person's need, and to hand that person a prescription which defines this new social role.[9]

Thus, this relationship of mutual dependency creates a social distance between the client and professional and reinforces the idea that one needs a service which is best provided by an expert. In essence, this is a *political* relationship, since it legitimizes the professional in the role of policy and decision-maker for the client. Rather than fostering a sense of shared responsibility for the problem, the professional behaves in ways which are designed to maintain awe of and respect for the profession.

Our daily lives are a source of constant confrontation with such professional enhancement. Haven't we all had the experience of waiting in line at an agency office and hearing a person introduce himself or herself as a Doctor, Attorney, or Professor? Is this done as a means of identification or is it a professional claim to be placed ahead of the people waiting in line? Perhaps it would be useful for all of us to try an experiment to test the reality of this system. Introduce yourself, either in person or on the telephone, using your usual name one time, and a professional designation another time. See if the tone of voice, the demeanor of the person to whom you are talking or the quality of service changes. For even more impact, try slurring your words or add a foreign accent and see if the response is any different.

This way of acting develops during a period of training in which the professional acquires a certain self-concept which gives legitimacy to these actions in her or his mind. This training consists of absorbing a particular way of thinking about oneself and one's society which emphasizes success over support and nurturing. We are taught to get to know people according to their accomplishments rather than for their human characteristics. Upon meeting someone, we are most often concerned about their status (assembly line worker, housewife, vice-president), rather than the possibility of a shared relationship or learning experience. Contacts such as these tend to reify and depersonalize human relations. This superficial way of interrelating becomes dominant in everyday interactions. It would require a very different way of thinking about ourselves and our society for us to become more humanly, and less technically, concerned about our fellow persons.

Those of us in professions know very well the narrow, procedural training we received. We can remember the emphasis on technical solutions to social problems and moral dilemmas. Jeffry Galper reflects upon the process of professional training.

Students, for example, are encouraged to think analytically, but not to connect the material before them to the major emotional dynamics in their lives. Similarly, the survival needs of many

305

workers dictate that they not feel, in any profound way, the emotional poverty of the work situations . . . . To encourage people to deny and compartmentalize their emotions, therefore, serves to maintain a public myth about the acceptability of the social order, since it encourages the belief that the pain people experience is idiosyncratic. (In addition) this serves to isolate the professional from the fullest awareness of the amount of pain that exists in the society and the relative powerlessness of the professional to deal with it.[10]

Certification is an attempt to ensure that professionals will acquire their profession's view of what is best for people. Unfortunately, both the client and professional too easily conform to expectations each has of the other and therefore both maintain the status quo. This established hierarchical form is generally restrictive and constraining to human development and human relationships.

UNDERLYING IDEOLOGIES

It is helpful to reflect on the dominant ideologies and values in our society which create and support this professionalized training. One underlying ideology emerges from the examination of worker alienation as technological changes are introduced into the workplace. The worker moving from being a crafts person to a babysitter on an assembly line illustrates this ideology.[11] Technology tends to dominate the workplace, thus allowing a system of cost effectiveness to emerge, which devalues human beings. Purpose and meaning give way to narrow productivity measures and work and leisure are subordinated to specialized, industrial functions. When this occurs, it is difficult for individuals and groups to feel a sense of control over their own lives. Rather than confronting this dilemma, professionals and others rationalize its necessity. Using this ideology of rationalization, professionals often focus upon facts, objective data, and procedures as a way of explaining social problems, rather than trying to understand the political-economic and human issues underlying a problem.[12] Unconsciously then, rationalization has become a way of explaining and resolving daily life issues.[13]

To what extent do recreationists accept the rationalization of leisure by assuming that play is what you do away from work? Does professional education for recreationists reflect the strong conservative bias which seems to dominate professions in general? Examining the leading books in a field is one interesting way to decipher these questions. Our reading of the recreation literature suggests a consistent theme, which focuses upon the present and future growth of leisure and recreation as a result of technology. Some textbooks on leisure services argue that diversion and escape from a highly complex industrial society are central to the growth of mass leisure.[14] Many recommendations for organized recreation emerge from this assumption. Based upon this material, one clearly gets the impression that social, political, and economic systems are accepted unquestioningly. This simplistic focus on leisure as diversion is contradicted by the increasing evidence about the impact of technology and unemployment on both body and soul.[15]

Recreationists educated in such a narrow focus will continue to promote recreation as a means of coping with or avoiding oppressive and alienating work. Our leisure, however, is hardly more fulfilling than our work. Workers currently employed in unsatisfying jobs know that the "frustration and tension of the job are not easily left at the plant gate."[16] It is in this sense that recreationists often use leisure as a way of placating people. For example, disabled people are offered recreation programs but not jobs, often with the rationalization, unlike normal expectations, that they are fortunate not to be working, and that free time should be used more constructively. As a second example, recreation focuses upon activity, skills, procedures, participation, and programs. It seldom, if ever, emphasizes self and community development, women's groups, workers' study groups, political, theatre, or participant-directed activities.

A second ideology is known as positivism. The positivist tends to accept the status quo and dominant ideology that emphasizes bureaucratic rationality, modern technology, centralized authority, and scientific control.[17] Thus both the positivist and rationalist way of knowing and organizing the world presuppose the existence of objective knowledge and decision-making, processes which devalue subjectivity in order to maintain control. This approach legitimizes technique at the expense of human interrelationships.[18] The contrast illustrated by the chart below, adapted from Harold Hodges Jr., clarifies the socialization process which occurs as young people become professionalized.[19]

THE CHILD	THE PROFESSIONAL
spontaneous, unrestrained	self-restrained, inhibited
risk-taking, adventuresome, change seeking	cautious, fearful of unfamiliar, security-oriented, stability seeking
intuitive, affective	logical, cognitive
open-minded	close-minded
innovative, exploratory	conventional, custom-bound
at ease with chaos, complexity, disorder, mystery	fearful of the unstructured, undefined

In our view, these dominant values represent social processes which create daily life situations which avoid the real problems, support hierarchical relationships, and view people as commodities. The irony for recreation and leisure is that while recreation professionals often are characterized by items in the right hand column they are at the same time supposed to nurture the values in the left hand column through play and leisure.

PROFESSIONAL DOMINANCE OF HUMAN SERVICES

In recent years there has been a rapid expansion in social, medical, and human services. Jeffry Galper, in a penetrating critique of social services in the United States, views current social services as a logical extension of capitalism.[20] Galper presents a great deal of data to support the viewpoint that social services allow the dominant ideology and commodity relationships discussed earlier to be maintained. Obviously, this approach will dismay many liberals who see welfare, homes for the elderly, and miminum wage laws as progressive and humane practices. In reality, however, many of these are band-aid arrangements which delay the implementation of fundamental changes in social services and political-economic structures. The myriad of existing human services which are constantly increasing to respond to yet another need is society's way of approving professionalism. In this sense, the human service industry serves as professionalism's stamp of approval.

Professionalism in human services is maintained by a belief in a political and value system which is supportive of competition as natural process, people as commodities, and hierarchies as the logical means of organization in people's lives. Thus, recreation departments teach primarily competitive values, slot people into programs, and force individuals and consumer groups to compete for artificially scarce resources. The cruel paradox of this value system is that individuals are often blamed for problems which are, instead, created by this unjust system. For example, in one community, a fitness program for senior citizens was run on Sundays from five to six-thirty. When few attended, the recreation department blamed the seniors for being poorly motivated.

Four practices help to maintain and institutionalize professionalism in human services.[21]

Narrow Focus
Professions develop a narrow frame of reference by focusing upon one aspect of a client or a problem. Such specialization narrows the range of solutions which are considered possible. In fact, real problems are often avoided and any solutions apply more to the symptom than to the cause of the problem. For medicine this means that a headache is viewed as the problem, and thus, treatment is aimed at eliminating the headache. In developing a broader frame of reference, professionals would spend less time trying to ameliorate existing problems and more time on prevention and self help. For example, in recreation, many problems and solutions tend to revolve around the issue of activity. We struggle to determine how to get and keep people active, but seldom do an analysis of meaning and purpose in people's lives.

Professional Detachment
Professions emphasize that their members should not become emotionally involved with their clients. It is ironic that many so-called "helping professions" train people and deliver services based upon these values. By "helping," we have come to mean doing something for someone without involvement. To *not* be neutral is to be involved and might mean cultivating a sense of wholeness. This includes playfulness, empathy, and support for enabling others to view their own oppression collectively and the facilitation of alternative courses of action. This issue creates a dilemma for

the recreationist. To be professionalized means the recreationist loses a certain degree of involvement and playfulness. Once these vital personal ingredients are lost, recreation becomes another commodity, another marketplace item to be packaged and sold. Thus, recreationists need to be deeply reflective about the growing professionalism in their field. Godbey is one of the few recreation professionals to express concern at the growing professionalization of recreation. He wonders whether:

> the recreation and parks movement, in seeking professional status, has moved toward an inappropriate model to bring about its initial ideals, such as restoring a sense of community through recreation, provision to the poor, and increased recreational self-sufficiency for citizens . . . (professionalism) may increasingly alienate the practitioner from the social reform ethic and "grass roots" approach to community involvement.[22]

We must ask ourselves whether increased professionalization in the field of recreation will lead to further degradation of play values which are inherent in the minds and spirits of children, but which have lost their impact and meaning for most adults.

Professionalized Service Ethic
Professionals develop an ethic of service based upon their standards and expectations. Lack of cooperative efforts between the professional and client ensures that this process continues. For example, games are not adjusted for *mutual* participation when disabled individuals, health-impaired persons, or children wish to take part. The standard of performance continues to be the professional sports player. Some recreationists segregate participants of unequal capabilities and do not even consider changing the rules to permit the inclusion of all persons. This is another illustration of the permeation of the competitive ethic in our society. For many participants socialized in this society, the game would lose its meaning if the rules were changed. Thus, service to others is most often seen as the service *needed by the client*, in order to adjust him/herself to the requirements of the existing structure of power in any society.

Impartial Service Delivery
Human service providers generally claim impartiality in terms of the allocation of their services. Race, creed, and sex, for example, are said to be irrelevant factors in distribution of resources. In practice, however, people start at very different levels when seeking

services, and thus require different degrees of support. As Galper puts it:

> To guarantee equality of opportunity without assuring equality in the places from which people start to compete is to assure that equal opportunity will mean unequal outcomes.[23]

In order to show how this is part of our social-economic lives, we need to examine the unequal basis from which people begin. First, we recommend the study of income distribution and poverty in North America.[24] Second, despite improvements in recent years, there is evidence that women and minority groups with equal training compared to white males earn considerably less on entry into the labor market.[25] Third, consider the claim many community recreationists make that their services are equally available to all citizens. In reality, few recreation facilities are physically accessible to all persons, costs are often prohibitive, and opportunities for particular age groups are lacking.

Professionalism reflects a strong conservative bias in human services. Professional control serves to dampen personal and collective action and to encourage dependence on professional remedies. The human service and leisure industries support this dependence by serving as a link in the institutionalization of professionalism. The diagram on the following page illustrates the relationships among several components which serve either to institutionalize or change professionalism.

WHY THE TRUST YET THE QUESTIONING?

In a society where professionalism has become dominant, people continue to have tremendous trust in the process of professionalism.

> It is one of the maddening facts of our time that people believe themselves incapable of dealing with the most ordinary human conflicts without the aid of a 'specialist.'[26]

Professionalism engenders trust because it penetrates and controls most aspects of our lives. Three of the ways in which professionalism affects people and gains trust follow.

Figure 1

FIGURE ONE – INSTITUTIONALIZING PROFESSIONALISM

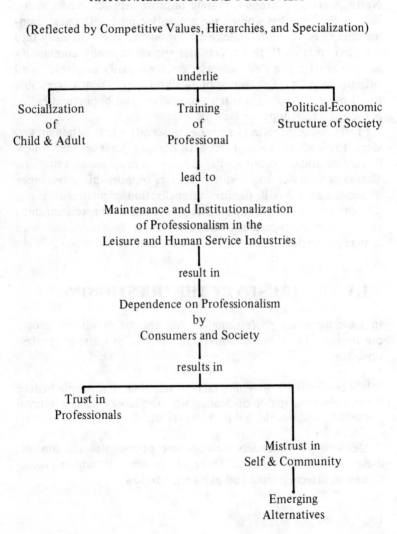

DOMINANT IDEOLOGIES

of

RATIONALIZATION AND POSITIVISM

(Reflected by Competitive Values, Hierarchies, and Specialization)

underlie

Socialization	Training	Political-Economic
of	of	Structure of Society
Child & Adult	Professional	

lead to

Maintenance and Institutionalization
of Professionalism in the
Leisure and Human Service Industries

result in

Dependence on Professionalism
by
Consumers and Society

results in

Trust in
Professionals

Mistrust in
Self & Community

Emerging
Alternatives

First, the institutionalization of professionalism has resulted in a trust of institutions rather than community, and a trust in professionalism instead of self and others. We have been taught to believe that institutions have something that we need. For example, knowledge is of value only when given by an expert; therefore, learning must occur at school. Thus, it has become difficult for people to self-generate or put trust in oneself for learning the essential nuances of our day. Similarly, we believe we can't play without a recreationist, get better without a doctor, or gain rights without a lawyer.

Second, the trust in professionalism should not be so surprising, when one considers how professional power is subtly and effectively enshrined in our common speech. In an excellent book by one of the few persons to examine the relationship between power and helping language, Murray Edelman wrote:

> Consider a common usage that staff, clients, and the general public all accept as descriptive of a purely professional process: the term 'therapy.' In the journals, textbooks, and talk of the helping professions, the term is repeatedly used as a suffix or qualifier. Mental patients do not hold dances; they have dance therapy. If they play volleyball, that is recreation therapy. If they engage in a group discussion, that is group therapy.[27]

In other words, the professional's relationship to the client is based upon controlling the other's context by defining the possibilities for the client in professionally advantageous ways. By calling a relationship or an activity therapy, an immediate power hierarchy is established which makes it difficult for the devalued client to develop any self-help skills except those sanctioned by the professional. The client comes to rely on a professional for cues which will indicate the appropriateness of behavior and thoughts. Linguistic support for this situation is emphasized in professional jargon: solitary confinement is called a quiet room; an attempted escape is referred to as attempted elopement; and compulsory personal revelations at group meetings are defined as "benefiting from peer confrontation."[28] There is implicit power in these new terms and clients readily respond to the professional's orders.

Third, public policy is shaped, to a large extent, by our dependence upon, and trust in, professionals. An example occurred during National Health Week in Canada, when the former Minister of Health and Welfare was discussing health problems. He emphasized that:

"... of all the problems we face, motivation of Canadians has to be singled out as the crucial one which will ultimately decide whether our strategy will be a success or failure ... public education therefore cannot be overemphasized. Although education alone has had only limited success in the past, there are exciting new approaches to be explored by scientists, psychologists, professional educators, social workers, and all professional workers."[29]

Professional intervention is thus seen as necessary for overcoming people's needs which have been described as deficient. By seeing the problem within the citizen, a fertile climate for professional dominance is maintained. Individualizing the problem leads to blaming the victim, when the root causes of health and leisure problems are much deeper. Examples of causes include: the dominance of professions and corporations in dictating our needs; political-economic priorities which devalue certain citizens; loss of citizen control of schools, the work place, and the community.

It is understandable why professionals are able to acquire so much trust and control in our society. It is people's feeling of personal powerlessness combined with an expectation that they should be able to get ahead and solve problems by themselves (individualism) that leave people susceptible to relying on professionals. When acting alone, we become the only integrators of our experience and our perceptions of ourselves become as fragmented as the world in which we live. We get caught in a vicious cycle of believing ourselves to be fragmented, and thus share with others in fragmented ways. It is at this point that we become even more susceptible to the influence of professionalism.

Despite this professional encapsulation of our lives, or possibly because of it, cracks are appearing in the dominant trust of professionalism. In our view, two major thrusts account for this questioning. First, citizens and their families who have been systematically devalued by the society have often had the courage to speak out about the oppressive nature of professionalism. For example, a young couple gives birth to a baby who is mentally retarded. They oppose the overwhelming advice of physicians and social workers to have their baby institutionalized. Such people are tired of professionalism and all its trappings, its bureaucracy, and its inequality. The result is a growing advocacy effort by parents, disabled persons, and their friends directed toward changing the human service industry.

A second attack on professions has come from social critics who see professionalism as avoiding the root causes of problems. In fact, some critics point out that professionalism contributes to our problems, rather than resolving them. For example, John McKnight asks:

> Why are we putting so much resource into medicine while our health is not improving?

> Why are we putting so much resource into education and our children seem to be learning less?

> Why are we putting so much resource into criminal justice systems and society seems less just and less secure?

> Why are we putting so much resource into mental health systems and we seem to have more mental illness?[30]

While many citizens are beginning to echo these concerns in their daily life experiences and dialogue, it is interesting to note the response of professionals to the growing criticism of professionalism. Some appear shocked and claim that any wrong-doing or problems in the profession are rare and must be the result of incompetent individuals. If one pushes the critique further, the professional may ask: "are you in this field?" This defense, which assumes that one must be certified in a field in order to understand and criticize, squelches any attempt to critique professionalism on the basis of human values and system problems. These defenses serve as excuses which function to limit the creation of new options.

BROADENING THE OPTIONS

Developing alternatives to professionalism means broadening the options which people believe they can create to transform our society and daily lives. We suggest three broad approaches which we believe can have an impact on daily life and leisure. We also trust that readers can generate more specific alternatives and applications which are appropriate to their contexts.

New Vision
Creating serious alternatives to professionalism involves developing a vision of a different kind of society. As Margaret Mead once said:

> Periods of social disorganization invite correction in two directions, one an order imposed by force . . . the other a radical

transformation of society that relies on the creation in individuals of a spirit of deep dedication to new social goals.[31]

A new vision would involve new social goals which enable *all* individuals to develop to their fullest capacities. Social reconstruction would entail a deep concern for the quality of life of every citizen. Society would no longer be based on the principle that the individual is respected only insofar as s/he is profitable.[32] We need to acknowledge that we have a very crucial identity as persons separate from our role in economic and institutional life. Valuing people as developing human beings would mean new goals and new priorities for human and leisure services. For example, elderly people, disabled people, minority group individuals, and native people would no longer be systematically devalued. We would link the oppression of these groups to our own lives. Professional practices would cease to assume that people's needs are best resolved by psychological and specialist answers. Recreationists would ensure strong consumer input and control in planning services. And quality of the leisure experience would take precedent over the quantity of services. Cooperation and collective understandings become central to these values. Too often, our sense of self is tied directly to our individual, professional goals. If we truly valued the potential of sharing with others, we would transform our work and leisure. Decision-making would become decentralized. Egalitarian relationships would replace professional domination and hierarchies. And leisure services would become a community and neighborhood project rather than a professional responsibility.

Changing Relationships

The professional-client relationship must change significantly. It must be viewed as an inter-relationship rather than a controlling relationship. In practice, professionals must not only share knowledge in a natural way, but struggle into the unknown with their clients through shared experiences and shared reflections. Barry Kaufman writes in a deeply human manner about his struggle with professionals in seeking effective approaches with his autistic son.[33] All professionals either had rigid prescriptions or responses which clearly indicated that nothing could be done. Finally, one professional was willing to explore the unknown and to converse with Kaufman about a range of options. It is in this sense that broadening the options means that professionals must be open to altering their theories in response to ongoing experiences in which alternative realities have been demonstrated. This also involves shared control over contexts rather than professional domination in relationships. Lack of consumer input into decision-making and planning in recreation makes it unlikely that recreation professionals either alter their perceptions or relinquish control through cooperative efforts with citizens.

Advocacy

Recreationists must advocate to ensure that professionalism does not dominate the field of recreation. The recreationist as an advocate can work to deprofessionalize recreation and to deindustrialize the leisure industry.

A deprofessionalized view of recreation restores community and play as central to the recreation movement. Advocates will cooperate with others to identify barriers to community and play. They will infuse their jobs and their lives with a sense of community and a sense of playfulness. In practice, this will mean having a support group of deprofessionalized friends and colleagues who share the commitment to create a more just and humane society. It also entails being comfortable with negotiation and confrontation about the practical issues in everyday life. Creating links with community groups to ensure that consumers gain control of community resources is one example.

Recreationists as advocates can also begin to deindustrialize the leisure industry. First, this requires a fundamental critique of who controls our leisure needs. Corporate permeation of our lives through television and advertising creates expectations in which pursuit of material things is the major goal.[34] Second, most people in the leisure field unquestionably accept the notion that a technological society frees people for more leisure. As we have emphasized, however, failure to confront this notion contributes to the technological permeation of our lives. Instead, we need to take learnings gained away from the job and vice versa and fuse them into the work-place. Common phrases such as "stop talking about the office, we are here to have fun" need to be confronted. And participating in a shared, cooperative venture in a leisure setting raises consciousness about the possibility of such sharing in other environments.

Is it possible that bottom-up change, with cooperative efforts of recreation advocates and others, could change the leisure delivery system? The alternative is more professionalization and more recreation leaders imprisoned within their allegiances and loyalties to the organization and the profession. Fortunately, alternatives are emerging in people's lives which involve cooperation, shared knowledge, and a different set of social goals. Change is fundamental to this search and struggle. It challenges us to reemphasize collectivity, self-worth, advocacy, and responsibility in social affairs. As Richard Bach states in *Illusions*, change is perfection; the sea and the sky are changing every second, but they are always a perfect sea and sky![35] Can we find security in changing ourselves and our society?

REFERENCES

1. For a delightful, yet extremely important, analysis of children's potential to grow and develop through play and natural learning, see Pearce, Joseph Chilton, *Magical Child: Rediscovering Nature's Plan for Our Children*. New York: E. P. Dutton, 1977, esp. pp. 138-145.
2. Orlick, Terry. *Winning Through Cooperation: Competitive Insanity: Cooperative Alternatives*, Washington, D.C.: Hawkins and Associates, 1978.
3. Sage, George H. "American Values and Sport: Formation of a Bureaucratic Personality," *Leisure Today*, October, 1978. p. 10-11.
4. Bledstein, Burton J. *The Culture of Professionalism*. New York: W. W. Norton and Company, Inc., 1976. pp. 21-22.
5. Illich, Ivan. "Disabling Professions." In: Illich, Ivan, et. al. *Disabling Professions*. London: Marian Boyars, 1977. pp. 15-21.
6. Heidenheimer, Arnold, Heclo, Huch, and Adams, Carolyn Teich. *Comparative Public Policy*. New York: St. Martin, 1975. p. 14.
7. Illich, Ivan. *Medical Nemesis: The Expropriation of Health*. New York: Bantam, 1977.
8. Smollet, Eleanor, "Schools and the Illusion of Choice: The Middle Class and the 'Open' Classroom." In: Martell, George (Ed.). *The Politics of the Canadian Public School*. Toronto: James Lewis and Samuel, Publishers, 1974. pp. 92-102.
9. Illich. "Disabling . . ." *Op. Cit.* p. 50.
10. Galper, Jeffry. *The Politics of Social Services*. Englewood Cliffs, N.J.: Prentice-Hall, 1975. p. 95. Jeffry Galper's book continues to be the primary reference for those interested in a radical critique of social service delivery systems. Our four practices in systematizing professionalism follow his suggestions with adaptations. See also Allan Moscovitch and Glenn Drover (Editors). *Inequality: Essays in the Political Economy of Social Welfare*. Totonto: University of Toronto Press, 1981.
11. Shaiken, Harley. "Craftsman into Baby Sitter." In: Illich, Ivan, et. al., *Disabling Professions*. London: Marian Boyars, 1977. p. 120.
12. Fay, Brian. *Social Theory and Political Practice*. London: George Allen and Unwin, 1975. p. 44.
13. For a valuable analysis of the rationalization of the conduct of life, see: Goldman, Robert and Wilson, John. "The Rationalization of Leisure." *Politics and Society*, 7:2, (1977). pp. 127-156.
14. See, for example: Sessoms, H. Douglas, Meyers, Harold D. and Brightbill, Charles K. *Leisure Services: The Organized Recreation and Park System*. Englewood Cliffs, N.J.: Prentice-Hall, 1975. And Shivers, Jay S. *Principles and Practices of Recreational Service*. New York: MacMillan Company, 1967.
15. Sharon, Kirsh. *Unemployment: Its Impact on Body and Soul*. Toronto: Canadian Mental Health Association, 1983.
16. Shaiken. *Op. Cit.* p. 122.

17. Quinney, Richard. *Critique of Legal Order*. Boston: Little, Brown and Company, 1974. pp. 2-4.
18. See especially two essays: "Technical Progress and the Social Life-World," and "Technology and Science as 'Ideology'." In Habermas, Jurgen. *Toward A Rational Society*. Boston: Beacon Press. 1970.
19. Hoedges, Harold M., Jr. "The Humanistic Intellegentsia." In Gella, Aleksander, (Ed.). *The Intellengentsia and the Intellectuals*. Beverly Hills, California: Sage Publications, 1976. pp. 157-158.
20. Galper. *Op Cit*.
21. *Ibid.*, p. 91-98.
22. Godbey, Geoffrey. "The Professionalization of Recreation and Parks in the Public Sector: Implications for Social Development." *Society and Leisure*, 1:2 (November, 1978). pp. 280-81.
23. Galper, *Op. Cit.* p. 98.
24. See for example, Johnson, Leo A. *Poverty in Wealth*. Toronto: New Hogtown Press, 1977.
25. Baker, Sally and Levenson, Bernard. "Earnings Prospects of Black and White Working-Class Women." *Sociology of Work and Occupations*, 3:2 (May, 1976). p. 123.
26. Henley, Nancy and Brown, Phil. "The Myth of Skill and the Class Nature of Professionalism." In: Radical Therapist Rough Times Collective (Ed.). *The Radical Therapist*. Middlesex, England: Penguin Books, 1974. p. 61.
27. Edelman, Murray. *Political Language:* Words That Succeed and Policies That Fail. New York: Academic Press, 1977. p. 59-60.
28. *Ibid.*, p. 61.
29. Lalonde, Mard. Quoted in: *Halifax Mail Star*, (March 18, 1978). p. 2.
30. McKnight, John. "Professionalized Service and Disabling Help." In: Illich, Ivan, et. al. *Disabling Professions*. London: Marion Boyars, 1977. p. 75.
31. Mead, Margaret and Heyman, Ken. *World Enough*. Boston: Little, Brown and Company, 1975. p. 56.
32. deBeauvoir, Simone. "Old Age: End Product of a Faulty System." *Saturday Review*, (April 8, 1972). p. 42.
33. Kaufman, Barry Neil. *Son-Rise*. New York: Warrier Books, 1976.
34. Hamelink, Cees. *The Corporate Village*. Rome: IDOC International, 1977. p. 138.
35. Bach, Richard. *Illusions*. New York: Delacorte Press, 1977.

Chapter Twenty-Two
Leisure Services and Social Control
Ronald P. Reynolds

. . . "To submit to however wise a master planner is to surrender an illusion that may be the bedrock on which life flourishes"[1]

While those concerned with the study of "leisure" and/or the provision of leisure services have yet to reach a consensus regarding its exact substantive definition, there is general agreement that the element of choice or freedom from constraint is one essential aspect of the phenomenon.[2] Conversely, *control* or imposed external influences affecting the leisure participant may preclude the achievement of the desired leisure state. With the notion of personal freedom as an atmosphere engendered by the absence of external control, the ideal society for promoting leisure is one which allows and encourages the individual to exert maximum autonomy over his or her own lifestyle. Sites[3] describes such a set of social conditions:

> A good society then is a society which is structured by allowing optimum control possibilities to each person of his own life experiences within the framework of an identity which he has been free to work out, maintain, or change on his own terms, so long as he does not infringe upon the possibility of others doing the same thing.

There are increasing indications which suggest that North Americans may not count themselves members of the "good society" nor perceive that they have adequate control over their own life experiences, including leisure. Cult organizations, Equal Rights Amendment movements and taxpayer revolts represent divergent attempts to regain or insure personal control of one's own religious ideology, human rights and monetary resources. Concern for leisure autonomy also prevails in our society as individuals turn to leisure counselors seeking dispensation to enjoy their free time and business executives forsake established careers to hand-fashion boats and sail the world.

In the midst of increasing discontent with personal and leisure lifestyles in a fast changing and unpredictable society, members of the leisure service profession must address several critical questions relative to the notion of social control. To what extent has the field of leisure services contributed to the personal autonomy of the individual? What has been and what will be the response of the leisure service profession to threats upon individual control and freedom as we move beyond 1984? Has our field in general functioned to maintain the status quo at the expense of the freedom of the individual? Are we subtly yet effectively selectively shaping and promoting subservient behaviors for our "clientele"?* In responding to those with special needs are our notions of therapy, as Angel[4] suggests, "obsolete, elitist, male-centered and obsessional, clinging to concepts often outmoded and rarely questioned?" Has recreation therapy today become a commodity? A means of social control?

THE INFLUENCE OF OUR "ROOTS"

As a profession, the Recreation and Parks field traces many of its historical ties to the discipline of social work as practiced in the early 1900's. Despite its eventual emergence from social work, the leisure service profession has retained and continues to model many practices exhibited by social workers who promote and perpetuate the social service system today. Recent critics of this system have charged that the social service delivery structure "fosters particular behavior patterns in clients both as a condition of usage and as a consequence of service,"[5] thus denying personal control and autonomy to individuals served by this system. Three such practices — economic responding, functionally specific professionalism, and "socio-psychologism" found in the social services also appear to permeate the field of leisure services. A brief examination of each concept reveals the potentially deleterious effect which adherence to these practices may have upon the type and quality of service provided by contemporary recreation and parks personnel. Also suggested are some future directions which leisure service providers might explore to insure the leisure autonomy of our "clients" in the 1980's and beyond.

---

*The term "client," when utilized, appears in quotes to symbolize the incongruous relationship those in the recreation and parks field have established with both disabled and non-disabled service recipients. As the basic methods and content of this interaction change over the next decades, it is hoped that leisure service professionals will develop alternative perceptions of individuals as "consumers" or "citizens."

ECONOMIC RESPONDING AND LEISURE SERVICES

A basic criticism of today's social service practices relates to the system's perception of the good society as one exhibiting an overriding commitment to economics and materialism which in turn causes the state to "view human needs as being primarily economic and serve the needs of private capital in many ways."[6] Competitive behavior is viewed as an inevitable part of the human condition and welfare programming is designed to prepare people to excel through practicing individualism and self aggrandizement. Work in turn is viewed as being a means to high levels of leisure consumption.

In several respects, the field of leisure services plays a major role in reinforcing a materialistic and competitive orientation to leisure thereby perpetuating a form of economic control on the recipients of its services. This practice is effected both through the *types* of activity offerings provided and the *method* in which participation in recreational experiences is structured. The largest proportion of content of our professional magazines is devoted to private and commercial enterprises proclaiming the necessity to install $100,000 fiberglass skateboard parks, purchase vanilla ice-cream bars "wrapped in attractive sports motif foil" for concessions or appropriate funds for peacocks as "exotic accents" for parks. This is symptomatic of our growing tendency to respond to the leisure needs of the public in an overly materialistic fashion.

Similarly, we frequently find ourselves in the uncomfortable position of denouncing the work ethic in our writings and teachings while continuing practices such as offering community recreational pursuits which stress activities requiring high initial monetary outlays, the purchase of expensive consumer goods, the consumption of fossil fuels and the construction of extravagant facilities. Practices such as these are particularly disconcerting in times of high inflation when rising prices and decreased discretionary income mean increased work hours to purchase leisure goods and services. The dilemma is apparent — individuals are encouraged to utilize their leisure in a more personally satisfying manner but to work longer and consume more in the process.

When scarce time is found for leisure participation, an inordinate emphasis is placed upon individualistic competitive pursuits. Recreation program texts suggest a plethora of competitive events varying from sports and drama tournaments, sandcastle sculpturing contests and spelling bees to baking contests, shingleboat races, flower arranging contests and sidewalk chalk art competitions. Elitist sport for disabled and non-disabled athletes consumes a disproportionate amount of our human and physical resources while comparatively little energy is expended for developmental activity programs for the non-competitor at the grass roots level. Our largest single effort to promote activity for mentally retarded persons, the Special Olympics, is modeled after the highest echelon of competition, the Olympic Games.

Lest there be misunderstanding relating to competitive endeavors between and among the sexes and disabled persons, current tests provide the following advice concerning sport:

> . . . there is organized support for recognizing limitations, which says that a big bosom and throwing things are incompatible. Menstrual cramps don't contribute to record-making physical outlays. But then these are foreseeable handicaps, perhaps more psychological than physiologically restricting. A fat boy doesn't throw too well either, nor does a mentally or physically depressed male rise to great efforts in recreational activity.[7]

Sports medicine clinics continue to cater to a younger and younger clientele. As a recent article points out "For the anxious mother of a little league player or a mosquito, a sports injury is a nightmare which she must hope is never played out."

Programmatic interventions designed to rehabilitate disabled persons have also fallen prey to the paradox extant in the economically oriented philosophy of the mental health field which defines emotional well being as "the active pursuit of a career, the engagement in competition within the rules of the game, the focus on recreation (asceticism) and on purposeful activity in general (utilitarianism).[8] The current controversy over the inclusion of recreation services in sheltered workshop settings for mentally retarded people speaks to our confusion regarding the relationship between work and leisure in "therapeutic recreation" service.

FUNCTIONALLY SPECIFIC PROFESSIONALISM AND LEISURE SERVICES

According to critics of the current Social Service System, professionalism, characterized by functional specificity, is a second critical issue threatening the autonomy and self control of its clients. Briefly, functional specificity may be defined as:

> the condition whereby professions are characterized by their development of technologies. As a result of the orientation clients and professionals are prevented and "protected" from

forming relationships which transcend this orientation. As a consequence of this ideology, the professional tends to concentrate on one facet of a client's life to the exclusion of other areas. In short, the person is viewed only in terms of their problem.[9]

Undesirable by-products of this orientation appear to be emotional indifference toward clients and faulty perceptions and practices relating to the delivery of service. The field of leisure services has in no way remained immune to the development of functionally specific professionalism or the undesirable consequences of this practice in removing control of personal leisure lifestyles from our "clients." As we move toward another decade of service, the following questions must be addressed: Have our technologies prevented us from forming meaningful relationships with colleagues in our own field, with others in related disciplines and with the individuals served by our profession? Does the leisure service field as a whole concentrate on certain facets of a "client's" life to the exclusion of other needs and interests? To what extent has our own "functional specificity" resulted in a loss of autonomy and control by the individual consumer? A brief examination of two current practices in our field — specialization of training and compartmentalization of services illustrate the extremes to which unchecked overspecialization may lead in the next decade.

Functional Specificity in Professional Preparation
Specialization appears rampant in professional training in the field of leisure services. A cursory glance at our professional preparation institutions reveals that individual curriculums provide program options in "Public Recreation," "Commercial Recreation," "Resource Planning," "Church Recreation," "General Programming," "Private Recreation," "Turf Management," "Vocational Corrections," "Recreation for the Socially Deviant," "Agriculture Teaching," "Ranger-Enforcement," "Naturalist-Historian," "Social Service Agencies," "Recreation for Minorities," "Youth-Family Leadership," "Maintenance," "Industrial Recreation," "Volunteer Management," "Community Schools." Junior colleges specialize in the training of "technicians." Four year curriculums spawn graduates who aspire as "leaders," "supervisors" or "administrators." Competency based graduate education attempts to develop "Educators," "Researchers," "Master Administrators" or "Clinicians." The "Researcher - Practitioner" dichotomy controversy periodically rears its head in our professional writings and conferences illustrating the real or imagined rift between "providers of service" and "generators of new knowledge." "Special groups" personnel segregate themselves

from "community recreators" in professional societies and universities. "Therapeutic Recreation Personnel" frequently see themselves as concerned exclusively with one particular "clientele" (visually impaired mentally retarded persons), setting (institutional, hospital or community), or media (art therapist, crafts specialist, physical activities instructor). The effects of this overspecialization on the autonomy and control of the individuals served by the leisure service profession can be profound. As therapeutic recreation specialists and community recreators isolate themselves, those trained in "T.R." will lack a working knowledge of leisure service provision in the public sector and consequently will be unable to influence this system and act as advocates for their "clients." Similarly, those trained in "community recreation" will not be imbued with an awareness and understanding of the needs and abilities of disabled persons. The current rift between institutions and community based services will remain thus, depriving disabled persons of the right to participate in generic services. While functional specificity reigns supreme, landscape architects and resource planners will continue to design aesthetically pleasing environments and facilities which are architectural nightmares to disabled persons. All leisure service providers lacking extra-disciplinary study in economics, political science, sociology and human development will continue to perpetuate economic control in leisure services as previously described.

Compartmentalization of Services
A second manifestation of functional specificity exhibited by those charged with the provision of leisure services concerns the fragmentation of leisure experiences offered to recipients of our program efforts. By limiting our attention to certain aspects of a "client's" life, we inadvertently assign and perpetuate stereotyped roles and sets of expectations on the basis of our preconceived notions of the characteristics of groups of individuals. Labeling, a commonly used technique to insure functional specificity in therapeutic recreation, controls peoples' lives and potential through:

> . . . categorical judgments about individuals' interests, skills, level of functioning and previous experience. This practice has the effect which I am sure we do not intend, of proving to others that persons with a particular illness are "within their category," "alike in all respects" and "distinctly different" from the non-ill, non-disabled, non special in all respects."[10]

Once this labeling process is complete, the removal of control from the disabled person is inevitable. The recreator provides "packaged programs" or activities based on the diagnostic label of the "client" which exist in a vacuum devoid of other skills, abilities or interests of the individual. Functional specificity prevails — mentally retarded people receive one regimen of activities, the aged another, and so on. Compartmentalization of activities also extends to the time frame in which leisure pursuits are scheduled. This condition is dramatically illustrated in the account of an ex-mental patient:

It's a pretty dull existence in which everything you need is handed out in neat little packages — even the therapy — not when you need it most, but again at specific times.[11]

While the labels utilized by the "community recreator" are not as mystifying as those adroitly adopted by the "therapeutic recreator" they too have the effect of perpetuating social control through stereotyped responding to the leisure lifestyle needs of the general public. A cursory examination of commonly used municipal recreation labels identifying program offerings include: Boys, Girls, Men's, Women's, Adult, Child, Novice, Advanced, Intermediate, Teen, Handicapped, Special. "Women's" programs are still offered primarily during the day ignoring the fact that over 40% of married women are now gainfully employed. Children's activities are scheduled at times so as not to interfere with adult activities or disturb family cohesion. Program levels such as beginner, intermediate and advanced stratify ability levels and promote competition. Specialized instructors are relied upon to provide technical expertise rather than general assistance in planning a leisure lifestyle. Leisure counseling and education necessitating personal contact and familiarization with all aspects of the "client's" life remain low priorities of parks and recreation agencies. "Handicapped" programs insure that groups of individuals sharing only one common feature will congregate at a certain place at a certain time. Functional specificity again promotes social conformity and control in leisure services.

"Socio-Psychologism," Leisure Services & Social Control
A third factor threatening the personal control of "clients" served by the leisure service profession is the profession's adherence to the concept of "socio-psychologism." Briefly stated, socio-psychologism is the practice or philosophy of emphasizing or focusing on the problems which an individual has in his or her personal interactions with the social order, rather than exhibiting a

concern for the underlying basic nature of the social order. In terms of the social services:

> If a diagnosis does not incorporate a concern for the way in which the whole society may be pathological and produce pathology in individuals as a normal condition of functioning, then the condition of pathology that is shared by all will be, paradoxically, the standard of behavior and existence toward which treatment is directed.[12]

The implications of the application of this orientation in the field of leisure services are obvious. If all existing values of society are embraced as a given, service efforts will center around the adaptation of the "client" to existing conditions thereby exerting a form of social control. Our professional interventions tend to be "time limited" and "technological" and treat symptoms of discontent within the "client" rather than dealing with the fundamental environmental sources of the person's discomfort. The following points will illustrate the prevalence and effects of socio-psychologism in the field of leisure services.

Like the social services, leisure service providers seem most willing to interact with individuals who do not exhibit major differences in behavior and lifestyle. By selectively excluding persons who manifest significant deviations from commonly accepted norms, leisure service providers are spared the cognitive dissonance which would be engendered if the environment instead of the individual was viewed as being pathological. For example: an individual of lower socio-economic status is parolled to a community from a correctional facility. He or she is motivated to become involved in community recreation and leisure opportunities. After locating the recreation department, the individual finds the program offerings foreign to his/her previous experiences. Secondly, no one is available in the department to offer assistance in developing the skills necessary for participation or to suggest alternative forms of leisure pursuits. The "parolee" returns to his or her former lifestyle, the environment influencing this deviance remains unchanged, and the socio-psychological orientation triumphs.

When the recreation field is involved in providing services to devalued or disadvantaged people, it also frequently adopts a socio-psychological "time-limited," "technological" intervention. To illustrate — leisure programs and services to delinquent youths are frequently aimed at altering the "clients" beliefs, values, attitudes and actions without attempting to change the pathological environment which may be responsible for the behaviors of the person. By ignoring economic, familial, and social conditions, such interventions are doomed to failure. Partington graphically illustrates the results of adopting a strict socio-psychological approach to aiding disadvantaged individuals. Commenting on the failure of a wilderness project to engender measurable changes in delinquent youths, he laments:

> Perhaps the most crushing inference to be drawn from this project is that in retrospect it is seen to rest on a suspect assumption; namely, that troubled youth can be helped by making them think more like "normals" — to expect that they can influence outcomes in their own lives. Unfortunately, changing expectations without changing realities may arouse frustration and resentment. The WILD program, like most current therapeutic interventions, was not designed to change the actual reward structures in the schools and communities to which these participants returned. Moreover, no efforts were made to change their future probability of success through social — economic — political engineering to create broader potential occupational opportunities. Maybe the 86% of WILD participants who chose not to complete the four trip program understood this conceptual error.[13]

Our approaches to leisure counseling and education are also frequently colored by a socio-psychological and technological orientation. If an individual becomes motivated to seek assistance in his or her leisure planning, what is frequently offered is a value laden "choice" of activities to fill the individual's time. Usually these pursuits are predominently middle-class in nature and are "prescribed" without concern for altering the environment which has caused the basic dissatisfaction with the person's current leisure lifestyle. For example, a counselor might urge a person in a disadvantaged area to select an activity or series of activities limited by the existing resources in the community rather than working with the individual to secure new and better leisure resources in the individual's neighborhood. Additionally, many recreation departments fall victim to the socio-psychologism approach in their attempt to assume sole responsibility for the provision of leisure opportunities in communities. This role is undertaken in lieu of providing services not currently offered by other existing generic agencies and organizations *and* instead of lobbying for leisure environmental changes which would ultimately result in improved services to all community members. As a result of this orientation, energy is expended providing "patchwork" diversional programs which could be better used in analyzing what services are needed and (if so) what agencies could best provide these services.

Meanwhile the practices of the public sector of leisure services exhibit a subtle socio-psychological approach. The area of leisure services to and for "special populations" blatantly embraces this orientation. Even a casual review of past and current literature reveals numerous examples of technological approaches aimed at changing the person to fit the environment rather than dealing with the pathology of the external conditions impinging on the individual. The social control function which is attributed to recreational activities in many institutions (and community based programs) is ample testimony to the orientation. Obvious examples are the diversional and inappropriate activities offered in correctional settings and residences for mentally retarded people. The purpose of these activities is the distraction of the individual from their living conditions (in which they may have cause for rebellion) and the release of surplus energy which they may misdirect toward themselves or their keepers. In both instances, social control prevails.

In psychiatric settings, a more clandestine form of social control through recreation exists. Individuals have the following idea communicated to them in many subtle (and not so subtle) ways.

Healthy people take part in recreation. You are currently unhealthy and therefore don't take part in recreation. Your participation in recreation will be taken as a sign of getting well. Therefore, if you want to get out of here, you had better participate!

Consequently, a great deal of stress is placed on participation in highly structured and controlled activities which are often inappropriate to time, age, and skill level of people. (Has anyone else observed "mentally ill" adults throwing bean bags in a day room at 9:00 AM?)

A more direct form of social control through socio-psychologism and technological intervention is evidenced by the persistent "prescription" of activities for disabled persons in institutional settings. This interventionist strategy by definition "precludes the voluntary aspect of recreational activity."[14] Ironically, this belief and practice may be the last remaining vestiges of choice, control and autonomy of the individual. Behavioral technology poses a similar threat to the personal freedom of the individual. Recent experimental investigations[15] in which participation in "client" preferred activities was made contingent upon participation in therapist "prescribed" activities raises some serious questions concerning our rationalization for mandatory activities and the degree to which individual choice (control) over participation must be respected in all leisure service settings.

RETURNING THE LOCUS OF CONTROL

With the previously outlined threats to client autonomy exposed, it is imperative that the field of leisure services develop new orientations and strategies resulting in more personally responsive, consumer-controlled leisure lifestyles. To meet this end, the following directions and practices are suggested:

1. *Future Recreators Must Encourage the Development of Leisure Lifestyles Which are Consistent With the Means and Therefore Under the Control of the "Client."* If the vicious circle of spiraling work and extended credit to meet high levels of leisure consumption is to be overcome, individuals must learn to locate, utilize and enjoy leisure opportunities which are geographically and economically accessible. Over the past decade, inflation and increases in the cost of living, including high gasoline prices, have plagued customers. Developments such as these will necessitate an increased use of leisure resources within the home, community and neighborhood, in which the individual resides. Trips of 500 miles in aerodynamically inefficient vehicles obtaining 5 miles per gallon of gasoline (if available) to distant facilities will become untenable. Vest-pocket parks, home-centered family leisure participation and low-budget "new games" will prevail. Leisure interest finders may be re-designed to emphasize non-commercial leisure activities which do not reinforce or create materialistic "wants" for their users. The artificial work/leisure dichotomy may disappear from our therapeutic interventions as occupational and recreational "therapists" de-emphasize professional boundaries in favor of providing opportunities meeting the total lifestyle needs of the individual. "Vocational" and "avocational" counseling interventions will merge into client-centered educational experiences fostering an integrated rather than fragmented lifestyle in which work and leisure needs are complementary, realistically achieved, and under the control of the "client."

2. *Recreators Must De-emphasize Limited Technological Interventions in Favor of Developing a Fundamental Understanding of the Phenomenon of Leisure.* By departing from traditional, functionally specific educational training and professional placement, several changes in service delivery would take place, resulting in increases in "client" autonomy. First, by emphasizing the exploration of the underlying human needs and motivations relevant to the leisure experience, future service providers

would be less likely to stress traditional facility planning and the provision of stereotyped activities. As concepts such as "activity substitution" are substantiated, consumers will be provided with *choices* of several leisure pursuits within cognates of low-cost, readily available activities which satisfy a basic human leisure need. This practice will be in sharp contrast with current practices of offering a finite number of highly structured "programs."

Secondly, "client" leisure autonomy will be enhanced as professional recreators are encouraged to view individuals' leisure and lives in total rather than as a series of compartmentalized activities. Those individuals involved in public and quasi-public agencies will take an interest in the consumer's leisure beyond the four walls of the agency. Activities within institutions will cease to be served up "in packages." Rather, opportunities for free play and social interaction of the "client's" own choosing will predominate. The role of the recreator must hence be shifted from that of a therapist or programmer to that of a facilitator.

3. *Recreators Must Recognize Participants as the Only Reliable Monitors of the Effectiveness of Their Services.* Contemporary leisure research[16] has tended to reaffirm early notions of leisure as being a state of mind or a personal perception of the individual engaged in a "leisure experience." Despite the growing recognition of leisure as being subjective (participant defined) rather than objective (second party defined), recreators continue to offer narrow, structured, time limited programs which ignore the subjective feelings of the "client." In seeking a solution to this situation, Ellis[17] admonishes recreators to "consult more with individuals regarding their leisure perceptions and reactions and abandon the orientation that any activity *we* provide for people is recreational." In the public sector, this may mean polling individuals as to *their* needs and wants and altering community centers from program facilities to places for consumer-centered leisure counseling and resource referral. In institutional settings, this orientation may involve the abandonment of the weekly activity schedule, the initiation of free choice of activity on the part of the "client" and the right to refuse recreational treatment. The "client" must in fact play the most significant part in the restoration of his or her own health if personal autonomy is to be insured.

4. *Recreators Must Engage in Reciprocal Relationships With "Clients" Which Stress the Development of Independent Leisure Skills.* A final step in insuring the personal leisure control of the individual involves a re-definition of our relationships with our "clients" in both public and "therapeutic" recreation settings. No longer must the recreator be seen as the mentor or ultimate source of expertise in handing down or prescribing activities for the consumer. Rather, the "client" must be viewed as having the primary responsibility for the quality of his or her own leisure. This does not suggest that the recreator has a diminished role to play in achieving this end. It does however, suggest a fundamental change in our interventions with our "clients." Fifty-minute-hour, counselor oriented leisure counseling sessions stressing computerized activity matching must give way to more personal reflection on the part of the "client." Counselors and other personnel in municipal recreation and institutional facilities must "de-mystify" their techniques to the point where the "client" may understand and adopt these practices to his or her own betterment. In short, recreation personnel in general cannot afford to become privileged and unaccountable at the expense of the freedom and control of the individuals they serve.

When man creates his own meaning he takes possession of the world; when he does it recreatively with style and dignity, he stages the dream of human life as only it can be staged.[18] Perhaps our greatest challenge of the next decades will be the creation of a climate of personal freedom in which this "dream" can be realized.

REFERENCES

1. Lefcourt, H. M. "The Function of the Illusions of Control and Freedom." *American Psychologist*, (May, 1971). p. 425.
2. Neulinger, J. *The Psychology of Leisure.* Springfield, Illinois: Charles C. Thomas, 1974.
3. Sites, P. *Control: The Basis of Social Order.* New York: Dunnellen Co., 1973. p. 214.
4. Angel, J. *The Radical Therapist.* New York: Ballantine Books, 1971. p. XV.
5. Galper, J. F. *The Politics of Social Services.* New Jersey: Prentice Hall, 1975. p. 47.
6. Galper, *Ibid.*, p. 22.
7. Tillman, A. *The Program Book for Recreation Professionals.* California: National Press Books, 1973. p. 63.
8. Galper, *Op. Cit.*, p. 54.

9. Galper, *Op. Cit.*, p. 92.
10. Meyer, L. "A View of Therapeutic Recreation: Its Foundations, Objectives and Challenges." Paper presented at New England Therapeutic Recreation Society Meeting, Durham, New Hampshire, October, 1976, p. 15.
11. Angel, *Op. Cit.*, p. 50.
12. Galper, *Op. Cit.*, p. 123.
13. Partington, J. "Project Wild: A Wilderness Learning Experience for High Delinquency Risk Youth." *Leisurability,* 4:2, (1977). p. 40.
14. Shivers, J. "Why Not Recreational Therapy?" *Leisurability,* 4(4), (1977). p. 4.
15. Quilitch, H. R. and de Longchamps, G. "Increasing Recreation Participation of Institutional Neuro-Psychiatric Residents." *Therapeutic Recreation Journal,* 8:2, (1974). pp. 56-60.
16. Shaw, S. "The Problem of Leisure: A Comparison of Subjective and Objective Methods of Calculating Leisure for Males and Females." Unpublished Master's Thesis. Dalhousie University, Halifax, Nova Scotia, Canada, 1978.
17. Ellis, M. J. "Some Leisure Studies — Review and Preview." Paper presented at the Allen V. Sapora Symposium on Leisure and Recreation. University of Illinois, Champaign, Illinois, May, 1977. p. 10.
18. Becker, E. *The Structure of Evil.* New York: George Braziller Co., 1968. p. 213.

Chapter Twenty-Three

Buckpassing, Blaming or Benevolence: A Leisure Education/Leisure Counseling Perspective

Peter A. Witt

There are several professional stances that can be taken toward an individual in need of service. One can, for example, act with benevolence, attempting to "do good" relative to meeting the expressed needs. On the other hand a posture of "it's not my concern or within my professional domain" can be adopted. Or we can blame the one in need for causing his/her own misfortune and subsequently hold them responsible for extricating themselves from the causes and consequences of their own actions. As recreation and leisure services begin to move toward "enabling" and "facilitating" services, adopting a philosophic stance toward the cause, responsibility and remediation of problems of leisure functioning will become an increasingly important concern. Whether to act with benevolence, pass-the-buck or blame the victim will become an increasingly difficult moral and practical issue.

Nowhere is this problem of focus more acute in the realm of recreation and leisure services than in the burgeoning attempts to conceptualize and initiate leisure counseling and leisure education services. (LC/LE).[1] In general, theory and practice have tended to develop along the twin paths of the "helping relationship" and educational models. Remediation or learning has been largely assumed to be client, student or participant focused. School systems, recreation programs and counseling relationships have been seen as the locus for some kind of intervention. All of these developments have emerged within a general framework that has emphasized individuals learning to cope with problems or barriers that block leisure fulfillment.

While there is every reason to believe that the LC/LE movement will further crystalize its methods and broaden its base of support over the next few years, there are several issues which it must come to grips with if it is to make a lasting impact on peoples' leisure functioning. Of particular concern is the fact that, to date, most of the attention has been focused on helping individuals change or modify some combination of their values, attitudes, skills or knowledge concerning leisure. Little attention has been directed toward dealing with systematic problems that support the work ethic, productivity, and societal definitions of usefulness as basic criteria for success, well being and meaning.

The belief within LC/LE seems to be that individuals need to be educated or counseled to fit into society and its institutional structures. Little attention has been given, however, to changing the basic social, economic and political conditions within the society that affect an individual's ability to undertake personally meaningful leisure experiences. It is not clear whether "changing" individuals will have any significant impact on the values and attitudes expressed by the institutional structures of the society as a whole. It seems more likely that efforts to educate or counsel individuals will be significantly over-ridden by the basically conservative and slow nature of social change that will continue to support the status quo and a work-ethic-dominated definition of purpose, success and personal well-being.

While not suggesting that we abandon attempts to help individuals develop the tools necessary for a personally meaningful leisure lifestyle, it is proposed that significant attention be directed toward reforming the social institutions that support the dominance of the work ethic (at least to the extent that it undermines leisure lifestyle). This stance does not necessarily imply supplanting work by leisure or the downgrading of attempts to create a society that meets the material needs of its populace. Rather, this position is aimed at helping to create a society that provides a climate conducive to leisure. While it is not being proposed that work be made obsolete, the work environment and its accompanying ethic of production, quantity and conformity does need to be humanized to make the possibilities of leisure more achievable and meaningful at the individual level. Significant attempts must also be made to make recreation environments more "hospitable" to human needs for play and leisure.

BLAMING THE VICTIM

Up to now, leisure education and leisure counseling have proceeded based on a "blame the victim" model. Thus, we blame individuals as the source of their own problems and "justify inequality by finding defects in the victims' inequality."[2] Ryan explains that the stigma, defect or fatal difference (whether it be an inability to read, the failure to obtain or maintain employment, or the failure to achieve a personally satisfying leisure lifestyle):

. . . is still located within the victim, inside his skin. With such an elegant formulation, the humanitarian can have it both ways. He can, all at the same time, concentrate his charitable interest on the defects of the victim, condemn the vague social and environmental stresses that produced the defect (some time ago) and ignore the continuing effect of the victimizing forces (right now). It is a brilliant ideology for justifying a perverse form of social action designed to change, not society, as one might expect, but rather society's victims.[3]

Thus, Johnny can't read because Johnny is not smart enough to read and is poorly motivated as opposed to looking at factors such as poor teaching methods and inadequate reinforcement (perceived value to bother learning). In the case of leisure "problems," we tend to overemphasize the "defects" in an individual's values, attitudes, skills and knowledge regarding leisure without giving proper attention to the service provisions and reinforcements provided by the society which influence leisure choices and outcomes. Further, we fail to give proper weight to factors such as unequal distribution of income, social stratification, inequality of power, plus mechanization and urbanization as the source of significant portions of the "leisure problem" for many individuals.

Overcoming the "blame the victim" mentality of LC/LE requires that we pay more attention to why, for example, poor leisure habits arise in the first place; why individuals are unprepared for increased free time; why playfulness is considered only the prerogative of children, and only then if it's the work of the child in his quest to grow up to be a productive adult; and why competition versus cooperation, and physical versus artistic and intellectual activity, are the socially accepted and reinforced bases of leisure involvements. We blame victims who turn to spectatoritis and noninvolvement through our tendency to overprogram and plan for people to the point where "many are almost incapable of creating their own satisfying activities or of finding lasting meaning in what they do."[4]

Orlick provides numerous examples of children, as they get older, dropping out of competitive, hierarchially based sports programs because these programs are not conducted at an appropriate skill and competitive level for their needs.[5] Of course, we can undo Orlick's evidence by "blaming" the drop-outs as being unmotivated and insufficiently competitive. We may even rationalize that they have learned an important lesson in life by failing and being rejected. It is in this context that some have argued for the need for LC/LE to help dropouts deal with rejection and failure when a better system of opportunity and matching skill or interest levels may be what is really required.

Preparing people to cope better with an unfit, dehumanizing and non-growth encouraging environment is only part of the answer. Rendering the environment more hospitable is the necessary correlate.[6] Lane goes even further by suggesting that we place too much emphasis on individuals as if they had personal power and choice and on human behavior as if it was primarily determined by enduring and consistent characteristics of the individual. "We perpetuate the cult of individualism by refusing to consider the existence of interrelated power structures as necessary if not sufficient variables in determining behavior."[7]

BLAMING THE ENVIRONMENT

In recent years several other authors have suggested more emphasis on a change (blame) the system versus change (blame) the individual approach in leisure services. Most have voiced their opposition to the medical model approach to the problems of special populations. For example, Rusalum suggested what he called the ecological model as an alternative to the therapeutic model in therapeutic recreation. This model:

. . . is built upon the belief that the overwhelming majority of disabled and disadvantaged persons do not need therapy. Despite their limitations and a denying society, they are relatively well-integrated emotionally healthy persons struggling to survive in a given unrewarding, unhospitable, environment . . . For example, America's urban areas are polluted, crowded, unattractive, inconsiderate of people's need for intimacy and warmth, poverty-stricken, inconvenient, dangerous, and most important from the vantage point of the exceptional individual, intolerant and inflexible in relation to extremes of human differences.[8]

The ecological approach would significantly "shift professional emphasis from the therapy of people to the therapy of environments."[9]

Thibault outlines three general approaches that can be taken to leisure education.[10] The first of these he labels the *traditional education model*. Under this model leisure activities are offered by service providers that are judged appropriate and good according to the dominant values of the society. Individuals are then informed via advertising of the availability of these opportunities and sensitized to the value of participating in them.

The *psycho-education model* assumes that individuals lack self knowledge regarding leisure values and attitudes. A variety of individual and group counseling methods are used to help individuals develop personally appropriate values and attitudes.

Finally, the *psycho-socio-education model* sees actual leisure involvement as a result of the interaction between economic, social and political influences of society and the individual's own will to actualize his needs, values and attitudes. The aim of leisure education is to demystify the actions of these social forces thus enabling the individual to perceive and act differently relative to his/her leisure. This demystification is accomplished by working to reduce the pressure of the social forces and impinging systems within the society as well as influencing the individual's perceptions by offering social alternatives that make real choice possible. Thibault seems to favor this model as it has the most potential for influencing the perception of options available and resultant outcomes for leisure lifestyle.

Edginton and Compton also have taken a middle ground position in the system versus individual change controversy by arguing for more attention to consumerism and advocacy as essential service approaches for those working with special populations. Consumerism will help individuals develop "personal competency in making qualitative and quantitative judgments about goods and services received and consumed."[11] Advocacy involves efforts to improve the quality of goods and services rendered to deal with the environment and bringing about significant environmental change to meet the needs of individuals.

To blame the victim or blame the environment is a controversial issue in a number of other helping professions as well. Of particular relevance is the controversy going on in both the psychology and the health fields. For example, Lewis and Lewis argue that a preventive or developmental approach to community mental health problems is more efficient than a remedial one.[12] The intent of prevention is "to anticipate future problems and move to prevent them by providing individuals or groups with needed skills or by creating changes in the environment so as to prevent the development of problems."[13] These authors do not argue against the validity of direct efforts to help people deal with the problems they confront in their lives. Rather they see the need for equal attention to changing the social surroundings that affect people's lives. To accomplish this Lewis and Lewis outline four programmatic approaches to intervention:

Extensive-experiential: programs that provide direct experiences available to the population as a whole.

Intensive-experiential: programs that provide special experiences to individuals or groups that need them.

Extensive-environmental: programs that attempt to make the entire community more responsive to the needs of all its members.

Intensive-environmental: programs that intervene actively in the environments of specific individuals or groups, so that their special needs can be met.[14]

Rappaport *et al.* suggest that we tend to place too much emphasis on problems, whether a victim or environment blaming model is adopted. As community psychologists, they argue that services should emphasize building on "community strengths and aiding in the development of those, while leaving amelioration of deficits to physicians, clergyman, social workers and clinicians."[15] This point of view may have a valuable parallel when trying to delineate the responsibility of recreation professionals to remove leisure deficits of individuals. Building on strengths via community development and enabling functions may be much closer to both the traditional roots and the training of most recreation professionals. Creating new avenues to desired goals and helping to transfer skills from areas of already existing competence via identification and utilization of community resources may be better avenues than attempts to repair weaknesses. In a sense, this calls for emphasis on a "what are you good at" versus a "what can I help you with" model.[16]

IMPLICATIONS AND FUTURE DIRECTIONS

The preceding ideas have a number of implications for the ways that the recreation and leisure services profession should conceptualize and deliver services aimed at dealing with people's leisure problems or deficits. Emphasis should change from trying to initiate person-centered remediation and counseling approaches to strategies emphasizing consumerism, advocacy, environmental change and education, particularly in community settings. Because it is new and sounds "professional," jumping on the leisure counseling bandwagon may appear to be a more attractive alternative than services aimed at redistributing opportunity, removing barriers to participation, and providing a humane environment in which people can make personally meaningful leisure choices. However, given the roots and basic expertise of the leisure service profession, our real mission lies in helping to reshape the opportunities available for leisure involvements, whether these be municipally, school or privately sponsored, as well as providing the supportive and skill training services that would facilitate participation.

In addition, the leisure services profession also has a vital role to play in educating itself, other professionals and citizens regarding a new outlook on the benefits and potential of leisure experiences. This education process should probably begin at home with the staff of existing recreation, park and leisure services. It is necessary that workers in these areas assess their own attitudes toward play, recreation, leisure and work. In the process, workers should analyze how their own biases and philosophies become a filter through which the problems and needs of others are viewed. As Friedson points out:

Embedded in the claims of each of the professions is a paradigm, a taken-for-granted conception of what the issue is, and how it is solvable. Each tends to see the world in terms of its own characteristic conception of problems and solutions.[17]

The paradigm within recreation and park services has been based on seeing the essential problems as 1) recreation, i.e. involvement in activity that would prepare an individual to go back to work refreshed; 2) idleness, i.e., people need something to do to fill the time freed from work due to automation; 3) catharsis and compensation, i.e., helping people act out frustrations derived from dehumanizing work and living environments. In a sense we've avoided blaming ourselves for our service conceptualization and provision failures by passing judgment on participants. This paradigm has led to a system of park and recreation services which has generally served the interests of a society committed to the work ethic. In many cases the profession has been the handmaiden of a bread-and-circuses social-control approach to serving the public good. Arguing that what is currently being provided is what people want ignores the process by which people learn to want. It ignores the fact that the delivery system is a value giving, reinforcing and reflecting entity that shapes and reinforces particular patterns of activity within the population.

Up to now, the recreation profession has had a basically conservative focus. It has been largely a civil service profession, allied closely with the purposes of preserving status-quo governmental priorities and assumptions. These assumptions have led to a mainstream system of park and recreation opportunities that tend to reinforce existing values and keep people busy or entertained. The profession must do some serious soul-searching and self-evaluation if a revised set of assumptions, and eventually services, is to become a reality. The "bankruptcy" warnings of Grey and Grebin[18] and the need to adopt a more holistic and humanistic perspective, as suggested by Murphy,[19] must be seriously examined.

Perhaps Charles K. Brightbill best summarized the basis for a new paradigm when he stated:

If we are to educate for leisure, it will be necessary to change many of our basic values. It will be necessary for us to revise our ideas of what constitutes success in life. We shall have to think less of bank accounts, fur coats and estates to leave to our children and cherish more the wonders of nature, the arts, the zest of leisurely physiological release, as well as service to our fellow man. We shall have to want more time not to produce and consume more material goods, but rather, to live more of life.[20]

In addition to adjusting our own paradigm, the profession must also place substantially more emphasis on becoming a catalytic change agent in the society at large. The profession must become more active in the political and social development process to help foster a better understanding of leisure needs and barriers to leisure fulfillment. The profession must also help to foster a social, political and economic environment conducive to leisure fulfillment. This will require the profession to become an active force in promoting an awareness of leisure's potential among political leaders, school officials, the clergy, business leaders and social service workers; an awareness that goes beyond a work ethic definition of recreation.

The profession must also help to overcome the emphasis on competition (to the detriment of cooperation), busyness (to the detriment of involvement and meaning) and consumption (to the detriment of experience and quality). On a wider scale, this involves seeing the role of leisure in fostering personal autonomy and growth; building a foundation for personal expression and self-defined meaning. It builds on the potential of leisure to add to an individual's life rather than repair problems created by interaction with the work or urban environment. Thus, increased emphasis is placed upon prevention and building on strengths rather than remediation and overcoming weaknesses.

REFERENCES

1. Epperson, Arlin, Witt, Peter A. and Hitzhusen, Gerald. *Leisure Counseling: An Aspect of Leisure Education.* Springfield: Charles C. Thomas, 1977. Compton, David M. and Judith E. Goldstein (Editors). *Perspectives of Leisure Counseling.* Arlington: National Recreation and Park Association, 1977.
2. Ryan, William. *Blaming the Victim.* New York: Vintage Books, 1976. XIII.
3. Ryan, William. *Op. Cit.* pp. 7-8.

4. Czurles, Arthur. "Art Creativity vs Spectatoritis." *Journal of Creative Behavior.* 10, 1976. p. 107.
5. Orlick, Terry. *Winning Through Cooperation: Competitive Insanity: Cooperative Alternatives.* Washington, D.C.: Hawkins and Associates, 1977.
6. Witt, Peter A. "The Art's in a State." In: D. M. Compton and J. Goldstein (Editors). *Perspectives of Leisure Counseling.* Arlington: National Recreation and Park Association, 1977. pp. 1-8.
7. Lane, Mary Kay. "A Reconsideration of Context: Perspectives on Prediction-Mote in the Eye." *American Psychologist.* 32 (12), 1977. p. 1056.
8. Rusalem, Herbert. "An Alternative to the Therapeutic Model in Therapeutic Recreation." *Therapeutic Recreation Journal.* 7, 1979. p. 12.
9. Rusalem. *Ibid.* p. 15.
10. Thibault, Andre. *La Situation Professionnelle des Travailleurs en Loisirs du Quebec comme Determinant de la Possibilite Differentielle de l'Education au Loisir.* These de Doctorat, Universite Laval, 1979.
11. Edginton, Christopher R. and David M. Compton. "Consumerism and Advocacy: A Conceptual Framework for Therapeutic Recreation." *Therapeutic Recreation Journal.* 9 (1) 1975. p. 27.
12. Lewis, Judith A. and Lewis, Michael D. *Community Counseling: A Human Services Approach.* New York: John Wiley Sons, Inc. 1977. p. 16.
13. Morrill, W. H., Oetting, E. R., Hurst, J. C. "Dimensions of Counselor Functioning." *The Personnel and Guidance Journal.* 52 (Feb.), 1974. p. 357.
14. Lewis and Lewis. *Op. Cit.*
15. Rappaport, J. *et. al.* "Alternatives to Blaming the Victim or the Environment." *American Psychologist.* 30 (4), 1975. p. 526.
16. Rappaport, *et. al. Ibid.*
17. Friedson, Eliot. "Professions and the Occupational Principle." In: Friedson, Eliot (Ed.). *The Professions and Their Prospects.* Beverly Hills: Sage, 1973. p. 31.
18. Gray, David E. and Seymour Grebin. "Future Perspectives." *Parks and Recreation,* 9, 1974 (July). pp. 26-56.
19. Murphy, James F. *Recreation and Leisure Service: A Humanistic Approach.* Dubuque: W. C. Brown, Co. 1975.
20. Brightbill, Charles K. *Man and Leisure.* Englewood Cliffs, New Jersey: Prentice Hall, Inc. 1961. p. 193.

Chapter Twenty-Four

Leisure Research and Park and Recreation Education: Compatible or Not?

Rabel J. Burdge

Assessment of the structural and organizational problems that confront the future of leisure and recreation research is critical to both those in academic settings and in recreation service agencies alike.[1] While discussion still persists within the academic community about whether or not leisure represents a body of knowledge, there is increasing agreement that leisure represents an important area of study both for its theoretical and practical implications. Among practitioners there is at least respect for the role that research can play in providing insights that can potentially lead to more effective and efficient service delivery. Yet acceptance of the value and role of recreation and leisure research is not universal and rarely unequivocal by either practitioners or academicians.

Problems in accepting leisure as an appropriate area of study may be traced to difficulties in defining the term and what the use of leisure means for the maintenance of a "healthy society." A well adjusted person uses free time properly for individual enhancement. Inappropriate use of free time can lead to breakdowns in the normative structure of society. If leisure time is not used properly by large segments of the population, it is seen as a social problem. Leisure research has become more important as we have sought to understand expressively and intrinsically motivated human behavior as opposed to maintenance or productive activity. Attempts to deal with the "leisure problem" are represented by the development and distribution of recreation programs and facilities.

Recreation and leisure research has had trouble finding a home in either traditional disciplines such as economics or sociology, or in academic departments focusing on professional park and recreation education. Nevertheless, recreation and leisure research has received increased attention over the last twenty-five years. But what of its future? Where will leisure research be "housed?" How well will it be supported and promulgated by academicians within degree programs focused on educating recreation professionals? Is there a place for recreation and leisure research within such traditional disciplines as sociology or economics?

Most of the early social science research on leisure and recreation came from persons trained and housed in traditional disciplines (mainly sociology) with little output from persons located in "park and recreation" type departments. However, few departments of sociology, economics, psychology or geography had the resources to devote portions of their programs to the study of leisure. As a result, Ph.D.'s from traditional disciplines with an interest in the study of leisure sought positions in park and recreation departments.

The renaming of traditional park and recreation departments to leisure studies, recreology or even leisure sciences, was an attempt to lay claim to the study of leisure while continuing to train professionals for park and recreation management careers. Furthermore, the emphasis on leisure as a topic of scholarly study is a reflection of the increasing need of these departments to achieve respectability within the larger academic community. The key question is: has renaming departments enhanced and expanded leisure research? To shed light on this question, I have reviewed the history of leisure research and the difficulties inherent in pursuing leisure education and leisure research within the same department.

THE BACKGROUNDS AND LOCATIONS OF RESEARCHERS

In the 60's, Kaplan, Burch, Dumazedier, Meyersohn, Foote, Berger, Parker, Clawson, and Brightbill, among others, were the dominant scholars in the emerging field of leisure research. A different generation is now writing the articles and doing the research. However, we are not so much interested in who is doing the work as the disciplines the researchers represent and the contribution of the different disciplines to the supply of refereed leisure research articles. Knowing the background of leisure researchers helps us understand the major theories and methods that have shaped the body of knowledge. In addition, it is useful to examine the disciplinary background and institutional location of editorial board members of major journals that publish leisure research. Editorial groups, which include editors, associate editors and book review editors, are important because they are both the promoters and the gatekeepers of research. Editorial groups decide what gets into print and what is kept out and promote their product by encouraging submissions.

Two journals are recognized as preeminent in the leisure research field: the *Journal of Leisure Research* (*JLR*) and *Leisure Sciences* (*LS*). The editorial boards of both *JLR* and *LS* reflect the multi-disciplinary and applied nature of the field. In the early 70's persons from the traditional social science disciplines were dominant. In the late 70's and early 80's persons with degrees from parks and recreation and forestry represented the emerging majority on the editorial boards.

The discipline of the authors whose articles were printed in these two journals has been, and through the early 80's remains, based within the traditional social sciences. Sociologists continue to hold the lead in authorships with persons from forestry a close second. Persons with degrees from park and recreation type departments increased their share of contributions in recent years, but continue to lag behind both forestry and sociology.

Articles published by economists dropped significantly in the last part of the 70's and that pattern continues today. Several of the applied disciplines not normally associated with leisure research, including urban and regional planning, landscape architecture, engineering and business administration/marketing, published a number of articles in the early years of *JLR*, but those contributions have since stopped.

Leisure research is done by persons in a variety of disciplines located in diverse institutional settings. The institutional location of scholars determines the constraints on their research, how they are rewarded and the type of research problem they select. Equally important, their institutional setting influences the way they review and select manuscripts for publication, thus also the focus of the publication.

In the first seven volumes of *JLR* (through 1975), persons from recreation and park departments had the most representation on the editorial boards, with forest experiment stations having significant representation. At about the time that *JLR* was established (1969), the U.S. Forest Service was expanding its recreation research program. This was also a period when attendance was increasing at federal recreation facilities and much research was focused on management problems. Sociology and agricultural/resource economics had the most representation on the editorial boards among the traditional social sciences.

During the late 70's and early 80's, departments of parks and recreation and forestry totally dominated the editorial group of *JLR*. Persons housed in traditional sociology and economics departments had measurably less involvement in the later part of the 1970's; leadership and control of the editorial group had shifted to persons in the applied departments. The institutional location of the *LS* editorial group is proportionally similar to the first seven volumes of *JLR* (through 1975), with the important exception that well over one-third of its members were located in departments of parks and recreation and leisure studies.

The institutional location of authors for both journals underscores the basic trend of where leisure research is done. There are more contributions from authors affiliated with applied departments and less from traditional social science departments. For example, forestry and parks and recreation made up about fifty percent of the authorships in *LS* through the first five volumes. Sociology and geography had slightly more contributions than *JLR* during the late 70's and early 80's, but that may have been because these represent the disciplines of the two founders and co-editors.

There are also important similarities between institutional location of the editorial group and authors of the two journals. The traditional social science departments of sociology and geography as well as the applied discipline of forestry are underrepresented in the editorial groups compared to the amount of materials they publish. On the other hand, parks and recreation departments and forest experiment stations have more editorial representation than authorships.

If these trends continue through the remainder of the 1980's, we can expect that more of the editorial group, at least of *JLR,* will be concentrated in departments of forestry and parks and recreation. Being an independently owned journal, the editorial board of *LS* will probably maintain a good diversity in institutional location. The authors of articles published in both journals will more likely come from the applied departments as rewards for multidisciplinary research decrease in traditional social science departments.

In total, the authors and the location of leisure research has shifted from traditional social science departments such as sociology and economics to applied departments like forestry and parks and recreation. But can leisure research be properly nourished in departments that must provide professional training for park and recreation practitioners?

THE LOCATION OF TEACHING AND RESEARCH PROGRAMS

The mission of park and recreation departments has been, and continues to be, one of training practitioners for positions in leisure services agencies. When research was added as a requisite for academic credibility, many faculty resented the additional requirement to publish, particularly if they had not obtained the research skills during their graduate student days. Professors in applied departments were accustomed to addressing problems defined by the practitioner or professional in the field. They were not as supportive of scholarly research directed toward the accumulation of knowledge about leisure. Furthermore, the interconnectness between research and teaching was not always perceived or understood by persons in departments that emphasized professional training. The quality and quantity of research produced by departments of recreation and parks may be characterized by an emphasis on application, a disdain for intellectualism and the lack of a research tradition.

In North America, and most particularly the United States, parks and recreation had its roots as a teaching program within Colleges of Education, generally housed within Departments of Health, Physical Education and Recreation. In many universities those departments are now colleges, with each area designated as a separate department. Recreation was taught as a series of skills, which were then combined into recreation and park programs. The content of the classroom materials was based on what seemed to work best for the practitioner.

Chronicling of individual experiences in developing good recreation programs was labelled as research. Research was defined in an "experience" sense rather than by scientific procedures of accumulating verified knowledge. Parks and recreation teaching materials tended to have narrow applicability and seldom could be generalized from one situation to the next. Being applied in orientation, the information base for recreation programs was not the stuff upon which a science is built.

However, teaching from experience is perfectly appropriate for professional training. No conflict would have been present if the graduate programs in parks and recreation that inevitably arose in the quest for academic respectability had not been increasingly staffed by faculty from traditional social science departments. When this happened, graduate programs that emphasized social science research bore little resemblance to undergraduate programs that trained managers to operate park and recreation programs. Park managers need skills ranging from turf management to accounting. The early graduate programs in parks and recreation had a tradition based in the College of Education, which taught methods and techniques. The shift to the study of leisure and recreation behavior represented an attempt to establish leisure as an area of scholarly concern. The process has produced faculties split between undergraduate professional education and graduate research programs.

The previous discussion raises a policy question: should park and recreation departments recruit and retain faculty who have a background in the study of leisure but not practical experience in the field? Perhaps so, but the realities of the university tenure system may not allow the retention of faculty immersed in park and recreation teaching and public service activity but not involved in scholarly research. A recent article by Sessoms helps to further clarify the dilemma.

". . . if departments of park and recreation administration continue to build faculties of an interdisciplinary nature, . . . rather than ones with training in parks and recreation, they might find themselves with faculties more inclined toward research and the traditional academic reward system. However, the field of parks and recreation may find that students trained under these faculties are ill-prepared as recreation and park practitioners. The profession may discover that universities are no longer preparing students for practitioner roles; university curricula may discover that their students are no longer as employable or interested in employment as recreation practitioners. The same phenomenon occurred in sociology some years ago as sociology ceased to be interested in the preparation of social workers. Consequently, social work evolved its own curricula and program of professional preparation."[4]

LEISURE RESEARCH AND PARK AND RECREATION PROGRAMS

If the amalgamation of parks and recreation and leisure studies is to be successful, then research generated under the umbrella of leisure studies should eventually translate into a body of useful and useable knowledge for the many practitioners in the field. Although accumulated knowledge about leisure has increased, the link to recreation programs has been spotty. Practitioners have complained that research such as that published in *JLR* and *LS* is incomprehensible and therefore useless for their programs or facilities. They seem much happier with the "research by experience" reported in *Parks and Recreation* magazine. There have been several abortive attempts to halt the publication of *JLR* by practitioner oriented groups within the National Recreation and Park Association (NRPA). However, all have failed, because publication of the journal provides legitimacy for the educational and research functions of NRPA.

Being housed in an applied curriculum, where the interests are practical, has limited the chances of leisure researchers to address important theoretical and methodological issues. Research is often funded by organizations interested in the improvement of leisure delivery systems or the removal of obstacles to program implementation. Under such a system, each researcher must identify a management problem and then look for a theoretical framework within which to study it. In essence, the research problem determines the selection of theory and methods. For example, if the management problem is campsite vandalism, then that behavior is singled out for study. The emphasis is on how to get rid of vandalism, rather than how leisure settings differ from other settings in the frequency and type of vandalism. The emphasis on management precludes the findings from the study being placed within the leisure literature. Under the pressure to be practical and relevant we may not be pursuing the theoretical and methodological advances that an emerging field so badly needs.

FUTURE DIRECTIONS

Can leisure research be conducted within the same department that conducts park and recreation education? In the late sixties the union seemed promising. "Leisure studies," a nebulous and uncertain problem area, found an organizational home within an already established university department. The university administration was excited because research and measurable publication standards would come to a department that previously had little taste for scholarly writing. The more thoughtful leaders among park and recreation educators saw a chance for practitioner oriented students to receive a more "liberal" education made possible by a broader leisure studies curriculum.

The discovery of an administrative home within the university community may ultimately prove to have hampered leisure research. Leisure is broader and research derived from its study has wider implications than simply the evaluation of park and recreation programs. In the process of coming under the parks and recreation umbrella, the number of persons interested in leisure research who felt they could fit within these units declined. As a result, many of the leisure researchers that were not inclined toward the park and recreation movement either sought different organizations or continued their research in the relative isolation of their disciplinary departments. At the same time, the departments of parks and recreation that attempted to label their graduates as leisure studies majors were having difficulty marketing students to practitioners who operated the leisure services systems.

Given the above problems, what steps need to be taken to insure the further development of leisure research? The following are a few suggestions on how the problem might be dealt with and perhaps provide the opportunity for both leisure studies and parks and recreation education to flourish in the decades ahead.

1. One solution, at least in the short term, would be for Institutes of Leisure Studies to be established. People trained in traditional disciplines could return to their home discipline and hold joint appointments in that department and the research institute. Thus, they could teach within their own field, while working with a multi-disciplinary research team in their interest area. Graduate students could receive training within these institutes but would earn their degrees within an established discipline. The institutes would retain ties to park and recreation departments but would not be identified solely with them. Parks and recreation departments could then concentrate on providing quality professional preparation for undergraduates and terminal master's degree students and be evaluated on that basis, rather than research productivity, assuming tenure and promotion criteria permit it.

2. The American Leisure Studies Association should be established as a meeting ground for scholars and scientists representing the breadth of disciplinary interests in leisure. Here they could meet, exchange ideas, and present papers on leisure and recreation theory, methodology and the substantive accumulation of findings. As the name implies, the Association would have as its central focus the theory and methods of leisure studies. One would attend the meeting to exchange research findings on that topic. The American Leisure Studies Association, like its counterparts in other parts of the world, would be supportive of organizations devoted to training leisure service delivery professionals as well as the applied aspects of leisure research.

3. A separate Department of Leisure Studies would, of course, be an optimal solution. However, in North America, only at Trois Riviere, in Quebec, has the study of leisure flourished on an independent basis. A few leisure studies type departments and institutes are active in Europe, where a distinction is made between theoretical and independent research in scientific institutes and applied research done by non-academic, commercial organizations.

In an earlier portion of this chapter, it was shown that editorial control of leisure research has shifted to persons housed in park and recreation and forestry departments. It may be that in a period of reduced funding levels and hiring freezes that the study of leisure as a scholarly pursuit can only be kept alive by support from an applied department. If those are the short-term political realities, then the issues raised in the later portion of this chapter must be understood and discussed by faculty members in departments where both "leisure studies" and "park and recreation education" is practiced.

Regardless of the location of leisure studies, the university research community, as well as state and federal governments, must recognize that the study of leisure is necessary for understanding social change in post-industrial societies. The importance of understanding leisure for individual and societal development has already been established for other countries and will become important in North America as all those trends in leisure we have talked about over the last three decades begin to come true.

REFERENCES

1. This chapter was adapted from: Burdge, R. J. "Making Leisure and Recreation A Scholarly Topic: Views of a Journal Editor," 1972-1982. *Leisure Sciences.* 1983, 6 (1), 99-126.
2. Discipline refers to the major department from which the Ph.D. or Ed.D was obtained, even though the place of employment may be different upon graduation. Data supporting the conclusions in this section are detailed in Burdge, R.J. *Op. Cit.* pp. 110-117.
3. Portions of this section are taken from: Burdge, R.J. "The Coming Separation of Leisure Studies from Parks and Recreation Education." Keynote paper for the annual meeting of the Leisure Research Symposium. Orlando, Florida, October 21, 1984.
4. Sessoms, H.D. "Research Issues in Park and Recreation Education: An Overview." *Leisure Sciences.* 1984, 6 (3), p. 333.

Chapter Twenty-Five
Spirits Sacred and Secular: Context as Bias in Leisure Research

Thomas L. Goodale

A professor at the California Institute of Technology has suggested a method for determining the credibility of works of a theoretical nature. So along with Murphy's Law, Parkinson's Law and Peter's Principle, David Politzer suggests what might best be called "The Volkswagon Criterion." It states:

> Never believe a theoretical paper unless you can fit all the authors into a Volkswagon. If there are more than that, it means no one person has thought the whole thing through.[1]

In science and in art, creative individuals often "think the whole thing through." The more precise the questions to be answered and problems to be solved, the more likely individuals can and do provide answers and solutions. But more questions and problems are complex. And so we have deliberative bodies, panel discussions, think tanks, and interdisciplinary teams for this and that. That is also why the search for relationships, understanding theories, facts and laws is conducted publicly. Thus research literature accumulates, publicly and communally, into a body of knowledge.

This exploration of the biases of (or in) the body of leisure research is an individual one, but also a public one. It is for sharing, perhaps also for shredding. Whatever the result, the more important matter is that the issue be joined. What are the biases in leisure research, where do they come from, and what difference does it make?

The perspective here is that of one neither immersed in nor divorced from leisure research. From that perspective, it appears that — all considered — the body of leisure research is in adequate health. To be sure, there remains some pseudo-sophistication, an example being a phrase like "peripheral parameters of the age cohort." (I have tried to figure that out: I think it means age range.) To be sure there is an air of stridency around some of it, including appeals to each other for constantly improving the quality of leisure research. To be sure there remain communications among researchers in which the art of civility appears to have been sacrificed to the faculty of criticism. All that is understandably the exuberance of a still young science.

In addition to that, leisure research encompasses a variety of viewpoints; perhaps biases is the appropriate term. Some, for example, are concerned that too few leisure researchers are well versed in multivariate statistical techniques;[2] others wonder whether or not the quantification imperative may not be too limiting for a young science.[3] Views as diverse as this are a sign of good health. Further, it is axiomatic that the skepticism integral to the practice of science be applied to one's own work as well as to the work of others. Thus when highly respected researchers note that perhaps it is fortunate that the research output is far behind attempts to formalize scientific planning and design of leisure experience,[4] one can be assured of a healthy skepticism and a healthy body of research.

Perhaps there is a health-maintaining system "built in" to leisure research. Since freedom, or at least perceived freedom, is a fundamental attribute of leisure, the pursuit of explanatory power by would-be autonomous persons is bound to incorporate a certain amount of ambivalence; most of us would like to be exempt from the laws we are trying to discover. Consequently, while appreciative of the analysis and insights of many informed commentators, it may be that leisure research is not seriously plagued with biases, or conversely, is plagued by such a variety of them that the body of leisure research remains in reasonably good health.

Three related observations, biases if you will, about leisure research are briefly discussed in the following pages. First, the bodies of leisure researchers are occupied by spirits other than the spirits of curiosity and inquiry. Second, the biases that may be evident in leisure research are not so much the biases of leisure research as the biases of the culture in which leisure research takes place. Third, the biases are evident not only in what is present in, but also what is missing from, the body of leisure research.

SPIRITS IN CONTEXT

Curiosity and the spirit of inquiry are the sacred spirits moving within us. Were there only sacred spirits, the body of leisure research would likely be different: probably smaller, conceivably better. The voluminous work on intrinsic and extrinsic motivation points to the likelihood of such an outcome.

However, extrinsic motivations, secular spirits if you will, are evident in a variety of ways. When Greg Buhyoff stepped down as editor of the *Journal of Leisure Research*, he observed cycles of recurring phenomena in the life of an editor. One such phenomenon was the increased number of telephone calls inquiring about the status of manuscripts during those weeks prior to up- dating vitaes and resumes for submission to deans and committees charged with assessing department, faculty and university person- nel.[5]

A second manifestation of secular spirits at work results from the pursuit of funding. In most universities the number and amount of grants received by individuals and departments is an important evaluation criteria. Thus there are, among researchers, whether in leisure or any other domain, those who do research on anything that can be funded. That is not necessarily a bad thing, but it is a force which shapes the kind of work undertaken, thus also the kind that is not. Individuals' research interests may be deferred or lost in the process.

This is an old argument, of course, though the state of the economy and the financing of universities raise the question anew. Many universities are redoubling efforts to attract private financ- ing, much of which takes the form of contract research. University overhead charges are often a substantial percentage of the contract amount. Too, the flow of funds available for academic or non- contract research has become a trickle, a highly politicized trickle.

In the quest for private-sector financial support, the dominance of faculties of medicine, science and engineering, law, and more recently commerce or business may become even greater than at present, probably to the detriment of the arts, humanities and social sciences. Even in psychology, private funding likely favors experimental psychology and such hyphenated fields as psycho- pharmocology; clinical psychology a poor second and social psychology a poorer third, and social psychology is one of the main disciplinary bases of leisure research. The concern, then, is the potential distortion not simply of leisure research as of the tradition and provision of liberal education. But even with funding, among those extensively involved in contract research on parks, recreation and leisure-related topics are those who perceive their own work as hack research, devoid of much of the intellectual challenge, creativity and fun. Without those attributes, academic undertak- ings of every kind become merely work, usually harried work.

Another manifestation of secular spirits at work is that leisure research is anything but leisurely and becomes, necessarily, geared more to production than discovery. As funding sources change their priorities, or as old sources are replaced by other sources with other priorities, research tends to become the result of sporadic forays into this subject or that. Conversely, when topics are pursued in a sustained, long-term fashion, articles appear which report not so much completed research as work in progress. Deans and personnel committees are singularly unimpressed with vitaes which report work in progress. So whether sporadic foray or work in progress, the result is a literature more fragmented than one might hope. Of course the breadth of the field and the limited number of outlets for some of the work contributes to producing the same effect.

Because secular spirits demand productivity, they also demand efficiency, especially of a researcher's time. Money for leisure research usually enables the researcher to buy the time and services of others. Thus within a research enterprise, specialization and division-of-labor increase efficiency. But they also tend to shape the methods and techniques employed. Not every kind of research lends itself to division of labor such as is possible, for example, with surveys. Perhaps that is one reason for the preponderance of surveys in leisure research, and the lack of other methods.

The other secular interest served by methods permitting such specialization is that the Volkswagon may be crowded, if not overflowing, with co-authors, thus dramatically increasing the passenger miles per gallon.

CULTURAL BIASES WRIT LARGE

This is not so much a criticism of leisure research as a gnashing at the secular bits by which it is held in tight rein: not so much a comment on the biases of leisure research as the cultural context which shapes it. Among the characteristics of that context has been the shift from monism to pluralism, perhaps extending even to atomism. So it is not surprising, then, that social philosophies like utilitarianism and pragmatism find expression at the individual level. It is also not surprising to find with the body of leisure research much diversity, leading to fragmentation and growing splits between this and that. The volume of information alone requires increasing specialization which reinforces the trend.

The growing split between leisure research and parks and recreation has been noted in the previous chapter. Not long ago Steven Smith and Arthur Haley commented on the apparent divorce of theory and empiricism, noting the atheoretical nature of much empirical work and the lack of empirical support for work of a theoretical nature.[6] One might also argue that research is increasingly divorced from scholarship or that scientific creativity and imagination is increasingly divorced from scientific methodology and techniques. The cultural dualism dividing the artistic and literary group from the scientific, noted by C. P. Snow some 25 years ago, seems also to have evolved to pluralism and perhaps atomism.[7] It is often jokingly observed that even within a discipline, sociology is the common example, those from one section of the country have trouble understanding those from other parts.

Yet there is much that is compelling in the parallels in the creative process in science and art and much compelling in depicting sociology, again by way of example, as an art form.[8] The best science and the best art does not sacrifice imagination, creativity or the desire to communicate to jargon or to the methods or techniques at hand. Among many possible examples are two from the work of colleagues in my region. A young psychologist, now at McGill University, observed how pleased those engaged in various self-improvement courses seemed to be with their progress, though empirical evidence was lacking. He discovered a strong tendency for people to depreciate their level of competence at the start of their self-improvement activities. His thesis, "Getting What You Want by Revising What You Had" was imaginative, technically sound, literate and fun.[9]

Another psychologist, this one at Carleton University, has been engaged the past few years in "personal projects" research.[10] Its focus is not upon subjects, instruments and experimental situations important to researchers but on the projects large and small that individuals are engaged in in the context of everyday life. One of the preliminary findings will be mentioned later on. The principal point is that the many splits and divisions that seem increasingly characteristic of the body of leisure research are understandable but not inevitable. Works that are imaginative, comprehensive and literate can be just as scientific as work in which some of these attributes are compromised by limiting designs to those projects for which methodological tools are available.

Other researchers have noted the fragmentation and have advanced suggestions and made efforts to help bring more coherence and comprehensiveness to the leisure research literature. In undertaking a book-review editorship, Tinsley, among others, encouraged comprehensive reviews of a body of literature rather than reviews of single books in which reference to other recent, related materials is usually absent. Similarly, Iso-Ahola, in assuming a journal editorship, expressed receptivity to review articles and to occasional theme issues.[12] These are encouraging efforts. But here again, secular influences may restrain such efforts. Review articles, however well done, do not have the status, in many quarters, of research articles. Reviews contribute much more than reward structures reward. The preparation of such reviews is difficult academic work which, once references have been gathered, does not lend itself to efficient divisions of labor. Book reviews, even comprehensive ones full of good insight and analysis, count little — if at all.

BIAS BY OMISSION

The volume of research articles published by those trained in psychology seems quite consistent with the dominant notion that leisure is an individual matter and the dominant socio-cultural trend toward individualism and individuation. Second largest in volume of articles published is from the area encompassing natural resources, resource economics, and forestry. This, too, is understandably part of traditional recreation resource interests and reflects the opportunity for research not only in academia but also resource-oriented agencies of government, particularly those at national, provincial or state levels.

The balance of the leisure research reported is scattered over a dozen or more fields of study.[13] Thus psychology and natural-resource orientations are predominant. Surely there are biases within these orientations though the greater bias appears to be not within what is present but between what is present and what is not.

Among the social sciences, the disciplines of economics and political science are notably under-represented in the leisure research literature. Yet leisure, which is generally operationalized as time free from work and other obligations, is a dependent variable. At the collective level it is profoundly dependent upon economic and political forces. No doubt there are a number of reasons for the comparative dearth of materials from these disciplines in the body of leisure research. But among those reasons may be the almost exclusive focus upon leisure as an individual as opposed to a collective phenomenon. Perhaps, too, except for econometrics, economics and politics are inextricably tied not only to each other but to value-laden social, political and economic philosophies. This is uncomfortable terrain for value-free inquiry. Again, there appears to be a parallel between tendencies in the culture and leisure research. The transition from monistic to pluralistic and perhaps atomistic value systems comes at some point to mean that there may be so many value systems as to have, essentially, none. There seems also a tendency in the culture to perceive human institutions as incapable of any right and individuals as incapable of any wrong.[15] Nonetheless, political scientists and economists have few difficulties wading into value-laden waters to explore human institutions including work, leisure, income distribution, welfare, democracy, community and so much more. Most of them are quite explicit about the values involved, often including their own value positions. Presumably we all value leisure, work, democracy, community and all the rest. Despite that, leisure at the collective level, deeply interpenetrated with social, political and economic forces, has not been incorporated into the body of leisure research.

This seems the case, at least, for the body of research reported in the *Journal of Leisure Research* and *Leisure Sciences*, arguably the two most prestigious North American leisure research journals. Work reflecting more of a collective focus and more of a political and economic orientation is more likely found in European and British publications such as *Leisure Studies* or even the publication emanating from (mainly French) Quebec, *Loisir et Societe*. This, in turn, appears to reflect if not biases then surely traditions of the different cultures.

The growing split between leisure research and parks and recreation may be in part a function of this void in the body of research. Parks and recreation, including both public- and private-sector involvment, is inextricably bound to political and economic forces. Secular as well as sacred spirits move among practitioners, too. And those secular forces make the gap between leisure research and park and recreation practice even wider.

The split may be unfortunate for all concerned for there seems to be much fertile ground upon which leisure research and parks and recreation could grow. At the present time, park and recreation practitioners are in great need of effectiveness measures. In recent years, evaluation research has become topical in many agencies and programs. In Canada, there is growing interest in "comprehensive auditing," particularly of public-sector activities. The comp-audit includes effectiveness, in addition to the traditional auditing of economy, efficiency, and accountability. Value for money is being demanded at all levels of government. Leisure research could contribute more. Practitioners' difficulties with evaluation, effectiveness or benefit measurement is partly the result of ill-formulated problems: that is, non-researchable problems. Yet implicit in most decision making are hypotheses of an if-then nature which can be reformulated in researchable ways. Problems of measurement, of course, are difficult. Further, limited resources and constant public and political surveillance may preclude much experimentation. They may also make it difficult to fail, and what kind of research is it that cannot support a null hypothesis?

Related to this is the fact that the concept of need has almost totally disappeared from both the research and professional literature. This is especially true at the collective level — how much of what service does this community need? — but also at the individual level — has someone's affiliation need, for example, been met? Rather we speak of wants, desires, preferences and demands. Perhaps the concept of need is simply too ambiguous. Perhaps people do not need much. But perhaps we have abandoned the concept of need because it begs a question that is evaluative. Wants and desires contain their own closures: that is, we want what we want because we want it. Need is without closure. The concept demands explication. We don't need something because we need it, we need something in order for something else. Whatever that something else is, it is value laden and collective in a way that parallels the process of counter reinforcement. We attempt or do not attempt to meet needs according to judgements about the purposes to be served by so doing. If we cannot be explicit about our purposes, we cannot engage in evaluation or effectiveness research.

The lack of work on recreation benefits and on service effectiveness is only one of many voids in the literature which leisure researchers might appropriately address. Matters related to the distribution of work and thus the distribution of both income and non-work time are clearly of interest, as are matters related to the political processes of distributing leisure resources. Technological impacts and assessments of them are impotrant to our understanding, such as the studies undertaken by the Office of Technology Assessment of the United States Congress. The Conference Board in Canada, a highly respected, private, economic research organization, has engaged in a major study of the implication of a three-day work week. Surely the lists of subjects which leisure research might encompass could be a very lengthy one.

One of my biases, related to leisure research and to university education, favors renewed emphasis on liberal studies and reduced emphasis on specialized training. In particular, subjects like history and anthropology should be stressed, and much more historical and anthropological research on leisure would be greatly appreciated. For it seems clear that a broader perspective of ourselves and our times would contribute much to leisure. Perhaps not, though on this matter the arguments of historians and anthropologists are persuasive. Mypoia surely contributes to anxiety, and anxiety is a fatal enemy of leisure.

Finally, the personal projects research, noted earlier, is very much a study of leisure, comprehensive and fully integrated into daily life. The starting point is whatever projects people are engaged in. Projects could range from getting some letters written to building a boat and sailing around the world or even to transforming western intellectual thought. Participants in the study also answer dozens of questions related to their projects and to other aspects of their lives, including verbal and other measures of health. Some interesting relationships are emerging from preliminary results. One of the correlates of poor health is that no one else seems interested in the projects engaging the respondents.[14] Are we beginning to identify the limits of individualism and atomism? Are we beginning to identify the break point between tolerance and indifference? Are these, indeed, some of the health hazards of our current cultural biases?[15] If that is so, then we should weigh very carefully the values and attitudes shaping our culture and thus our work.

REFERENCES

1. Politzer, David. Cited in: *The University of Ottawa Gazette*, 19:12 (July) 1984. p. 13.
2. Tinsley, Howard E.A. "Application of Multi-Variate Analysis Procedures in Leisure Reaearch." *Journal of Leisure Research*, 15:4, 1983. pp. 285-289.
3. Cf. Kelly, John R. "Leisure and Quality: Beyond the Quantitative Barrier in Research," In: Goodale, Thomas L. and Peter A. Witt. *Recreation and Leisure: Issues in an Era of Change.* State College, Pennsylvania: Venture Publishing, 1980. pp. 300-314.
4. Mannel, Roger. "The 'Psychologization' of Leisure Services," In: Goodale, Thomas L. and Peter A Witt, *op. cit.* p. 107.
5. Buhyoff, Greg. Editor's Notes. *Journal of Leisure Research*, 15:3, 1983. p. iv.
6. Smith, Steven L.J. and Arthur J. Haley. "Ratio ex Machina: Notes on Leisure Research." *Journal of Leisure Research*, 11:2, 1979. pp. 139-143.
7. Snow, Charles P. *The Two Cultures and the Scientific Revolution.* New York: Cambridge University Press, 1959.
8. Nisbet, Robert. *Sociology as an Art Form.* New York: Oxford University Press. 1976.
9. Conway, Michael. "Getting What You Want by Revising What You Had." (Unpublished Master's thesis) University of Waterloo, Department of Psychology, 1983.
10. Little, Brian R. "Personal Projects: A Rationale and Method for Investigation." *Environment and Behavior*, 15:3 (May) 1983. pp. 273-309.
11. Tinsley, Howard E.A. "Some Parting Thoughts." *Journal of Leisure Research*, 10:1, 1978. p. 5.
12. Iso-Ahola, Seppo. "Editorial Philosophy and Policy." *Journal of Leisure Research*, 15:3, 1983. p. v.
13. Cf. Burdge, Rabel. "Making Leisure and Recreation Research a Scholarly Topic: Views of a Journal Editor 1972-1982." *Leisure Science*, 6:1, 1983. pp. 99-126.
14. Little, Brian. In a graduate research seminar, Department of Psychology, University of Ottawa (April) 1982.
15. Cf. Vickers, Geoffrey, "The Future of Morality." *Futures*, VII:5 (October) 1979. pp. 371-382.

Chapter Twenty-Six

Recreation and Park
Professional Organizations
in an Era of Change

Charles E. Hartsoe

In order to gain perspective on the future of professional organizations in the recreation and park field it is helpful to understand why they exist at all. The most prominent national organization on the scene today is the National Recreation and Park Association, thus scene today is the National Recreation and Park Association, thus the historical focus and commentary will be about that organization. It is important to note that NRPA, in its present organizational form, was created some two decades ago, through the consolidation of several professional and service organizations in the recreation and park field.

The purposes for which NRPA exists today are not new and differ little from those which led to the creation of its predecessor organizations at the turn of the century. Briefly stated, the goals of NRPA are to promote public awareness of, and support for, the value of recreation and parks in the lives of individuals and to provide services that contribute to the development of its members.[1] As the importance of leisure increases, it is assumed that NRPA's role and importance will expand.

To gain insight into the current structure of NRPA and the internal issues the organization must deal with in the future, it is helpful to understand something about the associations that merged to form NRPA. Also, it is useful to examine the motivations that led to merger as well as the principal issues that needed to be resolved to accommodate the unification that was achieved. First, a discussion of the predecessor organizations.

DIVERSE ORIGINS

The National Recreation Association (NRA) created in 1906, was by far the largest in terms of financial resources and staff. Its budget at the time of merger was $924,000, or $2,206,512 expressed

361

in 1984 dollars. The NRA staff was made up of approximately one hundred full-time members of which some thirty were professional. The Association had an endowment fund just short of one million dollars and owned a headquarters building in New York City valued in 1963 at approximately a half-million dollars. Most of the NRA's financial support was from philanthropic sources with only 3 percent of its budget coming from membership fees. In addition to its New York Headquarters, the Association maintained a staff in Washington, D.C. and in eight regional offices throughout the country. The National Recreation Association, working primarily with local governments, was governed by a self-perpetuating board of citizen leaders who were committed to the goal of expanding constructive leisure time opportunities for the American public. NRA, as a citizen organization, advocated professional standards in employment, programming and physical planning as a means of increasing the quality of community recreation and parks. Its nonvoting membership numbered eighteen thousand and consisted of professionals, citizens and individual contributors.[2]

The American Recreation Society (ARS), established in 1937, had, by the time of merger, increased its membership to 4,200 professional recreation personnel. ARS was recognized as a professional organization for recreation personnel whereas NRA was considered a service organization. The ARS was organized into special interest sections which included armed forces recreation; hospital recreation; public and park recreation; professional education; county, state, and federal recreation; private and voluntary agencies; and religious organizations. An executive director, an administrative assistant, and a secretary made up the ARS staff. The annual operating budget was approximately $50,000 or $119,400 measured in 1984 dollars. Seventy percent of its revenue came from membership dues and the remainder from the sale of advertising and publications. The ARS published its own magazine, *The American Recreation Journal*, and jointly sponsored an annual national convention with the NRA. The ARS governance structure was highly democratic with the membership electing an 88 member administrative council. The majority of ARS members were employed by municipal recreation and park departments.

The American Institute of Park Executives (AIPE) had been established in 1898 primarily to gather and disseminate information on public parks and recreation areas. By the time of consolidation, AIPE membership included some two thousand park and recreation administrators who constituted the voting membership of the organization. In addition there were about a thousand local park and recreation board members affiliated in a nonvoting capacity.

The AIPE's operating budget was just under $190,000 ($453,720 in 1984 dollars) of which approximately 22 percent was derived from membership dues. Much of AIPE's income was generated from a strong commercial exhibit component of their national conference and from an especially successful publication program. While AIPE was regarded essentially as a park-oriented organization, it had attracted a sizable group of recreation administrators to the point where its membership was almost evenly divided between park and recreation practitioners. The orientation of its program was clearly toward the park and recreation administrator rather than toward the broader membership thrust of both NRA and ARS. The American Institute of Park Executives was governed by a small, six member, board and its headquarters was located at Oglebay Park in Wheeling, West Virginia.

Closely affiliated with the park executives was the American Association of Zoological Parks and Aquariums, an autonomous organization created in 1924 and dedicated to wildlife conservation. Many of the general services of AAZPA were jointly operated for purposes of economy with AIPE out of Oglebay Park. The zoological group was not particularly active in the merger negotiations but merely followed the leadership of AIPE. The AAZPA pulled out of NRPA shortly after the merger. Apparently, the somewhat unique and diverse concerns of the zoological managers could not be adequately accommodated within the structure of NRPA.

The National Conference on State Parks had been formed in 1921 by national park pioneer Stephen Mather and other leading conservationists for the purpose of encouraging the states to acquire and preserve scenic areas of importance. Its membership included professional resource managers and citizens concerned with the development of state parks. Its budget and staff resources were small and comparable to those of the American Recreation Society. Like ARS, the headquarters for the National Conference on State Parks was located in Washington, D.C.

CONSOLIDATION

The incentives to unify the recreation and parks profession in the 1960's were varied. At that time consolidation appeared not only a desirable course of action but also a necessary one for the survival and future growth of the profession. A closer look at some of the incentives for merger is instructive.

The decades of the 1950's and 1960's which created the environment for merger were ones of action and opportunity for the recreation and park field. There was a strong trend toward centralizing power and authority as an approach to solving problems and providing services. Municipal recreation and park departments which initially had been organized as separate units of local government were being consolidated at a rapid pace. Following the continued growth of the New Deal philosophy, there was a growing interest in an expanded role for state and federal government in the park and recreation field. A major stimulant was the completion of the Outdoor Recreation Resources Review Commission Report (ORRRC) with the subsequent enactment of its recommendations, including the creation of the Land and Water Conservation Fund and the establishment of a federal recreation agency.

The ORRRC report pointed out that the overall demand for outdoor recreation in this nation would triple by the year 2000 and called for expanded roles by all levels of government in acquiring and protecting needed recreation resources. The study helped to reinforce the fact that the recreation and park field was growing so rapidly that no one organization had the resources and following to exercise overall leadership. Dr. Luther Gulick, nephew of one of the founders of the playground movement and a long time citizen leader of the recreation movement summed up the changing situation of the 1960's by stating, "The nation stands on the threshold of tremendous developments in recreation and parks, greater than for two generations; it is important to develop a whole new general strategy, to take a broad look and start anew, concentrating on positive moves."[3]

By the time of the ORRRC study, competition between national professional organizations in the park and recreation field had become more intense. In order to attract broader support, organizational philosophies and goals became somewhat similar, resulting in duplicate institutional services, such as national conferences, magazines, and membership promotion. It was not uncommon for the same recreation and park professional to belong to the National Recreation Association, the American Recreation Society and the American Institute of Park Executives. The increasing confusion and competition between recreation and park groups prompted many professional leaders to speak out openly in favor of consolidating organizations.

The idea of eliminating competition through unification or consolidation of national recreation organizations was not a new one. The suggestion had been made as early as 1909 that the fledgling Playground Association of America (early predecessor to NRPA) merge with the American Physical Education Association.[4] Pioneer Luther Gulick had suggested in 1911 the formation of a public recreation federation. His plan at that time had called for changing the Playground and Recreation Association to a "Public Recreation Federation." Under his proposal the general association would have retained control over a majority of the board, the field staff, and common finances. Each special interest organization was to retain its own name, have representation on the overall board, raise the special expenses for its own program, subject to approval by a general finance committee, and select its own paid specialized staff.

The basis for his concept of a coordinating recreation corporation had been to eliminate the "considerable duplication between different national organizations having to do with the leisure time among the people of America."[5] In addition to the playground movement, Gulick had proposed including public school athletic leagues, commercial recreation, social centers, boys' clubs, the Boy Scout movement, the Camp Fire Girls (of which Gulick was also founder), and an agency to censor motion pictures. PAA president Joseph Lee had rejected the proposal on the theory that four of the areas (public school athletics, commercial recreation, playgrounds, and social centers) already were more or less being looked after by the Playground Association. Lee also had felt that the Boy Scouts and the Camp Fire Girls would eventually come into the PRAA structure after leaders of each had "made their own ideas clear and incisive as a separate organization."[6] Regardless of this early concern, it was not until some fifty years later that a major consolidation of national organizations was actually accomplished. The unification did not come about easily, but rather was the product of years of intensive and at times bitter negotiations.

Professionals and Laymen
One of the early obstacles encountered in the formulation of a plan for merger was the question of how to reconcile the unique differences that existed between the organizations. The ARS and AIPE were both professional membership societies with voting members who elected their officers and board members, who in turn staffed their committees. On the other hand, the National Recreation Association was a national voluntary service organization with no voting members but rather service associates (individuals) and service affiliates (agencies). Committee members were appointed on the recommendations of staff. Professionals who joined the NRA had no voting power over its board of trustees or its budget. Thus, the issue of professional rights and governing power versus lay control became a dominant issue in the merger negotiations.

With this merger, leaders in the recreation and park field were trying to accomplish something that no other social movement had done successfully — to mold together in one organization the citizen and professional leadership of the nation concerned with recreation and parks. The rationale for such a consolidation was to build strength through unity and to combine overlapping resources into a more effective and cohesive organization to better serve the park and recreation movement. It is important to remember that citizen leaders had been the early activists in creating most municipal recreation and park departments throughout the nation and that citizen leaders still held extensive external power in public recreation and park systems. It is equally important to note that all of the organizations involved in the merger negotiations had public recreation and parks as their primary orientation.

The assumption was made that the layman and professional could develop a mutually supportive organizational relationship where policy and programs could be developed harmoniously. Susan Lee, one of the principle citizen negotiators, viewed the layman's contribution to be in the areas of public education, interpretation and finance with the special place of the professional being in the areas of professional expertise, skills and services.[7]

One of the most technical aspects of the lay/professional issue was its perceived relationship to the tax status of any new organization created through the merger. One of the strong prerequisites for the NRA's involvement in merger discussions was preservation of the full tax-exempt status of the Association, the most favored tax status among the organizations discussing merger. The Association was tax-exempt under Section 501(c) (3) of the Internal Revenue Code. The major benefit of this particular tax classification was that contributions to such designated organizations were deductible for federal income, estate, and gift tax purposes. The AIPE and ARS, on the other hand, were both classified for tax purposes as trade or professional associations under a different section of the Internal Revenue Code, which prohibited donors from deducting contributions as tax-deductible gifts. Under federal regulations, the NRA thus was characterized as a charitable, educational, and scientific organization operating exclusively in the public interest while the ARS and AIPE were interpreted to be professional associations operating to promote the specific interests of their own members.

The NRA board maintained a strong stance that any unified organization must direct its board programs to the recreation interests of the nation through public education and service to both lay and professional interests, communities throughout the country, and public and private recreation agencies. In NRA's view, this broad based public service philosophy would insure the continued tax exempt status of a unified organization.

On the other hand, APIE and ARS leaders questioned the continuing need for voluntary charitable support in a merged organization, particularly in view of the growing profession and the increased activity of the federal government. They advocated the importance of the professional recreator becoming more self-sufficient and having at least an equal share in policy determination. The value of the franchise and the individual professional member's right to representation was emphasized. The professional groups maintained that a top policy board equally balanced between laymen and practitioners would not in itself jeopardize the ability to gain tax-exempt status. This question of equal representation became an issue of paramount importance to the professional groups and on several occasions during the three years of negotiations threatened to scuttle the proposed merger.

The lay-professional issue was subsequently resolved by creating a policy making board of 63 members, twenty-one of whom were laymen selected at large, twenty-one professional persons and twenty-one laymen nominated by the professional group. This unique compromise satisfied the NRA requirement of a predominantly lay board and provided the professionals with a sense of controlling two-thirds of the board through the right to nominate one-half of the lay trustees.

Thus, the National Recreation and Park Association became operational in January 1966. The offices of the merging organizations were consolidated in Washington, D.C. and a new era of unification began within the recreation and park field.

A Cumbersome Unity

Consolidation did not mean simplification. In order to accommodate the varied philosophical and political interests of each organization, NRPA, by necessity, began with a cumbersome and somewhat complex organizational structure. There was an expectation that with time many of the special interest philosophical differences would fade and that the governance and committee structure would be simplified. However, by 1975, NRPA, in an effort to meet the needs of its continuing diverse membership, had created an even more elaborate and unwieldy organizational bureaucracy. Its overall governance structure included a 63 member national board, a 240 member national council, seven branches with 150 plus board members, 160 different committees, 8 districts and 63 affiliates.

Subsequent organizational studies and constitutional revisions that have taken place have modified the lay/professional dichotomy and have strengthened regional and special interest representation on the governing board. Despite these changes, there is a growing realization that further reorganization is needed if NRPA is to achieve the overall leadership role which, presumably, would result from merger.

RE-EMERGENT DIVERSITY

There are some developing trends that are of special significance to the National Recreation and Park Association as it seeks to define its role and develop an organizational structure for the future. The first of these is the increased proliferation of professional organizations in the park and recreation field. There are more professional recreation and park associations in existence today than prior to the merger in 1965 that created NRPA. Among the more recently established organizations are the International Military Recreation Association, International Military Club Executives Association, Resort and Commercial Recreation Association, American Academy for Park and Recreation Administration, American Academy for Leisure Sciences, National Association of County Recreation and Park Officials, Travel and Tourism Research Association, National Intramural Recreational Sports Association, American Association of Fitness Directors in Business and Industry, and the American Therapeutic Recreation Association.

The growth in the number of new professional organizations may be in response to the realization that NRPA cannot be "all things to all people." Initially, perhaps it was unrealistic to expect that the diverse elements of such a broad occupational field as parks and recreation could work together harmoniously in a homogenous organizational community. Indeed, the professional needs and concerns of a park and recreation administrator in a political environment are quite different from those of a recreation therapist in a clinical setting heavily influenced by milieu therapy.[8]

One lesson learned through the 1965 merger experience is that the process of professional segmentation will continue regardless of organizational structure. As occupational ideology develops within specific agency settings, the need for professional identity increases as does the need for a strong professional support system to enhance that identity.[9] In the case of NRPA, professional identity is defined in many different ways and under many different institutional formats. Moreover, NRPA has the added mandate to maintain an appropriate balance of citizen involvement if its tax status and public service image are to be preserved. Perhaps NRPA could be more effective by narrowing the scope of its constituency and encouraging organizational spin-offs of such special interest groups as clinical recreation therapists.

Of equal interest to the proliferation of professional organizations is the recent growth of state recreation and park associations. At the time of the NRPA merger in 1965 perhaps no more than one or two state associations had full time executive directors. Today, some twenty states have full time executives and most state societies conduct conferences, publish a journal and provide other membership services similar to those provided by NRPA.

The trend of decentralizing government under concepts of New Federalism is having an important impact on a wide range of national associations. The increasing power that is shifting to state and local government brings with it new opportunities and challenges for state professional and service organizations.[10] It is inevitable that NRPA will be required to re-think its relationship with state recreation and park societies. Such issues as the allocation of revenue from dues, legislative liaison and the delivery of membership support services provide areas of great opportunity for building a strong, mutually supportive relationship between state organizations and NRPA.

Recently, the Texas Recreation and Park Society passed a resolution calling for the redefinition of roles, relationships and funding mechanisms between state societies and NRPA. The Pennsylvania and Virginia Recreation and Park Societies have developed model chapter agreements that call for stronger state roles in the development of national policy. The pressure is growing at the state level for some reorganization of NRPA to accommodate the expanding needs and opportunities of the state associations. The increasing strength and vitality of state organizations may provide NRPA with one of its best opportunities for growth and leadership in the future. The question of how to share power and resources in a mutually supportive way is the key issue that must be resolved.

A REVISED ROLE

Today, NRPA has a staff of approximately forty professional and clerical employees. At a time of increasing demand for services, this is less than half the staff resources available at the time of merger. It would appear to be to NRPA's advantage to explore ways to decentralize some membership services to the state societies. This would enable limited national staff resources to be utilized for high priority programs. Such a reallocation of service responsibilities would almost certainly require NRPA to provide state societies with a voice in association policy determination. This may be difficult for NRPA with its partially self-perpetuating board. A more democratic board might well re-energize the entire organization.

A reconceptualization of the national role cannot ignore the increasing importance of international contact in the recreation and park field. The information explosion is international in scope as is the technology to communicate. For many years the National Recreation Association (predecessor to NRPA) was active in promoting recreation on an international basis. The NRA organized the first International Congress on Recreation in conjunction with the 1932 Los Angeles Olympic Games. In 1956, the NRA was responsible for the creation of the World Leisure and Recreation Association. However, since the merger, NRPA has virtually ignored the international arena.

John Naisbitt, social forecaster and author of *Megatrends* has predicted that the trend toward a global economy will make international associations and international meetings more important in the future.[11] Over thirty nations have established national programs to foster active participation in leisure and recreation. National and regional recreation and park associations have been established in various parts of the world and work is underway in developing international guides to literature in the leisure and recreation field. A broader and more international perspective is but one direction that might provide NRPA with the type of new frontier that could expand the horizons of the entire park and recreation field. There is a growing interdependence between what happens in an expanding leisure service field whether it takes place in Japan, Brazil, England or America. NRPA must become more effective in sharing and interpreting world wide developments to its members. Moreover, it should initiate student and professional exchange programs to develop networks and foster international understanding.

The greatest opportunities for NRPA in the future may grow out of the realization that as an organization it cannot be "all things to all members." Much has been learned from the experience of the merger. There is a strong argument for NRPA to reinvest its resources in a leadership commitment to the public recreation and park field and to support the independence of special interest groups whose principal mission may be in related areas. This is not to suggest that NRPA abandon its concern for the broad field of recreation and leisure, but rather that as an organization it focus its limited resources on building a strong support system to foster the growth and development of public recreation and parks.

In such a role, NRPA would be in an excellent position to lend its strength and leadership to re-establishing a coordinating mechanism similar to the now defunct Federation of National Professional Organizations for Recreation.[12] A federation or council of national organizations in the recreation and park field could then develop work programs and legislative support on matters of common interest that would serve the broad field of recreation, parks and leisure services.

The field of recreation, parks and leisure is far too broad an area from which to expect a single organization such as NRPA to provide overall leadership. The powerful trends of decentralization and expanding body of knowledge are encouraging the growth of new special interest organizations. State recreation and park societies are getting stronger possibly at the expense of the national organization. New international opportunities are emerging. It is an opportune time for NRPA to reconceptualize its mission, role and services to accommodate these major changes.

REFERENCES

1. Constitution and By-Laws, National Recreation and Park Association, May, 1984.
2. Material on background of merging organizations from Knapp, Richard F. and Hartsoe, Charles E. *Play for America*. Arlington, National Recreation and Park Association, 1979; for additional information on the American Recreation Society see *The American Recreation Society: Its Early Years (1937-1952)*. Washington, D.C. 1953; on the National Conference on State Parks see "Fifty Years: The Origin and Development of the National Conference on State Parks", *Parks and Recreation*, December 1970, pp. 18-21, 53.
3. Minutes, NRA Board of Directors, January 24, 1962.
4. Mabel Lee and Bruce L. Bennett, "This is Our Heritage", *Journal of Health, Physical Education and Recreation*, April 1960, pp. 42-43.
5. Letter from Luther H. Gulick to Joseph Lee, April 5, 1912.
6. Letter from Joseph Lee to Luther H. Gulick, April 23, 1912.
7. Memorandum from Susan M. Lee to NRA Board of Directors, March 10, 1964.
8. For an extensive discussion of professional priorities of a clinical therapeutic recreation specialist see Peterson, Carol Ann. "A Matter of Priorities and Loyalties", *Therapeutic Recreation Journal*, Third Quarter, 1984, pp. 11-16.
9. For an extensive discussion of organizations and the process of professionalization see "Professional Associations and Colleague Relations" (Chapter 5) In: Vollmer, Howard M. (Ed.). *Professionalization*. Englewood Cliffs, N.J.: Prentice-Hall, Inc. 1966, pp. 153-196.
10. Porter, Margo Vanover. "Get Ready for Decentralized Government", *Association Management*, June, 1982.

11. Sabo, Sandra, "Be Ready To Be Surprised," *Association Management* (Leadership Supplement), December, 1983, p. A-16.
12. The Federation of National Professional Organizations for Recreation was created in 1953; it met semi-annually and had ten affiliated organizations as members. The federation became inactive following the merger.

Chapter Twenty-Seven
Leisure and Recreation
an International Perspective

Cor Westland

Whenever one attempts to deal with a subject from an international perspective, one cannot escape generalizations or the risk of creating an impression of uniformity and homogeneity which may not exist to the degree implied. This is especially true for phenomena such as leisure and recreation which are (a) strongly influenced by cultural, political, demographic, educational and economic conditions, (b) highly personal in perception and interpretation and (c) subject to an infinite variety of forms of expression. Yet these conditions determine to a large degree the place and role of both leisure and recreation in a given society and make it possible to identify general characteristics that are peculiar to the various regions of the world.

The intent of this chapter is to highlight some of these characteristics. The nature of the available data does not permit a systematic and rigorous treatment of each of the world regions under discussion, nor is a thorough comparative analysis possible. In spite of these limitations, one can derive some interesting insights into the leisure and recreation practices in Europe, Latin America, and the Far East. This review is limited to those three regions for practical purposes and because they show the differences in approach and practices most clearly, assuming that the reader is familiar with the North American scene.

CONCEPTS OF LEISURE AND FREE TIME

Leisure

In spite of the apparent lack of conceptual consensus among the English speaking peoples, there is a high level of agreement worldwide on an operational definition of leisure.

Increasingly, *leisure* is seen as time; more specifically unobligated or discretionary time; time that is left after physiological needs have been met and work, family and social obligations fulfilled. Thus, leisure is time one can occupy as one wishes.

Acceptance of this concept has been greatly facilitated by the absence of the equivalent for leisure in most languages. For instance, although the German language does know the word "Musze," which comes close to leisure (Joseph Pieper uses it in his classic, *Leisure, The Basis of Culture*), in contemporary German it is virtually extinct and replaced by a new noun "Freizeit," composed from "die freie Zeit" (free time).

Spanish speaking peoples use the expression "Tiempo libre," the Scandinavians speak of "Fridit" and the Dutch talk about "Vrijetijdsbesteding," all indicating an element of time.

Although in academic circles of the French speaking world "Loisir" is generally interpreted as identifying "the totality of activities," popular usage of the word relates it to time (le temps de loisir), not unlike "leisure time" among English speaking peoples.

Free Time
Given that leisure, on the international scene, has increasingly come to be equated with free time, it is important to stress that it also has come to mean not only free time quantitatively, but especially qualitatively. Although freedom "from" precedes freedom "to," the latter is increasingly placed central to the concept, meaning free from anxieties, concerns for basic needs, war or social unrest and therefore free to choose without undue restraint or compulsion.

This is well expressed in the *Charter for Leisure,* composed by a committee representing all the world's regions and adopted by the World Leisure and Recreation Association. When referring to the right of people to "certain periods of time during which they can freely choose how to occupy themselves," the Charter states:

"Peace, a minimum of social stability, the opportunity to establish meaningful inter-personal contacts, and the reduction of social inequality are some of the major prerequisites for the full implementation of that right."[2]

The primacy of quality over quantity was vividly illustrated by Fruto Vivas Barquisimeto at the Conference on "Non-formal Education through Recreation," held in Venezuela in 1979. When discussing the problem of lost children in the large urban centers of Venezuela, she said:

"Go to a hillside neighbourhood and take any child at random and any other person at random in this neighbourhood and he will tell you that this child is the child of a laundress and that she arrives home at such and such an hour. This child is not lost. He is part of a miserable and poor social milieu. He is integrated into a social space in the middle of great misery, of great problems of the neighbourhood, of serious food and sanitary control problems, without knowing his father perhaps, but, sociologically, he is a liberated child. He is a child less poisoned by television, by comic books and, above all, by foreign dependence. He is a Venezuelan child who plays, spins tops, flies kites, knows poisonous animals, knows the trees, plays with butterflies and ants, has contact with the soil, makes his own toys. He is creative."[3]

The Paradox

The quote underscores the fallacy of the question that seems to preoccupy many on the North American continent: "Who is ahead?" It is quite clear that this is the wrong question. What does "ahead" mean? If we are thinking of the consumption of recreation goods and services, North Americans probably are. Unfortunately, the North American society, characterized by abundance and professionalization of services, has frequently deviated from the essence of the recreation concept which stresses human growth and development and which, therefore, must include involvement and commitment.

It is important to realize that the consumer model is a byproduct of industrial development; consumerism is following industrialism across the world. This pattern creates an almost tragic paradox: while on the North American continent a growing awareness develops that materialism, competition, individualism and passive consumption ought to be replaced by an emphasis on the individual's responsibility, voluntary effort and community involvement, the parts of the world that are in the process of industrialization can hardly wait to adopt the North American model. While North Americans cast nostalgic looks at the cooperative ethic of the Indonesian villages with their "gojong-rojong,"[4] this is in danger of being swept away by the wave of recreation consumerism that accompanies industrial "progress." And so the pendulum swings.

IN EUROPE

If one can define a "post-industrial" society as one where the majority of the labor force is employed in the service industry, most of the countries of Europe have only recently achieved post-industrial status. Some of the consequences are that:

— leisure and recreation have generally a lower priority than in North America;

— the individual's responsibility is central and activities are predominently concentrated in clubs and associations;

— government involvement is largely limited to the provision of facilities;

— leadership is mainly of a voluntary nature;

— policy development, if existent at all, is sectorial.

Another interesting characteristic stems from the origin of the study of leisure and recreation as social phenomena. In North America, this has a very practical base, having grown from child welfare concerns as expressed in the community centers and playground movements and youth serving agencies like the YMCA. By comparison, in Europe leisure was seen primarily as a theoretical problem, and its study based on the sociology of leisure. One of the consequences is that European researchers have almost exclusively a sociological background, whereas their North American colleagues originate from a wide variety of disciplines, increasingly including that of leisure itself.

A third general observation is that, as the North American "industrial pendulum" swings towards Europe, the recreation consumer model is becoming the norm which means that in virtually all countries, governments become increasingly involved, not only in the provision of facilities, but also in the organization and direction of activities, perhaps to the detriment of the initiative and commitment of the individual citizen.

Furthermore, in a region as diversified as Europe, with some 34 countries and more than 34 languages, the development of conceptual consensus and commonly accepted terminologies meets with serious difficulties. A study group of the European Leisure and Recreation Association, charged with the study of professional preparation in Europe, has, on different occasions, attempted to catalogue the various approaches and to identify common trends. Its efforts, together with the Congresses organized by the ELRA, have contributed significantly to greater understanding and closer cooperation between those who are involved in the provision of recreation opportunities in the various European communities.[5]

Another cooperative achievement is the *Leisure, Recreation and Tourism Abstracts Journal,* published under the auspices of the Commonwealth Agricultural Bureau, England and the World Leisure and Recreation Association. It publishes abstracts of research projects and articles from all over the world although, due to continuing problems of communication and structure, still with an emphasis on Europe.

Program Development

Whereas in the past the development of program activities was the exclusive responsibility of the individual, primarily through voluntary clubs and organizations, the emergence of the consumer society has caused governments to become involved. As a result, most European communities now have within their structures a department charged with the provision of sport and recreation opportunities.

Influenced by the rehabilitation programs following the destruction of the Second World War, a number of countries have embarked upon programs of standardized facility construction. The most thorough among these has been the "Goldene Plan" in the Federal Republic of Germany which has, on the basis of detailed criteria and a financial support program between Federal, Land (Provincial) and Municipal governments, managed to provide the country with an impressive number of swimming pools, playgrounds, sportsfields and indoor sporthalls.

The Government of the Netherlands developed a support-program for the construction of sporthalls: this, too, has grown to be eminently successful.

An interesting example of involvement on the part of local school boards comes from Sweden, where "leisurehomes" are attached to the schools. These facilities, where the children can go before school, after school hours and during holidays, usually include facilities for indoor and outdoor games and cafeteria type rooms. The leaders (Fritidpedagogs) organize trips and excursions during the holidays.

Leadership and Professional Preparation

As a general observation, one can say that the emphasis is on pedagogics; the "Freizeitpedagoge" in Germany, the "Fritidpedagog" in the Scandinavian countries and the "Vrijetijds agogie" in Flemish Belgium, all have a strong pedagogical base and are closely connected with teacher training. More recently, the "Animateur," originating from the community development movement in France, has become a popular model, with its emphasis on assisting people in discovering their talents and developing new interests in a non-directive way.

The number of leisure oriented curriculae is growing rapidly, although professional recreation programs, such as the ones common on the North American continent, are still virtually unknown at the university level. One of the exceptions is the Thurrock DPL Course in the United Kingdom which is the only full time course in English leading to a degree in play leadership. An interesting development in this area, furthermore, is a proposal prepared by the "Interuniversitair Overleg" (inter-university dialogue) in which a number of universities of the Netherlands participated, suggesting the creation of a new field of study, called "Vryetydskunde" (leisure science). The Universities of Tilburg and Amsterdam in the Netherlands have developed undergraduate programs in that new discipline, making them the first universities in Europe to offer leisure and recreation studies. The curricula are, by and large, patterned after those of the Universities of Illinois in the United States and Ottawa in Canada.

Some countries, like Sweden and the Netherlands, have developed two or three year courses resembling those offered at community colleges in Canada and the United States.

At the European universities, leisure oriented courses are often spread over a rather broad spectrum; for instance, theory, research and practical application are often part of departments of education; administration and tourism are taught in departments of economics; free time activities are taught in departments of physical education. An interesting exception is to be found at the Vrye Universiteit in Brussels, Belgium, which offers at the graduate level a course in "Vryetydsagogiek," which can be compared with "education for leisure."

The number of professionally employed people has grown by leaps and bounds; in 1982, Sweden, with a population of 8,000,000 people, counted 13,000 fritidsledare (recreation leaders) and 6,000 fritidpedagogs (recreation educators).[6]

Policies and Structures
This has been dealt with in greater detail in the chapter, "Development of National Recreation Policies." We will, therefore, refer to that and restrict ourselves to noting the differences between the countries of Western Europe and those belonging to the Eastern Block. Whereas in the former the individual is central and the point of departure of policy development, the socialist countries see as the main function of leisure and recreation the development of "socialist man" and leisure time primarily in its connection with economic tasks. Social policy is equated with economic policy.

As a consequence, the private person plays a much less dominant role in the planning process and group activities are stressed over individual participation. The State, professional cooperatives, and a large number of agencies occupy themselves with the organization of worker holidays, school holidays and tourism. The goal of the free time policy in countries like the German Democratic Republic is to prevent free time behavior which, from a party standpoint, is undesirable. One of the ways to achieve this is to have people, whenever possible, spend their free time collectively.[7]

Structures at the national level reflect the emphasis of the policies. In the Netherlands, where the emphasis is on outdoor recreation, the responsible department is Agriculture: in Norway, where sport and recreation are considered to be part of the culture, it is the Ministry of Church and Education: in the Federal Republic of Germany, where health and family are the main motivators, the responsible Ministry is Family, Youth and Health.

American and Canadian recreation professionals often express the desire to spend some time in European municipal parks and recreation departments, obviously under the assumption that they resemble the North American model. But one must realize that the Recreation Director, common in North American communities, is unknown in most European countries. Although European communities are gradually creating departments dealing with sport and recreation, those who are employed have a much stronger administrative responsibility than is the case in North America. The absence of specific training opportunities and the fact that recreation, as a separate area of study, is still virtually unknown, results in a wide variety of educational backgrounds of those responsible for these departments.

LATIN AMERICA

Latin America is no longer the "sleepy neighbor in the South." Oil finds in Mexico, Peru and Venezuela and industrialization in Argentina, Brazil and Columbia have pulled it towards central stage from a global point of view. Although, with its roughly 370 million people, it is not the most densely populated region of the world, it has the second fastest rate of population growth, which makes its population among the youngest of the world's regions. A staggering 42% of its population is under 14 years of age (compared to 9% for Canada). The median age in Brazil is 19 years. Only 6.4% of the population of the region is 60 years old and older.[8]

At the present time there are some 150 million youngsters of school age, which poses an impossible task for the education authorities. In many countries, if the children can go to school at all, they only go for half-days. One of the consequences is that recreation in Latin America has strong utilitarian overtones; a great deal of importance is attached to "formal education through informal activities." Recreation, in the sense of systematically provided opportunities, is still in its infancy and government involvement is only just beginning.

That this large concentration of young people will have a profound impact on the demographic picture of the North as well as South American continent in the next ten to fifteen years is clear. While the populations of the United States and Canada are "greying," the millions of young adults of the Latin American countries, increasingly concentrated in the urban centers, will undoubtedly look to North America for the living space that will become progressively scarce in their part of the world.

Program Development
There are a number of different approaches to the provision of recreation services. Several of these demonstrate a deep concern for those segments of the population that are virtually deprived of opportunities. Many also demonstrate attempts to create linkages with the cultural roots of the people and to meet with the growing resentment against cultural colonialism exemplified by the impact of the North American model.

a) The first one is the program operated by the "Corporacion para la Recreacion Popular" of Cali, which is one of the fastest growing population centers in Colombia. This program represents a unique blend of public and private involvement in the provision of city-wide recreation services. The organization is built along corporate lines and governed by a Board of Directors in which government, business and the community are represented. The corporation's policies are executed by a staff, headed by a management team.

The goals of the corporation are to promote and develop active and passive recreation activities, to develop cultural and educational programs, to conserve natural resources and to protect the environment in the city of Cali. The working capital consists of 50% private funds, 30% public sector contributions and 20% contributions generated within the local community. Private sector participation is encouraged by means of substantial tax incentives for companies contributing financially to the Corporation. To date, the Corporation has erected five centers and there are fifteen more in the planning stage.

b) An interesting example of non-formal education through recreation comes to us from Peru, which uses play and other recreation activities as teaching tools. Around the periphery of Lima, Peru, a swath of dwellings built by very poor migrants has been growing. These are the Peruvian "Pueblos nuevos" or new towns. A private social service group, the "Team for Human Development," has developed a program aimed at the children of these very poor barrios. To compensate for the lack of educational services of any kind, the team has developed a highly successful program of teaching the basic skills of reading, writing and arithmetic through the use of recreation activities. The activities take place in some earthen structure made available by one of the families. Children set up the "classroom" with wooden tables, piles of bricks for chairs, a kerosine stove to cook the meal, and other material. The learning process is guided by a team member assigned to the area and follows a syllabus prepared in cooperation with volunteer educators who contribute technical input to the program.

c) An interesting playstreet initiative is the one of San Fernando, near Buenos Aires, Argentina. Here the municipal government has decreed that the streets adjacent to the city square be closed to traffic on week-ends. Without the usual motor traffic, these streets immediately become an important means of socialization. The city has hired a team of professionals in the fields of recreation, physical education and arts, who run a series of organized activities. In addition, schools in the area are encouraged to form teams in a large variety of activities to compete in many Sunday competitions.

d) The last examples deal with recreation services for workers. The first comes from Brazil, where the government created, as far back as 1946, an institution which translates as "Social Service of Commerce." This organization is decentralized to the state level (there are 21 states in Brazil) and operates with a great deal of independence. The Service provides its programs through a number of recreation centers built, for the most part, in the densely populated urban areas of Brazil. They cover virtually all aspects of life, from medical and dental care, through informal education classes to arts and crafts as well as physical activities.

They are architecturally, efficiently and attractively designed, with playing fields, swimming pools, gymnasia, medical clinics, day care centers and craft rooms. The programs are financed through worker contributions, amounting to 1.5% of their salaries. The centers provide a broad range of activities, including fitness, arts, health programs, education and nutrition information programs. To give an impression of the financial resources these State Services possess, the one in Sao Paulo, Brazil's richest State, has a total budget of the equivalent of 60 million dollars (U.S.), of which nearly half is devoted to recreation activities and opportunities.

The second example originates from Mexico, where the government, through the Social Security program, makes funds available for the development of recreation complexes which are, at a very minimal cost, available to the workers and their families on week-ends and holidays.

One such center is located in the province of Flaxcala, reputedly the poorest province of Mexico. The center is developed in an old and deserted textile mill and is a real oasis in a barren landscape. It contains in- and out-door swimming pools, gymnasia, tennis courts, meeting rooms, an excellent dining room and very attractive bedrooms. The entire center is surrounded by manicured parklands, containing man-made lakes and waterways for boating and canoeing and a large number of ducks.

Leadership and Professional Preparation
As is to be expected, professional preparation is rare and primarily directed towards activity leadership. Leadership, in general, is still a rather elitist concept; there is a considerable gap between the well educated who run the affairs of the few national recreation organizations and those they intend to serve.

The relatively few well equipped and efficiently run multipurpose centers appear to be based on the North American model; this is probably to be expected since the people who have received formal training obtained it almost exclusively in the United States. The population at large, which has no, or very limited access to the "show-cases," occupies its free time with the traditional, culturally specific activities. This dichotomy causes increasing opposition, especially among the youth leaders, who deeply resent the "cultural colonialism" to which they feel victim.[9]

Formal preparation for full-time employment in recreation is a rather recent phenomenon in Latin America. The oldest program is that of the Federal University of Rio Grande du Sol in Brazil. This institution has, since 1963, offered courses in what is called, "Specialist in Leisure and Recreation." It is a program offered at the graduate level, modest in size (a total of 150 graduates since its inception with currently 30 students), oriented towards social psychology, supervision, continuing education and theories of leisure and recreation; it aims to develop generalists in the area.

More recent examples are the "Studies for the Formation of Technicians in Recreation," offered by a private, non-profit organization in Bogota, Columbia, preparing students for jobs in a wide range of areas, such as industrial and therapeutic recreation. "Professional Preparation in Recreation," a course offered by the Foundation for Higher Education and Social Recreation, a division of the Colombian Recreation Association, was founded in 1975.

Other examples include the "Bachelor's Program in Administration of Free Time and Recreation" under the auspices of the Mexican YMCA, instituted in 1976, the "Recreation Professional" program initiated in 1983 at the University of Costa Rica, and two programs offered in Puerto Rico; a "Bachelor's Program in Arts and Secondary Education, with Specialty in Recreation" at the University of Puerto Rico and another undergraduate program concentrating on "Recreation Management" offered by the American College in Puerto Rico, a relatively new private university.

Virtually all of these programs are patterned after the American model and, if one projects them against the young, 370 million strong population of the region, only a very modest beginning of what is potentially an area of phenomenal growth.[10]

Policies and Structures
Although one cannot speak of a uniformly applied Latin American model in these areas, there is a pattern developing that is increasingly becoming universal. Growing numbers of cities have created departments responsible for the development of recreation. Some of the previously mentioned examples reflect this. However, this development is virtually restricted to the municipal level; in other words, there is no "hierarchy," including regional, provincial and/or national government involvement.

The recent formation of ALATIR, the Latin American branch of the World Leisure and Recreation Assocation, has given some impetus to the development of national associations in a number of countries and, as our examples from Mexico and Brazil showed, national governments are beginning to develop recreation oriented programs.

THE FAR EAST

In spite of the enormous area covered by this region and the undoubtedly significant cultural and demographic differences of its component parts, a few general observations are applicable to all. The level of economic development of the region is low; the industrialization process being only in its initial stages. What is important, however, is that in spite of this, all parts are reached by the messages from the modern means of communication, a fact that has a profound influence on the traditionally high level of life satisfaction. The constant bombardment with advertising of consumer goods and the enormous gap between the demand this creates and the chances of ever satisfying that demand, have resulted, according to a Gallup poll conducted some years ago, in the highest levels of unhappiness and frustration of all countries surveyed. This in a region where serene happiness and satisfaction with the quality of life have, traditionally, been the norm.

The strong influence from the western world has had a profound impact on the traditional culture and the conflict between that and what has come to be considered desirable has resulted in a mixture of traditional and western ideas; the latter accessible to and adopted by the affluent, the former still characteristic of the population at large.

An important aspect of life in the region, as in Latin America, is the fact that "time" is a totally different notion from that of the highly industrialized world. Time, in countries like Indonesia (which we have taken as a model for this discussion), is not very valuable in an economic sense; time is not yet money. As a matter of fact, money is rare and time available in abundance. Therefore, time can be dispensed with freely and generously, a notion that is demonstrated in all aspects of life. For instance, it dominates the shopping ritual. "Boleh tawar" is an essential practice meaning that, before buying an item, one is supposed to enter into negotiation with the merchant, who would be very disappointed if one were to pay the asking price without lengthy discussion. That one would pay in money rather than time would be insulting.

Another aspect of this "cyclical" time concept is to be found in the popular "Gamelan" music, to western ears a rather monotonous type of music, performed in a leisurely manner for many hours at a stretch as well as in the picture (Wajang) shows, consisting of legends of Hindu origin, told and illustrated by means of puppet-like images projected as shadows on a screen.

An important part of the recreation activities of the population is oriented towards cultural and religious life, based on the extended family and a cooperative ethic, illustrated by the "gojong-rojong" mentioned earlier.

Program Development
This is almost exclusively left to private initiatives. The more affluent part of the population, the ones who can afford to, belong to the private clubs, play tennis, golf and go to the theatre, while the population at large plays soccer and attends wajang, gamelan or other traditional performances. Government involvement in program development is limited mainly to manifestations at "national holidays" or participation in international events.

Leadership and Professional Preparation
It is virtually impossible to draw general conclusions from a situation so diverse as that in the Far East, other than to note that, in each of the countries concerned, recreation leadership is primarily indigenous and formal preparation next to non-existent. Starting

from that condition, it must be said that, the more a given area has been touched by western oriented industrial development, the more policies and practices from those parts of the world have penetrated.

Therefore, in Hong Kong, for example, models resembling the British and American ones have gotten a foothold, with strong ties with physical education and sport. The American influence is noticeable in the Philippines, whereas recreation leadership in the formal sense is virtually unknown in a country like Indonesia. Interesting examples are the neighborhood organizations or "barangags" in the Philippines. These serve as instruments for the provision of training programs to develop leadership in recreation and leisure activities from the community to the national level.

Policies and Structures

It will be clear from the foregoing that the development of recreation policies follows a similar pattern. Here too, we see a continuum with a total absence of policy development at one extreme and the emergence of the American model at the other. However, the emphasis is at the "no policy" end of the continuum.

Among the rare examples of government involvement in some aspects of recreation development are a few measures adopted by the Philippine government as reported by Mrs. Fortuna Marcos Barba at the First World Conference of Experts on Leadership for Leisure, held at Michigan State University in September, 1977.

"One measure was Presidential Decree No. 604 issued on December 10, 1974. The decree integrated nation-wide youth development, physical fitness and amateur sports development programs and created for the purpose the Department of Youth and Sports Development. The measure was a recognition by the Philippine Government of the vital role of physical fitness and amateur sports programs in the development of a healthy and alert citizenry for national progress. It also indicated the government's recognition of the urgent need to intensify fitness and recreation programs for the population at all ages and in all levels of the community in order to serve as a strong foundation for the inculcation of national discipline. The government also thereby recognized the need to adopt an integrated approach in the physical fitness and amateur sports programs involving all sectors of the citizenry.

Among the functions of the Department of Youth and Sports Development are: to develop and/or maintain recreational facilities, playgrounds, and sports centers in strategic places in the country, and a modern sports complex adequate for major international sports competitions; to administer the existing

National College of Physical Education in accordance with the regulations of the Department of Education and Culture; and to perform such other functions as may be directed by the President or provided by law."[11]

EMERGING ISSUES

1. Probably the most important issue the so called "developing nations" face is that of creating a balance between the preservation of their traditional cultural identity and the behavior patterns and activities that accompany the industrialization process. It is becoming increasingly clear that the growing influence of the "American Model" is felt with resentment. Expressions like "cultural colonialism" and "imposing foreign models" are being heard with growing frequency when one participates in conferences and study sessions in, for instance, Latin American countries.

    On the other hand, the "communications society" cannot help but have a standardizing influence on all world regions; new demands and desires will be created and behavior patterns all over the world will increasingly show comparable characteristics. Developing dogmatic attitudes will only result in the creation of cultural ghettos and sharpen differences within regions.

    Whether one likes it or not, a certain amount of "foreign domination" is inevitable and need not endanger people's cultural identity. After all, the spread of soccer pitches all over the world, including the Indonesian jungle, did not make cultural puppets out of people. The issue rather is for the leadership to be aware of the dangers involved and to provide guidance to the people concerned.

2. Another issue, related to the first, is that of leadership. Leadership is a comprehensive concept, involving not only the "hands on" relationship with people vis-a-vis the occupation of their free time, but also matters of state intervention and government control.

    The highly industrialized regions of the world have virtually completed the cycle and are "re-discovering" the dominant role of the individual as his/her best leisure resource, whereas the developing nations, which by and large have strong central governments, demonstrate a tendency towards state intervention if and when the provision of recreation opportunities becomes an issue.

As soon as competent professional leadership emerges, the nature of this intervention tends to change and human growth and development become more prominent among the motives, reflected in a desire to meet expressed needs, desires and expectations.

Formal recreation leadership is very much in its infancy in most of the non-industrialized regions of the world. Developed regions show a pattern of increasing specialization which has in recent years brought forth the cry for holistic approaches and multidisciplinary treatment of issues. One wonders if and how the developing regions can avoid having to go through the same developments.

3. In the absence of formally trained leadership, the motives for the involvement of these governments are predominantly political, often of the "panum et circensus" (bread and circuses) variety of the Roman Empire. The question of government motives is an important one, regardless of level of industrialization and economic development. In addition, consequences may not always match motives and the motives announced publicly may not always tell the whole story. Each government and each culture is unique in these respects.

4. A similar question is raised when one considers the paradox noted at the beginning of this chapter. To what degree can and should those not already touched by it, counter the onslaught of recreational consumerism? Do the developing regions of the world have to follow the patterns of the industrialized nations? Are the consequences of industrialization inevitable and will the developing nations too, in time, have to re-discover the essence of the recreation notion?

5. Economics are and probably will be a major issue when we talk about participation patterns. Dr. Swampo Sie expressed this quite clearly at the First World Conference of Experts on Leadership and Leisure. According to him,

Any overview of recreational forms and opportunities available to the people of Indonesia reveals an immediate dichotomy between urban and rural, rich and poor. Since Indonesia lacks the large middle class characteristic of industrialized countries, this vivid contrast is not surprising.

On the one hand are the recreational activities available to the rich, including wealthy citizens, resident foreigners and foreign tourists. These range in scope from highly luxurious activities, such as semi-private clubs requiring membership fees of $1,000 and more per year, to paid admission to local dance performances. In this category also can be included the luxurious movie theatres, amusement parks, stadiums and youth centers of the largest cities, many of which are within the financial reach of the upper middle class, at least on an occasional basis. In short, the rich have access to almost every recreational opportunity known to the Western world and some — the highly traditional modes of recreation — which are not. It should be noted, however, that the demand for recreational facilities far exceeds their availability. This tends to push prices outside the financial limitations of the middle class despite an eagerness to participate. For instance, there is a long waiting list for tennis courts in Jakarta and other large cities and even when top prices can be paid, there is often difficulty in locating a court which is not completely booked up for months ahead, much less one which is conveniently located to work or home.[12]

6. The final major issue emerging is the large proportion of young people in many of the developing regions, notably Latin America. This phenomenon has important consequences for the regions concerned. Many of these youth move to the urban centers in search of employment, creating shanty towns and problems of overcrowding, hygiene and control.

But perhaps more fundamental than this is the problem of education; how to accommodate the staggering number of school-age children in the chronically insufficient number of schools. Hence, the utilitarian emphasis on many of the recreation activities in those parts of the world, with recreation designed very purposefully for educational outcomes.

Another aspect of this demographic development is, in the view of many, the inevitable push of millions of Latin American people northward and the concomitant problems of accommodation, feeding and, especially, integration. That such an influx of people from different cultural backgrounds will have significant impact on the provision of recreation opportunities in the receiving regions is clear. Also, higher levels of adaptability and tolerance on the part of both leadership and participants will be required than have been demonstrated traditionally.

Tolerance represents probably the most important requirement one can distill from this overview. Prerequisite for the development of this attitude is an awareness and understanding of different cultures and different perceptions of time, work and life.

It is imperative that those operating on the international scene sharpen their insights into these issues, that they make extra efforts to facilitate the exchange of information and experiences, that they help develop programs of inter-cultural exchange and educational opportunities, in short, that they help develop the "global conscience" in leaders and participants alike, without which many of the potential advantages of development will be lost.

REFERENCES

1. The scope of an article of this nature simply does not permit a thorough treatment of all regions of the world. A selection had to be made; therefore, primarily due to biases and limitations of the author, countries like Japan and India and a region like Africa, fascinating as these might be, were excluded from this overview.
2. World Leisure and Recreation Association, *Charter for Leisure,* New York, World Leisure and Recreation Association, 1981, prologue.
3. Fruto Vivas Barquisimeto, The Importance of Recreation in the non-formal education of the child. In: *Non-Formal Education Through Recreation,* Proceedings of the First Latin American Regional Symposium, Venezuela, 1979, p. 24.
4. "Gojong-rojong" is a cooperative principle that governs Indonesian village life. It is the practical expression of the inter-dependence of the villagers and demonstrates itself in assisting neighbours in the construction of homes, working the land, sharing the burden of disasters, etc.
5. Examples are:
    — European Leisure and Recreation Association, *Leisure Policy in Europe,* Edition Freiseit, Dusseldorf, 1975.
    — European Leisure and Recreation Association, Social Development and Leisure Policy, report of the third European expert conference on leisure and recreation, Stavanger, Norway, 1977.
    tion, Stavanger, Norway, 1977.
    — Wolfgang Nahrstedt and Gustav Ungglin, editors, *Freigeit padagogik und Animation in Europa,* Edition Freiseit Dusseldorf, 1977.
6. Wolfgang Nahrstedt, *Professional preparation for leisure and animation in Europe,* paper presented at the Annual Congress of the National Recreation and Parks Association, Kansas City, 1983.
7. Stundl, Herbert, *Freizeit Und Erholungssport In Der DDR,* Schondorf, Verlag Kars Hofmann, 1977, p. 21.
8. Nelson Melendes, *Leisure in the developing world: A Latin American perspective,* paper presented at the Annual Conference of the Canadian Parks/Recreation Association, August 13-15, 1981, p. 1.
9. This sentiment forms an ever recurring theme at regional conferences; the resentment and frustration may be best expressed by one of the Mexican delegates at the Second International Conference on Recreation Leadership, held in San Juan, Puerto Rico, in 1979, when she exclaimed "What is the use talking about freedom and culture to people who are already contaminated?"
10. Examples taken from Nelson Melendes, *op. cit.*

11. Fortuna Marcos Barba, New Philippine Directions in Leisure and Recreation, in *Proceedings and Papers,* First World Conference of Experts on Leadership for Leisure, Michigan State University, East Lansing, Michigan, U.S.A., 1977, p. 30.
12. Proceedings and papers of the First World Conference of Experts on Leadership for Leisure, *op. cit.,* p. 48.

Chapter Twenty-Eight
The Development of National Recreation Policies

Cor Westland

INTRODUCTION

With the increasing importance of free time in our society and the growing number of agencies offering opportunities to occupy that time, the concern about the cohesiveness of the ensuing delivery system causes many to demand the development of national policies in this area. Fundamental to this is the question whether governments should have any involvement in the leisure aspect of people's lives.

Critics of the welfare state maintain that we have already reached the point where being taken care of has become an inalienable right in the minds of many, that current social policies have made people powerless because every problem has to be solved for them and that, therefore, they no longer can make decisions on their own. Futhermore, "freedom" and "choice" are central notions to the recreation concept and governments are commonly identified with restriction of freedom and limitation of choices.

Convincing as these arguments may be in some quarters, the existing precedents have made it abundantly clear that government involvement in the provision of recreation services and opportunities has not only been accepted but is increasingly considered essential, to the point that the development of specific government policies is being demanded with growing vigor.

This acceptance is primarily due to our concept of government, which creates the interesting paradox that the notions of "freedom" and "choice" are precisely the reasons why governments should be involved. In our society, the role of government is "to do those things that ought to be done and that can not be done by each person individually."

This principle makes government an instrument of collective action, dealing with collective goods such as justice, freedom and welfare. Free time is such a collective good: the freedom to occupy it is not unlimited, lest one person's freedom becomes someone else's un-freedom. Therefore, there ought to be an agency that has the power to limit the freedom of some in order to extend that of others. In other words, there is a need for an authority with the power to allocate society's scarce resources; hence the rationale for the creation of governments.

Other reasons justifying the involvement of government in the recreation field include the fact that:

— government has a responsibility to *all* citizens, in contrast to a private agency or club which, by its nature, limits its services to its membership;

— government has the required financial, physical and personnel resources or, if needed, the means to acquire them through taxation, expropriation or other legal means;

— government has continuity, thus ensuring a degree of permanence in the provision of services, a permanence often lacking in private agencies which, frequently, depend on the efforts of a limited number of dedicated people;

— government has the potential to provide services more economically than the private sector is able to do;

— government possesses the mechanism needed for the planning, administration and management of its services;

— the public has come to expect and demand government services.

NATURE OF GOVERNMENT INVOLVEMENT

Having thus established why governments are involved in the provision of recreation programs and services, the next question we must address is the nature of this involvement. Traditionally, government's activity in major social phenomena has been re-active rather than pro-active; in other words, governments have become involved as a result of pressures brought to bear by interested groups or individual citizens, thus responding to expressed demands. This is the essence of the political process.

Rare are examples of pro-active behavior of governments, consisting of programs or initiatives developed on the basis of perceived or expected social changes or perceived needs. Current government initiatives in the field of preventive medicine are good examples. Pro-active behavior, useful as this may be, inevitably raises questions about the ethics of this type of involvement and is, especially in the so highly subjective field of recreation, only acceptable if and when it is based on extensive consultative processes.

The most desirable type of government involvement in the recreation field is, in my view, the re-active one, based on the principle of support to groups and/or individual citizens. The most appropriate model for this principle is that developed in *The Elora Prescription* which sees individuals acting as "their own best leisure resource" and which establishes that all "support services operate under the residual principle."[1] The authors argued that the bulk of these support services ought to be provided by groups at the local level with, if need be, more specialized services emanating from the more senior levels of government. Therefore, this principle of service delivery follows a hierarchy of support services. That hierarchy should also be followed in those cases where a senior level of government considers it advisable to launch initiatives inevitably involving the other levels.

POLICY PRINCIPLES

Once governments have decided to become involved in certain fields, they develop policies or "consciously chosen courses of action, directed towards some end."[2] It is important to realize that although politicians, pressure groups and other segments of the political system play a significant role in the policy making process, the bureaucratic agencies are the central elements. As a result of this, policies often suffer from the bureaucratic tendency to consider policy making as nothing more than one of the many aspects of public administration.

In addition, all actors in the process must realize that policy making is seldom a rational, intellectual process aimed at reaching clearly defined goals. Policies frequently are the result of complex and often arduous interplay between all economic, social, cultural and political forces of a given socio-political environment.

The values and beliefs in this environment provide the basic philosophies by which policy makers must be guided; the specific details are the result of difficult and often time consuming analysis of frequently conflicting interests and objectives of the many elements involved.

The purpose of recreation policies should be: *the creation of conditions under which all citizens can develop their full potential as human beings.* To quote the "Charter of Leisure," adopted by the World Leisure and Recreation Association: "Recreation opportunities must be provided on a universal basis, reasonable access ensured, and appropriate variety and quantity maintained." They should, furthermore, stress "self-fulfillment, the development of international relationships, the fostering of family and social integration, international understanding and cooperation and the strengthening of cultural identities."

To achieve this, three conditions must be met:

1. The policies must aim at the *elimination of existing barriers;* these can be financial, legal, social, physical or psychological. Such barriers must be studied carefully and their impact assessed, especially in relation to special segments of the population, such as the poor, youth, native peoples, the aged, the handicapped and women. Furthermore, the effects of the rapidly growing leisure industry and of the commercialization of culture must be analyzed and measures designed to curb their negative effects.

2. The policies must make provision for the *supply of adequate and varied opportunities on a universal basis.* These include, other than physical facilities, the development of leadership, the strengthening of organizational structures and communication networks, and the allocation of financial resources.

3. The policies must make provision for *full participation in the decision making process* by those who will be affected by them. Central to all policies in the recreation field must be the fact that recreation is a personal concept, and that its focal point is the individual as a total human being; a being who is not only worker, but also player; who is not solely a rational being, but also a creature with emotions, dreams, fantasies, spontaneity, needs and aspirations; who is not simply a cog in the social hierarchy, but also a communicator, living in relationship with his/her environment, with interpersonal relationships and experiences and with an increasing quest for the quality of life.

Especially in an area that is characterized by so many individual interpretations as the field of recreation, a few prerequisites emerge which are essential for policy development:

1. There must be consensus on what it is we are talking about; a clear understanding about what recreation is and what constitutes a recreation program is essential. Based on that understanding the programs and activities must be clearly identified. Unless this is done, it does not make a great deal of sense to talk about policy development because, if the

dialogue is based on "eyes of the beholder" understandings, all discussion about coordination and cooperation will be futile and lead to a never ending series of conflicts, making the development of effective policies impossible.

2. The purpose must be defined as clearly as possible. Although we are dealing with broad goal definitions, attempts must be made to avoid meaningless generalizations and vague statements; policies should be formulated in such a way that a series of measurable objectives can be developed with reasonable ease.

3. A consciously chosen course of action means that the policy must give not only some indication of *how* the goal is to be achieved, but also *who* is to do *what*. The various actors ought to be identified and their responsibilities outlined, including their respective financial responsibilities.

4. Whenever coordinating mechanisms are to be developed, the policy must clearly indicate what is meant by coordination. It must indicate who coordinates what, but especially how that is to be done. This means that the coordinator must not only be identified, but must also be given the authority required to effectively accomplish this task. One of the major problems with most policies is that far too many agencies are given coordinating roles, almost as blanket statements, which makes effective execution of these roles impossible and quickly becomes counter-productive and ineffective. De-emphasizing coordination and replacing it with cooperation produces, in general, much better results since it is less threatening for the agencies involved and maintains their operational independence.

POLICY OPTIONS

In the process of development of recreation policies, governments have the choice of three basic philosophies:

1. They can look at recreation from an integrated perspective and develop "umbrella" type policies, covering all aspects in a comprehensive way. This approach results in overall recreation, leisure or human services policies, providing one set of basic principles and procedures from which individual policies affecting the various activity areas flow.

2. They can deal with the issue in a sectorial manner and treat each aspect in a separate policy. This approach produces individual sport, tourism, outdoor recreation, cultural and other policies.

3. Governments may have developed, over the years, a great variety of programs dealing with recreation, each one as part of policies having a non-recreation primary purpose, without, therefore, having adopted separate recreation policies. This option, therefore, is that of deciding not to have a policy.

The Integrated Approach
Some of the apparent advantages of this approach are:

1. The reciprocal influence among the various supply elements is recognized; an increase in theatre attendance, for instance, may be related to a decline in weekend and vacation travel and a sudden upswing in cross-country skiing may affect cinema attendance. Judging the effectiveness of a given program in isolation is extremely difficult, especially in an area in which subjective value orientations play such an important role. In addition, this policy approach demonstrates a "holistic" philosophy, underlining the fact that "man" cannot be subdivided into "physical man," "intellectual man" and "spiritual man." It recognizes the fact that it is impossible to pigeonhole recreation, just as it is impossible to pigeonhole health, education or welfare.

2. The answer to a number of questions are of importance to all supply elements and influence all. For instance, the relationship between free time and work time, the influence of education, income, work and other variables on the choice of an activity, the trends in the availability of free time, expected economic developments, energy prospects and many more, have an impact on all aspects of recreation.

3. Integrated treatment of all offerings avoids many of the conceptual and definitional problems. This is an especially sensitive issue in North America where the recreation concept, largely derived from playground activities, has expanded over the years to include aspects of culture, tourism, adult education and much more. Since this has been mainly an extension advocated and promoted by those employed in the recreation field, it has received little or no positive response from those who feel threatened by what they often feel as attempts to take over and as unjustified infringements on their territory. Consequently, people spend many hours "defining" concepts but, since most of this is done in an unilateral fashion, the final decisions still depend mainly on vested interests.

However, one must not get the impression that the European countries do not struggle with conceptual issues. Professor P. Thoenes, moderator of a recently held congress of the "Stickting Recreatie" in the Netherlands, probably touched on the major problem when he said, "It has struck me how much discussion at this Congress has been devoted to the old words and concepts; the new words have not yet emerged in our language . . . . We are still stuck with the old image of recreation . . . . If free time moves from the periphery to the center, that concept and the recreation notion will have to be reviewed . . . . We must begin to think in other terms . . . . If recreation is going to direct itself to the wider context, many people will feel this as a loss of identity."[3]

4. A comprehensive approach is the most effective way to achieve a balanced program. Recent Canadian history provides evidence of the difficulties created when comprehensiveness is lacking. It has proven to be virtually impossible to strike a reasonable balance between, for instance, public expenditures on cultural activities and those related to sport development, as these programs are governed by different departments and separate budgets. The sectorial approach harbors the danger of the individual sectors becoming the end, rather than the means to an end. Again, the development in the cultural, but more specifically the sport, sphere has shown ample evidence of that danger.

5. A comprehensive policy can more easily be responsive to changes in societal conditions such as energy, mobility, and changes in the workweek. Especially in a society in which rapid change is a permanent feature, a comprehensive approach makes it easier to change emphasis in the overall policy if and when circumstances require it. Governments can put more weight on the development of activities close to the urban centers and reduce its support to tourism, for example, should energy problems and overall value change make this necessary.

6. Finally, it appears that a comprehensive approach is more in line with the thinking of the general public. The distinction policy makers and professionals try to make between culture, tourism, recreation and others, have little significance for the consumer. People go to the theatre, play sports and travel because that is what they want to do, and very few ask themselves whether this is a cultural, sport or tourist activity. Their main interest is that the opportunity be available when they want it.

The Sectorial Approach

Advocates of the sectorial approach might point to the following advantages:

1. The existing policies are already so tangled and fragmented that it would be virtually impossible to untangle or integrate them. The only practical approach, therefore, would be to refine the process as it exists, to develop separate policies in the various areas, to make sure that all are based on the same philosophic principles, and that effective mechanisms for cooperation and coordination are developed and implemented.

2. One of the major problems of a comprehensive approach is to determine what, and who, comes under the umbrella. After having operated in relative isolation for a long period of time, the free time world, following the example of the field of knowledge, has developed an ever growing number of specializations, each with its own terms of reference, staking out its own domain, and adopting its own criteria. In the course of this process they have begun to consider each other as competitors and as infiltrators into their exclusive territories rather than as complementary parts of a much larger whole.

3. Each sector has its own specific problems requiring specific solutions. Comprehensive policies risk attempting to standardize for the sake of efficiency, losing in the process much of that which makes the component parts specific.

4. The various composing elements of an overall policy are for the most part still in the developmental stage and there is still a need to deepen and strengthen the knowledge of the various areas before an effective, comprehensive system can be developed.

5. Finally, there is the argument that one must go from the specific to the general in order to develop a proper perspective.

The No Policy Option

Judged on the surface, the third option, not to develop policies at all, is highly unrealistic because leisure would remain the privilege of the "idle rich" and, therefore, totally out of tune with government's role in modern society, or it would assume a utopian situation where all people have the resources and ability to make judicious choices for their free time behavior. Still, it can be argued that the development of either comprehensive or sectorial free time policies is not as essential as it is considered to be; that policies may even be counterproductive, in that they might accentuate specialization and further fragmentation; that instead, we must work towards the development of leisure centered national *philosophies*, which must form the bases of all policies. Advocates of this option maintain that the ultimate objective ought to be the development of "quality of life," "lifestyle," or "human services" policies, providing an overall framework for all government action. They point to arguments such as made by Bennett M. Berger, who noted:

> "The problem of leisure is difficult to treat intelligently because it lies in an area that is not amenable to our genius for organized solutions . . . . If leisure is time free of merely instrumental obligations, it is not subject to the criteria of efficiency and hence is immune to the power of rationality and organization."[4]

POLICIES IN EUROPEAN COUNTRIES

How this problem is approached in a number of European countries may give us an interesting insight into the various models that have developed.

The Netherlands
The national ministry having primary responsibility for recreation is the Ministry of Agriculture. Its activities are restricted primarily to the provision of subsidies for the development of facilities. Recreation is identified as outdoor recreation, protection of the natural environment, radio, television and press, and recreation sport. Youth, youth organizations and clubs fall under the jurisdiction of the "social development" sector.[5]

Although the Netherlands is administratively divided into eleven provinces, these have little or no political role, and, therefore, national grants are made directly to communities. Most communities have a section for "Youth, Sport and Recreation." Again, these are primarily administrative units, involved in the provision of grants and the maintenance of facilities. Therefore, Dutch communities do not have Recreation Directors in the North American sense, although the public servants heading up the Youth, Sport and Recreation departments are increasingly selected from those with a sociology, sport or youth work background. They have virtually no program responsibility; that is left to the many clubs. Clubs for practically every interest and activity imaginable develop and execute programs for their memberships. Clubs form the framework of all program activity, which implies that those who do not belong to a club are often deprived from participating in certain activities.

This limiting factor is of concern, and attempts are made to alleviate it. For instance, in the Netherlands, which has a strong emphasis on the out-of-doors, the parks, beaches and lakes, being public property, are open to all. Policy development in the Netherlands is sectorial, although a special study group recently made a strong plea for the development of comprehensive policies, a plea which had surfaced from time to time in the past.[6]

Federal Republic of Germany
The coordinating agency at the federal level is the Ministry of Family, Youth and Health. The prime responsibility for the development of policies and facilities rests at the provincial (Land) and municipal level, where comparable political structures have been developed. Clubs, churches, trade unions and industries are extremely active in developing programs and offering activities.

It is probably still out of a reaction against a history of domination by a strong centralized and totalitarian regime, that West Germany shows a reluctance against government involvement in the affairs of its citizens, especially in the area of free time. The attitude appears to be: "as many organizations as necessary; as little organizing as possible."

For instance, the West German Sports Federation, of which practically the entire recreation movement is a part, is very careful to point to the absence of government assistance. Also, the "Trimm" program, a motivational program aimed at encouraging people to become physically active, finances all its activities from private contributions and donations.

Although the emphasis for program development lies at the municipal level, the involvement of municipalities is still highly sectorial, and although the need for coordination of all these individual activities is increasingly felt, it is generally not considered necessary to develop study programs for those charged with this responsibility. The serious study of leisure and the development of professionals in the area are very recent phenomena; professional preparation is directed towards the development of "leisure educators" (Freizeitpedagogue).[7] Policy development is also still at a very basic level; the approach appears to be an integrated one.

Sweden

The Swedish example is almost the opposite of the West German one. Whereas in West Germany there is a strong emphasis on the individual and down-playing of structures, in Sweden there is a high level of organization and reliance on "Volksbewegungen" as the basic participation structure. The difference is one of political philosophy and development. The Swedish society is very much oriented towards the welfare state, towards a classless society in which the many organizations occupy a place between government and people. Up to 80% of the citizens between 12 and 25 years belong to some organization or another. The many youth organizations are considered key elements in the development of the Swedish democracy.[8] Leisure in Sweden is, other than a personal, also a socio-political issue. Sweden is probably the only western country where the educational objectives include the preparation for leisure. Here, too, one notes the emphasis on assistance programs at the municipal level; the federal and provincial governments can in no way influence the decisions taken at that level.

Virtually all Swedish municipalities have special leisure departments, which coordinate all municipal services having an impact on free time opportunities. Policy development has been, up to now, sectorial, with a clear distinction between leisure (freizeit) and culture, but with strong emphasis on cooperative planning.

Switzerland

Although the prime responsibility for the provision of facilities and opportunities lies at the canton and municipal levels, the federal government has become increasingly involved. Examples include the "Federal Law on Area Planning" which has as purposes, "to preserve the uniqueness and beauty of the landscape and to ensure the continued existence of the recreation areas." The Federal Government is also developing a tourist concept for the whole of Switzerland.

The peculiar political relationships which exist in Switzerland, and which place specific emphasis on the municipalities as centers of decision making, result in the emphasis on the construction of local facilities. As virtually everywhere in Europe, the operation of programs is left to private clubs and individuals. Dr. A. Ledermann, former Executive Director, Pro Juventute and past President of the European Leisure and Recreation Association, indicated that the Swiss see the role of government as limited to the provision of space, money and facilities, to which recently has been added the employment of "animateurs" to encourage broader participation.[9] Policy development has been sectorial, dealing with specific aspects of the overall free time area.

Norway
Norwegian policy is integrated; the concept of culture includes youth work, sport, and recreational pursuits. One of the basic aims of policy is to promote cultural democracy, to decentralize activities as well as decision making, to remove social barriers and to "build a society in which each individual may develop his talents and inclinations in an environment where he is free to make his choices on his own premises."[10] Emphasis is on amateur activities and on local club work.

At the present time all countries, and practically all municipalities, have a cultural committee, appointed by their respective Councils. These are advisory agencies, with a few executive functions. The state authority is the Ministry for Church and Education. The Ministry receives advice from the Norwegian Cultural Council, the State Youth Council and the State Sport Council. The public sector, through the Ministry, supplies the major part of the finances for all free time programs. Leadership development in Norway seems to be more systematically undertaken than in most European countries, especially with the education of consultants in leisure and cultural work.

German Democratic Republic
When reading this short overview, one must realize that in accordance with the socialist ideology, the development of the socialist image of man is the ultimate objective of the G.D.R. Based on this, man must, through work and leisure, develop into a socialist personality. The citizens' free time activities are part of the activities of the socialist policy; they must be planned and, whenever possible, executed collectively. As Bauermeister states, "in accordance with the collective social development, the utilization of free time must not be left to its own devices."[11]

The intent of policy is to integrate, as much as possible, the use of free time into the overall education and development process. Consequently, the goal of the free time policy in the G.D.R. is to prevent free time behavior which, from the party standpoint, is undesirable. The state attempts to achieve this purpose by: a) making free time behavior secondary to political plans; b) concentrating on free time activities for children and youth; and c) having people, wherever possible, spend their free time collectively. Free time policy in the G.D.R. is an integral part of social policy and essential for the existence of the system; it serves to increase productivity and facilitate adjustment to the norms of the party.[12]

Canada

The Federal Government of Canada seems to have returned to the "no policy option," its position of the early 1970's. At that time, the Federal Cabinet decided not to become directly involved in the provision of recreation programs and services, but to continue its policy of limiting its involvement in the recreation field to those activities which are a consequence of mandates with a different primary purpose.[13] Some of the best known examples of that period are the Fitness and Amateur Sport program, the main objective of which is to "encourage, promote and develop participation by Canadians in fitness and amateur sport activities"[14] and the National Parks program, initiated with the primary purpose of the preservation of Canada's natural heritage. In spite of the fact that these, and other programs had, and still have, a significant impact on the Canadian recreation scene, involvement in these areas is considered secondary to the main objectives of fitness and preservation.

In the latter half of the 1970's it seemed that the Government of Canada might be prepared to work towards the development of a National Recreation policy; the creation of the Recreation Canada Directorate in 1973, although with a mandate limiting its involvement to "Physical Recreation," acknowledged at least a shared jurisdiction in the area. That was confirmed by then Prime Minister of Canada, the Right Honorable Pierre Elliot Trudeau who expressed his opinion in a letter to the President of the Canadian Parks/Recreation Association:

"I believe recreation services to be the domain of no single government jurisdiction. Recreation is a very personal activity which demands the same recognition, respect and encouragement as is afforded to all other basic social concerns. No one jurisdiction can fully provide for all the recreation services required by the citizens and no jurisdiction can operate effectively without some impact on recreation."[15]

Furthermore, the "green paper," published by the Minister of State for Fitness and Amateur Sport, published in 1979 and entitled "Towards a National Policy on Fitness and Recreation" was seen as a clear indication that, indeed, the Government of Canada was prepared to join with those of the Provinces in a national dialogue on the subject.[16]

It would soon become clear, however, that the political realities and expediencies appeared to dictate otherwise. As early as 1974, the Federal Government had declined to take an active part in the Edmonton Conference of Provincial Ministers responsible for Sport and Recreation. From that moment on, the Provinces followed an independent course, culminating in an "Inter-Provincial Recreation Statement," adopted by the Provincial Ministers responsible for Recreation and Sport at their Conference in Fredericton, New Brunswick, in October 1983. In that document, the provinces reiterated that "Recreation in Canada in common with other social services lies within the jurisdiction of Provinces."[17] However, after having made that statement, the provinces recognized that "the resources and the cooperation of all jurisdictions and a wide variety of private and community agencies are required to meet the recreation needs of all citizens,"[18] thus leaving the door open for federal participation in future dialogue.

The developments that were outlined in the preceding paragraphs illustrate an accelerating move towards conceptual understanding and cooperative approaches between the provinces, accentuated in their resolve to institutionalize the cooperative mechanisms developed over the years consisting of Ministers' Conferences, Deputy Ministers' Conferences, and Inter-Provincial Sport and Recreation Council meetings (the latter consisting of senior provincial officials).[19] As far as the Federal Government is concerned, however, the past decade has demonstrated that that there is no intention to become formally involved in recreation from a policy development point of view and, given the political climate of the day, it is highly unlikely that a change in this situation will occur in the years ahead.

CONCLUSIONS

1. Policy making is not a rational process and should not be primarily entrusted to the bureaucratic system. It must reflect the dominating values of a given social environment, reconcile the often conflicting interests and objectives of all elements concerned, and correspond with the political climate of the day.

2. An integrated approach to policy development is probably the most desirable one, in spite of the many difficulties involved.

3. Irrespective of the option selected, serious efforts must be made to achieve conceptual clarity. It is imperative that this not be attempted by the various elements in isolation but, in a multi-disciplinary and multi-agency fashion, resulting in consensus and commitment to the conclusions reached.

4. Free time policy development around the world shows a variety of models, each born from the peculiar situation within the country concerned.

5. In view of the policy options discussed and different models adopted by various countries, the central question appears to be, "What difference do these approaches make in the behaviors and attitudes of individual citizens?" Is it true that one option provides better opportunities for human development than another? Or are policies, particularly at the national level, necessarily so broad and general that differences between the philosophies and options are negligible? Does this not re-enforce the personal aspect of the recreation concept and the overriding responsibility the individual has in meeting his/her own recreation needs? Has too much of this responsibility been delegated to governments who cannot and perhaps should not deal with it?

6. The *main issue* appears to be not that of policy development as panacea, but of redirecting the locus of responsibility from governments to the individual. The *main problem* will undoubtedly be how to bring this about in a society where still "to have" seems to be more important than "to be," "to consume" more significant than "to produce" and "to withdraw" more popular than "to participate."

REFERENCES

1. *The Elora Prescription: A Future for Recreation.* Toronto: Ontario Ministry of Culture and Recreation, 1979. p. 15.
2. Simeon, Richard. "Studying Public Policy," Canadian Journal of Political Science, IX:4 (December, 1976). p. 557.
3. Thoenes, P. "Congressamenvatting," *Congresversla Recreatie '98,* (June, 1979). p. 55.
4. Berger, Bennett M. "The Sociology of Leisure." In Smigel, Erwin O. (Ed.), *Work and Leisure.* New Haven, Connecticut: College and University Press, 1963. p. 37.
5. Ministerie Van Cultuur, Recreatie En Maatschappelyk Werk, *Informatie Van De Hoofdafdeling Openluchtrecreatie,* (November, 1978). p. 43.
6. Commentaar Van Het Interuniversitair Werkverband Sociologie Van Het Vryetydsgedrag, *Recreatie,* 17:3, (March, 1979). p. 68.
7. Nahrstedt, Wolfgang. "Aus-Und Fortbildung Von Mitarbeitern In Freizeiteinrightungen In Der Bundes - Republik Deutschland." *Freizeitpadagogik Und Animation In Europa.* Dusseldorf: Edition Freizeit Verlan GMBH, 1975. p. 43.
8. Nahrstedt, Wolfgang. *Freizeit In Schweden.* DUsseldorf: Walter Rau Verlang, 1975. pp. 10-45.
9. From a conversation with Dr. A. Ledermann, Zurich, June, 1979.
10. Royal Norwegian University of Foreign Affairs, *Norwegian Cultural Policy.* Oslo, May 1977. pp. 1-12.

11. Stundl, Herbert. *Freizeit-Und Erholungssport In Der DDR.* Schorndorf: Verlag Karl Hofmann, 1977, p. 19.
12. Stundl, *Op. Cit.,* p. 21.
13. Memorandum to Cabinet. Cab. Doc. 697/71, June 10, 1971.
14. Fitness and Amateur Sport Act, Art. 1.
15. A letter from the Prime Minister of Canada to the President of the Canadian Parks/Recreation Association, dated July 12, 1978.
16. Campagnolo, Iona, Minister of State for Fitness and Amateur Sport, *Toward a National Policy on Fitness and Recreation,* Ottawa, Minister of Supply and Services, 1979.
17. Provincial Ministers responsible for Recreation and Sport, *An Interprovincial Recreation Statement,* Fredericton, New Brunswick, 1983, p. 3.
18. Ibid., p. 3.
19. Ibid., p. 15.

Chapter Twenty-Nine
Back to Our Radical Roots
Mary Duncan

The most dangerous woman in America, a civil-rights newspaper columnist, a man who started a playground at his own expense, a publicist who exposed filthy tenement conditions and advocates of socialism and leftist politics are frequently cited as being the founders or cornerstones of the park and recreation movement. Unfortunately, these facts are seldom stated in our recreation text-books. One has to read biographies, autobiographies and other publications before these facts become evident.

Why haven't our textbooks dealt with the personalities, commitments, failures, and political views of our professional predecessors? Is it because the authors were not aware of it? Has there been an unspoken conspiracy to make our new profession more "respectable" by glossing over our founders' sometimes unsavory and controversial pasts?

In order to fill these voids in our literature, herewith is a brief foray into the lives of Frederick Law Olmsted, Jacob Riis, Jane Addams, Luther Gulick and Joseph Lee. In many ways they were the radical counterparts of Eldridge Cleaver, Jane Fonda, Caesar Chavez, Gloria Steinem and Ralph Nader. They continually fought city hall, organized labor strikes, marched in the streets, gave public speeches, and wrote award-winning articles deploring the living conditions of the poor. The issues and problems they faced were well defined: slavery, the aftermath of the Civil War, thousands of new immigrants, slums, child labor, disease, the suffrage movement, World War I, and a rapidly industrializing nation. America was striving to develop its abundant natural resources and was also enjoying a booming economy. The work ethic and the free-enterprise system flourished, thus creating a paradox of strong economic growth at the expense of human suffering and exploitation.

Our founders faced these issues. They were not meek and mild, easily intimidated or swayed by local politicians. They worked in, around, and with the political system. The political battles they fought gave them the skills needed in order to establish the park, playground and recreation services we enjoy today. With these thoughts in mind, let's look at their radical pasts. Perhaps it will provide some insights into the present, and hopefully provide a model for the future.

FREDERICK LAW OLMSTED (1882-1903)

Frederick Law Olmstead, a political columnist, writer, traveler, farmer, and landscape architect, was also an abolitionist who later became one of the designers of Central Park. His biographer, Elizabeth Stevenson, states that his early years laid the groundwork for his dedication to public service.

His childhood was unusual and set the course for his interest in landscape architecture. Even though his family were prominent merchants and lived in Hartford, Connecticut, Fred was allowed to roam free in the nearby woods. At the age of seven, he was sent to live with a series of ministers where his formal education vacillated between very good and very bad. He was not always happy, but learned to cope by escaping to the woods for solitude and adventure.[1] Later he visited England where he was impressed with her parks and wrote that in "democratic America there was nothing to be thought of as comparable with this People's Garden."[2]

Even though he was not a good student, writing his thoughts seemed a natural habit for him. This ability led the liberal editor of the *New York Daily-Times* to employ Olmsted to travel South and write his impressions about slavery. While Olmsted's columns were simple and unemotional, they vividly portrayed the brutalities, both physical and psychological, of a slave society. Writing in a letter to a friend he said, "I would take in a fugitive slave and shoot a man that was likely to get him." One of his columns was attributed to influencing Abraham Lincoln to emancipate the slaves.[3]

Prior to the Civil War, Olmsted, who had "tried being clerk, tried being sailor, and failed at farming," was determined to be the Superintendent of Central Park. He succeeded and immediately ran into opposition from Chief Engineer Egbert Viele. When Calvin Vaux's and Olmsted's plans for Central Park were later adopted, Viele charged them with stealing his plans. Viele had designed a drainage system for the park, and based on that was initially awarded a court settlement of $8,000.[4] But the jealousies between the men did not deter the progress of Central Park.

For a while, Olmsted resisted entering the Civil War. He considered Lincoln to be "lacking in firmness and dependent upon others for direction." Later he changed his mind and became Secretary of the Sanitary Commission, which dealt with the health needs of Northern soldiers.

Following the war, Olmsted designed numerous other private and public parks. Almost as if he were psychic, he recommended that San Francisco's Golden Gate Park be designed to act as "a barrier of protection to large districts . . . during great conflagrations." Although he didn't design Golden Gate Park, his suggestions were followed and during the fire that followed the 1906 earthquake, the park served as a firebreak and later was used to house thousands of homeless people.[5]

Both Vaux and Olmsted served as consultants to the New York City Park Department, but were fired in 1870 when the Tweed Ring took over New York City. In spite of the political setbacks, they were later reinstated and continued to guide the development of Central Park.

During these years, his wife Mary cared for their children and also advised him on professional matters. Partially because of this he was not upset by the Suffrage Movement. "If an occasional woman was found to be doing a man's work . . . he was not alarmed." He welcomed Elizabeth Bullard, of Bridgeport, Connecticut, into the "brotherhood" of landscape architects and recommended her for several jobs.[6]

Conservation and preservation were also Olmstead's concerns. He continued to fight for maintaining the natural scenery of such places as the Niagara Falls area and Yosemite.

The tumultuous years of Civil War, corrupt politicians, suffrage, and increasing urban problems did not deter the thousands of immigrants who flooded our shores. Among them was twenty-one-year-old Jacob Riis, a Danish citizen.

JACOB RIIS (1849-1941)

Jacob Riis was a troublemaker. Using his position as a police reporter, he expanded his beat to include dramatic stories about the horrors of slum conditions in New York City.

Stressing the theme of two Americas, he wrote that "slums were an evil cancer born of public neglect and nurtured by private greed."[7] His book, *How the Other Half Lives*, recommended tighter health laws, the prohibition of child labor and improvement of public schools.

Lectures, photo displays and articles facilitated his meeting influential people. Together they conducted tours of the tenements and pressured politicians to clean up the filth. Philosophically he wanted to solve the problems by going further than simple charity but stopped short of socialism. His biographer stated:

"Riis's programs of social, economic, political and humanitarian reform aimed to beautify the environment and to reestablish the position of the home, the school, and the neighborhood in the lives of the poor . . . Riis wanted school buildings to be open in the evenings, on weekends, and during the summers for recreational, cultural and civic use."[8]

Highly critical of organized religion, he admonished the churches to wipe the soot from their windows and take up the gospel of service. Settlement houses to him were the best example of practical Christianity.

Parks and playgrounds were high on his priority list of urban needs. He believed cities should provide parks for "the rest and recreation of the poor," rather than "for the pomp and parade of the wealthy."[9] Like other members of our movement, he wrote that creative play was necessary for teaching proper citizenship. As local politicians grew tired of his crusades, Riis resorted to other methods. One of his favorites was to send women to the mayor's office because "they could worm a playground or small park out of him."[10]

Jake's concern for parks and play areas was undoubtedly a result of his rural youth environment. Like Olmsted, he preferred rivers, hills or trees to the structured classroom. The son of a school master, he enjoyed high social status but on an austere family income. He once commented that his father "was the one link between the upper and lower strata in our town . . . enjoying the most hearty respect of both."[11] In order to support fourteen children, the elderly Riis wrote columns for a local newspaper. It was as his father's young assistant that Jacob decided he wanted to be a news reporter.

Distressed by the rejection of his sweetheart, Elisabeth, and the lack of work, he travelled by steamer to New York in 1870. From that time until 1877, he lived on the brink of poverty, hunger, loneliness and humiliation. Cheated by several employers, Riis finally turned to the Danish consul who gave him shelter, clothes and a job.

His social life revolved around the Lutheran Church where the young people played "particularly energetic kissing games" because the pastor despised dancing.[12] But he still longed for Elisabeth, who was now engaged to another man in Denmark. Finally, after years of effort and taking classes at a business school, he secured a job as a reporter. From here he embarked on his career as a social reformer and, when established, was able to marry Elisabeth.

Throughout his life he struggled to bring the "two Americas" that he knew so well — one rich and the other poor — into harmony with one another. Believing in the integrity of neighborhoods, he emphasized community rehabilitation by the families, schools and churches rather than distant experts.

On these points, he and his friend Jane Addams concurred.

JANE ADDAMS (1860-1935)

Jane Addams is frequently lauded for having started a playground next to Hull House in Chicago. Photos of her depict a kindly woman chatting with children. Addams was also a "woman's libber" who helped organize labor unions for women garment workers, investigated child-labor practice, established a day nursery for the children of working mothers and struggled to help women gain the right to vote. In spite of her personal wealth, she chose to work among the poor. Her clientele consisted of immigrant settlers, sweatshop toilers, unwed mothers, the hungry, sick and aged. Programs at Hull House encompassed a myriad of social, educational and recreational services.

As an ardent supporter of Theodore Roosevelt, she seconded his nomination for president under the now defunct leftist Progressive Party. Her endorsement of him waned when he became a "hawk" regarding World War I while she was an avowed pacifist. Along with several other women she organized the Women's Peace Party and organized a large peace demonstration in Washington. Later in 1931 she was awarded the Nobel Peace Prize for her efforts.[13]

Psychoanalysts could offer some insights into what motivated Jane Addams. She was the daughter of a wealthy man whom she adored, but his attention to her was diverted by her stepmother. Marriage probably did not seem appealing because her mother died in childbirth; her father's remarriage disrupted her emotional ties to him and her sister's marriage was marred by much bitterness and recrimination. Her personal relationships revolved around Mary Rozet Smith, who was a donor to Hull House and Jane's closest friend, confidante and companion. For many years they lived together and when apart exchanged what only can be described as love letters. Her biographer Daniel Levine wrote, "there can be no doubt that each of the women filled some of the emotional requirements a spouse might have filled had either married. Whether emotional intimacy ever led to physical intimacy no one can say. Probably the strong sexual inhibitions of the age and of both women prevented it."[14]

What really matters, though, is that she channeled her energies into projects like Hull House and into creating a more humanistic society. Other wealthy women might have succumbed to their tensions, and retreated to a pampered, self-indulgent lifestyle. Jane Addams dealt with her world and in the process touched many lives including Joseph Lee, the father of the American playground movement.

JOSEPH LEE (1862-1937)

Joseph Lee and Jane Addams both served as officers in the Playground Association of America and he, like her, came from a wealthy, prominent family. While Lee would not be considered as radical as Riis or Addams, he continually fought to make recreation a viable part of American life. Appalled by the jailing of children for playing in the streets, he established, at his own expense, an experimental playground in Boston.

His Harvard education, law degree, European travel and happy childhood provided a solid foundation for pursuing his interests in youth, delinquency and family life. His book, *Constructive and Preventive Philanthropy*, stressed the importance of recreation in molding youth development. Another of his books, *Play and Education*, focused on the relationships between play, recreation and the social problems facing our cities.[15] Lee, philosophically, felt that recreation was an integral part of everyone's life, both adults and children. His definition of recreation included many aspects of leisure time activities such as visiting museums, use of school fields and parks as well as children romping on playgrounds. Recreation, to him, was one important factor in life which also had to be integrated with the educational, political, social, religious and economic realities of neighborhoods and cities. To use today's terminology, Lee advocated utilizing an holistic approach to recreation services. This approach was shared by Luther Gulick, a pragmatic man who identified needs in our society and then created organizations or programs to meet those needs.

LUTHER GULICK (1865-1918)

The dignified and moustached Luther Gulick was shoved into the swimming pool, along with several other officers of the newly created Playground Association of America. Graham Taylor, who wrote "Everybody Played," cited this as the high point of that organization's first Chicago convention in 1907.[16] This playful and spontaneous prank was indicative of Gulick, who was described by his son as a "great initiator, a vigorous man who was fun, jovial, very inventive, and an energetic outdoorsman. He derived his greatest satisfaction from working with youth-serving agencies and once established, moved on to other projects." Halsey goes on to recall that his father "had a great interest in the suffrage movement. He fought battles with the New York City School Board in order to incorporate girls into the physical education classes, and organized an elaborate girls folk-dance festival at a time when dancing was considered immoral."[17]

Frustrated by the lack of recreational opportunities for his three daughters, Gulick and his wife started a camping program which later became the Camp Fire Girls. He was also instrumental in promoting the YMCA and designed the triangle which symbolizes that organization.

As the first president of the Playground Association of America, the forerunner of the National Recreation Association, and the National Recreation and Park Association, Gulick struggled along with Jane Addams, Jacob Riis, Joseph Lee, Henry S. Curtis and Howard Braucher to establish recreation services as a proper function of government. President Theodore Roosevelt, honorary president of the Playground Association of America, heartily supported their efforts.

Gulick's parents were medical missionaries in the South Seas. One can only guess at the influence this had on Gulick's sense of strong moral purpose and commitment to the recreation movement. In spite of his strict, biblically based religious childhood, he was an evolutionist, a man with world vision. Many of his thoughts and ideas are expressed in his book, *Philosophy of Play*, and in his formal address at the Chicago Convention. Unlike many other people, Luther felt that play was an absolute necessity for the maintenance of democracy in an industrial society. He and Addams both espoused a new social ethic which stressed society's responsibility to recognize and solve social problems.[18] This differed significantly from the prevailing philosophy that problems were separate, and segmented and could be examined on an individual basis.

Gulick argued that this social ethic could only be learned by experience and in an atmosphere of considerable freedom. Playgrounds and sandpiles were where children learned about self-control, mutual rights and the awareness and importance of group effort.

As a professor at Massachusetts's Springfield College he taught this philosophy and continued until his sudden death to promote progressive camping, physical education and recreation programs.

SUMMARY

In many ways, Olmsted, Riis, Addams, Gulick and Lee represented the left wing of Theodore Roosevelt's Progressive Party. They advocated government support and regulation of parks and playgrounds while Riis and Addams in particular wanted government to also control nickelodeons, penny arcades and pool halls. Many of the problems they faced have been solved only to create a fascinating paradox. Immigrants and foreign laborers are now actively discouraged from entering our country. Our efforts to industrialize were so successful that now, in the '80's, we face dramatic energy shortages. Children who were once exploited in the factories are now economically dependent on their parents until their late teens or early twenties.

The slavery issue has been resolved, but racial injustices still exist. Others feel that white people or Anglos are discriminated against and have filed reverse discrimination suits involving college admissions and employment opportunities. Antibiotics and modern sewage systems have irradicated most communicable diseases only we now find that cancer and stress-related diseases like heart attacks have taken their place. Government at all levels has recognized its role in providing park and recreation services for the people but a growing taxpayers' revolt now threatens some of those same services. Women have been able to vote for many years but are still struggling to pass the controversial Equal Rights Amendment which guarantees equal rights to everyone regardless of sex. High infant-mortality rates have been replaced by abortion laws which allow women to control their own bodies. Even the traditional family concept has been broadened to include the alternative lifestyles of singles, couples without children, divorced people and gay or homosexual relationships.

It's difficult to second guess how our founders would have dealt with these issues. But based on their past records one can imagine Riis marching with the Mexican migrant farm workers; Addams leading the fight to ratify the Equal Rights Amendment and opposing the Vietnam War; Olmsted an active member of the Sierra Club and writing columns opposing nuclear reactors and the commercialization of our state and federal parks; Lee financing adventure playgrounds with his own money and Gulick initiating recreation programs on rooftops and under freeways and continually lobbying with government officials for better recreation services.

Some people may question if these leaders were really radical. When looking at definitions of "radical" one finds the following explanations: "A person favoring drastic political, economic or social reforms; advocates extreme change of the social structure."

It would be difficult to deny that there have been "drastic political, economic and social reforms" since the early 1900's. Our founders were an integral part of those reforms. Now as we look to the future, what role will park and recreation professionals play in addressing today's issues?

REFERENCES

1. Stevenson, Elizabeth. *Park Maker: A Life of Frederick Law Olmsted.* New York: The MacMillan Company, 1977. p. 113.
2. *Ibid.*, p. 55.
3. *Ibid.*, p. 72, pp. 112-131.
4. *Ibid.*, p. 335.
5. *Ibid.*, p. 268.
6. *Ibid.*, p. 383.
7. Lane, James B. *Jacob A. Riis and the American City.* New York: Kennikat Press, 1974. p. 50.
8. *Ibid.*, p. 91.
9. *Ibid.*, p. 113.
10. *Ibid.*
11. Riis, Jacob A. *Making of an American.* New York: The MacMillan Company, 1904. p. 22.
12. *Ibid.*, pp. 14-16.
13. Levine, Daniel. *Jane Addams and the Liberal Tradition.* Madison, Wisconsin: State Historical Society of Wisconsin, 1971. p. 203.
14. *Ibid.*, p. 71.
15. Lee, Joseph. *Play and Education.* New York: The MacMillan Company, 1916.
16. Taylor, Graham R. "How They Played at Chicago." *Charities*, XVIII (August 3, 1907). pp. 471-480.
17. Gulick, Halsey. Personal interview with the author, May 1979.
18. Gulick, Luther H. "Play and Democracy." *Charities*, XVIII (August 3, 1907). pp. 481-486.

CONTRIBUTORS

Serena E. Arnold is Professor Emeritus, having recently retired as Chair of Kinesiology from the University of California at Los Angeles where she served for nearly 30 years as teacher, researcher, consultant and administrator. Before entering teaching she was Superintendent of Parks and Recreation and a state recreation consultant. Her main interests are administration and analyzing the conceptual basis of leisure services.

Joseph J. Bannon is Head of the Department of Leisure Studies, University of Illinois, and founder of the Management Learning Laboratory. Author of three texts and numerous articles, he has given dozens of workshops on problem solving, human resource management, decision making and delegation, and other management related topics. Active in professional organizations, he has been a trustee of the National Recreation and Park Association and Chairman of its National Council; president of the Society of Park and Recreation Educators and recipient of its Distinguished Fellow award as well as a similar award from the American Park and Recreation Society. His Ph.D. was earned at the University of Illinois.

Doyle Bishop is currently Senior Research Analyst at National Demographics and Lifestyles, Denver, Colorado. He holds a Ph.D. Degree in Psychology from the University of Illinois and was a professor and research associate there. He has an extensive background of research and writing in psychology and leisure research and has been an editor and reviewer for several research journals. His research interests focus upon personality as it influences leisure pursuits, creativity, physical and mental health, and lifestyles as they relate to consumer behavior.

Francis J. Bregha, Professor in the Department of Recreology at the University of Ottawa, was for several years Professor and Chairman of the Community Development and Social Change Program, School of Social Work, University of Toronto. He has been writing about leisure since 1970 when he analyzed the impact of changes in demography, employment and social security on free time. Interested also in social planning and community development, recently he has been examining the philosophical and ethical basis of our ideas about leisure. Member of several federal and provincial commissions and task forces in Canada, he was recently the first Canadian representative of the Inter-American Development Bank in Central America.

Rabel J. Burdge is Professor of Rural Sociology at the University of Illinois and is affiliated with the Institute for Environmental Studies, the Department of Agricultural Economics, the Department of Leisure Studies, and the Faculty of Urban and Regional Planning. Dr. Burdge holds degrees from the Pennsylvania State University and Ohio State University. Former editor of the *Journal of Leisure Research*, he was a founding editor of *Leisure Sciences*. Author of scores of articles and co-author of a text in rural sociology, he has taught at universities in the Netherlands and Australia as well as at the Universities of Kentucky and Washington and the U.S. Air Force Academy.

John L. Crompton is Associate Professor of Recreation and Parks at Texas A&M University. He holds degrees from Loughborough College (England), the University of Illinois, and a Ph.D. in Recreation Resource Development from Texas A&M. Co-author of *Financing, Managing and Marketing Recreation and Park Resources*, his most recent book is *Marketing Government and Social Services*. He has given dozens of workshops and lectures throughout the United States and several other countries in Europe and elsewhere.

Mary R. Duncan received her Ph.D. from the United States International University and currently chairs the Department of Recreation at San Diego State University. She has published several articles regarding recreation and violence in Northern Ireland and co-authored *Supervision of Leisure Services*. She also wrote *The Underground Guide to Job Interviewing*. She has traveled extensively and lectured in Europe, India and the Arab Gulf as well as the Smithsonian Institution in Washington, D.C., where she lectured on "Play, Terrorism, Revolution and Radical Politics."

Garry D. Ellis is Assistant Professor of Recreation, Department of Physical Education and Recreation, Western Kentucky University. His major interests are research methods, measurement and statistics, and the social-psychology of leisure. He played a major role in developing the leisure diagnostic battery. Ellis received his doctorate from North Texas State University. He is an Associate Editor of the Therapeutic Recreation Journal and author of numerous articles in recreation and park related publications.

John Farina recently retired as Professor of Social Work at Sir Wilfred Laurier University, having taught previously at the University of Toronto and the Chinese University of Hong Kong. He earned the Doctor of Social Work degree at Washington University, Saint Louis. Prior to teaching he was Assistant Superintendent of Recreation in Tacoma and Superintendent of Recreation in Edmonton, Alberta, and was Executive Secretary for Group Work of the Canadian Welfare Council. He has authored numerous articles and reports on social work and social welfare, as well as leisure and recreation.

Geoffrey Godbey is Professor of Recreation and Parks at The Pennsylvania State University. He is the author or co-author of four books and numerous articles concerning leisure behavior and services. His interests include aging and leisure, leisure ethics, urban parks and recreation services, second home development, research methodology, international aspects of leisure services, futures research and histories of leisure behavior. He has given invited presentations in twelve countries and is the Managing Editor of Venture Publishing.

Seymour M. Gold is Professor of Environmental Planning at the University of California, Davis. He holds the Ph.D. degree from the University of Michigan and has engaged in teaching and research at Michigan State University and the Universities of Illinois, Michigan, and California-Berkeley. He has a variety of experience as a planner at municipal and state levels and as a planning consultant. He is the author of *Recreation Planning and Design* and *Urban Recreation Planning* along with scores of articles on recreation and park related subjects, and is extensively involved in reviewing and editing materials for planning and leisure research journals.

Thomas L. Goodale is Professor and Chairman, Department of Recreology at the University of Ottawa, having taught previously at the State University of New York-Cortland and the University of Wisconsin-Green Bay. He received the Ph.D. degree from the University of Illinois. The author of numerous articles and chapters on recreation and related topics, he has also written reports on recreation services for federal and provincial government agencies and for professional associations and is currently directing a Senior Management Institute for professionals in the field.

Charles E. Hartsoe is Chairman of the Department of Recreation at Virginia Commonwealth University. He is co-author of *Play for America*, a historical account of the development of the organized recreation movement in the United States. He served as Assistant Executive Director of the National Recreation Association and was involved in the planning process that led to the creation of the National Recreation and Park Association. Previously he served as Chairman of the Department of Recreation and Leisure Studies at Temple University.

Peggy Hutchison, Assistant Professor in the Department of Recreation at the University of Waterloo, is active in research and practice related to community involvement of disabled persons. She co-authored the book *Recreation Integration* and *The Community Integration Game*, has been Editor of the *Journal of Leisurability*, recently conducted a national study entitled *Curriculum Guide: Leisure and Disabled Persons*. She is also affiliated with the Centre for Research and Education in Human Services.

Claudine Jeanrenaud, formerly an Associate Professor in the Department of Recreology, University of Ottawa, earned her Bachelor's of Art Education degree at the University of Lausane, Switzerland; her M.S. and Ph.D. at the University of Illinois, Department of Leisure Studies. Her main interests lie in the area of conceptual and creative development as reflected in graphic expression of adults and children, as well as the environmental and personality determinants of such development. She is currently a candidate of the C.G. Jung Society, studying analytical psychology, and she has a private practice providing individual psychotherapy and group art therapy.

John R. Kelly is Professor of Leisure Studies at the University of Illinois. His Ph.D. in Sociology is from the University of Oregon, and he has received master's degrees from Yale, Southern California, and Oregon. He is author of three books: *Leisure; Leisure Identities and Interactions*; and *Recreation Business*, as well as over 50 published papers. His current research on leisure and social integration among over-40 adults is funded by the National Institute on Aging. He chairs the Research Commission of the World Leisure and Recreation Association.

John Lord is currently with the Centre for Research and Education in Human Services in Kitchener, Ontario. John has been a school teacher, a recreation worker, and has worked in program development, planning, and evaluation. He was, for seven years, faculty member at Dalhousie University. John has published several articles, and two books in the area of integration, advocacy, recreation, community development, and human service planning. He is also an Associate of the National Institute on Mental Retardation.

Roger C. Mannell is an Associate Professor in the Department of Recreation and Leisure Studies at the University of Waterloo. He is a research psychologist having received a doctorate in Psychology at the University of Windsor. Previously he directed the government and university sponsored Center of Leisure Studies at Acadia University in Nova Scotia. His teaching and research interests include the psychology of leisure and program evaluation.

Bill Michaelis received his Ph.D. in Education from the University of California Berkeley and is currently a Professor and Chair of the Department of Recreation and Leisure Studies at San Francisco State University. He has written, taught and consulted extensively in the area of play and its applications to learning and development. He is a former member of the Board of Directors for both the American Adventure Play Association and The New Games Foundation, and the founder of The Family That Plays Together, a creative play/community development/leisure education enterprise. He is the co-author of *Learning Through Non-Competitive Activities and Play* and most recently was one of the editors of *More New Games.*

Ronald P. Reynolds received his Ph.D. from the University of Illinois in 1973. He has held faculty positions at California State University-Chico and Dalhousie University, Halifax, Nova Scotia, Canada, and is currently Associate Professor and Coordinator of Therapeutic Recreation at Virginia Commonwealth University, Richmond, Virginia. He has authored over two dozen book chapters, journal articles and monographs related to leisure services for disabled persons. He is currently co-authoring a textbook on issues in therapeutic recreation. Dr. Reynolds has served as Editor of the *Journal of Leisurability* and the *Therapeutic Recreation Journal.*

H. Douglas Sessoms is Chairman and Professor of Recreation Administration, University of North Carolina at Chapel Hill. He has authored or co-authored three textbooks and published in a variety of research and professional journals. He is a member of the American Academy of Leisure Sciences, the National Recreation and Park Association, and the American Association for Leisure and Recreation. He has served as President of the Society of Park and Recreation Educators, the American Academy of Leisure Sciences, and the North Carolina Recreation and Park Society. He is a recipient of the J.B. Nash Scholar Lecture Award. His special interests are the sociology of leisure, group dynamics as applied to leisure services, and the conceptual basis for the professional preparation of recreation and park personnel.

Stephen L. J. Smith, Associate Professor and Chairman of the Department of Recreation, University of Waterloo, completed his bachelor's and master's degrees in Geography and his Ph.D. in Recreation and Resources Development from Texas A&M University. His research activities include the geography and economics of leisure, park planning, tourism, and the philosophy of leisure research. He is the author of *Recreation Geography and Tourism Analysis*, and former editor of *Recreation Research Review*.

Irene M. Spry is Professor Emeritus of Economics at the University of Ottawa. Educated at the London School of Economics, Girton College of Cambridge University and Byrn Mawr, she previously taught at the University of Toronto and University of Saskatchewan. She represented, for many years, the Federated Women's Institutes of Canada with the Associated Country Women of the World, an international non-governmental organization engaged in community development and continuing education activities, serving as administrative chairman and Deputy President as well as member of Council. Co-editor of *Natural Resource Development in Canada*, she was a Senior Research Associate of GAMMA, contributing a study on non-renewable resources to its multi-university, multi-disciplinary work on the prospects for a conserver society. An article on "The Tragedy of the Loss of the Commons in Western Canada" was recently published in *As Long as the Sun Shines and Water Flows*.

Cor Westland is currently Executive Vice-President of the World Leisure and Recreation Association, having recently retired from the Department of Recreology, University of Ottawa. Previously he was Director of Recreation Canada in the Department of National Health and Welfare. Co-author of *Playing, Living, Learning*, he has traveled and lectured throughout most of the world's regions, often as official representative of Canada or of major national and international associations. A forceful advocate of leisure and recreation, he has worked extensively in the formulation of government policy and role in leisure service provision.

Peter A. Witt is Associate Vice-President for Research at North Texas State University and Professor and former Chairman of its Division of Recreation and Leisure Studies. He previously taught in the Department of Recreology, University of Ottawa. He completed his Ph.D. degree at the University of Illinois. He was the founding editor of *Leisurability* and currently edits the *Therapeutic Recreation Journal* and *Leisure Commentary and Practice*. Author or editor of numerous articles and books, his main interests are psycho-social determinants of leisure, leisure education, and recreation for special populations. He is a member of the American Academy of Leisure Sciences and the 1985 recipient of the AALR Outstanding Achievement Award.

Fred Van Derbeck had been involved in policy and advocacy related to child development services for disabled and non-disabled children. He worked with the East Mountain Centre, an integrated preschool in Westfield, Massachusetts. He also has an extensive background in political science.

CREDITS

While nearly every chapter was prepared especially for this book, a few are revised or expanded versions of papers or articles initially prepared for another forum. We, and the authors noted below, believed the subject matter timely and pertinent to the issues orientation we have tried to develop, and we wish to cite and thank those for whom the subject matter was initially developed. The chapter by Doyle Bishop and Claudine Jeanrenaud is an expanded version of a chapter in *Play and Human Settlements* (1979) and appears here with the kind permission of the editor of that volume. Seymour Gold's chapter is an expanded version of an article reprinted from the May, 1979, issue of *Parks and Recreation* by special permission © 1979, National Recreation and Park Association. Portions of Tom Goodale's chapter (14) appeared in an article in the *Journal of Park and Recreation Administration*.